BERTRAND RUSSELL
Critical Assessments

Russell in 1938

BERTRAND RUSSELL
Critical Assessments

Edited by A. D. Irvine

VOLUME I: LIFE, WORK AND INFLUENCE

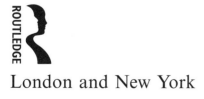

London and New York

First published 1999
by Routledge
11 New Fetter Lane, London EC4P 4EE

Simultaneously published in the USA and Canada
by Routledge
29 West 35th Street, New York, NY 10001

Typeset in Times by J&L Composition Ltd, Filey, North Yorkshire

Printed and bound in Great Britain by T. J. International Ltd,
Padstow, Cornwall

British Library Cataloguing in Publication Data

A catalogue record for this book is available from the British Library

Library of Congress Cataloging in Publication Data

A catalogue record for this book has been requested

ISBN 0-415-13054-9 (boxed set)
ISBN 0-415-13055-7 (Vol. I)
ISBN 0-415-13056-5 (Vol. II)
ISBN 0-415-13057-3 (Vol. III)
ISBN 0-415-13058-1 (Vol. IV)

Contents

VOLUME II *Logic and Mathematics*

VOLUME III *Language, Knowledge and the World*

VOLUME IV *History of Philosophy, Ethics, Education, Religion and Politics*

Preface

These four volumes provide an introduction to the secondary literature surrounding one of the most influential philosophers, logicians, essayists and social critics of the twentieth century. As such, Bertrand Russell is one of only a handful of intellectuals who has captured the imagination of the popular press, the thoughtful layman and the professional philosopher alike. It is the goal of these volumes to provide an entry point into the literature surrounding Russell, his philosophical work, his life and influence.

This project would not have been possible without the generous consent of the many contributors involved. Their contributions to the field of Russell scholarship, as well as their often life-long interest in Russell, stand in strong testament to the influence which Russell has had on this century's philosophical and social development. I extend my warmest thanks to each of them and, in some cases, to their estates and heirs as well.

Very special thanks is also due to Kenneth Blackwell, formerly of the Russell Archives at McMaster University, for his many generosities too numerous to catalogue; to Adrian Driscoll, Sarah Brown, Alan Fidler, Emma Davis and Anna Gerber at Routledge for their guidance and assistance; to Stuart Shanker at York University and John Slater at the University of Toronto for advice on the overall conception of these volumes; to Tony Anderson, Jonathan Berg, Stewart Candlish, Bill Demopoulos, Jim Dybikowski, Nicholas Griffin, Peter Hylton, Gregory Landini, Bernie Linsky, Alan Richardson, Francisco Rodríguez-Consuegra, Harry Ruja, Steven Savitt, Kate Talmage, and Ed Zalta for advice with regard to the selection of individual papers; and to Jim Dybikowski, Anne Harland, Joan Irvine, Monica Muller, Dawn Ogden, Roger Seamon and Shannon Shea for library and editorial assistance.

Support for this project came from Stanford University's Center for the

Study of Language and Information (CSLI) and the University of British Columbia's Killam Memorial Fellowship Committee. I would like to take this opportunity to extend my warmest thanks to both CSLI and the Killam Trust for their respective generosities.

A. D. Irvine
Vancouver, Canada

Acknowledgements

The publishers have made every effort to contact authors/copyright holders of works reprinted in *Bertrand Russell: Critical Assessments*. This has not been possible in every case, however, and we would welcome correspondence from those individuals/companies we have been unable to trace.

Routledge Limited for its kind permission to reprint the manuscript page of Bertrand Russell, 'Prologue: What I Have Lived For', © 1956, Bertrand Russell.

Routledge Limited for its kind permission to reprint Bertrand Russell, 'Prologue: What I Have Lived For', © 1956, George Allen and Unwin. Reprinted from *The Autobiography of Bertrand Russell*, vol. 1, London: George Allen and Unwin, 1967, 3–4.

Continuum 1 Limited for the use of Barry Feinberg and Kenneth Blackwell, 'A Short Chronology, 1872–1970', © 1967, 1998, Continuum 1 Limited. Reprinted with revisions from 'A Short Biography/Bibliography' in Barry Feinberg (ed.), *A Detailed Catalogue of the Archives of Bertrand Russell*, London: Continuum 1 Ltd, 1967, 11–15. Used with permission.

London Mathematical Society for its kind permission to reprint C. D. Broad, 'Bertrand Russell, as Philosopher', © 1973, London Mathematical Society. Reprinted from *Bulletin of The London Mathematical Society*, 5, 328–341. Used with permission.

London Mathematical Society for its kind permission to reprint R. O. Gandy, 'Bertrand Russell, as Mathematician', © 1973, London Mathematical Society. Reprinted from *Bulletin of The London Mathematical Society*, 5, 342–348. Used with permission.

The Royal Society for the use of Georg Kriesel, 'Bertrand Arthur William Russell: 1872–1970', © 1973, The Royal Society. Reprinted from *Biographical Memoirs of Fellows of the Royal Society*, 19, 583–620. Used with permission.

Lady Ayer for her kind permission to reprint A. J. Ayer, 'Bertrand Russell as a Philosopher', © 1972, The British Academy. Reprinted from *Proceedings of the British Academy*, 58, 127–151.

The British Academy for the use of A. J. Ayer, 'Bertrand Russell as a Philosopher', © 1972, The British Academy. Reprinted from *Proceedings of the British Academy*, 58, 127–151. Reproduced by permission.

Routledge Limited for the use of Alan Wood, 'Russell's Philosophy: A Study of its Development', © 1959. Reprinted from 'Russell's Philosophy: Summary and Introduction', in Bertrand Russell, *My Philosophical Development*, New York: Simon and Schuster, 260–272. Used with permission from Routledge and the Bertrand Russell Peace Foundation.

Blackwell Publishers for the use of Kenneth Blackwell, 'The Early Wittgenstein and the Middle Russell', © 1981, Blackwell Publishers, MIT Press. Reprinted from Block, I. (ed.), *Perspectives on the Philosophy of Wittgenstein*, Oxford: Blackwell, 1–30.

MIT Press for the use of Kenneth Blackwell, 'The Early Wittgenstein and the Middle Russell', © 1981, MIT Press, Blackwell Publishers. Reprinted from Block, I. (ed.), *Perspectives on the Philosophy of Wittgenstein*, Cambridge, Massachusetts: MIT Press, 1–30.

Paul Delany for the use of 'Russell's Dismissal from Trinity: A Study in High Table Politics', © 1986, Paul Delany. Reprinted from *Russell*, n.s. 6, 39–61.

Barry Feinberg and Ronald Kasrils, 'A Chair of Indecency', © 1973, George Allen and Unwin. Reprinted from 'A New York Appointment' and 'The Chair of Indecency', *Bertrand Russell's America*, vol. 1, London: George Allen and Unwin, 135–151, 152–167.

Peters Fraser and Dunlop for the use of Alan Ryan, 'War and Peace in the Nuclear Age', © 1988, Alan Ryan. Reprinted from *Bertrand Russell: A Political Life*, New York: Hill and Wang, 172–206; 216–217. Reprinted by permission of The Peters Fraser and Dunlop Group Limited on behalf of Alan Ryan.

Katharine Tait for her kind permission to reprint 'Portrait of the Philosopher as Father', © 1983, Katharine Tait. Reprinted from *Russell*, n.s. 2, 21–30.

Kenneth Blackwell for his kind permission to reprint portions of *A Bibliography of Bertrand Russell*, edited by Kenneth Blackwell and Harry Ruja (1994), London: Routledge, from which much of the Primary Bibliography in Volume I is drawn.

Prologue.

What I have lived for.

Three passions, simple but overwhelmingly strong, have governed my life: the longing for love, the search for knowledge, & unbearable pity for the suffering of mankind. These passions, like great winds, have blown me hither & thither, in a wayward course, over a deep ocean of anguish, reaching to the very verge of despair.

I have sought love, first, because it brings ecstasy — ecstasy so great that I would often have sacrificed all the rest of life for a few hours of this joy. I have sought it, next, because it relieves loneliness — that terrible loneliness in which one shivering consciousness looks over the rim of the world into the cold unfathomable lifeless abyss. I have sought it, finally, because in the union of love I have seen, in a mystic miniature, the prefiguring vision of the heaven that saints & poets have imagined. This is what I sought, & though it might seem too good for human life, this is what — at last — I have found.

With equal passion I have sought knowledge. I have wished to understand the hearts of men. I have wished to know why the stars shine. And I have tried to apprehend the Pythagorean power by which number holds sway above the flux. A little of this, but not much, I have achieved.

Love & knowledge, so far as they were possible, led upward toward the heavens. But always pity brought me back to earth. Echoes of cries of pain reverberate in my heart. Children in famine, victims tortured by oppressors, helpless old people a hated burden to their sons, & the whole world of loneliness, poverty, & pain make a mockery of what human life should be. I long to alleviate the evil, but I cannot, & I too suffer.

This has been my life. I have found it worth living, & would gladly live it again if the chance were offered me.

25. 7-56

Manuscript page from Russell's 'Prologue: What I Have Lived For', 1956.

Introduction

Three passions, simple but overwhelmingly strong, have governed my life: the longing for love, the search for knowledge, and unbearable pity for the suffering of mankind.

Bertrand Russell (1956)

It is difficult to read these words without being moved by them. They strike a chord which resonates within each of us. That someone could articulate these sentiments so easily and clearly helps to explain Bertrand Russell's lasting influence as a writer. That he succeeded – and to the extent that he did – in organizing his life around these ideals also helps explain his appeal as a person.

So much has been written about Russell that approaching the literature surrounding him can be a daunting task. Thousands of books and articles have been written about the man and his ideas. That such a large secondary literature exists concerning someone who has been dead for barely a quarter of a century speaks to Russell's importance as well as to his influence.

Of course, if one wants to learn about Russell's ideas, the natural place to begin is with Russell's own writings. Yet even here one is faced with an overwhelming selection: Russell is the author of over 50 books, as well as some 4,300 articles, book chapters, reviews, pamphlets, letters to the editor, press releases and other publications. Simply deciding where to begin is no easy task. The purpose of these four volumes is thus to provide the serious student with a compact springboard into the literature surrounding Russell. Here, in one place, the reader will find informed, critical commentary on Russell's life and influence, as well as on his work in logic, the philosophy of mathematics, metaphysics, epistemology, the history of philosophy, ethics, education, religion and politics.

In outline, Russell's life is well known. Russell's grandfather, Lord John

Russell, had been created Earl Russell and Viscount Amberley in 1861 after twice serving as Prime Minister. Russell's parents, Lord and Lady Amberley, both died when Russell was young. Orphaned four months before his fourth birthday, Russell and his brother Frank were raised primarily by their grandmother, Russell's grandfather also having died two years after Amberley's death. In his will, Russell's father had appointed two atheists to serve as guardians for his sons, but the will had been contested by Russell's grandparents and informal custody had been granted to them.

Educated first privately and then at Trinity College, Cambridge, Russell became interested in mathematics and, later, in philosophy. The story is often recounted how, at the age of eleven, Russell was disappointed to be told by his brother that the axioms of geometry had to be taken on trust, rather than being proven. It was at the same age that he began to develop religious doubts. While an undergraduate, he became a member of the exclusive Cambridge society known as "The Apostles" and together with another undergraduate, G. E. Moore, he rebelled against the idealism then in fashion at Cambridge.

As a result, during the first decade of the twentieth century Russell was at the forefront of the new realism being advanced in English-speaking philosophy. He also became famous for his defense of logicism – the view that mathematics is in some important sense reducible to logic – and for his advocacy of what was soon to become known as analytic philosophy. Together with his former teacher, Alfred North Whitehead, he published the monumental *Principia Mathematica*. His two articles "A Free Man's Worship" (1903) and "On Denoting" (1905) are among the most widely read and cited philosophical works of the century.

Russell's opposition to British participation in the First World War led to his involvement in anti-war activities and to his eventual conviction on the charge of making "statements likely to prejudice the recruiting and discipline of His Majesty's forces". He was fined £100, with £10 costs, and was dismissed from his lectureship at Trinity College as a result of his conviction. In 1918 he was again convicted for a publication relating to his opposition to the war effort. This time he was sentenced to six months' imprisonment. While in Brixton Prison, he wrote his *Introduction to Mathematical Philosophy* and began work on *The Analysis of Mind*.

Following the war, Russell remained controversial. Together with his second wife, Dora, he opened an experimental school. Seven years later, in 1936, he returned to professional philosophy, taking up a teaching post at the University of Chicago for one year, followed by a three-year appointment at the University of California, Los Angeles. In 1940 he was offered a position at the College of the City of New York. However, prior to his taking up the position, the offer was withdrawn when the New York State Supreme Court revoked Russell's lectureship. At issue were not only Russell's personal morals, but his jail term in England and his views about education. In the judgment revoking Russell's appointment, Justice John McGeehan concluded that, were the appointment to come into effect, it would be "an insult to the people of the City of New York" and equivalent to the establishment of "a chair of indecency". Following Russell's dismissal, offers for speaking engagements were withdrawn and Russell found himself stranded in the United States, unable to return to Britain because of wartime travel restrictions. With no significant source of support for himself and his family he eventually found work when, through the intervention of John Dewey, he was offered a position by the Philadelphia millionaire, Albert Barnes, at the Barnes Institute of Fine Arts. When the eccentric Barnes fired Russell two years later, Russell successfully sued him for $20,000.

Returning to England in 1944, Russell accepted a lectureship at Trinity College. Here he occupied rooms previously used by Newton. He remained a Fellow of Trinity for the rest of his life. During this time he continued his anti-war efforts. He received the Order of Merit in 1949 and the Nobel Prize for Literature in 1950. In 1955, together with Einstein, he released the Russell–Einstein Manifesto which called for the curtailment of nuclear weapons. Together with a number of other leading scientists, Russell also initiated a series of conferences through which high-profile academics would be able to lobby their respective governments for world peace. After the first such meeting was held in 1957 at the summer home of Cyrus Eaton in Pugwash, Nova Scotia, these conferences became known as the Pugwash Conferences. A year later Russell became founding President of the Campaign for Nuclear Disarmament (CND). Eventually frustrated by the CND's lack of effect, Russell helped form the splinter group, the Committee of 100, in 1960.

On Hiroshima Day, August 6, 1961, Russell was prohibited by police from speaking with a loud-speaker in Hyde Park, London. Shortly afterwards, he and Edith, his fourth wife, along with other organizers of the Committee of 100, were brought to trial and convicted on charges of inciting acts of civil disobedience. Upon appeal, Russell's original two-month prison sentence was reduced to one week in the prison hospital. After establishing the Bertrand Russell Peace Foundation in 1963, he remained a prominent public figure until his death at the age of 97.

As is often the case in philosophy, Russell's many admirers have been united over the years, not so much by agreement with his views but by admiration for the man and his goals.

This volume contains some of the most interesting material published on Russell's life and influence. The biographies by Broad, Gandy, Kreisel and Ayer not only detail the major events in Russell's life, they also introduce the reader to many of the main themes in Russell's writings. Wood and Blackwell tell us about Russell's philosophical development, as well as about the remarkable relationship which Russell had with that other well-known Cambridge philosopher, Ludwig Wittgenstein. The chapters by Delany, Feinberg and Kasrils, and Ryan give additional insight into several of the more controversial issues with which Russell was associated. The last word is given to Katharine Tait, whose moving portrait of her father tells us much about the private man behind the public figure.

Prologue

What I Have Lived For

Bertrand Russell

Three passions, simple but overwhelmingly strong, have governed my life: the longing for love, the search for knowledge, and unbearable pity for the suffering of mankind. These passions, like great winds, have blown me hither and thither, in a wayward course, over a deep ocean of anguish, reaching to the very verge of despair.

I have sought love, first, because it brings ecstasy – ecstasy so great that I would often have sacrificed all the rest of life for a few hours of this joy. I have sought it, next, because it relieves loneliness – that terrible loneliness in which one shivering consciousness looks over the rim of the world into the cold unfathomable lifeless abyss. I have sought it, finally, because in the union of love I have seen, in a mystic miniature, the prefiguring vision of the heaven that saints and poets have imagined. This is what I sought, and though it might seem too good for human life, this is what – at last – I have found.

With equal passion I have sought knowledge. I have wished to understand the hearts of men. I have wished to know why the stars shine. And I have tried to apprehend the Pythagorean power by which number holds sway above the flux. A little of this, but not much, I have achieved.

Love and knowledge, so far as they are possible, led upward toward the heavens. But always pity brought me back to earth. Echoes of cries of pain reverberate in my heart. Children in famine, victims tortured by oppressors, helpless old people a hated burden to their sons, and the whole world of loneliness, poverty, and pain make a mockery of what human life should be. I long to alleviate the evil, but I cannot, and I too suffer.

This has been my life. I have found it worth living, and would gladly live it again if the chance were offered me.

A Short Chronology, 1872–1970

Barry Feinberg and Kenneth Blackwell

1872   Born May 18 at Ravenscroft, near Trelleck, Monmouthshire, Wales; the second son of Lord and Lady Amberley.

1874   Death of his mother and his sister Rachel.

1876   Death of his father. Bertrand and his brother Frank go to live with their grandparents Lord and Lady Russell at Pembroke Lodge, Richmond, after the courts reject the guardianship of T. J. Cobden-Sanderson and Robert Spalding, both being atheists.

1878   Death of his grandfather Lord John Russell.

1883   Tutored in mathematics by his brother.

1888   Records in diary his doubts as to the existence of God.

1889   Studies at a crammer and wins a minor mathematical scholarship to Cambridge.

1890   Enters Trinity College, Cambridge.

1893   Obtains 1st class degree in mathematics, begins systematic study of philosophy.

1894   Obtains 1st class in Moral Sciences examinations. Appointed attaché at the British Embassy in Paris. Marries Alys Pearsall Smith on return to England.

1895   Travels to Germany to study economics at Berlin University. Meets Social Democrats. On his return wins Fellowship at Trinity with dissertation on 'The Foundations of Geometry'. Second visit to Germany. Studies Social Democratic movement. First signed published writing: a review in *Mind*.

1896   Appointed one of first lecturers at London School of Economics. Publication of his first book *German Social Democracy*. Travels to USA and lectures on non-Euclidean geometry at Bryn Mawr College and Johns Hopkins University. Member of Fabian Society and Aristotelian Society.

1897   Publication of *The Foundations of Geometry*.

1898   Influenced by G. E. Moore into rejecting the philosophies of Kant and Hegel.

1899   Lectures on Leibniz at Trinity College. At first, supports the British cause in the Boer War.

1900   Publication of *The Philosophy of Leibniz*. Attends International Congress of Philosophy in Paris with A. N. Whitehead. Meets Peano, whose work provides him with a technique of logical analysis. Drafts *The Principles of Mathematics*.

1901   Lectures on Mathematical Logic at Trinity. Beginnings of *Principia Mathematica*. A 'mystic insight' changes his views on war and personal relationships. Begins life-long friendship with Gilbert Murray.

1902   Writes *The Free Man's Worship* after realizing his love for Alys has died.

1903   *The Principles of Mathematics* published.

1903–4   Intellectual deadlock over 'Russell's paradox'. Writes and speaks on Free Trade.

1905   Discovers his 'Theory of Descriptions'.

1906   Discovers the 'Theory of Types'. Elected to London Mathematical Society.

1907   Stands for parliament in Wimbledon by-election, campaigning for Women's Suffrage and Free Trade, and is defeated.

1907–9   Working 10–12 hours a day for 8 months in the year on *Principia Mathematica*.

1908   Elected Fellow of the Royal Society. Attends International Congress of Mathematicians in Rome.

1909   Criticizes William James's philosophy of Pragmatism.

1910   Publication of 1st volume of *Principia Mathematica*. Appointed lecturer in Logic and Principles of Mathematics at Trinity College for 5 years. Active in politics on behalf of the Liberals but rejected as candidate for Bedford because of his lack of religion. *Philosophical Essays* published.

1911   Break-up of marriage after falling in love with Lady Ottoline Morrell. Lectures at Sorbonne in Paris. Meets Wittgenstein. Elected President of the Aristotelian Society.

1912   Criticizes Bergson's philosophy. Publication of *The Problems of Philosophy* and of 2nd volume of *Principia Mathematica*. Re-elected President of the Aristotelian Society. Presides over a section of the International Congress of Mathematicians held at Cambridge.

1913   Beginning of friendship with Joseph Conrad. Publication of 3rd volume of *Principia Mathematica*.

1914   Second trip to USA. Delivers Lowell lectures on *Our Knowledge of the External World* (subsequently published under the same title) while visiting professor of philosophy at Harvard. T. S. Eliot one of his students there. Public speeches in England against the war. Helps to organize Union of Democratic Control, an anti-war organization. Herbert Spencer Lecturer at Oxford.

1915   Delivers course of public lectures in London called 'Principles of Social Reconstruction'. Brief, explosive friendship with D. H. Lawrence. Awarded Nicholas Murray Butler Medal of Columbia University for outstanding work in philosophy. *Justice in War-Time* published. Public controversy with Gilbert Murray. Ceases to be a Liberal and becomes a Socialist.

1916   Active with the No-Conscription Fellowship. Meets Lady Constance Malleson. Open letter to US President Wilson appealing to him to use his influence to obtain peace. Writes leaflet on behalf of an imprisoned conscientious objector; is prosecuted and fined £100. Dismissed from lectureship at Trinity. War Office restricts his movements. *Principles of Social Reconstruction* published.

1916–17   Edits *The Tribunal*, organ of No-Conscription Fellowship.

1917   *Political Ideals*, containing public lectures banned by the War Office, published in USA only. Rejoices in Russian revolutions.

1918   Imprisoned for 5 months as a result of an article he wrote for *The Tribunal*. Writes *Introduction to Mathematical Philosophy* and begins *The Analysis of Mind* in prison. Delivers public lectures on the Philosophy of Logical Atomism. *Roads to Freedom* and *Mysticism and Logic* published. The war marks a change in Russell's outlook on life. As a result he becomes increasingly involved in social as opposed to purely intellectual problems.

1919   Beginnings of relationship with future second wife Dora Black. *Introduction to Mathematical Philosophy* published. Meets Wittgenstein at The Hague to discuss *Tractatus Logico-Philosophicus*. Public lectures on philosophy in London. Accepts offer of five-year lectureship in Logic and the Principles of Mathematics at Trinity College.

1920   Lectures at Barcelona. Visits Soviet Union with Labour delegation, has interview with Lenin. Writes and publishes *The Practice and Theory of Bolshevism*. Visits China with Dora Black.

1921   Divorce from Alys finalized. Lectures as professor of philosophy at National University of Peking. Visits Japan. On return to England marries Dora Black. Birth of his first son John Conrad. *The Analysis of Mind* published. Lectures in London and Manchester on 'International Problems of the Far East'. Resigns from Trinity lectureship without having lectured.

1922   Family life in Sydney Street, Chelsea, and Porthcurno, Cornwall.

           The Problem of China published. Stands for parliament in Chelsea as Labour candidate and is defeated. Delivers Moncure D. Conway Memorial Lecture. Writes Introduction to Wittgenstein's *Tractatus*.

1923   Daughter Katharine born. *The Prospects of Industrial Civilization* and *The ABC of Atoms* published. Stands again as Labour candidate in Chelsea and is defeated. Delivers 'Vagueness' paper to Jowett Society, Oxford.

1924   *Icarus, or the Future of Science* published. Lecture tour in USA, including public debates. Presidential address to Student Union of London School of Economics.

1925   *What I Believe* and *The ABC of Relativity* published. Volume I of 2nd edition of *Principia Mathematica* published.

1926   *On Education, Especially in Early Childhood* published (in USA, as *Education and the Good Life*). Tarner Lecturer at Trinity College on the Analysis of Matter. Lectures at British Institute of Philosophy.

1927   With Dora, starts experimental school at Telegraph House, Petersfield. Lecture tour in USA. Delivers lecture on *Why I Am Not a Christian*. Publishes *An Outline of Philosophy* (in USA, as *Philosophy*), *The Analysis of Matter*, and *Selected Essays of Bertrand Russell*.

1928   *Sceptical Essays* published.

1929   Lecture tour in USA. *Marriage and Morals* published. Meets 'Peter' Spence.

1930   *The Conquest of Happiness* published. Dora gives birth to child not fathered by Russell.

1931   Lecture tour in USA. Dictates draft of *Autobiography* to 1921. Becomes 3rd Earl Russell on his brother's death. Begins four-year series of weekly articles for Hearst press. *The Scientific Outlook* published.

1932   Dora gives birth to 2nd child not fathered by Russell. Separates from Dora. Publishes *Education and the Social Order* (in USA, as *Education and the Modern World*). Awarded Sylvester Medal of the Royal Society. President of the India League.

1933   Awarded the de Morgan Medal of the London Mathematical Society. In fortnightly articles for the *Sunday Referee*, reacts strongly to advent of National Socialism in Germany and also writes on economic causes of the Depression. Champions Roosevelt's domestic and foreign (especially disarmament) policies.

1933–4   With Patricia Spence, his research secretary, writes and publishes *Freedom and Organization, 1814–1914*.

1935   Divorce from Dora Black. Publishes *In Praise of Idleness* and *Religion and Science*. Begins research with Patricia Spence for

	The Amberley Papers. Decides to regain his philosophical reputation. Elected to 3rd term as President of the Aristotelian Society.
1936	Marriage to Patricia Spence. Delivers Earl Grey Memorial Lecture. *Which Way to Peace?* published. Advocates pacifism in next war in speeches and articles.
1937	Birth of second son Conrad. *The Amberley Papers* published. Lectures on social philosophy at London School of Economics. Discusses foreign affairs in maiden speech in House of Lords. Presidential address to Conference of Educational Associations. Introduction to 2nd edition of *The Philosophy of Leibniz*.
1938	Special lecturer at University of Oxford on 'Words and Facts', an early version of *An Inquiry into Meaning and Truth*. *Power: A New Social Analysis* published. Supports British policy at Munich. Introduction to 2nd edition of *The Principles of Mathematics*. Travels with Patricia and Conrad to USA, appointed visiting professor of philosophy at University of Chicago and lectures on 'Words and Facts'.
1939	Appointed professor of philosophy at University of California at Los Angeles. Outbreak of war prevents return of John and Kate to England. Lecture tour of USA.
1940	Offered professorship at New York City College. Appointment revoked in controversial court case. Declares his support for the Second World War. Delivers William James lectures at Harvard, published as *An Inquiry into Meaning and Truth*.
1941–2	Lectures at Barnes Foundation in Pennsylvania on the History of Philosophy (these lectures provide the basis of his *History of Western Philosophy*).
1942–3	Dismissed from Barnes Foundation – later wins court case claiming breach of contract by Dr Barnes. Lectures at Rand School of Social Science on 'The Problems of Democracy' and 'Philosophies in Practice'.
1944	Friendship with Einstein while at Princeton. On return to England appointed lecturer for five years and Fellow of Trinity College. Publication of P. A. Schlipp's *The Philosophy of Bertrand Russell*, to which he contributes. Begins long participation on BBC *Brains Trust* programme.
1945	*A History of Western Philosophy* published. Predicts development of hydrogen bomb in speech to House of Lords. Writing *Human Knowledge*. Campaigns for World Government for next decade.
1946	Delivers Henry Sidgwick Lecture at Newnham College, Cambridge. Delivers National Book League Annual Lecture.
1946–8	Frequent lecturing on the Continent for such organizations as the New Commonwealth and the Foreign Office.

1947   Attends International Congress of Philosophy in Brussels. Pamphlet *The Faith of a Rationalist* published.

1948   Many broadcasts for the BBC. Sent to Norway by British Government to encourage Norwegians to join alliance against the Soviet Union. *Human Knowledge* published. Controversy over his advocacy of threatening USSR with atomic weapons to join a world government.

1949   Delivers 1st Reith Lectures on BBC, published as *Authority and the Individual*. Awarded Docteur Honoris Causa by the Université d'Aix-Marseille. Awarded the Order of Merit by George VI. Delivers Lloyd Roberts Lecture to Royal Society of Medicine. Lectures at Ruskin College, Oxford. Expands and updates his *Autobiography*. Separates from Patricia.

1950   Lectures at the Sorbonne. Travels to Australia as visiting lecturer and then to the USA where he lectures at Mt Holyoake College and Princeton, and gives Matchette Foundation Lectures at Columbia University. Awarded Nobel Prize for Literature. *Unpopular Essays* published. Shares new home with son John and family.

1951   Matchette Foundation Lectures published in USA as *The Impact of Science on Society*. *New Hopes for a Changing World* published. Lecture tour in USA.

1952   Divorce from Patricia Spence. Marriage to Edith Finch. Expanded version of *Impact of Science on Society* published in England. Publicly criticizes increasing illiberalism in America. Elected to Athenaeum Club.

1953   His first book of stories, *Satan in the Suburbs*, published.

1954   The Bikini hydrogen bomb tests lead to his 'Man's Peril' broadcast on the BBC. *Human Society in Ethics and Politics* and *Nightmares of Eminent Persons* published. Delivers Herman Ould Memorial Lecture on 'History as an Art'.

1955   Attends International Congress of Parliamentarians for World Government in Rome, World Assembly for Peace in Helsinki (*in absentia*), International Congress of the World Movement for World Government in Paris, and the World Conference of Scientists in London. Einstein agrees to sign manifesto based on 'Man's Peril'. London press conference on Nobel Prize scientists' manifesto (known as the Russell–Einstein statement).

1956   Dinner in his honour given by World Government Association at House of Commons. Campaigns on behalf of Morton Sobell. *Portraits from Memory* and *Logic and Knowledge* published. Condemns British intervention in Suez and Russian intervention in Hungary.

1957   Elected President of 1st Pugwash Conference of Scientists from both East and West. Wide publication of his Open Letter to Khrushchev and Eisenhower urging cooperation between East and West. Awarded Kalinga Prize by UNESCO. Publication of *Bertrand Russell, The Passionate Sceptic*, a biography of Russell by Alan Wood, and of *Why I Am Not a Christian* and *Understanding History* (in USA only). Participates in founding of Campaign for Nuclear Disarmament. Criticizes current linguistic trends in English philosophy.

1958   Launches Campaign for Nuclear Disarmament of which he is President. Devotes most of his time henceforth to advocacy of nuclear disarmament and international peace. *The Vital Letters of Russell, Krushchev, Dulles* published.

1959   *Common Sense and Nuclear Warfare, Wisdom of the West* and *My Philosophical Development* published.

1960   Addresses CND demonstration at Trafalgar Square. Resigns from Presidency of CND. Becomes President of the Committee of 100. Writes pamphlet *Act or Perish* advocating mass civil disobedience. Awarded the Sonning Prize in Denmark. *Bertrand Russell Speaks His Mind* published. Begins working with Ralph Schoenman and soon hires him as secretary.

1961   Leads mass sit-down outside Ministry of Defence to protest against British Government's nuclear policies. He and his wife sentenced to 2 months' imprisonment; reduced to one week for reasons of health. Publication of *Fact and Fiction, Has Man a Future?* and *The Basic Writings of Bertrand Russell*. Elected Honorary Fellow of London School of Economics.

1962   His 90th birthday celebrations include a concert and luncheon in his honour at the House of Commons. Discussions with U Thant about world nuclear and disarmament policies. Acts as intermediary between Khrushchev and Kennedy in Cuban Crisis and between Nehru and Chou En-lai in Sino-Indian border conflict.

1963   Presented with American Emergency Civil Liberties Union's Tom Paine Award. Launches Bertrand Russell Peace Foundation, designed to institutionalize his increasing international activity. Increasingly devotes himself to opposing the war in Vietnam. *Unarmed Victory* and *Essays in Scepticism* (in USA only) published.

1964   President of the British 'Who Killed Kennedy?' Committee. Writes articles attacking American policies in Vietnam.

1965   Delivers two speeches on 'The Labour Party's Foreign Policy'. Resigns from British Labour Party.

1966   Addresses founding conference of Vietnam Solidarity Campaign and preparatory meeting of International War Crimes Tribunal.

1967   Publication of Volume I of *The Autobiography of Bertrand Russell* and *War Crimes in Vietnam*.

1968   Publication of Volume II of the *Autobiography*. Sells his archives to McMaster University.

1969   Publication of Volume III of the *Autobiography* and *Dear Bertrand Russell* . . . Authors 'Private Memorandum on Ralph Schoenman' after severing ties with his former secretary.

1970   After a short illness dies on February 2 at Plas Penrhyn, Penrhyndeudraeth, Merionethshire, Wales.

Appendix: Chronological Table of Reprinted Articles

Date	Author	Article	Journal Reference	Vol.	Chap.
1903	G. Frege	The Russell Paradox	*The Basic Laws of Arithmetic: Exposition of the System*, Berkeley and Los Angeles: University of California Press, 1964, pp. 127–30	II	1
1904	E. Wilson	The Foundations of Mathematics	*Bulletin of the American Mathematical Society*, vol. 11, pp. 74–93	II	2
1912	J. Shaw	What Is Mathematics?	*Bulletin of the American Mathematical Society*, vol. 18, pp. 386–411	II	3
1915	J. Dewey	The Existence of the World as a Problem	*The Philosophical Review*, vol. 24, pp. 357–70	III	3
1915	G. F. Stout	Mr Russell's Theory of Judgment	*Proceedings of the Aristotelian Society*, n.s. vol. 15, pp. 332–52	III	4
1916	C. E. Van Horn	An Axiom in Symbolic Logic	*Proceedings of the Cambridge Philosophical Society*, vol. 19, pp. 22–31	II	4
1926	F. P. Ramsey	Mathematical Logic	*Mathematical Gazette*, vol. 13, pp. 185–194	II	5
1927	T. S. Eliot	*Why I Am Not a Christian*	*The Monthly Criterion*, vol. 6, pp. 177–9	IV	11
1928	H. A. Prichard	Mr Bertrand Russell's *Outline of Philosophy*	*Mind*, vol. 37, pp. 265–82	III	5
1928	P. Weiss	The Theory of Types	*Mind*, vol. 37, pp. 338–48	II	6
1930	E. M. Kayden	A Tract on Sex and Marriage	*The Sewanee Review*, vol. 38, pp. 104–8	IV	5
1931	R. Carnap	The Logistic Foundations of Mathematics	*Philosophy of Mathematics*, P. Benacerraf and H. Putnam (eds), 2nd ed., Cambridge: Cambridge University Press, 1983, pp. 41–52	II	10
1938	W. V. Quine	On the Theory of Types	*The Journal of Symbolic Logic*, vol. 3, pp. 125–39	II	7
1944	K. Gödel	Russell's Mathematical Logic	*The Philosophy of Bertrand Russell*, P. A. Schlipp (ed.), New York: Tudor, pp. 125–53	II	9
1947	I. Berlin	*A History of Western Philosophy*	*Mind*, vol. 56, pp. 151–66	IV	3

Appendix continued

Date	Author	Article	Journal Reference	Vol.	Chap.
1949	P. Edwards	Russell's Doubts about Induction	*Mind*, vol. 58, pp. 141–63	III	18
1950	P. F. Strawson	On Referring	*Mind*, vol. 59, pp. 320–44	III	11
1954	B. Russell	Prologue or Epilogue?	*Human Society in Ethics and Politics*, London: George Allen & Unwin, pp. 235–9	IV	
1956	G. Bergmann	Russell's Examination of Leibniz Examined	*Philosophy of Science*, vol. 23, pp. 175–203	IV	2
1956	B. Russell	Prologue: What I Have Lived For	*The Autobiography of Bertrand Russell*, vol. 1, London: George Allen and Unwin, 1967, pp. 3–4.	I	
1956	L. Wittgenstein	*Remarks on the Foundations of Mathematics*, II §§ 1–14	*Remarks on the Foundations of Mathematics*, Oxford: Blackwell, pp. 65e–72e	II	11
1957	A. Wood	Marriage and Morals	*Bertrand Russell: The Passionate Sceptic*, London: George Allen & Unwin, pp. 166–74	IV	6
1959	A. Wood	Russell's Philosophy: A Study of its Development	*My Philosophical Development*, Bertrand Russell, New York: Simon and Schuster, pp. 260–72	I	5
1960	D. H. Monro	Russell's Moral Theories	*Philosophy*, vol. 35, pp. 30–50	IV	4
1962	A. Church	Mathematics and Logic	*Logic, Methodology and Philosophy of Science: Proceedings of the 1960 International Congress*, E. Nagel, P. Suppes and A. Tarski (eds), Stanford: Stanford University Press, pp. 181–6	II	21
1963	J. Park	The Beacon Hill School	*Bertrand Russell on Education*, Columbus: Ohio State University Press, pp. 138–57	IV	9
1966	S. Hook	Lord Russell and the War Crimes Trial	*The New Leader*, vol. 49, 24 October 1966, pp. 6–11	IV	14
1967	B. Feinberg and K. Blackwell	A Short Chronology, 1872–1970	*A Detailed Catalogue of the Archives of Bertrand Russell*, B. Feinberg (ed.), London: Continuum 1 Ltd, pp. 11–15	I	

Date	Author	Article	Journal Reference	Vol.	Chap.
1967	I. F. Stone	To Oppose the Stream	*Bertrand Russell: Philosopher of the Century*, R. Schoenman (ed.), Boston: Little, Brown and Company and The Atlantic Monthly Press, pp. 56–60	IV	17
1970	H. Hochberg	Strawson, Russell, and the King of France	*Philosophy of Science*, vol. 37, pp. 363–84	III	12
1970	D. Kaplan	What is Russell's Theory of Descriptions?	*Physics, Logic, and History*, W. Yourgau and A. D. Breck (eds), New York and London: Plenum Press, pp. 277–88	III	10
1971	A. J. Ayer	His Conception of Philosophy	*Russell and Moore: The Analytical Heritage*, Cambridge, Mass.: Harvard University Press, pp. 10–15	III	2
1972	A. J. Ayer	Bertrand Russell as a Philosopher	*Proceedings of the British Academy*, vol. 58, pp. 127–51	I	4
1972	E. R. Eames	Russell on 'What There Is'	*Revue internationale de philosophie*, vol. 26, pp. 483–98	III	8
1973	C. D. Broad	Bertrand Russell, as Philosopher	*The Bulletin of the London Mathematical Society*, vol. 5, pp. 328–41	I	1
1973	B. Feinberg and R. Kasrils	A Chair of Indecency	*Bertrand Russell's America 1896–1945*, B. Feinberg and R. Kasrils (eds), New York: The Viking Press, pp. 135–67	I	8
1973	R. O. Gandy	Bertrand Russell, as Mathematician	*The Bulletin of the London Mathematical Society*, vol. 5, pp. 342–8	I	2
1973	G. Kreisel	Bertrand Arthur William Russell, Earl Russell: 1872–1970	*Biographical Memoirs of Fellows of the Royal Society*, vol. 19, pp. 583–620	I	3
1974	R. M. Chisholm	On the Nature of Acquaintance: A Discussion of Russell's Theory of Knowledge	*Bertrand Russell's Philosophy*, G. Nakhnikian (ed.), London: Duckworth, pp. 47–56	III	13

Appendix continued

Date	Author	Article	Journal Reference	Vol.	Chap.
1974	W. C. Salmon	Russell on Scientific Inference or Will the Real Deductivist Please Stand Up	*Bertrand Russell's Philosophy*, G. Nakhnikian (ed.), London: Duckworth, pp. 183–208	III	19
1974	R. Schoenman	Bertrand Russell and the Peace Movement	*Bertrand Russell's Philosophy*, G. Nakhnikian (ed.), London: Duckworth, pp. 227–52	IV	15
1974	E. F. Sherman	Bertrand Russell and the Peace Movement: Liberal Consistency or Radical Change?	*Bertrand Russell's Philosophy*, G. Nakhnikian (ed.), London: Duckworth, pp. 253–63	IV	16
1974	R. Wollheim	Bertrand Russell and the Liberal Tradition	*Bertrand Russell's Philosophy*, G. Nakhnikian (ed.), London: Duckworth, pp. 209–20	IV	7
1975	J. Pitt	Russell on Religion	*International Journal for Philosophy of Religion*, vol. 6, pp. 40–53	IV	12
1976	A. Church	Comparison of Russell's Resolution of the Semantical Antinomies with that of Tarski	*The Journal of Symbolic Logic*, vol. 41, pp. 747–60	II	8
1981	K. Blackwell	The Early Wittgenstein and the Middle Russell	*Perspectives on the Philosophy of Wittgenstein*, I. Block (ed.), Cambridge, Mass.: MIT Press, pp. 1–30	I	6
1981	G. Hellman	How to Gödel a Frege-Russell: Gödel's Incompleteness Theorems and Logicism	*Nous*, vol. 15, pp. 451–68	II	12
1981	W. Lycan	Logical Atomism and Ontological Atoms	*Synthese*, vol. 46, pp. 207–29	III	15
1981	D. Pears	The Function of Acquaintance in Russell's Philosophy	*Synthese*, vol. 46, pp. 149–66	III	14
1982	N. Griffin and G. Zak	Russell on Specific and Universal Relations	*History and Philosophy of Logic*, vol. 3, pp. 55–67	III	7

Date	Author	Article	Journal Reference	Vol.	Chap.
1982–3	K. Tait	Portrait of the Philosopher as Father	*Russell: The Journal of the Bertrand Russell Archives*, n.s. vol. 2, pp. 21–30	I	10
1984	T. C. Kennedy	Nourishing Life: Russell and the Twentieth-Century British Peace Movement, 1900–18	*Intellect and Social Conscience: Essays on Bertrand Russell's Early Work*, M. Moran and C. Spadoni (eds), *Russell: The Journal of the Bertrand Russell Archives*, n.s. vol. 4, Hamilton, Ont.: McMaster University Library Press, pp. 223–36	IV	13
1985	W. Demopoulos and M. Friedman	The Concept of Structure in *The Analysis of Matter*	*Philosophy of Science*, vol. 52, pp. 621–639	III	17
1985–6	H. Woodhouse	Science as Method: The Conceptual Link between Russell's Philosophy and His Educational Thought	*Russell: The Journal of the Bertrand Russell Archives*, n.s. vol. 5, pp. 150–61	IV	8
1986	P. Delany	Russell's Dismissal from Trinity: A Study in High Table Politics	*Russell: The Journal of the Bertrand Russell Archives*, n.s. vol. 6, pp. 39–61	I	7
1987	W. Hare	Russell's Contribution to Philosophy of Education	*Russell: The Journal of the Bertrand Russell Archives*, n.s. vol. 7, pp. 25–41	IV	10
1987	L. Linsky	Russell's 'No-Classes' Theory of Classes	*On Being and Saying: Essays for Richard Cartwright*, J. Jarvis Thomson (ed.), Cambridge, Mass.: MIT Press, pp. 21–39	II	18
1988	A. Ryan	War and Peace in the Nuclear Age	*Bertrand Russell: A Political Life*, New York: Hill and Wang, pp. 172–206, 216–217	I	9
1988	J. G. Slater	Russell's Conception of Philosophy	*Russell: The Journal of the Bertrand Russell Archives*, n.s. vol. 8, pp. 163–78	III	1
1988	R. E. Tully	Russell's Neutral Monism	*Russell: The Journal of the Bertrand Russell Archives*, n.s. vol. 8, pp. 209–24	III	16

Appendix continued

Date	Author	Article	Journal Reference	Vol.	Chap.
1989	W. D. Goldfarb	Russell's Reasons for Ramification	*Rereading Russell*, C. W. Savage and C. A. Anderson (eds), *Minnesota Studies in the Philosophy of Science*, vol. 12, Minneapolis: University of Minnesota Press, pp. 24–40	II	15
1989	A. D. Irvine	Epistemic Logicism and Russell's Regressive Method	*Philosophical Studies*, vol. 55, pp. 303–27	II	13
1989	G. Landini	New Evidence concerning Russell's Substitutional Theory of Classes	*Russell: The Journal of the Bertrand Russell Archives*, n.s. vol. 9, pp. 26–42	II	19
1990	P. W. Hylton	Logic in Russell's Logicism	*The Analytic Tradition: Meaning, Thought and Knowledge*, D. Bell and N. Cooper (eds), Oxford: Blackwell, pp. 137–72	II	14
1990	B. Linsky	Was the Axiom of Reducibility a Principle of Logic?	*Russell: The Journal of the Bertrand Russell Archives*, n.s. vol. 10, pp. 125–40	II	16
1992	P. Simons	On What There Isn't: The Meinong–Russell Dispute	*Philosophy and Logic in Central Europe from Bolzano to Tarski*, Dordrecht: Kluwer Academic Publishers, pp. 159–91	III	6
1993	G. Hunter	Russell Making History: The Leibniz Book	*Russell and Analytic Philosophy*, A. D. Irvine and G. A. Wedeking (eds), Toronto: University of Toronto Press, pp. 397–414	IV	1
1993	F. Rodríguez-Consuegra	Russell, Gödel and Logicism	*Philosophy of Mathematics: Proceedings of the 15th International Wittgenstein-Symposium*, J. Czermak (ed.), Vienna: Verlag Hölder-Pichler-Tempsky, pp. 233–42	II	20

Date	Author	Article	Journal Reference	Vol.	Chap.
1994	G. Boolos	The Advantages of Honest Toil Over Theft	*Mathematics and Mind*, A. George (ed.), Oxford: Oxford University Press, pp. 27–44	II	17
1995	B. Linsky	Russell's Logical Constructions	*Studies in Dialectics of Nature*, supplementary vol. 11, pp. 129–48	III	9

1

Bertrand Russell, as Philosopher

C. D. Broad

Bertrand Arthur William Russell was grandson on the paternal side of the Whig statesman Lord John Russell (1792–1878). The latter was a younger son of the sixth Duke of Bedford (1766–1839), and was created Earl Russell and Viscount Amberley in 1861. Lord John Russell's eldest son (by his second wife Frances Anna Maria Elliot, daughter of the Earl of Minto) was John Russell (1842–1876). The latter bore the courtesy title of Viscount Amberley; but, dying before his father, never became Earl Russell. He married in 1864, becoming the father in 1865 of Bertrand Russell's elder brother John Francis Stanley Russell (1865–1931) and, in 1872, of Bertrand Russell himself. The former became second Earl Russell in 1878, on the death of his paternal grandfather. He died, much married but without legitimate male issue, in 1931, whereupon his younger brother Bertrand succeeded as third Earl Russell.

Bertrand Russell's mother was Katherine Louisa Stanley (1842–1874). She was a daughter of the second Lord Stanley of Alderley (1802–1869) and the latter's wife *née* Henrietta Maria Dillon (1807–1895). The former was a descendant of Gibbon's Lord Sheffield (1735–1821), and the latter was a highly original and outspoken member of a noble family of Irish Jacobites. Through his mother Bertrand Russell was nephew to Rosalind Stanley, who became Countess of Carlisle, and was a celebrated and highly cranky *grande dame* in her day. Through the latter he became related by marriage to that eminent classical scholar Gilbert Murray (1866–1957), whose wife, Lady Mary, was a daughter of Lady Carlisle.

On the death of his father in 1876 Bertrand Russell, then four years old, went to live with his paternal grandparents at their house Pembroke Lodge in Richmond Park, which had been presented for life to his grandfather in the 1840s by Queen Victoria. Two years later his grandfather died at the age of 86. Bertrand's elder brother Francis was sent in the normal way to boarding schools. But Bertrand himself was educated within the home, under the control of his grandmother and her unmarried daughter Lady Agatha Russell, by a sequence of governesses and tutors until the age of 16. The religious atmosphere of the home was that of broad-church Protestant Christianity.

From the age of about 14 to 16 Russell, as a result of much private reading and reflexion, came to reject first revealed religion, and then the standard philosophical arguments for theism, for human survival of bodily death, and for free-will. Naturally, he felt obliged to conceal all this from his grandmother and his aunt Agatha. In his *Autobiography* he sums up the situation as follows: 'After the age of 14 I found living at home only endurable at the cost of complete silence about everything that interested me.'

Just at the beginning of his 17th year Russell was sent away from home for educational purposes for the first time. It was not to an ordinary school, but to a cramming establishment at Southgate, then in the country, in Middlesex. Here he was to be specially coached for the Entrance Scholarship Examination at Trinity College, Cambridge. Most of his companions were rather stupid and backward young men, being crammed for entrance examinations which were a necessary hurdle in the way of becoming professional officers in the army. He found little in common with them, was much more shocked by their habitual conversation than a boy of more normal upbringing would have been, and was subjected at first to a certain amount of rough teasing and minor bullying. However, he managed to keep his end up; and the coaching in mathematics which he received must have been pretty efficient.

In the December of 1889 Russell took the Entrance Scholarship Examination at Trinity. He was awarded a Minor Scholarship in mathematics, and he took up residence as a freshman in October 1890.

A. N. Whitehead (1861–1947), who was to be so much associated with Russell's later work in logic, had been one of Russell's examiners. He had noted the outstanding ability of Russell and of another successful candidate, C. P. Sanger, who soon became one of Russell's closest friends. Whitehead therefore recommended them both (of course without their knowledge) to those running the ancient Cambridge society of intellectual *élites* known to those who were aware of its existence as 'The Apostles'. Russell was elected to it in 1892, and it played a very important part in his early life in Cambridge. Among those other members who already were or were destined soon to become distinguished philosophers, were, beside Whitehead himself, J. E. McTaggart (1866–1925) and G. E. Moore (1873–1958).

Russell first studied mathematics, and was classed as seventh Wrangler in the Mathematical Tripos. He then switched over to the study of philosophy and took a first class in Part II of the Tripos in 'Moral Science', as Philosophy was then termed in Cambridge. In 1895 he was elected to a

Fellowship of Trinity under the then Title (α). Such a Fellowship, popularly known as a 'Prize Fellowship' was awarded on the result of an annual competition, at which candidates were confined to members of the College below a certain age, and at which each candidate submitted a dissertation on a subject chosen by himself. Such a Fellowship lasted for six years, and involved no duties of residence, teaching, or research. The dissertation on which Russell was awarded his Fellowship, combined his mathematical and his philosophical interests, and it became the basis of his first published philosophical book *An Essay on the Foundations of Geometry* (1897).

At this point it will be convenient to append a list of Russell's main philosophical publications. Some of these were books, and others were important papers in various philosophical journals. In the case of the latter I attach the name of the journal in which the paper first appeared.

Year	Title
1897	*An Essay on the Foundations of Geometry*
1900	*A Critical Exposition of the Philosophy of Leibniz*
1903	*The Principles of Mathematics*
1904	Meinong's Theory of Complexes and Assumptions (*Mind*)
1905	On Denoting (*Mind*)
1906	The Monistic Theory of Truth (*Mind*)
1910	*Principia Mathematica* (with Whitehead) Vol. I
1911	Knowledge by Acquaintance and Knowledge by Description (*Proceedings of the Aristotelian Society*)
1912	*Principia Mathematica* (with Whitehead) Vol. II
	The Problems of Philosophy
	On the Relations of Universals and Particulars (*Proceedings of the Aristotelian Society*)
1913	*Principia Mathematica* (with Whitehead) Vol. III
1914	On the Nature of Acquaintance (*Monist*)
	On the Relation of Sense-data to Physics (*Scientia*)
	On Scientific Method in Philosophy (*Herbert Spencer Lecture* in Oxford)
	Our Knowledge of the External World
1915	The Ultimate Constituents of Matter (*Monist*)
1918–19	Philosophy of Logical Atomism (*Monist*)
1919	*Introduction to Mathematical Philosophy*
	On Propositions: What they Are and How they Mean (*Proceedings of the Aristotelian Society*)
1921	*The Analysis of Mind*
1924	Logical Atomism (Contribution to *Contemporary British Philosophy* Vol. I)
1927	*The Analysis of Matter*
	An Outline of Philosophy

The above list represents Russell's most important contributions to philosophy in a period of some 50 years, during which he had many non-philosophical interests and occupations.

The first point to note is the fundamental breach between the philosophical position of *An Essay on the Foundations of Geometry* and that of all Russell's later works.

Up to about 1897 Russell's philosophical views, like those of most of his British contemporaries, might be described as in general idealistic and in particular semi-Kantian. *The Foundations of Geometry* is dedicated to McTaggart, who was to become the most eminent of English idealist philosophers. And in the Preface Russell says that his main obligations in Logic are to Bradley, Sigwart, and Bosanquet. Kant had held that Space is an innate form which each human percipient imposes on everything that he can perceive as external. Russell's doctrine is on these lines, though it is much more abstract and hypothetical, and is based on a much deeper knowledge than Kant had or could have had of the various different types of geometry.

Very soon after this Russell's general philosophical position changed fundamentally, and it never reverted to anything of the nature of idealism. This was due largely to the influence of his slightly younger contemporary G. E. Moore. Russell, when in his third year at Cambridge, met Moore, then a freshman at Trinity, and was immensely impressed by him both as a person and as a thinker. Moore himself was for a while, under the influence of McTaggart, a kind of Hegelian. He emerged from this position through his own reflexions earlier than Russell, and it was through Moore's conversation that Russell came to abandon idealism. (Moore's famous article 'The Refutation of Idealism' appeared in *Mind* in 1903.) This influence is apparent in Russell's *The Principles of Mathematics* (1903), where it appears in a rather crude naive 'realism' (in the mediaeval sense) concerning universals and their necessary connexions and disconnexions, which are held to be knowable *a priori*, either by direct inspection or indirectly by logical demonstration.

In this book Russell accepted Meinong's very literal view of the relations between words and phrases and sentences, on the one hand, and various kinds of non-verbal entity, on the other. But very soon afterwards he rejected this, in view of the difficulties to which it leads in connexion with such sentences as 'Round squares do not exist'. This was in his paper

'On Denoting' (1905). This negative conclusion soon led on to a certain positive doctrine, which was one of Russell's most important contributions to philosophy in general, and which was destined to have a profound influence on the further development of his own philosophical views. This began with the analysis of 'Definite Descriptions' (e.g., such a phrase as 'The man in the iron mask'), and developed into the wider theory of 'Incomplete Symbols'. This positive doctrine is fully stated and argued in Russell's classical paper 'Knowledge by Acquaintance and Knowledge by Description' (1911).

The essential point of the analysis of Definite Descriptions is this. One starts with an intelligible sentence in the indicative (e.g., 'The man in the iron mask was French'), containing as grammatical subject or object a definite description (e.g., 'The man in the iron mask'). One substitutes for it a set of inter-connected sentences having the following properties: (a) none of them contains the original, or any other, descriptive phrase; (b) together they convey all the essential information which the original sentence would convey to a person who used it understandingly himself or who understood it when used by others.

Russell argues that a person can understand a descriptive sentence only if he knows *by acquaintance* every term (particular or universal) which is named in any of the sentences which together constitute the analysis of the original sentence.

Now Russell's theory of 'incomplete symbols' and of 'logical constructions' may be regarded as a general philosophical method, of which his analysis of definite descriptions was the first outstanding instance. The general theory may be put very roughly as follows. Certain words or phrases (e.g., 'point', 'chair', 'mind', 'atom', etc.) occur frequently in sentences which we all often use and in some sense understand. In many cases, moreover, one claims to know, or to believe with reasonable conviction, that there are entities corresponding to such words and phrases, and that there are facts corresponding to such sentences. But, when one considers what could be the nature of such entities, one often finds that it is of a highly speculative and doubtful kind, and that such an entity (e.g., an atom), would be very unlike anything that we know by acquaintance or could describe in terms so known.

So far as I can see, Russell's general recommendation in such cases is this: Try to replace any sentence which contains such a word or phrase by a set of inter-connected sentences having the following properties: (a) none of them contains the word or phrase in question or any mere substitute for it; (b) together they convey all the essential information conveyed by the original sentence; (c) the names and phrases which occur in them either are, or approximate as nearly as possible to, the names of such entities as one is or could be directly acquainted with.

Russell's philosophy consists largely in successive attempts to carry out this general recommendation in more detail and further and further. An important and typical example in *pure logic* and the theory of mathematics is Russell's anlaysis of sentences in which the word 'class' or any particular class-name (e.g., 'man') occurs. This appears first in *Principia Mathematica*, Vol. I, (1910). Here any such word is treated as an incomplete symbol. Any sentence in which it occurs is replaced by a certain set of inter-related sentences, in which it does not occur, but which are about the values of certain *propositional functions*. Russell does not deny that there may be entities of a special kind denoted by class-names. But he regards this as doubtful, and on that ground prefers to treat all such names as incomplete symbols and to analyse them away on the lines suggested.

We are concerned here rather with Russell's *ontology* than with his theories of logic and of pure mathematics. By this I mean his philosophy of (a) the common-sense beliefs which a person has about himself, about other men, and about the non-human things and events in the external world; and of (b) the development and organization of these beliefs provided by such sciences as physics and psychology. Now, as we have seen, an essential feature in the general procedure recommended by Russell is this. The names and phrases which occur in the sentences substituted for one containing an incomplete symbol should approximate as nearly as possible to those which denote such entities as one is or could be *directly acquainted with*. The development of Russell's ontology has consisted in trying to reduce more and more the number of different kinds of entity fulfilling the above conditions. I will now trace this process in more detail.

We may consider in turn the following two *prima facie* dualisms, namely, (1) that of universals and particulars, and (2) that of material and mental particulars.

(1) *Universals and Particulars.* The question here is whether it is necessary to hold that there are *universals*, i.e. qualities and/or relations, or whether we can get on with only particulars. Russell has argued throughout that universals, of one kind or another, are an indispensable factor in reality; though his views have varied considerably in detail in his various successive publications. Essentially his final position is that at the very least we must admit the reality of the *relation of similarity*; that, if one does this, there can be very little ground for denying that of other *relations*; and that, if one goes so far, there is no very good reason for doubting the reality of *qualities*.

(2) *Different Kinds of Particular.* Russell has never doubted that there are *particulars*. On his view anything that a person is 'acquainted with' (in his technical sense of that phrase) in sense-perception is a particular; and it is certain that each of us is acquainted from time to time in sense-perception with this or that object. The questions for him have been: What are the ultimate different kinds of particular? How few different kinds need to be accepted? How many of the various allegedly different kinds can be

dispensed with by means of appropriate logical constructions in terms of the one or the few which have to be accepted?

We may distinguish the following three different kinds of question which have arisen for Russell in this connexion. (i) A distinction has commonly been drawn, both in the case of material particulars and in that of mental ones, between, on the one hand, 'things' or 'substances' or 'continuants', and, on the other hand, 'events' or 'processes' or 'occurrents'. (An example would be the difference between a chair or a mind, on the one hand, and a flash of lightning or an experience of a twinge of pain, on the other.) (ii) Whatever decision we may reach on the above *categorical* distinction, as it might be called, we shall be left with another distinction which is commonly drawn between two kinds of particular, namely, *material and mental ones*. These have been alleged to be fundamentally different. (An example would be the difference between two such things as a chair and a mind, or two such events as a flash of lightning and an experience of feeling a twinge of pain.) (iii) Whatever conclusion may be reached as to (i) and (ii), the following questions, which may be called *epistemological*, remain for Russell. In the case of (a) *material* particulars a distinction is drawn between (α) the alleged immediate data of *sensation* (e.g., a roundish-looking, red-looking, visual sense-datum); (β) ordinary everyday *perceptible* things and events (e.g., a chair or a flash of lightning); and (γ) the *imperceptible* things and events postulated by physical science (e.g., a proton or an electron, or the motion of one of the latter about one of the former). And in the case of (b) *mental* particulars a sharp distinction is often drawn between (α) *one's own* mind and *one's own* experiences, on the one hand; and (β) on the other hand, the minds and the experiences of persons *other than oneself*. It is often held that one is directly acquainted with the former, and that one can know about the latter only very indirectly. How is one's alleged knowledge of the more remote and out-of-the-way of such objects related to one's knowledge of those with which one is directly acquainted?

Now Russell is concerned with questions arising under each of the above three headings. In the immediate sequel I will consider the development of his thought on topics concerned with (i) and (ii).

(i) *'Things' and 'Events'*. The position in regard to this question which Russell reached fairly early, and which he never afterwards saw reason to abandon, is this. The fundamental particulars, whether material or mental, are *events or processes*. Substance-names are incomplete symbols. The sentences to be substituted for one containing such a name contain only the names of *events*, and of certain complicated relations between the latter, which Russell endeavours to specify. When Russell asserts this, his statements must be understood as follows. By a 'particular' he means something which exists in time; and which, if it also exists in space, cannot occupy more than one place at any given time. And by an 'event' he means something that exists for a short stretch of time; and which, if it is extended, occupies a small finite region for such a stretch of time.

(ii) *Material and Mental Particulars*. On this topic there is a fundamental change in Russell's views with the publication in 1921 of his *The Analysis of Mind*. Up to then he had held that there are two different kinds of particular, namely, material and mental; though he had altered his views from time to time as to what were the ultimate kinds of mental particular. Thus, in *The Problems of Philosophy* (1912) he held (though with some hesitation) that each of us at each moment is acquainted with *himself* as subject of various experiences, existing at any rate for a brief period ending with that moment. By 1914, in 'On the Nature of Acquaintance' he had come to hold that one is *not* acquainted with oneself as subject, but is acquainted only with certain *mental states*. One's 'self' becomes a logical construction out of these latter standing in certain relations to each other. Russell expresses substantially the same view in his latest pronouncement on the question before 1921, namely, 'The Ultimate Constituents of Matter' (1915).

One may summarize the final position on this topic before 1921 roughly as follows. The ultimate particulars for the logical construction of the *material* world are *sensibilia*. These are short-lived, extended events. When a person is having a *sensation* he is being acquainted with a certain sensibile, and is aware by acquaintance of certain of the latter's qualities (e.g., its sensible blueness, roundness, etc.) and of certain of its relations (e.g., its being to the right of a certain other sensibile in his visual field at the time). When a person is thus being acquainted with a certain sensibile the latter is said to be a *sense-datum* for him. There is no reason to doubt that there are other particulars, of the same general nature as those which from time to time become sense-data to a person who is having a sensation, which never become sense-data. These may be called 'unsensed sensibilia'. Sensibilia (some sensed, and the vast majority unsensed) are the ultimate particulars in terms of which all logical constructions of statements about 'matter' must be made.

Now any sensation involves, beside the sensibile which is its immediate object (i.e. its sense-datum), an act or state of *sensing* (i.e. one of being acquainted). This is essentially *mental*. One is acquainted from time to time not only with this or that sensibile, when one has such and such a sensation. One is also acquainted from time to time, by introspection, with this or that occurrence (e.g., a sensation of one's own) which is, or which involves, a certain mental act or state (e.g., one of sensing). For any statement containing such words as 'mind' one should substitute appropriate sets of statements which do not contain any such word, but which do contain names of various mental acts or states, such as one is from time to time acquainted with by introspection.

The essential change in Russell's position which appears for the first time in his *The Analysis of Mind* is this. He drops the analysis of sensation into *act of sensing* (mental) and *sensed object* (non-mental), on the ground that the former can neither be observed nor legitimately inferred from anything that can be observed. He now recognizes only one ultimate kind of particular, namely, short-lived events of the kind which he formerly called 'sensibilia'. These are in themselves neither material nor mental; but they are the common stuff out of which are logically constructed both what we call 'minds' and/or 'mental events' and what we call 'material things' and/or 'physical events'. These are at least two fundamentally different kinds of ordered sets of such neutral particulars. One kind is ordered in accordance with laws of a *physical* sort, and the other kind in accordance with laws of a *psychological* sort.

As regards any one of the ultimate particulars there are the following three possibilities. (a) It may be *at once* a member of two sets, one ordered in accordance with physical laws and the other in accordance with psychological ones. In that case it will count as so-and-so's perception of such and such a material thing or physical event; and it will also count as such and such a state of so-and-so's brain, namely, as that one which physiologists would regard as the brain-state immediately correlated with that perception. (b) It may be a member *only* of a set ordered in accordance with *physical* laws. In that case it will count as an element in such and such an *unperceived* material thing or physical process. (c) It may be a member *only* of a set ordered in accordance with *psychological* laws. In that case it will count as a *purely mental* occurrence. (In his *The Analysis of Mind* Russell regards what we call 'mental images', whether arising spontaneously or called up deliberately, as instances of this third possibility.)

It is plain that at this stage the dualism which Russell formerly held to exist between two kinds of *particular*, namely, mental and non-mental, has been dropped. It has been replaced by a dualism between two kinds of *law*, namely, psychological and physical. There is no need here to elaborate the notion of physical laws, but something must be said about what Russell at this stage took to be the peculiarity of a psychological law.

At the time when he wrote *The Analysis of Mind* Russell had been much impressed with the notion of 'mnemic causation'. This he derived from two works by Semon, *Die Mneme* (1904) and *Die mnemischen Empfindungen* (1909). The idea of mnemic causation is this. There are plenty of instances in which there is a finite interval of time between a certain earlier event (e.g., meeting a certain person) and a certain later event (e.g., having an experience of remembering the incident), where the earlier event is certainly a necessary causal condition of the later one. Now it is commonly assumed that in all such cases the earlier event initiates a sequence of events, each of which is an effect of its immediate predecessor and a cause-factor in producing its immediate successor; that this sequence occupies the temporal gap between the earlier event and the later one; and that the later one is *immediately* caused by that one in this sequence which *immediately* precedes it. The essential feature in the doctrine of mnemic causation is to hold that there are cases in which the above common assumption is *false*. According to it, an earlier event may be an essential causal condition of a remotely later one *without* there being any such sequence of intermediate events as is commonly assumed to fill the temporal gap between the two. In such cases, where an essential factor in the *immediate* cause of an event is something that happened *at a finite period before* the latter began, we have mnemic causation.

Now, according to Russell in 1921, a 'mental image' may or may not have mnemic causes, but it always has mnemic effects. A sensation, on the other hand, has only physical causes, though it may have mnemic effects. This theory of mnemic causation is, I believe, peculiar to *The Analysis of Mind* among Russell's writings. It is certainly quite definitely given up in *Human Knowledge, its Scope and Limits* (1948).

It remains to mention one other characteristic feature of *The Analysis of Mind*. Russell has been reading carefully the writings of the American behaviourists, who claimed to get rid of everything that seemed *prima facie* to be specifically mental. With much of the programme of this school he found himself highly sympathetic. But they were not, and did not pretend to be, philosophers; whilst Russell was steeped in the problems of philosophy, had wrestled with many of them, and had offered various solutions to some. So a good deal of *The Analysis of Mind* may fairly be described as a strenuous attempt by a supremely able and well-informed philosopher to get as near to behaviourism as his philosophic conscience would allow. This tendency, like the neutral monism and unlike the mnemic causation, remained henceforth a permanent feature in Russell's philosophy.

I pass next to Russell's *The Analysis of Matter*, published in 1927. This work falls into three interconnected parts, which are concerned respectively with the following questions: (1) What is the logical structure of theoretical physics, considered simply as a hypothetical-deductive system? (2) How are the terms (e.g., atoms, electrons, electro-magnetic waves, etc.) and the laws (e.g., Maxwell's equations) of physics connected with the data of sense-perception, which must constitute the ultimate evidence for them? (3) What is the most plausible view of the contents and the structure of nature which shall be compatible with the answers given to the logical questions under (1) and to the epistemological questions under (2)?

Here we are concerned mainly with the questions discussed in Part II. The principal points which emerge are these:

(i) The common-sense view of an ordinary grown person is roughly this. The world consists of more or less permanent bodies, each of which combines many different qualities and passes through a sequence of various states. All these things exist in a common space; they interact with each other; and their changes have dates and durations in a common time.

Now this view, though practically universal, is by no means primitive. We can see infants painfully acquiring it by practice in their tender years. Russell suggests that the acquirement of conditioned reflexes in infancy is the physiological analogue of the use by a grown person of inductive arguments, and he holds that it plays an essential part in building up the common-sense grown-up view of the world.

(ii) If we take 'inference' in a wide sense, to cover the acquirement of conditioned reflexes before the use of speech and reasoning, it is difficult to point to anything that is a pure datum unmodified by inference. But we can still arrange various kinds of judgment in a hierarchy in this respect. We can see, e.g., that 'This is a sensibly red occurrence' involves much less inference than 'This is a red material thing'. So the problem is to show how judgments involving more 'inference' are based upon ones involving less.

(iii) Russell holds that the essential change in passing from the common-sense view of perception to the view of it taken by physical science is this. One abandons naive realism and adopts a *causal* theory.

The causal theory of perception has two sides to it, one negative and the other positive. The negative side is that what each of us is acquainted with in sense-perception is always something *private to himself*. Russell does not here trouble to consider the arguments for this. The positive side has the following two main features: (a) That various percepts of one's own which are correlated in certain ways with each other, and various correlated percepts of different persons, are all due to a common remote cause. (Examples would be those percepts which are taken as so many different visual appearances to oneself of one and the same thing from various points of view; and those percepts which are taken as visual appearances of the same thing to different persons.) (b) That some of the properties of such a remote cause can be inferred from the nature and inter-relations of such a set of correlated percepts.

(iv) The main conclusions which Russell reaches as to the positive side of the causal theory may be summarized as follows:

(a) It cannot be demonstrated. But, if we accept the validity of induction and of inverse hypothetical reasoning, it can be shown to be highly probable.

(b) The course of the argument would be roughly as follows:

(α) Each percipient can supplement the percepts which he actually has by other correlated ones which *he would have had if* he had followed up his actual percepts by a certain series of sensations of movement. This is an induction from cases in which such series were actually experienced and such and such correlated percepts actually followed.

(β) The next step is from the existence of *one's own* actual and possible percepts to that of others which are *not* one's own. It is at this stage that each of us constructs the notion of a space common to many percipients. Russell thinks that the argument, if set out, is one by analogy, and that it is very strong.

(γ) The last step is from the actual and possible percepts of oneself and of others to events which happen where and when there is *no actual percipient* (e.g., an explosion miles beneath the earth's surface, or a rain-storm before any men or animals existed); or which are such that no actual percipient *could* perceive them (e.g., an electromagnetic wave, an atom, etc.).

(c) Granted that we can legitimately infer to events which are not, and which perhaps from their nature could not, be perceived by anyone, how much can we know about the character of such events? Russell holds that we can infer with high probability from the *structural* features of our correlated percepts a good deal as to the *structural* features of unperceived and even of imperceptible events. But he holds that we can infer little or nothing from the *qualities* of the former to the *qualitative* character of the latter.

I think that we may fairly summarize the main content of 'The Philosophy of Matter' as follows. It is a very thorough attempt to carry out in detail a view of sense-perception and of the physical world such as was adumbrated by John Stuart Mill in his theory of material things as 'permanent possibilities of sensation'.

Of Russell's two later philosophical works, *An Inquiry into Meaning and Truth* (1940) and *Human Knowledge, its Scope and Limits* (1948), I shall consider only the latter, and only a part of that. Of the six sections into which the latter work is divided, those on 'Language' (Sect. II), on 'Science and Perception' (Sect. III), and on 'Scientific Concepts' (Sect. IV) cover much the same ground as does the former book. Russell's conclusions are essentially the same, though there is an increase of caution as to what we can reasonably conjecture about the detailed nature of the entities postulated by mathematical physics. Sect. V is concerned with Probability. All five lead up to Sect. VI, entitled 'The Postulates of Scientific Inference'. It is with this that I shall be mainly concerned, but I will first say something about Russell's views on Probability.

Probability, as discussed by pure mathematicians, is characterized by a set of axioms, from which theorems can be deduced. These axioms admit of various interpretations, and the pure mathematician is not concerned with these. The practical importance of the axioms is that we can give such interpretations to them as will bring the degree of probability of a statement into correlation with its degree of *credibility*. The notion of 'credibility' is a different one from that of 'probability', however the axioms may be interpreted; and there are kinds of statement which have a high degree of *credibility*, but to which the notion of *mathematical probability* (however interpreted) does not apply.

Russell's own interpretation of mathematical probability may be called the 'Finite Frequency Interpretation'. According to it, the probability of an A being a B is the ratio of the number of things which are both A and B to the number of those which are A. Now Russell holds that the notion of such a ratio is meaningless except on the assumption that the number of things which are A is *finite*. He therefore explicitly rejects the kind of *limiting* class-frequency interpretation which has been proposed by von Mises and by Reichenbach.

This brings us to Russell's conclusions about the logical status of *Induction*. They may be summarized as follows. No reasoning in terms of probability can validate the use of inductive argument *in general*. But such reasoning may raise the probability of a *particular inductive generalization* (e.g., 'All crows are black'), if and only if the latter already has some finite initial 'probability', in the sense of credibility. Now we cannot assign such an initial degree of credibility to any generalization unless we assume one or more general postulates as to the nature and structure of the external world. (So far Russell's position is essentially similar to that of J. M. Keynes in the latter's *A Treatise on Probability*. Keynes's suggested postulate is that of 'Limited Variety'.) Such postulates cannot, without logical circularity, be shown to be certain or even probable by any argument from experience.

The above forms the natural preliminary to Section VI, which is entitled 'The Postulates of Scientific Inference', and this is probably the most important part of the book.

Russell gives five postulates about the 'make-up' of the world, which he considers to be tacitly presupposed, though not usually explicitly formulated, in scientific research and in the construction of scientific theories.

The first of these is a form of the assumption that the world is composed of various more or less *permanent* 'things', with varying states and varying mutual relations. The second is a form of the following assumption. The causes of a given event are confined to a certain *limited part* of the total state of affairs immediately preceding it; and similarly its effects are confined to a certain limited part of the total state of affairs which will immediately follow it. The third postulate is essentially the denial of *actio in distans*. (Amusingly enough, it involves the denial of 'mnemic causation', which would be a kind of *actio in distans* in *time*.) It may be put as follows. If there is a spatial gap, or a temporal gap, or both, between two events which are causally connected with each other, then that gap must be filled by a causal chain of events forming a series of spatially and temporally *contiguous links*, starting from the earlier and ending with the later of the two.

The fourth postulate is considerably more specific than any of the first three. It may be stated as follows. Suppose that a number of complex events, all of which are alike in structure, occur in various regions which all lie in various directions from a common centre. Then it is to be assumed that there is at this centre an event of the same structure, and that each of these structurally similar events is on a different causal line emanating from this common central event. (For example, the various events in question might be so many heard bangs, each sensed by a different person at a different place and time. And the central event might be the discharge of a gun at a certain place at a certain earlier date.)

The fifth and last of these postulates is called by Russell that of 'Analogy'. It may be formulated as follows. Consider events of two kinds, say A-events and B-events. Suppose that, when *both* a certain A-event and a certain B-event can be observed, there is reason to believe that the former is an essential factor in causing the latter. A case may arise in which one observes an A-event, but where the circumstances are such that one would *not* be able to observe a B-event even if one were to follow. Then it is assumed to be highly probable that a B-event *will in fact* follow. (Similarly, if one observes a B-event under circumstances in which one could *not* have observed an A-event even if one had preceded, it is assumed to be highly probable that an A-event *actually did* precede.)

It is to acting in accordance with the fifth postulate that Russell ascribes *inter alia* the belief which each of us acquires in the existence of other conscious beings more or less like himself.

Russell appears to hold that the higher non-human animals and human infants have innate dispositions to behave in accordance with each of these five postulates. He says that the formation of inferential habits which lead to expectations which are in the main true is part of that adaption of a creature to its environment on which biological survival depends. But *deliberate* thinking and action, which is in fact in accordance with these postulates, can occur only in mature and suitably trained human beings. And *recognition* that thinking and action are taking place in accordance with such and such postulates can occur only in the course of philosophic reflexion on the nature of scientific practice and theory.

Human Knowledge: Its Scope and Limits had a respectful but relatively tepid reception by contemporary philosophers. Philosophic fashion in England at that time was mainly centred on what was called 'Logical Positivism'. The problems treated in the book, and the solutions proposed for them, lay outside this then fashionable area; and the interests and energies of most of those who could have understood it and have made intelligent criticisms on it were directed elsewhere.

In the above account of Russell's philosophy I have traced the gradual change in his opinions from what might be termed Platonic realism to naturalism and empiricism, and I have pointed out various specially marked stages in this. It would not be fair to end without mentioning certain qualifications which Russell has himself explicitly made. I can best do this by referring to certain remarks which he makes in the volume *The Philosophy of Bertrand Russell* (1944). I think that he would have been inclined to repeat them up to the end of his life; and I conclude by quoting some of them.

(1) 'even after I had abandoned Hegel, the eternal Platonic world gave me something non-human to admire. I thought of mathematics with reverence, and suffered when Wittgenstein led me to regard it as nothing but tautologies' (p. 19).

(2) 'I have always ardently desired to find some justifications for the emotions inspired by certain things that seemed to stand outside human life and to deserve feelings of awe . . . Those who attempt to make a religion of humanism, which recognizes nothing greater than man, do not satisfy my emotions. And yet I am unable to believe that, in the world as known, there is anything that I can value outside human beings and to a much less extent animals . . . ' (pp. 19–20).

(3) 'Suppose, for example, that someone was to advocate the introduction of bullfighting into this country. In opposing the proposal I should *feel*, not only that I was expressing my desires, but that my desires in the matter are *right*, whatever that may mean. As a matter of argument I can, I think, show that I am not guilty of any logical inconsistency in holding to' (a purely emotive) 'interpretation of ethics and at the same time expressing strong ethical preferences. But in feeling, I am not satisfied. I can only say that, while my own opinion as to ethics does not satisfy me, other people's satisfy me still less' (p. 724).

(4) 'What makes my attitude towards religion complex is that, although I consider some form of personal religion highly desirable, and find many people unsatisfactory through the lack of it, I cannot accept the theology of any well known religion, and I incline to think that most churches at most times have done more harm than good' (p. 726).

2

Bertrand Russell, as Mathematician

R. O. Gandy

Bertrand Russell is now and always will be chiefly remembered by mathematicians for his paradox concerning the class of all classes which are not members of themselves and for his creation of the theory of types. He will be remembered by historians of mathematics as co-author of *Principia Mathematica*, as a persuasive advocate for mathematical logic and logicism, and as a superb expositor and populariser of mathematical philosophy.

Russell had a brilliant, original and fertile mind. He devoted ten years (1900–1910) primarily to work in mathematics and its philosophy. So his actual and lasting contribution appears a poor return on capital invested; all the more so when we recall that Russell himself said ([20; p. 228]) of his work on the paradoxes and their solution: 'What made it more annoying was that the contradictions were trivial and that my time was spent in considering matters that seemed unworthy of serious attention.' Why was there such a gap between promise and achievement? One reason is accidental: in his discovery of logicism and his development of mathematical logic he had been anticipated by Frege. (And in many respects Frege's treatment is sharper and more lucid than Russell's.) But the main reason lies, I believe, in the *framework* of his philosophy. Although his philosophical beliefs changed substantially through the years, this framework remained the same from 1898 to his death. And the effect of maintaining it was continually to divert his attention from problems of mathematics and mathematical philosophy to more general philosophical questions. So this framework will be discussed first, then his contributions to mathematical philosophy and finally his contributions to mathematics.

Philosophical Framework

In [19] he describes his brief period (1894–1898) as an idealist. During it he wrote *An Essay on the Foundations of Geometry*, a study in the Kantian tradition in which it is shown that geometry is only 'possible' in a space of constant curvature. In 1898 he (together with G. E. Moore) abandoned idealism, and became convinced that there is an objective real world of which we can have exact knowledge. In what follows I shall refer to this simply as 'the world'. Initially his view was platonistic: the world contained abstract objects, such as numbers and points of space–time. But he moved, at first rapidly, and then with a gentler drift *towards* (not *to*) nominalism. The following tenets represent more or less constant features of his philosophy from 1900 to his death.

(1) There is a real world independent of human thought.
(2) By philosophical analysis we can, at least in principle, discover how the world may be described in terms of a certain minimum of irreducible constituents.
(3) The description will take the form of the assertion or the denial of atomic propositions. Each such proposition expresses that a particular primitive relation holds between certain particulars. Russell's views on the sort of things which will be counted as primitive relations or as particulars have varied greatly.
(4) By means of logical constructions we build up complex propositions and complex objects. This process covers not only the whole of logic, mathematics and physics, but also everyday objects.
(5) Russell's views on what should count as legitimate logical constructions also varied. But, except for the brief period during which he considered the 'no classes' theory (see below), the *minimum* apparatus considered was that provided by the ramified type theory of *Principia*.

An absolutely fundamental feature of this framework is that although the logical constructs need not themselves belong to the world,[1] they are built up from the constituents of the world and the atomic propositions which describe it. When Russell wrote 'The fact that all Mathematics is Symbolic Logic is one of the greatest discoveries of our age' ([3; p. 5]), he had in mind, I believe, not only the fact that the abstract objects of mathematics could be reduced to logical constructions, but also that the reduction answered, almost trivially, the question: why does mathematics apply to the real world? Indeed, Russell writes that *The principles of mathematics* grew from a question in the philosophy of dynamics ([3; p. xvi]). This is a strength of Russell's logicism; but, as we shall see, it is this anchoring of mathematics to 'the world' which helped to make his work so unproductive for mathematics.

Philosophy of Mathematics

(a) The Principle of Abstraction

Russell was proud of his discovery (also due to Frege) of, as we should now say, the notion of equivalence class. It is obviously an advance on the vague '*the* property which equivalent things have in common' (used, for example, by Peano). And unlike Cantor's method of postulation, the method does not call for new abstract objects other than classes. Russell worked it out in some detail in [2], and expounded its advantages in [3]. After the discovery of the contradiction, and the adoption of the theory of types it had to be reworked. This is done briefly in [7], and in great detail (for cardinal, ordinal, order-type and relation-number) in *Principia* – of which it forms indeed one of the main themes.

(b) The Contradictions and their Solution

Russell discovered his paradox in 1901 ('Never glad confident morning again' quoted Whitehead). From then until 1906 he searched for a solution; the miseries, both intellectual and personal, of this period are movingly described in the *Autobiography* ([20; Chapter VI]). He published many discussions of the paradoxes and possible solutions; the most important are in [3] (especially Appendix B), [4], [6] and [7]. Of these, [4] is the most profound and the most interesting mathematically. (It is the only paper which he published in the *Proceedings* of this Society.) In it, for once, the requirements of the mathematical imagination take precedence over those of the philosophical framework. (For a quotation, see below.) He describes very clearly three solutions.

(A) The Zigzag Theory (the name is misleading). The idea is that only straightforward, non-tricky propositional functions may determine classes. The difficulty is how to define 'straightforward'. This was overcome by Quine in 'New Foundations' ([Q1]). But as Russell foresaw the restrictions are not *intrinsically* plausible; they would look artificial to anyone ignorant of the paradoxes.

(B) The Theory of Limitation of Size: a propositional function shall only determine a class (i.e. a set in current terminology) if its extent is not too large. This is now the accepted solution. It was first suggested (but not published) by Cantor in [C1]. It is formalized in Zermelo–Fraenkel set-theory. Russell's objection to it has a point. Namely, axioms are required to determine what is *not* too large. The theory is essentially an *open* one: from time to time new and more powerful axioms of infinity may be proposed and accepted. For this reason, and also because it introduces objects which are neither logical constructions nor represented (for non-platonists) in the world, Russell never accepted this theory.

(C) The No Classes Theory: this has little connection with Russell's later view that classes are logical fictions. It says, essentially, that propositional functions, and variables for them shall not appear as arguments, but only through their values. Russell soon abandoned it.

His final solution was the theory of types (first described in [7], elaborated in [8] and revised in [14]). Propositions and propositional functions (relations in intension) are to be classified through the expressions which describe them into a hierarchy of types so that the type of a function (or a proposition for (b)) is: (a) above the type of any of its arguments and (b) above all the types over which quantified variables in its expression range. The Axiom of Reducibility says, in effect, that every function has the same extension as one which can be expressed by using quantifiers whose ranges are not of higher type than its arguments. Condition (a) is satisfied by ordinary mathematical practice, where variables always have well-defined ranges. But Russell, because of his concern with the philosophic framework, never appeals to this fact. Condition (b) is only required in two extreme cases:

(1) Platonist: if the world or the logical constructions contain *absolute* semantic notions (such as 'is true' or 'defines'), then (b) is necessary to avoid the semantic paradoxes. On this view (which seems to be that of the first edition of *Principia*) the axiom of reducibility is plausible. Russell later accepted the suggestion of Ramsey [R1], where (b) is dropped, and semantic notions are not absolute, but are assigned various linguistic levels.

(2) Nominalist: if propositional functions arise *only* by the finitary logical constructions of quantification theory then (b) is needed to avoid genuinely *vicious* circularities. In this case the axiom of reducibility is totally implausible. This is the position taken in the second edition of *Principia*. It is not adequate for classical analysis. Indeed, in [G1], which contains the most penetrating discussion of all these matters, Gödel casts doubt on its adequacy for number theory.[2]

Finally, it should be remarked that if only finitely generated types are used, then the theory is inadequate for the theory of cardinals not less than $\aleph_\omega$. Russell, as far as I know, never publicly discussed this limitation.

(c) Criticism

In [4] Russell expresses a moderate platonist viewpoint:

> When a new entity is introduced Dr. Hobson regards the entity as created by the activity of the mind, while I regard it as merely discerned; but this difference of interpretation can hardly affect the question whether the introduction of the entity is legitimate or not, which is the only question with which mathematics as opposed to philosophy is concerned.

But (because of his increasing concern with philosophical problems?) Russell gave up these admirable sentiments. In *Principia* the comment on the axiom of infinity is:

It seems plain that there is nothing in logic to necessitate its truth or falsehood, and that it can only be legitimately believed or disbelieved on empirical grounds.

([**8**; vol. II, p. 183])

This view is reiterated (and applied also to the axiom of choice) in 1937 ([**16**; p. viii]). It is a consequence of his philosophical framework, and 'empirical' must surely mean that abstract objects are not to be counted as existing in the world. If that world is finite, then mathematical objects, which are constructed from the constituents of the world, are also finite. But this is absurd. Suppose it were discovered that Eddington was right and that there are only $2.136.2^{256}$ fundamental particles in the universe. Would mathematicians immediately abandon classical number theory and analysis? Surely not; it would be the philosophical interpretation that might change. Indeed *Principia* itself exhibits the mathematician's indifference to empirical matters: by using typical ambiguity the authors ensure that their theorems do not depend, if the world *is* finite, on its exact size.

Russell's view is not only absurd, but it is also stultifying. This is because it denies the significance of the mathematical imagination and the value of mathematical experience. The mathematical ideas and results (not just the philosophical opinions) of, for example, Cantor, Hilbert, Brouwer, Zermelo, Skolem, Gödel, Tarski have totally transformed the philosophy of mathematics and our understanding of abstract and infinite objects. To be fair to Russell, he was not as dogmatic as the above quotation suggests. Also in [**16**] he writes:

It seems to me that these axioms either do or do not, have the characteristic of formal truth which characterises logic.

([**16**; p. xii])

He then suggests that the notion of 'logical form' points to a solution. If this is true, then new logical notions will be required (e.g., infinitary constructions). But these (and the types in the hierarchy) are abstract objects and, in general, infinite. Further investigations of them will lean heavily on *purely mathematical* results concerning infinite sets, or infinite constructions.

To sum up: Russell realized that for deciding the truth of certain crucial axioms the logic he had developed was inadequate. But he remained blind to the moral of this failure: an adequate logic must be based on *mathematical* imagination and knowledge.

Mathematical Content of Russell's Work

Almost all of Russell's mathematical work is represented in *Principia*. He felt that its mathematical content had been unduly ignored by other mathematicians (see Chapter 8 of [**19**]). It is not, of course, easy to use the book for rapid reference; though complete mastery of the elaborate notation is not in fact necessary for an understanding of the summaries which precede each section. But does it contain interesting *results* not available elsewhere? By and large the answer is: no. In particular, Hausdorff's book [**H1**] (1914) not only contains almost all the mathematically important theorems about cardinals, ordinals, and the order-types of linear orderings which appear in *Principia*, but much more – e.g., the theory of exponentiation for ordinals. The reason for this limitation is plain: the richness and rigidity of the notation and the superficial complexities with which the formal proofs have to cope, were obstacles for the authors, just as much as they are for the reader. For example, they refer to their proof of Cantor's theorem concerning the isomorphism of two countable open dense linear orderings as 'long and complicated' (vol. III, p. 299). It takes five closely packed pages as compared with the two leisurely pages of Cantor's original ([**C2**; pp. 505–506]) on which it is modelled. Complications arise because types have to be adjusted, disjointness of certain sets has to be secured, and (with a view to applications to the real world) the two orderings are not given enumerations, but are merely allotted orderings of type ω. The devices necessary to deal with these complications have been frequently used earlier in the book; at this stage they are purely routine. Interestingly, the authors do *not* introduce the genuine simplification of a back *and* forth argument (which is often, erroneously, attributed to Cantor).

Why didn't Russell and Whitehead content themselves with some sample complete formal proofs, while leaving much of the development informal? Besides the natural inertia which a large-scale project has, reasons are to be found in the mathematical climate of Cambridge in the 1890s. In ([**19**; p. 38]) Russell writes, 'The proofs that were offered of mathematical theorems were an insult to the logical intelligence. Indeed the whole subject of mathematics was presented as a set of clever tricks by which to pile up marks for the Tripos. The effect of all this upon me was to make me think mathematics disgusting.'[3] The metamathematics in *Principia* is not always quite precise. But every theorem is given a formal proof from the axioms; use of the axioms of infinity and of choice is always made explicit; great care is taken not to use unnecessary premises. In these respects it *is* a pioneering work – much more rigorous than was Peano, and covering a much wider range of subject matter than did Frege (as well as being based on a consistent class logic). It records a triumph of logic. Above all, it is a monument to the fortitude and perseverance of its authors.

Notes

1 In 1960 in conversation Russell recalled: 'When I met Professor Gödel I discovered that he was a complete platonist. I asked him if he believed that the real world contained the operation of negation. He said "yes", and, do you know, he gave a very good account of himself.'
2 J. Myhill has shown that with any reasonable definition of natural number in the ramified theory of types there will be instances of induction that cannot be proved. Gödel's suggestion is that this might be the case even for purely *arithmetic* propositions.
3 Russell still felt resentment against his teachers in 1960. In conversation he recalled that though they only proved the binomial for a positive-integral exponent, they stated and used it with a real exponent. 'I asked them how the general case could be proved. "We prove it" they replied, "by the principle of permanence of form"!'

Bibliography

1. *References to Papers by Other Authors*

C1 G. Cantor, Letter to Dedekind, 28 July 1899, reprinted in *Gesammelte Abhandlungen* (ed. E. Zermelo), Berlin 1932, 443–447. A translation appears in *From Frege to Gödel* (ed. J. van Heijenoort), Cambridge, Mass., 1967.
C2 —— 'Beiträge zur Begründung der transfiniten Mengenlehre', *Math. Ann.* 46 (1895), 481–512.
G1 K. Gödel, 'Russell's mathematical logic' in the *Philosophy of Bertrand Russell* (ed. P. A. Schilpp), The Library of Living Philosophers, Evanston, Ill., 1946.
H1 F. Hausdorff, *Grundzuge der Mengenlehre*, Leipzig, 1914.
Q1 W. V. Quine, 'New foundations for mathematical logic', *Amer. Math. Monthly* 44 (1937), 70–80.
R1 F. P. Ramsey, 'The foundations of mathematics', *Proc. London Math. Soc.* 25 (1925), 338–384.

2. *Articles and Books by Russell*

We list only the most important references about mathematics, mathematical logic and philosophy of mathematics. A complete bibliography is being prepared by H. Ruja. [This has now appeared as *A Bibliography of Bertrand Russell* (London, Routledge, 1994), by K. Blackwell and H. Ruja.] An incomplete, but extensive, version of this appears in *Bertrand Russell*, Ed. D. Pears, Anchor Books, London–New York, 1972.

1 *An Essay on the Foundations of Geometry*, Cambridge, 1897.
2 *Sur la logique des relations avec des applications à la théorie des séries*, Rivista di Matematica (Turin) 7 (1900–1), 115–48. (Translation appears in [17].)
3 *The Principles of Mathematics*, Cambridge, 1903.
4 'On some difficulties in the theory of transfinite numbers and order types', *Proc. London Math. Soc.* 4 (1907), 29–53.
5 'The theory of implication', *Amer. J. of Math.* 28 (1906), 159–202.
6 'Les paradoxes de la logique', *Revue de Métaphysique et de Morale* 14 (1906), 627–650.

7 'Mathematical logic as based on the theory of types', *Amer. J. of Math.* 30 (1908), 222–262.
8 *Principia Mathematica* (with A. N. Whitehead), Cambridge, Vol. I (1910), Vol. II (1912), Vol. III (1913).
9 'La théorie des types logiques', *Revue de Métaphysique et de Morale* 18 (1910), 263–301.
10 'The philosophical importance of mathematical logic', *Monist* 23 (1913), 481–493.
11 *Our Knowledge of the External World as a Field for Scientific Method in Philosophy*, London, 1914.
12 *Introduction to Mathematical Philosophy*, London 1919.
13 Introduction to L. Wittgenstein's *Tractatus Logico-Philosophicus*, London 1922.
14 Introduction and appendices for 2nd edn of [8] Vol. I, Cambridge, 1925.
15 'On order in time', *Proc. Cambridge Philos. Soc.* 32 (1936), 216–228.
16 Preface to 2nd edn of [3] Cambridge, 1937.
17 *Logic and Knowledge: Essays 1901–1950* (ed. R. C. Marsh), London 1956.

3. *Autobiographical Material*

18 'My mental development', in *The Philosophy of Bertrand Russell* (ed. P. A. Schilpp), The Library of Living Philosophers, Evanston, Ill., 1946.
19 *My Philosophical Development*, London, 1959.
20 *The Autobiography of Bertrand Russell: 1872–1914*, London, 1967.

3

Bertrand Arthur William Russell, Earl Russell

1872–1970

Georg Kreisel

Russell left an autobiography in three volumes and two earlier autobiographical essays. These works were widely read. The style is fresh and lucid, perhaps unequalled since Bishop Berkeley or Hume; and as memorable. So the reader may be assumed to know the general outline of Russell's life and thought. Since the complete bibliography of his writings is said to run to 500 pages there can be no question of attempting a full account here. The selection below, from his life and works, is made on the following principles.

The well-known aspects of his life, including his activities as a publicist and reformer, are described only briefly. For balance part I presents in more detail those aspects which, though perhaps equally important and sometimes quite explicit in his writings, have not become widely known. (Since Russell was a controversial figure, the selection made here may also be controversial.) Part II goes into 'his researches concerning the Principles of Mathematics and the Mathematical Treatment of the Logic of Relations' – to use the wording of the proposal for his election to the Royal Society. Some of Russell's views on points of general philosophic interest related to his scientific work are sketched in part III. Many of his later general writings do not always respect Hooke's warning (to the Royal Society) against 'meddling with Divinity, Metaphysics, Moralls, Politicks, Grammar, Rhetorick, or Logick', in the sense in which Hooke understood those words. To compromise with Hooke's law, the memoir confines itself to describing Russell's view of the world, how questions in the forbidden subjects presented themselves to him, without going too closely into the sense of the questions or the validity of the answers. This is done at the end of part III.

I. Russell's Life

Childhood

Russell was born on 18 May 1872 at Trelleck, Monmouthshire, Wales. His parents died before he was four, and he spent his childhood and adolescence at his grandparents', on his father's side, at Pembroke Lodge in Richmond Park. His grandfather, the first Earl Russell, had been Prime Minister, and was famous for having used the immense power of the British Empire with discretion. In his writings on education, Russell often referred to his own childhood, hoping to correct what he remembered as unsatisfactory. At least occasionally, he warned against drawing general conclusions from his limited experience; for example $(A_1\ 26)^1$ his diet was atrocious by current views and yet, as he goes on to point out, he never had a day's illness except for a mild attack of measles – and lived to be nearly 98, most of the time in excellent health and full of vigour. His psychological diet was, it seems, mildly unusual even for his time and class. Unlike, say, Churchill, he does not seem to have formed strong attachments to any of the people who actually brought him up; his nannies, governesses or tutors. He liked some of them well enough $(A_1\ 31)$, but they do not seem to have stayed on for a long time; possibly, as Russell himself suggests $(A_1\ 49)$, because of the child's own nature and its effects on the people around him. All this may be relevant to the more painful episodes of Russell's life. For at least statistically, his kind of childhood goes with long periods of loneliness in later years and, above all, a very schematic understanding of human nature which brings one unpleasant surprises; not only at other people's conduct (always doubly unpleasant if one likes to have good psychological judgement); but also at one's own feelings (when one is, so to speak, moved by one's own emotions rather than by their objects). Be that as it may, Russell's childhood was certainly not wholly unrewarding. He obviously had a great deal of affection for his family, in particular, for the remarkable collection of independent and, perhaps, formidable female relatives who must have enjoyed young Russell's attentions more than they let on $(A_1\ 33–34)$. In any case they did not spoil his gifts for entertaining and scintillating in company. He describes their foibles mockingly, but the mockery is good humoured and gentle – in sharp contrast to his acid indiscretions about the dons at Trinity $(A_1\ 89–90)$; 'in contrast' even if one allows for the objective differences between the foibles involved. As Russell was to find out, experience of his relatives had not prepared him adequately for some of the women he encountered later, at home and abroad.

Adolescence

He was educated privately, with plenty of free time to pursue those grand traditional questions which occur to us when – ontogenetically or

phylogenetically – we begin to reflect. To some extent this was family business: John Stuart Mill was his godfather.

Almost inevitably in the circumstances, questions about Euclid's axioms crossed his mind. But, it seems, even at this early stage, he showed robust good sense. He did not dismiss the questions – and surely was much more articulate about them than the average schoolboy as is evident from his diary (P.D. 28–34) – but did not let them cramp his style; he greatly enjoyed doing geometry (M.D.7).

Studies and Research

At Cambridge he studied mainly mathematics and philosophy, and was soon recognized to have exceptional talents. He was awarded a fellowship at Trinity for an essay on the foundations of geometry. It expounds fairly orthodox views, familiar since Kant and the German idealists; naturally without Kant's gratuitous stress on Euclidean geometry. But it exhibits already one of the most striking qualities of Russell's later work: a light and sure touch in marshalling an immense amount of erudition, which produces the very pleasant conviction that it is possible to have a broad view; both of the subject and our knowledge of it – a conviction very much in keeping with Hegelian doctrine.

In 1894, between the tripos and his fellowship, he married Alys Pearsall Smith, whom he left in 1911 and from whom he was divorced in 1921. They made two extended visits to Berlin, where he studied German social democrats in action, by attending meetings of their party. One day, in the Tiergarten and very much under the influence of Hegel, he decided to write a series of books organizing, more or less, all knowledge. This decision left a deep impression on him; he referred to it repeatedly, for example, in M.D.11 and in the reflections on his eightieth birthday (A_3 329). Even if the plan was not wholly realistic, it shows the proper spirit for embarking (some years later) on the more limited enterprise of writing the three volumes of *Principia*; with Whitehead listed as first author, in anti-alphabetic order, presumably because Whitehead was older.

After his return to England, Russell worked on mathematical logic and the foundations of mathematics. He was proposed for election to the Royal Society in 1907, by A. N. Whitehead (presumably seconded by) A. R. Forsyth, W. Burnside, E. W. Hobson, George H. Darwin and H. Head who knew him personally, and also K. Pearson, Robert S. Bell, and E. Divus. He was elected the following year. He was awarded the Sylvester Medal of the Royal Society in 1932, and the de Morgan Medal of the London Mathematical Society in 1933.

He found much of the work on P.M. exhausting and depressing, and remained reluctant to return to the subject; of course, he did return to it, for example when preparing its second edition. This important work is the principal subject of part II, where also some further relevant biographical material is given. But two 'objective' qualities of P.M. must be mentioned here because they may have affected his relations with the academic world.

P.M. is not polished enough to be really useful, not even to trained mathematicians. They cannot dip into it and work with it easily, not even with the theory of relation arithmetic which Russell liked particularly (P.D. 101). Professional reputations depend less on the general intrinsic value of ideas than on specific memorable results of more or less immediate use to other professionals; in accordance with the principle that – intrinsic – virtue is its own reward. This accounts for much of the lack of interest in P.M. of which Russell complained, for example in (P.D. 86): lack of interest on the part of others, not only his own. Of course in some isolated centres such as Warsaw, P.M. was studied enthusiastically.

A second problem, which lies beyond Russell's purely subjective description of his relief at being rid of P.M. (A_1 234), is this: What were the objective possibilities of improving or developing P.M.? There were two ways. One was to review P.M. in the light of criticism from 'without' (P.D. 112), by so-called formalists and intuitionists. Russell did not do so but chose to 'repel their attacks' (which was not hard because the opponents' dialectics were pitiful). As a matter of fact, as will be seen in part II, a great deal of work which has built on P.M. made essential use of such criticism from 'without'. The second kind of criticism, from 'within', had had to come from Russell himself: Whitehead's role in the work, though obviously substantial, consisted in developing and consolidating Russell's ideas. Especially in the light of a letter by F. H. Bradley (A_1 307) this intellectual loneliness, this lack of support by constructive criticism, may have been more exhausting to Russell than the actual writing of P.M.

Wittgenstein

Just about the time when P.M. was completed, Wittgenstein came to Cambridge and soon began to criticize some of the views in P.M. from 'within' – as Russell stresses repeatedly, for example, in P.D. 112. Without doubt he had great hopes of profound help from W. Also, while according to one of his brother's letters (A_2 85) many of the dons were uncongenial to Russell, he found W. an impressive human being (A_2 140). Indeed, his mockery of W.'s eccentricity has something of the same gentle quality noted earlier on in connexion with his own family. In an outburst of anger (P.D. 214, 215) Russell criticizes W. for 'abnegation of his talents' in later years, comparing him to Pascal and Tolstoy. Even remembering Russell's dislike of religion, one imagines that he could have found harsher things to say about others. (Besides, in some circles similar criticisms had been made of Russell.)

Actually, Russell introduces his criticism, in 1957, by first speaking of his own envy of Wittgenstein's reputation. The passage strikes me as quite unconvincing, just as many other references by him to envy and jealousy. Rutherford found them a bit facile (A_2 280), and the subject will turn up again in connexion with Russell's Nobel Prize lecture. Could it be that he was so surprised to discover that he was capable of jealousy at all (A_2 33) that he forgot other, less banal motives? – such as the feeling of being let down, intellectually, by W. (In the footnote on pp. 33–34 of A_2 he himself has late second thoughts on jealousy.)

Wittgenstein too showed a good deal of affection when he spoke to me of Russell (in the forties when I first met W.). W. was quite furious that Russell had involved himself in America with some universities and their administrators who, realistically speaking, simply did not belong to Russell's world. Not likely to let a chance of an apt, but malicious observation pass, W. proposed the defence, *Look at this face*! to the charge made against Russell (A_2 334): roughly speaking, Russell's personal appearance at City College of New York would be 'dangerous to the virtue' of the tender souls that grow up in, say, Brooklyn. Both Russell and Wittgenstein, though very different, had splendid faces and great style. They were a little below average height, and delicately boned, but generally quite free from the jumpy nervousness that often goes with this physique. Their gestures were always sure, often graceful, and sometimes beautiful.

First World War

Except for a period in Brixton jail, when Russell wrote I.M.P., he devoted much of his energy to – and, perhaps, derived it from – politics and the kind of social life he missed during his first marriage. He was strongly opposed to England's participation in the war. But the theory behind his opposition, especially as he saw it later (A_2 288), and his practical politics did not quite match.

He was not a doctrinaire pacifist, not a conscientious objector. He thought that *ceteris paribus* peace was better than war – like most people, even those whose wartime experiences constitute the most fulfilling part of their lives. His own activities show that he himself sometimes found it necessary to resist. At the time he was particularly struck by the possibilities of non-violent resistance (of Gandhi's followers against the British); but according to (A_2 288), Russell had overlooked that such resistance presupposes 'certain virtues in those against whom it is employed'. Actually, he later advocated the use, or threat, of force; not only during the Second World War (M.D. 17), but also after. In short, Russell objected to a specific war.

So much for theory. His anti-war propaganda pursued many different lines. In particular he was not jailed (in 1918) for pacifist convictions nor even for advocating non-violent resistance but for 'disaffecting' the troops. He had warned that America – reluctant as she was to enter the war at all – would send over troops to break strikes. (It is a moot point which was more far fetched: his warning or the charge against him that – presumably loyal – miners or soldiers were likely to be so easily 'disaffected'.) In any case, he liked jail quite well, in particular, smuggling love letters in volumes of the *Proceedings of the London Mathematical Society* (A$_2$ 31). Incidentally, Russell was in his mid-forties, not of military age. He most certainly was not a mere coward; and nobody – including himself – had to ask himself if he was.

After a conviction in 1916 under the Defence of the Realm Act, Trinity College deprived him of his lectureship, a shabby act by any standards. So quick to see shabby motives, like envy, in himself, he seemed to think of the dons as moved solely by political 'passions' and bigotry; and of himself as a 'martyr'. The realities of the situation seem different from the public debate which concerned of course the formal, legal merits of the case. There was a clash of temperament between Russell and those dons who opposed him (or, most of them; the matter is statistical since it concerns a vote). For many dons college life provided not so much a place for the pursuit of knowledge, but simply a shelter from practical life where one's opinions have to be put to the test of experience. Russell, full of dash and vigour, had little respect for the opinions of those who had 'no knowledge of life' (A$_1$ 240). The dons did not think lightly of their opinions. They happened to constitute a majority, and exercised their vote. Apart from formal rights and motives, there is a further point – however far it may have been from the minds of the opposition: realistically speaking, the normal duties of a college lecturer were hardly fitting for someone of Russell's standing at that time. Besides, as mentioned already, P.M. was not in a suitable shape for immediate consumption by his academic colleagues.

Russell, who had long found the dons uncongenial, cannot have expected them to behave differently, let alone more generously than they actually did. But, like Kierkegaard before him and others since, he may have had the illusion that it ought to be possible to make his smug opponents 'take notice' (even if he took little notice of them).

Between the Wars

During the twenties Russell engaged in diverse activities; he lectured, wrote books on general philosophy, and pursued his interests in social questions. He travelled in many countries, including the USSR and China. He was critical of the Soviet regime, unlike others in his circle, in particular, Dora Winifred Black whom he married in 1921, left in 1932 and by whom he was divorced in 1935. An unsatisfactory interview with Lenin, who showed little interest in Russell's political views, may have helped Russell see other defects of Lenin's judgement. As has long been known, prejudice sometimes permits us to see the mote when love blinds us to the beam. In contrast, China enchanted him, particularly the human qualities, of wit and finesse, which he found among Chinese intellectuals. In a memorable letter to Ottoline Morrell (A$_2$ 202), he spoke of political and 'bureaucratic machines [that] cared nothing for human values'. He meant the values of those particular qualities, of the Chinese and Oscar Wilde, which he himself possessed in the highest degree; not those surely much rarer qualities which permit a man to be both successful in public life and humanly impressive.

Russell and his second wife had 'advanced' social ideas. They also had the courage of their convictions. They decided, jointly (A_2 222), to try out some of them; a free school and a swinging marriage. He wrote *Marriage and Morals*, which, though mentioned among his principal publications in the Nobel Prize *vita* on p. 129 of Holmberg (1951), was not stated to be a, let alone the sole, reason for the prize – contrary to Russell's memory of it (A_3 25). His advanced views became widely known.

His change of views, though expressed in the clearest possible terms, is less well known. He discovered that the views were trivially wrong (at least for him) inasmuch as they were refuted by commonplace events. The children were difficult; when told to brush their teeth, they would sometimes say 'Call this a free school!' (A_2 227). As regards marriage, he had apparently completely forgotten to consider the case when the wife turns up with a child fathered by another man (A_2 228); as he says (A_2 288), he had been 'blinded by theory' – his own, not Hume's who goes into this sort of matter in section 195 on chastity (Hume, 1777). Russell did not try to refine his views; neither by the scientific method of making more actual or imagined (Gedanken) experiments nor by analysing the factors involved in happier historical precedents; for example, it has long been said, for good reasons given on pp. 210–211 of Bernard (1973), that the painter Eugène Delacroix was Talleyrand's natural son; Eugène had the full blessing of M. Charles Delacroix, Talleyrand's predecessor (in office).

Actually, Russell hardly ever refined his views. He dropped them, replaced them by new views and usually – both in his younger days and later when he was nearly 90 (P.D. 41) – had 'an almost unbelievable optimism as to the finality of [his] own theories'. But now, pushing 60, he was less confident. In particular, he remained an agnostic on the subject of marriage (A_2 228). And especially his last marriage, to Edith Branson Finch in 1952, seemed a good deal more peaceful – without theory and with 80 years behind him. He also wrote no more books like *Marriage and Morals* which, in a sense, could induce a wife to be naughty out of sheer loyalty to her husband's views (though one would not wish to be too dogmatic in such matters).

During these difficult years, in the early thirties, he wrote several articles surveying his past. He even tried to find out about his genetic make-up, as it were, by assembling the *Amberley Papers*; in collaboration with Patricia Helen Spence, whom he married in 1936, and divorced in 1952 after she had left him in 1949. Perhaps the most critical point that struck him at the time (1931) is contained in the article 'Christmas at Sea' (A_2 229); on the extent to which his life and his view of the world had depended 'on a superabundant vitality'. Clearly life had been simpler when there was plenty of energy to spare; the satisfying 'unity between opinion and emotion' in the First World War, of which he speaks nostalgically later (A_2 289), goes naturally with vitality and with the conviction that one will solve problems as they come along, a conviction produced by vitality. For this very reason the inconveniences directly due to vitality (such as the clash of temperament with the dons at Trinity) were not too disturbing. The decrease in vitality created different problems; most prosaically, presumably, the very marital problems that had taken him so badly by surprise. His writings give the impression that the decrease in the level of vitality to which he had been accustomed for nearly 60 years, had taken him by surprise too. If so, this must have created its own additional difficulties.

In 1939 he emigrated to America with his third wife and their young child born in 1937. He describes most vividly his experiences there and his reactions to them. They seem to be of general interest and will be taken up in part III as a typical example of Russell's contributions to what might be called literary social philosophy.

Return to England

He was happy to return and happy with his reception. He was now the third Earl Russell, having inherited the title when his older brother Frank died in 1931. In 1949, he was appointed to the O.M., described as 'this odd miscellaneous order' in T. S. Eliot's letter of congratulation (A_3 57). In the same year, Russell was awarded the Nobel Price for literature. This unexpected honour pleased him too, but, understandably, not the somewhat absurd citation, mentioned already, on pp. 57–59 of Holmberg (1951). It is not recorded whether Russell's own Nobel Prize speech was meant to be repayment in kind. On p. 261 of N.P. he suggests that the Kaiser wanted the First World War because he was literally jealous of his Grandmamma, Queen Victoria, on account of her Navy.

Russell's untiring efforts for nuclear disarmament, after both East and West possessed nuclear weapons, are well known. It is, perhaps, less well known that in the late forties he advocated the threat of the atomic bomb against Stalin's Russia (A_3 7–8). Whatever the merits of the proposal, many of the people I knew at the time were taken aback by it – some of us, but not all, much more so than by the proposals of preventive war ascribed to some Hungarian scientists (who had had a dose of communism – albeit the local variety – under Bela Kun). In the early sixties, at the beginning of a conversation partially reported on pp. 129–130 of Crawshay-Williams (1970), I asked Russell about his old proposal; admittedly in general terms. He immediately assumed that I objected to 'inconsistency', and answered (his own objection) with disarming logic: He did not want the bomb to be dropped on him; as long as the Russians did not have it, the proper thing was to prevent them from getting it; and when they had it, the proper thing was to persuade them not to use it. Obviously, he was quite fearless, in big things and in small ones. He was no more afraid for his own skin than he was afraid of my going out and telling his answer to some of his more fanatical admirers.

By this time he and his face had become part of our lives; organizations and foundations built up around him. One of them was the Bertrand Russell Peace Foundation. It is no doubt memorable for many things that it has done. But it was memorable even before it started, uniting among its sponsors Nehru of India and Ayub Khan of Pakistan, Albert Schweitzer and Kwame Nkrumah (whose political bible (Nkrumah 1970) contains a final chapter on set theory).

The touch of irreverence in the last paragraph is not unexpected from one who has been reading Russell a good deal, and writing about his life. But, perhaps inevitably in such circumstances, the irreverence is mixed up with a more personal note. Nobody reading the reflections which Russell wrote on his eightieth birthday, and reprinted 17 years later in A_3 (326–330), can fail to be impressed by his strong sense of failure. At least as far as his scientific work is concerned, his disappointments are not founded on objective facts, but – as will be clear from parts II and III – mainly on a failure of memory and lack of knowledge; mistaken memory of the aims he actually formulated for his scientific work, and lack of knowledge of the remarkable 'extension of the sphere of reason to new provinces', as he put it in M.D. 20, by the work of others who built on his scientific ideas and achievements. As far as moral and political problems are concerned, the disappointments are understandable. As he put it (A_3 328): in regard to those problems he did not 'pretend that what [he had] done . . . had any great importance'. It is far beyond the scope of this memoir to analyse to what extent this failure was due to the nature of these problems, to Russell's conceptions of them, and to his particular human qualities. His brother Frank considered these matters back in 1916 in a – for him – remarkably sombre letter (A_2 85–86). Also Russell's own letter to Lady Ottoline quoted on p. [29], may be relevant here.

Russell died on 2 February 1970, at his home in Penrhyndeudraeth, Merionethshire, Wales. He is survived by his last three wives and by his three children, John Conrad, Katharine Jane (Tait) and Conrad Sebastian Robert.

II. Mathematical Logic and Logical Foundations of Mathematics

Some mathematical background will be assumed. Basic issues involved here, such as the meaning of 'foundations', are best discussed in the general context of part III, in connexion with the scope of (scientific) philosophy. But a few general remarks may be useful here to avoid misunderstanding.

Foundations: Loaded Terminology

The word 'foundations' suggests a firm basis for a superstructure, which is to be 'secured'; here, the superstructure of mathematical practice. Evidently it is not in need of greater 'security' or reliability if it is already 100 per cent secure. Besides, ordinary clear exposition may well be the best method to achieve greater reliability where this is possible. Actually the term 'foundations' or 'Grundlagen' belongs to the familiar doctrines of finitism or formalism (rivals to Russell's school) which claim that the abstract principles of mathematical practice are not reliable. Thus, according to these doctrines, to be capable of reliable proof, an assertion about an abstract concept has to be reinterpreted in their doctrinaire terms. Since, in point of fact, long formal calculations have to be checked by means of short abstract considerations, clearly some kind of idealized reliability is meant; what 'should' be reliable, not what is reliable. And if the idealization is not realistic the doctrines are themselves questionable. Be that as it may, Russell's own aims were originally different though he occasionally used the word 'foundations', for example in I.M.P. 2. He did not assume that the basic (logical) notions would be particularly easy to grasp nor, *a fortiori*, that our assertions about them would be particularly 'reliable'. According to P.M. 12:

> It will be found that owing to the weakness of the imagination in dealing with simple abstract ideas no very great stress can be laid upon their obviousness. They are obvious to the instructed mind, but then so are many propositions which cannot be quite true, as being disproved by their contradictory consequences. The proof of a logical system is its adequacy and its coherence.

Even if Russell's views on the conclusions to be drawn from those contradictory consequences (paradoxes) are questioned as on p. [40], the passage shows that *he* did not expect the basic logical propositions to be obvious or obviously reliable. In any case his original aim was not to cleanse mathematics of the paradoxes because he started his work before he discovered them.

Russell's own work in the logical analysis of mathematics, that is, in building up mathematics from a few logical primitives, would seem to be better compared to fundamental science such as the atomic theory of matter. The principal aim of that theory is hardly to 'secure' our ordinary physical knowledge – despite dramatic assertions, for example, by Eddington who thought that it was correct to think of a table as being like a swarm of flies but false not to think about any micro-structure at all (which is what we normally do). Atomic theory builds up matter from a few elements and tries to derive the macroscopic laws from simpler laws for these elements. Correspondingly logical foundations 'build up' mathematical concepts by defining them from a few logical ones. Since Russell did not mention this comparison in his publications, I once asked him about it (in the conversation mentioned on p. [31]); he agreed – whatever weight one may attach to spontaneous agreement during a pleasant conversation.

Views differ on the pedagogic value of the comparison since, to some, it suggests that mathematical objects are physical substances. Here it is only intended to prepare the reader for some peculiar difficulties of foundations which are similar to those of the fundamental sciences, not to those in the bulk of everyday scientific practice; in particular, the special kind of *incompatibility* between rival schemes, corresponding to strategic and tactical differences. Fundamentally different schemes or different analyses within the same scheme may be compatible with familiar practice to an extremely high degree of approximation; and apparently, that is formally, insignificant differences in the basic schemes have enormous consequences. In short, we have here all the advantages and defects of an all-or-nothing approach to life, a point which Russell stressed (bottom of H.W.P. 643).

The next few sections describe briefly the background to Russell's logical anlaysis of mathematics; the tools (logical concepts) used for the analysis, and examples of analyses of familiar mathematical objects.

Background: Logical Language

Today elementary, also called first order, language (of predicate logic) is familiar. It builds up expressions from given ones by means of

$$\neg \text{ (not)}, \land \text{ (and)}, \lor \text{ (or)}, \rightarrow \text{ (implies)}, \forall \text{ (for all)}, \exists \text{ (there exists)}.$$

The intended meanings of these operations are not very common in ordinary usage, particularly of $\lor$, $\rightarrow$, $\exists$. As a matter of discovery, the chosen meanings lend themselves better to theory. Some of the discrepancies are most easily removed by suppressing $p \lor q$, $p \rightarrow q$, $\exists x A$ altogether and replacing them by $\neg[(\neg p) \land (\neg q)]$, $\neg(p \land \neg q)$, $\neg \forall x \neg A$ resp. which are equivalent (for the chosen meaning; actually, in ordinary usage not all meaningful sentences p, q can be 'sensibly' combined in to, say, $p \lor q$; for example, if p is: this glass is blue, and q is: this glass is 8 cm high). Frege (1879) contained this language.

Although Russell had Frege's book for many years before the International Congress of Philosophy in Paris in July 1900 (A_1 91), he could not make out what it meant till he met Peano in person at that unusually useful congress. Peano inspired a great deal of confidence in Russell, enough for him to master Peano's logical notation; and soon after, also Frege's.

It is often said that Frege's notation was 'cumbrous' and 'difficult to employ in practice' (P.o.M. 501). This may be true – though after all Frege did employ it quite a bit. The differences in the purposes for which Frege and Peano employed their symbolisms seem more profound, as hinted at by Russell *loc. cit.* and stated more explicitly by Gödel on p. 125 of Schilpp (1944). Peano established that his simple vocabulary with a perfectly precise grammar had great expressive power throughout all of mathematics. Frege used his for the analysis of (logical) thought and for a particularly detailed derivation of arithmetic from pure logic – Peano's aim and even the details have a permanent place in mathematical culture. But while the penetrating analysis of the most basic steps in logic was immensely fruitful for Frege, leading (him) to distinctions and notions of permanent value, we should not nowadays follow his own line of exposition; it is much easier and more convincing to explain his logical discoveries by means of examples taken from more 'advanced' mathematics where differences are greatly magnified; plain for all to see, not subtle as in elementary logical contexts. Besides, perhaps by mischance, logical analysis has so far been less rewarding for arithmetic than for many other branches of mathematics, even those existing at Frege's time. (Gauss did quite well in his *Disquisitiones* without knowing Peano's axioms.) It was left to Russell to set caution aside and to search for Principles of (the whole of) Mathematics, not only of Arithmetic.

Analogues to the facts just described are easy to find in the development of the atomic theory of matter.

Background: Sets and Predicates

Cantor, after studying the (mis)behaviour of trigonometric series at certain peculiar sets of points in the plane, went on to develop the properties of such sets more abstractly. Many familiar operations on sets of points or on finite sets (in the theory of combinations and permutations) were seen to be meaningful in a far more general context too. One operation, which turned out to have a particularly rich theory was the so-called *power set* operation $\mathfrak{P} \colon x \mapsto 2^x$, which associates to any given set x the collection of all its parts (subsets). It provided examples of infinitely many infinite cardinals.

Just because Cantor's study began with (infinite) sets of points, it cannot be supposed that he relied on his experience with finite sets to develop the general theory. But it is true that many of his results, in particular those concerning the power set operation, are very well illustrated by finite sets; even by so-called hereditarily finite sets (also called the cumulative hierarchy of type ω) which are obtained from the empty set $\varnothing$ by iterating the power set operation finitely often. (In symbols: $C_0 = \varnothing$, $C_{n+1} = \mathfrak{P}(C_n)$ and $C_\omega = \bigcup_n C_n$). Only, as Russell put it (P.M. vi), the 'general laws [of C_ω] are most easily proved without any mention of the distinction between finite and infinite'. (To be quite precise, Russell's remark applies to purely universal laws; for existential statements one has to look at the axioms used in the proof to verify in addition that a *finite* set realizes the statement.) One might add that the general laws are often better understood, for example by a child who has not yet convinced himself that the sets he knows – such as forests of trees or heaps of sand – can be counted at all.

Cantor gave some very general indications of the kinds of objects for which his assertions hold, for example, in Cantor (1899) or p. 282 of Zermelo (1932); saying that a set is a variety of objects (*Vielheit*) which can be grasped or comprehended as a unity (*Einheit*); but he did not draw many conclusions from this. Indeed, as far as (even today's) mathematical practice goes, little would be lost if Cantor's work were applied only to $C_{\omega+\omega}$; that is, to the sets obtained from the collection of hereditarily finite ones by finitely many applications of the power set operation. Only, by P.M. vi, it would be 'a defect in logical style to prove for a particular class ... what might just as well have been proved more generally' – as usual, $a \in X$ will mean: the object a is an element of the set X.

Frege considered a *prima facie* much more general notion, much farther removed from mathematical practice (then or now) than segments of the cumulative hierarchy described above. It is the logical notion of *predicate*, with no *a priori* restriction on the kind of thing to which the predicate may apply. Such predicates are very common in ordinary life; for example, *blue* is understood without any clear idea of all the things past, present or future, mental or physical, that may be blue (in contrast to mathematical practice, where one has predicates or sets *of* something; of numbers, of points etc.). We shall write $a\eta P$ for: the predicate P applies to (the object or predicate) a. Instead of 'predicate' (P.M.) uses 'propositional function' which, as Russell says on pp. 69–70 of P.D., 'sounds perhaps unnecessarily formidable. For many purposes one can substitute the word "property" ... but, except in ultimate analysis, it is perhaps easier to ... use the word "class".'[2] We use 'predicate'. To each set X corresponds of course a predicate P_X where

$$a\eta P_x \text{ if and only if } a \in X.$$

However, Cantor's explanation of 'set' shows clearly that there is no reason to assume the converse. Nevertheless operations on (Cantor's) sets often have analogues for predicates. Suppose we start with a variety V_0 which is not a set, and form varieties V_n by an analogue of the cumulative hierarchy construction, where

$$a\eta V_{n+1} \text{ if and only if } a\eta V_n \text{ or } a \subset V_n \text{ and } a \text{ is a set,}$$

that is, a can be grasped as a unity. Whatever doubts there may be about the notion of predicate, the V_n are predicates if any sense is given to Cantor's explanation and there should be a variety V_0 which is not a set if Cantor's distinction is to be of use at all. (The hierarchy will be cumulative if V_0 consists only of sets.)

There will be frequent references to various versions of this hierarchy construction. This is not *ad hoc*, but connected with Cantor's explanation of 'set', if not only the variety in question, but also its elements, their elements, etc. are required to be 'unities'. The only quite unproblematic way of achieving this is to build them up from the variety of 'individuals' which are simply given as unities. This variety takes the place of V_0 above (and the sequence V_1, V_2, . . . may be continued beyond ω).

Actually most formal laws discovered at an early stage of the subject hold equally for sets and predicates ($\in$ and η), about unions, differences, Cartesian products and the like; and again one 'might just as well' prove them generally. But this does not exclude basic differences between the notions; nothing could be simpler than the predicate, say V, which applies to everything; but it is hardly plausible that this variety V can be grasped as a unity.

Background: Definitions of Natural and Real Numbers

We begin with the natural numbers. In Dedekind (1888) there is a definition of the natural numbers in logical terms; that is, in the logical language built up from η or $\in$. It does not define specific numbers 0, 1, . . . but, as we should put it now, the class of structures (X, S) where S is a binary relation on X which are isomorphic to the natural numbers with the successor relation. This is accepted as a definition not because of some arbitrary decision but because of a *discovery* (made in the last century). Even when we think of the natural numbers as specific objects, the results we prove about them in pure mathematics turn out to be true for all those (X, S) described above. And this empirical observation becomes a theorem if we confine ourselves to results formulated in logical formulae (not necessarily of first order languages) built up from the successor relation.

Russell had two objections (I.M.P. 10). First, Dedekind's procedure 'does not even give the faintest suggestion of any way of discovering whether there are such sets', specifically, sets X and S satisfying Dedekind's conditions. One may think that we do not need to discover them, because we already know the familiar natural numbers, and Russell's demand, for a logical foundation, may be considered a luxury. It becomes a necessity when we pass from arithmetic to problematic notions. His second objection is this: 'we want our numbers to be . . . used for counting common objects, and this requires [them to] have a *definite* meaning, not merely . . . certain formal properties'. This matter is more delicate (and in any case, as will be seen below, the analogous requirement is not satisfied by Russell's own definition of the real numbers). But it is quite evident that not all isomorphic images of the natural numbers can be used for counting. Suppose a_0, a_1, . . . is an ω-ordering (of say the usual words for numbers), but we do not *know* the value of say a_5. We could not use the isomorphic image of ω above, that is, a_0, a_1, . . ., for counting in the literal sense because we should not know the numerical label for a set of 5 objects. (In current logic this remark is developed by use of recursion theoretic notions.)

Frege (1884), four years before Dedekind's publication as is pointed out on p. 1 of Frege (1893), does give definitions, in logical terms, for each natural number; for example of 1 as 'the class of all classes with a single element' in Russell's formulation. It would be idle to speculate whether we 'need' these definitions; we evidently do not, as long as we are concerned with results that hold for all structures defined by Dedekind. The question is rather whether, at least sometimes, we can do better when we do have such definitions. Amusingly, developments of arithmetic in current set theory introduce such definitions: the empty set is taken to be *zero*, and either of the two functions:

$$s_1: x \mapsto \{x\}, \; s_2: x \mapsto x \cup \{x\},$$

for the successor; s_1 and s_2 generate the structures in which $\in$ is the successor and the order relation resp. A pedant would say that s_1 analyses the notion of natural number, s_2 the notion of finite ordinal (tacitly assuming that $\in$, evidently the simplest relation of the set theoretic language, is to realize the successor, resp. order relation).

Dedekind (1872) also gave conditions, in logical language, for a structure (X, O) to be isomorphic to the real numbers; more precisely, to the ordering of the real numbers. Russell supplements the definition by treating each specific real number ρ as a set of rationals ($< \rho$) and verifying that Dedekind's condition is satisfied if these sets are ordered by inclusion. The questions raised by Russell (I.M.P. 10) about *applications* of natural numbers (to counting) have their analogues here. But he does not discuss them. His definition is not particularly useful for applications *within* mathematics; for example for computing, Cauchy sequences, satisfying $\forall n (\forall m > n)(|a_m - a_n| < 2^{-n})$, are better in the sense that we can effectively find sums, approximate Euler's constant γ and so forth, while it does not seem to be known if one can effectively decide for any rational r whether $r < \gamma$.

In short, there has not been much progress with Russell's (and Frege's) aim of finding 'privileged' structures in Dedekind's classes; perhaps the most one can hope is that relatively few specific structures will turn out to be well adapted for many uses (a topic for the philosophy of applied mathematics).

New Theories: Russell's Paradox

By the end of the nineteenth century it was known that then current mathematics could be 'reduced' to the natural and real numbers. So definitions of these objects in logical terms made it plausible that the grand old question: What is mathematics? had a satisfactory answer (relative to the knowledge at the time). Russell saw this clearly soon after that exciting congress in 1900. Whatever the formal defects of (P.o.M.), it put the grand old question back on the map when the time was right. When actually carrying out the work, Russell and Whitehead were naturally led to rethink parts of the mathematics of the day, and to develop the new subject, the Mathematical Treatment of the Logic of Relations, mentioned by Whitehead as one reason for electing Russell to the Royal Society.

The critical problem was to find significant laws satisfied by the basic logical notions; a minimum requirement being that these laws provided logically defined structures which are isomorphic to the familiar mathematical notions. Frege (1893) contained already such laws which he himself used specifically in the case of natural numbers. His laws were amazingly simple since there was essentially just *one* principle: In modern notation, for each formula A of the language considered

$$\exists X \forall Y (Y \, \eta \, X \leftrightarrow A)$$

provided A does not contain the variable X. It is called comprehension principle, X 'comprehending' all objects Y which satisfy A.

Frege himself was quite aware that the principle was problematic: 'Ich halte [das Prinzip] für rein logisch', on p. vii of Frege (1893). He certainly considered the possibility that it might be contradictory (*ibid*. xxvi). He obviously thought it wasn't and made the – for him! – weaker prediction: 'Aber [daraus einen Widerspruch abzuleiten] das wird Keinem gelingen'. An even more convincing symptom of Frege's *malaise* was this 'evidence': 'Es ist unwahrscheinlich, dass ein solcher Bau sich auf einem fehlerhaften Grunde aufführen lassen sollte'; Frege insisted on the objectivity of logic and mathematics, and knew quite well from physics that there were grand, but false theories.

Cantor's review of Frege (1884) in Cantor (1885) was extremely critical of the comprehension principle. This is quite natural given his explanation of set (to which, however, he did not refer there explicitly). Within the context of Frege's language, the only way to talk about varieties was to introduce such formulae as A above, and so according to the principle *every* variety could be comprehended as a unity! (neglecting the distinction between η and $\in$). Cantor's own objection was quite specific; the extension of a concept, defined by the formula A, is in general quantitatively quite undetermined. But Cantor did not derive a contradiction at that time. When he did, in Cantor (1899), he did not publish it.

Russell derived a simpler contradiction (in 1901 some 15 years after Cantor's review) and did publish it. He arrived at it by analysing Cantor's proof of $|2^x| > |X|$ applied to $X = V$ where V is the 'universal' class obtained by taking some true formula A in the comprehension axiom, for example A of the form $B \vee \neg B$.

Russell's analysis reduced the number of applications of the axiom (to derive the existence of V and the various operations involved in Cantor's proof) to the single case where

$$A \text{ is } \neg Y \eta Y.$$

One can put the argument a little more positively. Suppose X_R is any predicate satisfying

$$\forall Y(Y \eta X_R \to \neg Y \eta Y). \tag{*}$$

Then the predicate X_R^+ determined by

$$Y \eta X_R^+ \text{ if and only if } Y \eta X_R \text{ or } Y = X_R$$

also satisfies (*); $X_R \subset X_R^+$ but not $X_R = X_R^+$ since

$$X_R \eta X_R^+ \text{ but not } X_R \eta X_R.$$

Thus there is no X satisfying $\forall Y(Y \eta X \leftrightarrow \neg Y \eta Y)$. (Amusingly this is literally the proof that there is no greatest integer if one takes the successor operation s_2 on p. [38]).

Frege wrote to Russell (M.D. 13), 'die Arithmetik ist ins Schwanken geraten' (meaning that Frege's analysis of arithmetic had turned out to be shaky). There was, unquestionably, a problem here; even if Frege's formulation was a mere oversight, the fact remained that neither he nor anybody else had a theory; just because in his presentation everything had depended on that one comprehension axiom. One had to make a fresh start.

These facts leave no doubt about the objective interest of Russell's discovery. But, in addition, his and similar paradoxes seem to have considerable psychological interest since the reactions to paradoxes are both strong and diverse; possibly indicating, in a reliable way, striking personality differences. But existing studies, for example, Hermann (1949), are not altogether convincing. Russell's own reactions, at least as he remembered them, seem very natural from what we know of his personality. 'It seemed unworthy of a grown man to spend his time on such trivialities, but what was I to do?' (A₁ 222). 'It was quite clear to me that I could not get on without solving the contradictions' (A₁ 228). He did not look for drama perhaps because he was able to get his 'kicks' elsewhere.

True, False, Meaningless

One of the reasons why paradoxes are so disagreeable is that it is hard to *locate* an error, to 'solve' the paradox by specifying an error. In the familiar paradoxes produced by dividing by zero, $a \cdot a^{-1} = 1$ is asserted. There are two alternatives: (i) to require, as is common in logic, that the functions used *must* be defined on the whole range of the variables, in particular, 0^{-1} must have a (numerical) value; then the correction is: $a \neq 0 \rightarrow a \cdot a^{-1} = 1$, (ii) to take 0^{-1} as undefined and simply assert $a \cdot a^{-1} = 1$ for those a for which this formula is significant. In isolation, the example does not decide convincingly between the alternatives. Just because – in this particular case and many like it – it obviously does not matter which decision is taken, we are liable to be unprepared when it does matter.

There is a further, more specific consideration which is perhaps more persuasive in the case of predicates, such as the formula A in the comprehension principle, than in the case of functions (where, as a matter of historical fact, Frege did use a type distinction from the start, as pointed out on p. 147 of Schilpp (1944)). Why should we not simply *decide* that a predicate P does *not* apply to an argument a if, by intention, $a \eta P$ is meaningless? As intended, 'the number 2 is blue' is meaningless; but one would rather have it false than true. More importantly, this remark shows why current systems of set theory, going back to Zermelo, are formulated without *explicit* type distinctions, although those systems are intended, in Zermelo (1930), to apply to segments of the cumulative hierarchy of types; cf. p. 140 of Schilpp (1944).

In the cumulative hierarchy on p. [35] it is natural to say – and explicit in Russell's doctrine of types – that $x_m \in y_n$ is meaningless, if x_m is introduced at stage m (of the hierarchy) and y_n at stage n and $m \geqslant n$, since x_m is not even a candidate for being an element of y_n. However, in current set theories $x_m \in y_n$ is meaningful but false; and assertions of a logically compound structure are interpreted accordingly, for example $\neg x_m \in y_n$ is put true.

How can this kind of convention conflict with others or with axioms? Most easily if we have an independent assertion relating such simple formulae. Specifically, in the instance of the comprehension principle used in Russell's paradox, consider the predicate P_R determined by

$$Y \eta P_R \text{ if and only if } \neg Y \eta Y;$$

in particular, $P_R \eta P_R$ if and only if $\neg P_R \eta P_R$ (predicates and the relation η are used in place of sets and $\in$ because, as pointed out in Cantor (1885), the comprehension principle is not even remotely plausible for the latter). Suppose then that, as intended, $P_R \eta P_R$ is meaningless; then so is $\neg P_R \eta P_R$. The convention above requires $P_R \eta P_R$ to be put false,

$\neg\,P_R\;\eta\;P_R$ to be put true and this conflicts with $P_R\;\eta\;P_R \leftrightarrow \neg\,P_R\;\eta\;P_R$. As in some other domains of life, once we allow ourselves to parley at all, to entertain the 'proposition' $P_R\;\eta\;P_R$, we are seduced.

A different matter, which Russell himself described as a *puzzle* in O.D., had drawn his attention to (the logical interest of) meaningless expressions; specifically the sentence 'The present king of France is bald'. Since there is no such king, the use of the definite article is improper. Here there is a relatively simple convention giving a manageable meaning to all such phrases, roughly speaking this:

If $P(x)$ and $Q(y)$ are formulae not containing unexplained occurrences of the definite article and $\iota_x P(x)$ stands for: the x which satisfies P then

$$Q[\iota_x P(x)] \text{ means } [\exists! x P(x)] \wedge \forall x[P(x) \to Q(x)],$$

and $\exists!$ means 'there is a unique . . .' (At the time it was satisfying to see that such matters could be expressed succinctly in Peano's language.) This meaning, due to Russell, was manageable in the sense that he found relatively precise and simple formal laws for expressions containing also ι-symbols.[3] Russell's work is to be compared to the surprisingly simple and, more importantly, well-determined extensions of such arithmetic functions as: $n \mapsto n!$ to a wider domain (Γ-function), but, as so often, the mathematical example is more interesting.

There is no guarantee that equally manageable meanings exist for such expressions as $P_R\;\eta\;P_R$ which occur in the paradoxes. If not, this would be consistent with the view of many mathematicians at the time that very general logical ideas do not lend themselves to theory (except perhaps at a very advanced stage). This could be compared to so to speak the opposite extreme: in physics, apparently accidental facts. They are quite objective, quite striking, and therefore literally make up the bulk of the world as we see it, but do not have a simple theory; for example, of the fact that (the substance having the chemical composition of) glass is transparent. Be that as it may, the fact remains that without some definite meaning for formulae containing the expressions involved, the adequacy of the marvellous logical language on p. [34] is in doubt. The particular simple interpretation of the logical particles which leads to the familiar laws, does not apply. If the logical words are reinterpreted so as to apply to meaningless expressions, the expressive power of the simple vocabulary must be expected to be very much limited. This matter is wide open. At any rate, Russell pursued a different line.

Doctrine of Types and Use of Types

Russell was always very quick to see, and formulate memorably, the ideas which naturally cross one's mind. He did this in D.T. in connexion with 'patching up' formally Frege's system. Some of his ideas have since been pursued, with varying success, as described by Gödel on pp. 132–133 of Schilpp (1944). Russell himself pursued less superficial aims:

> To describe objects, that is, predicates and contexts involving them, that are clearly meaningful, and to state some of their properties.
>
> To give reasons for supposing that those objects and contexts are exhaustive. (If the reasons given are not convincing, one speaks of a *doctrine.*) The objects described may of course have *uses* even if they are not exhaustive.

The idea was that the predicates (considered) occur in a hierarchy, and that a context of the form $P \, \eta \, P$ or $Q \, \eta \, P$ is meaningless (excluded) if P is, roughly speaking, 'involved' in Q, the so-called vicious circle principle. Though, of course, it was important for Russell's own research to attempt a general formulation of the idea, it cannot be excepted that his wording remains satisfactory after more than half a century. Russell was too much of a pioneer for that. As Gödel explains carefully on pp. 133–135 of Schilpp (1944), Russell's formulation of the 'vicious circle' principle was defective. Formulation apart, even if there is circularity in some sense, it is not clear that it is vicious. We understand perfectly well many grammatical laws which patently apply to themselves: 'In basic English the verb follows the noun'. Again, in mathematics, we understand defintions of Dedekind cuts, which are predicates of the rationals, even if the definition contains variables over Dedekind cuts. The same applies, of course, to definitions of integers of the form:

$$n = 0 \text{ if } A \text{ is true and } n = 1 \text{ if } A \text{ is false,}$$

where A contains a variable over the integers. Of course, we have to understand 'basic English', 'predicate of the rationals' (or 'set of rationals') or 'integer'.

The logical 'essentials' of Russell's idea – which are related to ideas mentioned but not developed by Poincaré – are most easily understood by comparison with the cumulative hierarchy described on p. [35] – and a little difficult to follow without understanding the latter. (So this hierarchy is fundamental.)

In the full cumulative hierarchy, at any stage $\alpha > 0$,

$$C_\alpha = \bigcup_{\beta < \alpha} C_\beta \cup \mathfrak{P}(C_\beta),$$

where, as on p. [35] $\mathfrak{P}$ is the power set operation; in particular

$$C_{\alpha+1} = C_\alpha \cup \mathfrak{P}(C_\alpha).$$

(If $C_0 = \emptyset$, each C_α is included in $\mathfrak{P}(C_\alpha)$, whence the simpler form on p. [35].) Speaking now of predicates instead of sets, Russell's idea[4] is realized if one passes from the predicates accumulated at stage α, say L_α, to the collection of only those predicates P_F which are defined by formulae F with all variables restricted to L_α; here F is in the logical language considered (with additional symbols for the predicates in L_α) and

$$X \; \eta \; P_F \text{ if and only if } F(X) \text{ is true } and \; X \; \eta \; L_\alpha.$$

This hierarchy is more difficult to understand than the (full) cumulative hierarchy because, for domains familiar in mathematics such as the set of integers, the idea of *arbitrary* subset (of the domain) is easier to think about than the idea of subset defined in some particular language. But for Russell it was perhaps natural to avoid the power set operation which led (him) originally to his paradox when he thought of applying this operation brutally to the 'domain' V of all things (p. [39]; 'brutally' since, in terms of Cantor's explanation (p. [35]), every subvariety of a familiar domain (or set, grasped as a unity) is a set, but of course, not every subvariety of V. The explanation of the predicates V_n on p. [36] takes account of this difference; thus if V_0 is the predicate of 'being a set', $V_n = V_0$ for $n = 1, 2, \ldots$

It may be difficult, though surely not impossible, to establish conclusively the role, in later research, of Russell's original, rather complicated, formulation. One reason for the difficulty is this: in P.M., the simple idea of the hierarchy is mixed up with the so-called reducibility axiom. This was introduced to derive formally the familiar properties of natural and real numbers as defined in P.M.; but the 'axiom' is just not true for the hierarchy here described (and Russell's lack of precision about the notion of 'predicate', its linguistic or abstract character (mentioned on p. [36]), was natural: he was thrashing about for a notion which satisfied the axiom). Gödel discovered a version, described on p. 147 of Schilpp (1944), which makes sense of this axiom.

He first extended the hierarchy L_α to transfinite α, and then showed, for example, that all subsets of L_ω, definable in any L_α, have already definitions in $L_{\omega 1}$ where ω_1 is the first uncountable ordinal. This is just what is asserted by the reducibility axiom applied to subsets of L_ω, if $L_{\omega 1}$ is taken to be the next stage of the hierarchy after L_ω. Roughly speaking, the axiom holds for the hierarchy L_α, if not all ordinals, but only *cardinals* α are considered. Gödel's discovery is particularly relevant to a comparison between *intensions* and *extensions*, which concerned Russell a great deal (P.D. 87–88). Specifically, new intensions (that is, definitions) of predicates of L_ω appear at arbitrarily high L_α; but, for $\alpha \geqslant \omega_1$, no new extensions $\subset L_\omega$, that is, no new subsets of L_ω. The 'totality' of all such intensions is far bigger than that of the corresponding extensions.

Interestingly enough, Gödel's formulation of his results refers to axiomatic theories and their consistency properties, not simply to, so to speak, *objective* properties of the sets definable in the L_α's. For example, he speaks of consequences C of the 'axiom' that all sets are definable in the L_α's and of its consistency relative to usual axiomatic set theory. But where C is stated to be such a consequence, often a stronger result is proved: C is true for the hierarchy of the L_α's even if some sets (of the full cumulative hierarchy) do not occur in any L_α.[5] Gödel's language comes from Hilbert's 'rival' foundational scheme, from 'without', to use Russell's words quoted on p. [27] of part I – and is necessary if the rival scheme is accepted.

P.M. and the Axiomatization of Mathematical Practice

As so often at an early stage of research, even the criticisms of P.M. were overoptimistic. The defects talked about most can in fact be corrected fairly easily (though, even now, these corrections are not as well known as the defects). The real difficulties were hardly discussed.

The first principal defect, particularly for the mathematician, was the complexity of the language of P.M. with its many types. Also the description of the syntax was not formally perfect; less so than Frege's as was pointed out on p. 126 of Schilpp (1944) – but of course, for this very reason, known to be corrigible. Ordinary mathematics provides many lessons for introducing a 'global' theory of objects of different types, which are, originally, arranged in stages; for example, of all those points in the Euclidean plane which are obtained from points with rational coordinates by means of n compass constructions. (Incidentally, the relation between this, Pythagorean, plane and the full Euclidean plane illustrates quite well many relations between the hierarchy of P.M. and the full cumulative hierarchy.)

The second principal defect, particularly for the logician, was the unsatisfactory status of the reducibility axiom which, together with a few others, took the place of the comprehension principle on p. [39]. A better formal correction was proposed by Zermelo at about the time of P.M., but after Russell's fundamental article (D.T.), and clearly interpreted in Zermelo (1930) by reference to the cumulative hierarchy. For definite properties P – not meaningless ones of p. [42].

$$\forall a \exists x \forall y [y \in x \leftrightarrow (y \in a \wedge y \ \eta \ P)];$$

the side condition $y \in a$ expresses explicitly the difference between properties of ordinary life and in mathematics (p. [36]): x is a set of a's. When one has type distinctions, the condition $y \in a$ is not needed because the type τ of the variable y automatically limits the range of y (to the class, say a_τ, of objects of type τ). Enough properties P could be recognized to be definite to develop familiar mathematics from Zermelo's axioms (and modern extensions).

The real difficulties are closely connected with the view expressed in P.M. v: 'The chief reason in favour of any theory on the principles of mathematics must always be inductive, i.e. it must lie in the fact that the theory in question enables us to deduce ordinary mathematics.' P.M. was the result. Instead of trying to analyse what is meant by logical validity and to *prove* that the rules of the calculus generate all logically valid formulae (in the language considered), P.M. deduces a lot of such formulae. Instead of looking for some global features of ordinary *mathematical concepts*, for example, that any proposition about some specific objects such as the natural numbers is either true or false, and comparing these features with the *formal properties* of the calculus, P.M. deduces a lot of arithmetic propositions. In short, P.M. contains no metamathematical theory *of* its system, no criticism from 'without' (p. [27]). Gödel's completeness theorem for predicate logic and his incompleteness theorem, for P.M. and 'related systems', with respect to quite simple arithmetic assertions, are perfect examples of successful metamathematics. To be precise his original form-ally undecided assertions had simple metamathematical content (consist-ency); nowadays, we have undecided assertions of relatively simple number theoretic content, of the form: a diophantine equation in 14 variables, with prescribed integral coefficients, has a solution. But the metamathematical assertions were easier to discover.

The incompleteness theorem is by no means in conflict with the inductive evidence! There are plenty of unsolved problems in number theory. But it raises problems which one had hoped to avoid. *What is a correct axioma-tization or definition of a mathematical concept?* As long as one believes that all true propositions (in the language considered) are formally derivable, the question above may be bypassed. Certainly often formally different definitions, say P and Q, are proposed. A minimum requirement is that both P and Q are satisfied by the same objects x. So $\forall x(P \leftrightarrow Q)$ must be true. If this equivalence is also formally derivable, every assertion derivable for P is also derivable for Q – and in this sense it does not matter which of the proposed definitions is chosen. A more sophisticated complication is very familiar from the current mathematical practice of 'enriching the structure', which applies here as follows. Suppose we wish to axiomatize the concept of *set in one–one correspondence with the integers*. Shall we define it as a set X with the side condition that there *exists* an enumeration? or shall we take a *pair* (X, F), where F is a mapping of ω onto X, that is, with the side condition

$$\forall x[x \in X \leftrightarrow \exists n(Fn = x)],$$

so to speak *enumerated sets*? or even triples (X, F, G) satisfying

$$\forall x(x \in X \leftrightarrow FGx = x),$$

where G takes values in ω? A moment's reflection shows that different classes of X, so-called retracts, are obtained without explicit appeal to choice principles. (The list of examples can be continued indefinitely.) Evidently such complications would be minor if all true propositions could be formally derived; that is, if not all (sound) formal systems were incomplete. In connexion with completeness, that is, the requirement that all true statements in the language considered should be formally derivable, the introduction of 'ugly' types is most natural: 'global' systems are *obviously* incomplete, for example, Zermelo's (without the addition of the so-called replacement axiom); one can express that there is a set of type $\omega + \omega$ but cannot derive this assertion since the segment of the cumulative hierarchy below $\omega + \omega$ satisfies the axioms and of course contains no set of type $\omega + \omega$.

All this does not discredit the idea of a correct axiomatization – or, as Russell prefers to put it, analysis – of ordinary mathematical concepts; nor even an appeal to inductive evidence. It only means that the use of such evidence would have to be a great deal subtler than had been thought (by logicians). The same applies, *mutatis mutandis*, to the choice of funda- mental system itself, the most simple-minded criterion, of completeness, being demonstrably inapplicable since no formal system is complete (for the usual language of arithmetic). Indeed, the sensitivity mentioned above to details of the axiomatization provides a rational means for finding a – or even the – *correct* axiomatization.

If one thinks of modern axiomatic mathematics, the hierarchy of P.M. – or rather, as always, its modern version L_α mentioned on p. [44] – seems to have potential interest for mathematics, in particular for the study of the full cumulative hierarchy. In modern mathematics one uses knowledge of the rationals and of other formally real fields to study the reals and, possibly, facts suggested by looking at the Pythagorean plane (p. [45]) to study the Euclidean plane. So one asks: Do we gain anything by examining those properties (in a suitable language) which are not only true in some long specific segment of the cumulative hierarchy, but also for many L_α, with relatively small (countable) α?; gain either because these L_α have an independent interest or because proofs which are valid for all these L_α provide a better analysis of the nature of the theorem proved? There is a good deal of work in this area, partly under the name of 'generalized recursion theory'. Though it has not yet provided a conclusive answer to the question above, this study of the L_α's, the direct descendants of Russell's hierarchy, still seems the best way of understanding higher set theoretical principles at all properly, and so use them effectively in mathematical practice. However natural the C_α's may be, we do not know enough about them for practical use; cf. note 5.

Finally and quite generally, as far as the analysis of mathematical prac- tice is concerned, it should be noted that P.M. is much more detailed about the analysis of mathematical concepts than of mathematical proofs, or, more generally, of processes. For example, there is really no machinery in P.M. for formulating relations between proofs expressed by different formal deductions (from given axioms) of, say, the same formula.

P.M.: A Parenthesis in the Refutation of Kant

According to P.D. 75, this is how Russell himself thought of P.M. initially. (Considering the space Kant takes up to make his points about mathematics, the parenthesis is not very long.) Specifically Kant was led to connect the *validity* of mathematical assertions with the properties of our combinatorial, spatio-temporal imagination (*Anschauung*). His examples came almost wholly from traditional geometry; he neglected the massive work, at his time, on algebra and the calculus, let alone attempts at non-Euclidean geometry. (This neglect annoyed Cantor who, to Russell's delight in A₁ 335 and again in P.D. 75, called Kant 'yonder sophistical philistine who knew so little mathematics'.) As always when psychological aspects are stressed, Kant's view suggested that mathematical experience did not lend itself to theoretical analysis.

Cantor's set theory made Kant's view extremely dubious (unless one regarded assertions about infinite sets as a mere *façon de parler*). P.M. and work building on it certainly refuted the suggested implications: put quite conservatively, such work showed firstly, how the logical properties of mathematical concepts could be built up systematically from a few primitives, and secondly, how much of *pure* mathematics was conserved if one confines oneself to these logical properties. Perhaps it should be added that not only Kant's personal convictions were refuted, but what most people would have said too; even a century after Kant the expressive power of a *few* primitives came as a surprise.

There are at least two respects in which, at the present time, Russell's view of the refutation would be qualified.

The first qualification is minor. We should not stress as much as Russell the *logical* (rather than mathematical) character of the primitive notions. Put more formally, no very significant assertions about the logical notion of predicate and the relation η (p. [36]) are known. Of course, a formalism for this primitive notion can be set up and the property, say 𝕮 (of predicates *P*)

P is built up in the cumulative hierarchy from the empty predicate

can be defined in the language (using the device, on p. [36], for associating a predicate to each set). Then we merely assert that the predicates in 𝕮 satisfy the known facts about the cumulative hierarchy. But this procedure would not introduce any specifically logical properties which *distinguish* η from ∈. If the assertions mentioned are the only axioms, we can consistently add:

$\forall P\mathfrak{C}(P)$. Here, perhaps more than elsewhere, it is slightly easier to formulate the facts if one confines oneself to the hierarchy built up from the empty set, instead of starting with some indefinite variety of objects which are not sets or predicates. (The restriction is not arbitrary: specific mathematical structures have isomorphic copies in that hierarchy, copies which can be defined in the usual set theoretic language.)

The second qualification is more serious though it applies *mutatis mutandis* to any foundational scheme. It concerns the passage from a familiar concept, for example, of natural number, to its logical (or set-theoretical) analysis. Russell put the matter very clearly in his discussion of *definitions* on pp. 11–12 of P.M.:

> when what is defined is (as often occurs) something already familiar, . . . the definition contains an analysis of a common idea, . . . Cantor's definition of the continuum illustrates this: . . . what he is defining is the object which has the properties commonly associated with the word continuum.

Evidently, this passage or analysis is not part of the set theoretic development. The passage may be compared to the analysis of familiar properties such as colours in terms of physical theory. Views may well differ on what is lost, at the present stage of knowledge, by excluding the passage in question from an analysis of mathematics. It cannot be denied that the passage involves a different *kind* of reasoning from logical deductions, but after all, it is made by mathematicians. Realistically speaking there is as much certainty (agreement) on such analyses, for example on the definition of the length of a curve, as on the correct result of a long formal computation. More remarkably still, at least to the outsider, there is often agreement on the proper 'enrichment of structures' (p. [46]).

III. Philosophy, Pedagogy, Literature

Scope of Philosophy

It is a commonplace that the aims, the proper 'meaning', of a study will change as we learn more about the objects studied. Around 1912 when Russell wrote P.P., he formulated his views on the proper scope of philosophy, distinguishing two broad areas.

One was philosophical contemplation which 'views the whole impartially' and thus achieves an 'enlargement of the Self' (P.P. 245). In less exalted language this involves taking a broad view, not forgetting other sides of a question, generally giving matters a second thought rather than simply 'forging ahead'. It should not be assumed, as Musil (1930) warns in

§72 of book II, part 1, that philosophic contemplation will necessarily help in business, war or science.

The other broad area, which we shall call *scientific philosophy*, is described as follows (P.P. 239):

> Philosophy, like all other studies, aims primarily at knowledge . . . the kind of knowledge which gives unity and system to the body of the sciences, and the kind which results from a critical examination of the grounds of our convictions.

The description is clear enough though it cannot be assumed that the common part of the various sciences (that which gives 'unity') will necessarily be particularly useful or interesting. As is to be expected of a science of philosophy, it is not so easy to be precise about the features which distinguish it from 'ordinary' sciences. All the more since, as a matter of historical fact (stressed by Russell, P.P. 240), many present sciences were formerly included in philosophy and some were created to answer such typically philosophical questions as: What is matter? Russell's dicta concerning those characteristic features vary. But the one he stresses most consistently is the *uncertainty* of philosophy, with different emphasis in different contexts.

Perhaps the most positive formulation occurs in H.W.P. xiv. Philosophy is to teach us 'how to live without certainty'. In the context (*loc. cit.*) Russell is preoccupied with the unfounded certainty of dogmatic theology; in the tradition of Kant, Russell looks to philosophy as a bulwark against the temptations of theology. Those of us who do not feel tempted will naturally interpret Russell's formulation more broadly and look to philosophy for help in the 'face of uncertainty'. There are two extremes corresponding to the two parts in Russell's description of scientific philosophy.

The passage from genuine uncertainty to moderate certainty; at the very beginning of scientific research when one really knows nothing about the nature of the objects considered (or the 'kind' of answers to be expected); and secondly the passage from theoretical uncertainty, that is, practical certainty, to some ideal certainty, which is the business of so-called critical philosophy; the aim of 'securing' mathematical practice, mentioned on p. [33], belongs here.

The next section concerns the first passage. The idea that there may be a distinct subject here is not discredited by ordinary experience of scientific work. There is a recognizable difference in the flavour of the kinds of arguments used for starting a science (in the 'face of uncertainty') and for developing (or finishing) it. This difference is particularly striking in the case of the so-called fundamental sciences which study the very large or the very small: here one could hardly start by following Francis Bacon's recipe for collecting data. In short, the arguments used within our ordinary sciences are not altogether homogeneous. Looked at this way, the first branch of scientific philosophy (in Russell's formulation in P.P. 239) would require us to *separate* different kinds of argument already used *within* science, and to see whether the arguments with a philosophical 'flavour' lend themselves to a systematic development.

The separation of pure mathematics, as a distinct study, from its uses in scientific arguments would be a concrete example of the project considered.

Uncertainty and Generality

Even if the laws to be used in the 'face of uncertainty' are themselves perfectly certain they would not necessarily provide a panacea. There would be uncertainty about how to apply them in a practical situation and, more importantly, whether the application is of practical interest. So the search for such laws is not absurdly utopian. Perhaps the most naive idea for finding such laws is this:

If the laws are to be used in the 'face of uncertainty' they should concern arbitrary objects. The more general the objects considered the better the chance that laws about them can be applied without knowing the nature of the objects.

Evidently, the existence of *valid* general laws is not in doubt: we do not dispute that p implies p, nor other logical laws. What is needed, in Russell's words (I.M.P. 2), is a genuine 'enlargement of our logical powers' by means of laws which are (generally valid and) at least sometimes useful. Russell repeatedly discusses how one sets about finding such laws. A favourite of his (P.o.M. 3) was 'a precise analysis of . . . the ordinary employment [of] a common word'. But unlike many of his would-be followers, he was less concerned with the so to speak literary aim of a faithful analysis than with scientifically fruitful analyses.[6]

Russell unquestionably understated the progress made in the branch of scientific philosophy which searches for general laws, progress very much based on his own work. Practically speaking he probably simply did not know the details (though he seemed pleased when he heard about developments, for example, in P.D. (101) and also in the conversation mentioned on p. [31]). But there was also a theoretical obstacle; his stress on the identification of logic and mathematics. This suggests that there is no 'qualitative' difference between ordinary mathematics, correctly interpreted, and modern logic. Many mathematicians have a different impression, and distinguish between different parts (in developments) of Russell's work described in part II. Set theoretic structures and operations are seen to be natural extensions of familiar mathematics; less so results involving (logical) languages, in particular, of first order predicate logic. Such results have been applied within mathematics; partly in a routine fashion to formulate explicitly the general character of some 'easy' facts, partly with great imagination to solve old conjectures. Nobody questions the validity of these applications of logic. But inasmuch as they are 'qualitatively' different from ordinary mathematics, they constitute a 'qualitative' enlargement of our logical powers. They certainly help us sometimes to make a routine start in mathematics: to prove trivial things trivially (a, if not the, most useful result of having sound *general* conceptions).

The search for an enlargement of our logical powers recalls the heroic days of Descartes (1637) or Leibniz, as quoted, for example, in P.L. (169–170, 283–284). Both said – and surely believed – that their general rules of thought had led (them) to their remarkable scientific discoveries. These claims may well be true, but they are difficult to judge – as it is difficult to judge the actual role of general principles which (rich) business-men believe to have led to their fortunes, as in Getty (1963); or those to which (healthy) centenarians attribute their vigour. The principles of first order predicate logic are easier to use; one need neither 'sincerely wish to be rich' nor have the iron constitution required to digest the health food which brings longevity.

The reader of part II will have noticed another, quite typical, *heuristic* value, for ordinary science (mathematics), of studying (mathematical) concepts with a philosophical 'flavour'. There is nothing particularly 'philosophical' about solving diophantine equations; but the concepts needed for establishing negative results were *discovered*, by Gödel, in connexion with logical problems (pp. [46–47]).

Critical Philosophy and Occam's Razor

We now come to the second branch of scientific philosophy (in the sense of p. [50]) about which Russell says (P.P. 233):

> The essential characteristic of philosophy, which makes it a study distinct from science, is *criticism* . . . it searches out any inconsistencies there may be in [the] principles [used], and it only accepts them when, as the result of a critical enquiry, no reason for rejecting them has appeared.

The formulation is not perfect. To be consistent with Russell's description of the scope of philosophy, one would have to assume that this kind of criticism is likely to give 'unity and systems to the body of sciences'. And, in any case, every (respectable) science rejects inconsistent principles. (Contrary to his memory in later years, for example (P.D. 11), at the time of P.M., Russell was not preoccupied with this kind of critical philosophy, at least as far as mathematical knowledge is concerned. This is clear from the quotation on p. [33]).

The formulation of PP. 213 is improved by Russell's description, on p. 13 of P.D., of the principal tool to be used in critical philosophy, Occam's razor to which he 'had become devoted':

One was not obliged to deny the existence of the entities with which one dispensed, but one was enabled to abstain from ascertaining it. This had the advantage of diminishing the assumptions required for the interpretation of whatever branch of knowledge was in question.

As is well known, *critical* philosophy goes farther in practice: having shown that it was possible to dispense with certain entities for the interpretation of (existing) knowledge, it assumes that it is permanently desirable or even necessary to do so. Incidentally, Russell realized that it was not easy to be precise about meaningful uses of Occam's razor, about choosing the particular assumptions to which Occam's razor should be applied, but oversimplified matters in P.M. 91, 1.5; also earlier (P.o.M. 15) and later (P.D. 71). He looked for a reduction in the *number* of assumptions or of undefined terms, as if one could not be as wrong about one unfamiliar or complicated thing, such as set, as about twenty familiar ones such as numbers, points, etc.

Occam's razor is also applied in ordinary science, but with fundamentally different aims (two of which will be mentioned below). They too concern the analysis of existing knowledge, but they are not negative, not essentially critical.

First of all, Occam's razor provides a tool for action in the 'face of uncertainty', complementary to the use of laws about arbitrary entities on p. [51]. Instead we see how far we can get without assuming anything about certain entities which we don't happen to understand. Here Occam's razor is generally of temporary heuristic use. In any case ordinary scientific knowledge is not static; as a given branch of knowledge develops, the entities in question may become 'indispensable'. In fact more is true: unless there is independent reason for suspicion of the entities dispensed with, one will try to *extend* existing knowledge in such a way that additional assumptions *are* required for its interpretation! just as the decision between (sensible) rival theories is rarely made by use of existing knowledge: one has to invent a novel *experimentum crucis*. In other words, in ordinary scientific practice one will often conclude from an application of Occam's razor that existing knowledge is inadequate for studying the entities in question, and no more.

A second, also positive use of Occam's razor has proved fruitful so to speak at the opposite extreme when a branch of science is in a very advanced state: the application of the axiomatic method, especially in mathematics. Having established a result about a specific mathematical object, say, the real numbers, one examines which properties of the object are used in the proof and 'dispenses' with its other properties which are superfluous for the given result. But the reason for doing this is not that those other properties are any more dubious. (The reasons vary from genuinely useful generalizations to what might be described as an analysis of the nature of the specific result.) However, it should be remembered that critical philosophy played an important heuristic role for modern axiomatic mathematics, even on a technical level! One of the early results which were most useful for its developments was the algebraic treatment of polynomials in Sturm (1835). His express purpose was to avoid continuity considerations which he believed to involve infinitesimals, and wanted to dispense with the latter; a perfect example for Russell's views (p. [53]) on Occam's razor. Sturm's treatment survives; the aim does not, since Cauchy made continuity considerations independent of infinitesimals (and, besides, Sturm's work applies to non-Archimedean fields too, that is, fields which do have infinitesimal elements). The reader of part II may wish to pursue the following parallel between Sturm's work and P.M. Inasmuch as P.M. served as a parenthesis in the refutation of Kant (p. [48]), its axiomatization also fits Russell's description of Occam's razor; one 'dispensed' with Kant's acts of intuition. (And as Russell could have said, one was not obliged to deny that such acts occur in actual mathematical reasoning.) The next step in the parallel is to compare Cauchy's analysis of continuity to Zermelo's analysis of the cumulative hierarchy and Gödel's of the reducibility axiom (described in part II). Possible uses of the hierarchy of P.M. in generalized recursion theory, mentioned on p. [47], correspond to standard practice of modern axiomatic mathematics.

To sum up; so far critical philosophy seems to have had considerable heuristic, but less permanent, value. Particularly as far as ordinary knowledge is concerned, views will differ on the interest of the following result of critical philosophy (P.P. 233, 234): 'as regards what would be commonly accepted as knowledge . . . we have seldom found reason to reject such knowledge as the result of our criticism'. Paranoids ought to be reassured. Indeed the methods of argument in critical philosophy may even have clinical value since paranoids are notoriously sensitive to logical rigour. (Some are certainly capable of conviction by the right kind of argument: one of the three Christs of Ypsilanti in Rockeach (1964) was convinced by the others that he was mistaken.) Less speculatively, critical philosophy may lead to more interesting results at the frontier of knowledge; as suggested by the example of Frege's analysis of thought on p. [35] and, particularly, by Einstein's success, on p. [55]. The questions of critical – and other traditional – philosophy would not be 'deep' if we really wanted to answer them in the context where they occur to us; they are exciting (and difficult to judge) because they draw attention to a new kind of study which is not forced on us by familiar experience.

From What We Know to How We Know

In the preceding two sections the stress was on objects (and not primarily on our assertions about them); on extending the class of objects considered to get general laws, and dispensing with entities by means of Occam's razor. This respects Russell's manifesto in P.D. 16:

> I reverse the process which has been common in philosophy since Kant, [which was] . . . to begin with how we know and proceed afterwards to what we know. I think this a mistake, because knowing how we know is one small department of knowing what we know.

This type of mistake is familiar from popular positivist philosophy which proposes to begin with methods of measurement (as means of knowing) while, in point of fact, one has to examine whether proposed methods are *correct*; whether they measure what we want to know about and not artifacts. Russell's work in logic, as was stressed at length in part II, certainly fits in with his manifesto, and so does the work on the atomic structure of matter with which the logical analysis of mathematics was compared there. It should be added that in these cases one hardly goes on at all to the second stage, of analysing realistically the processes which bring us knowledge. It should not be assumed that this last omission is a mere accident. Observation of the facts of our intellectual experience shows that we can often be more sure of what we know than of how we (come to) know it; however strange this may seem on the so-called empiricist or any similarly simple-minded conception of our intellectual apparatus (wie sich der kleine Moritz das Denken vorstellt).

Russell, according to P.D. 13–14, did want to proceed to the second stage (how we know) – though, apparently, not in the case of mathematical or logical knowledge – 'in the years from 1910 to 1914, I became interested not only in what the physical world is, but in how we come to know it'. But, to quote Einstein's remark on p. 290 of Schilpp (1944) concerning Russell's theory of knowledge, the latter was infected by a touch of bad intellectual conscience. This came about because Russell looked for an empiricist analysis in the style of Hume, where our concepts are 'reduced' to, that is, obtained inductively from, sense experience. (In the case of mathematical knowledge – more or less sophisticated – versions of this style of empiricist analysis are required by the doctrines of formalism and finitism mentioned on p. [33].) Russell, reluctantly, came to the conclusion that many of the concepts we constantly use could not be so reduced, and remained troubled about them – in contrast to Einstein. It should perhaps be added that Einstein makes these concepts a little too mysterious, on p. 286 of Schilpp (1944), by insisting that they are *free* creations of our minds. The concepts would be less mysterious if, practically speaking, we had no choice: there would be little to distinguish them from what (we believe) is externally given.

When looking back (P.D. 12) at his change in interest, from what we know to how we know, Russell connected it with his having 'done all that

[he] intended to do as regards pure mathematics'. But the change is also in keeping with one of the great events of the first decade of this century, Einstein's special theory of relativity. Einstein's own presentation did begin with an analysis – in accordance with P.D. 16 quoted above – of how we know (simultaneity), for the critical purpose of searching out serious inconsistencies in the accepted principles of determining simultaneity; at least, when objects move at high relative speed. From that analysis one could then proceed to ask what we know (not space, nor time, but space-time). Incidentally, Einstein's reservations mentioned above about the positivist or empiricist theory of knowledge were not due to ignorance of its – occasional – advantages; on the contrary, Einstein was initially strongly attracted by the positivist views of Mach, but abandoned them after closer reflection. Russell's later ideas on how we come to know the physical world (as summarized in chapter II of P.D.), refer quite explicitly to the physiological apparatus of perception – in contrast to Einstein's exposition of his, perhaps, singular success with critical philosophy. Views differ on whether the properties of this apparatus are essential for Russell's aim. But if they are, the time is hardly ripe for pursuing this aim. Judging whether the time is ripe for a problem is of course essential for all research, but especially in philosophy; perhaps not surprisingly because the questions occur to us when we know very little. With wit and literary skill something of interest can no doubt be said about them at any stage; but at a given stage there is often – demonstrably – nothing significant or conclusive to be done. The physicist will here think of such a natural question as: What is matter (made of)? at the time of Galileo or Newton, who both had brilliant arguments for some kind of a micro-structure. The mathematician will think of questions about the need for abstract ideas in mathematics when all we know is numerical arithmetic or even elementary geometry.

Pedagogy in the Large

We now turn to two social changes which are, at least formally, connected with Russell's writings – on logic, not on war and peace. These changes, which literally affect the lives of many of us, the way we spend our time, come from the introduction of the New Maths and from the use of computers, particularly for so-called non-numerical computation. The connexions are clear.

P.M. is about logic and classes (sets), and claims that they provide the means for the correct analysis of other mathematics. The New Maths teaches children about these things before teaching them sums and what Russell called 'childhood's enemy' (P.o.M. 90).

P.M. expresses a great number of sophisticated mathematical concepts in terms of those logical primitives in a formally precise, that is, purely mechanical manner. The effective use of computers patently depends on the possibility of this kind of mechanization.

The actual, causal, role of Russell's writings in bringing about these social changes is less easy to establish, and perhaps not even important for understanding social history, for example, if good ideas may be expected to be 'in the air' (a view which could be connected with rushing into print). Be that as it may, there are some outstanding qualities of Russell's writings which have surely influenced the details of those social changes.

First, as Einstein stressed on p. 278 of Schilpp (1944), there are few scientific writers and certainly no contemporary logicians who catch the reader's imagination so vividly and so agreeably as Russell; incidentally, not only by form but also by content. Specifically, though the earlier work of Frege (1884) and (1893) is, in some respects, more satisfactory to the professional logician, the fact remains that Frege wrote about arithmetic, about the question: What is a natural or real number? while Russell asked: What is mathematics? (By p. [35], even formally Frege's caution was hardly justified, at least on present knowledge.) The bold sweep of Russell's presentation may well have impressed some of the educational reformers who worked for the New Maths, at least in Anglo-Saxon countries. After all, educational reforms can hardly be based wholly on empirical evidence since their effects are difficult to trace, let alone to predict. So it ought to be a comfort to know that one *should* begin with logic because, as Russell taught, mathematics *is* logic. As suggested above, this factor influenced details and the style of the reform. But also the principal factor involved is not unrelated to Russell: the success within mathematics (in establishing mathematical facts and mathematical fashion) of the logical and set theoretic notions first treated systematically in P.M.

Secondly, in connection with the exploitation of computers, which require an artificial language, Russell's writings must have helped by establishing confidence in the expressive power of such languages. Before him there was little practical evidence for this power (or, at least, not widely known). Of course there were highly mechanized languages, for example, for military orders, but these were not thought of as a sophisticated business. And there were theoretical arguments against artificial languages, for example, the dispute with Condillac described in Maistre (1821) – with interesting political overtones which will come up again on p. [60]. In short, it is suggested that Russell's writings established a favourable intellectual climate for the use of computers. Naturally, it is more difficult to be sure about effects on any particular scientist such as von Neumann, perhaps the principal pioneer of computer science; his early work concerned a theory related to Russell's D.T. and, of course, P.M. Here again it is suggested that Russell's writings affected the details in the development of computer science; but, in this case, not the principal factor (which is, presumably, the technological advance in electronics).

Russell himself does not seem to have written about the two social changes here considered. He certainly would not have liked all aspects of these changes. Perhaps he would have had – to use his own words about 'The Conquest of Happiness' (A₂ 228) – 'commonsense advice' for atomic scientists, divided between the (moral) agony of responsibility and a (wicked) sense of power; of having been responsible for something sufficiently powerful to merit the agony.

Pedagogy in the Small

Russell's writings, particularly on logic, are distinguished also by another, apparently quite intimate, didactic quality. A host of memorable metaphors, aphorisms and analogies relieves the reader of all anxiety about the knowledge he has and about the work to come. Russell formulates the questions that occur to the reader at the moment when they arise; even the right irrelevant ones, confusions. In short, Russell has great understanding of the feelings we have about our scientific knowledge. Descriptions of these, as of other feelings are liable to be tedious and banal. Russell avoids this because he always sees the, so to speak, universal element in these feelings – like such novelists as Musil or Solzhenitsyn. Incidentally, the quality under discussion of Russell's scientific style is relevant to a principal gap between science and current literature: the characters of most novels go through life without any thoughts or feelings about (their) scientific knowledge, in conflict presumably with the actual experience of those readers who happen to be scientists. (Evidently such a literary treatment of our feelings about knowledge may be satisfying at a stage when, objectively, there is nothing significant to be done; in contrast to the view about scientific philosophy on p. [56].)

Russell himself, quite explicitly, attached great importance to the universal element mentioned above. As early as 1900, he devoted §1 of P.L. to 'reasons why Leibniz never wrote a *magnum opus*', concluding that Leibniz did not use sufficiently impersonal, universal arguments because he was too much concerned with persuasion of some particular person; and quite specifically, according to p. vi of the second edition of P.L., of 'Princes and (even more) Princesses'. Some of us may have doubts about the validity of Russell's explanation; but we can have no doubt about his view on such matters.

Actually, a good deal of Russell's pedagogic skill is used on subjects which nowadays, when more facts are known, are easy to present; it is not necessary to spend nearly 20 pages on the notion of order (P.o.M. 199–217). The skill would, presumably, be more essential for a task which Russell often mentioned as a principal job of philosophy: the discussion of indefinables, as he called them in P.o.M. xv and P.D. 81, or, better, of primitive ideas (P.M. 91):

> primitive ideas are *explained* by means of descriptions intended to point out to the reader what is meant; but the explanations do not constitute definitions, because they really involve the ideas they explain.

(Of course, 'description' is not used in the technical sense of the ι-symbol on p. 66 or p. 172 of P.M. and 'definition' is not used in the informal sense of analysis of a familiar notion, top of p. 12.) More precisely (P.D. 81), the reader's attention is to be drawn to the entities concerned (as in pointing a finger at an object in front of us). One way of doing this is to state striking formal properties of these entities, so-called axioms which can often be relied upon to indicate the entities (and can be misunderstood, like pointing). Presumably, pedagogic skills like Russell's can sometimes be used more effectively than those axioms for conveying primitive ideas.

The 'intimate' pedagogy here described seems to be similar to the other, non-scientific, area of philosophy which was mentioned at the beginning of part III. It is perhaps of interest to go briefly into Russell's views on these matters at different times.

Philosophic Contemplation

On the face of things Russell changed his mind about the efficacy of philosophic contemplation. When he was forty, he was most positive (P.P. 243–250); twenty years later (A_2 230) and again in M.D. 20 he said: 'the "consolations of philosophy" are not for me'. On closer inspection the conflict disappears. In P.P. he meant by 'contemplation': reflection on unfamiliar possibilities (P.P. 243), viewing 'the whole impartially' (P.P. 245). Later he meant: gazing at the stars or admiring the universe for its size, and found that *these* activities did not console him. Views differ on whether one should look for consolation at all or be an activist; also on the extent to which philosophic contemplation presupposes a suitable temperament. But there is no doubt that the later Russell hardly ever engaged in philosophic contemplation in the sense of P.P. The two examples below are chosen because of their connection with the work described in part II.

The cornerstones of Russell's logical theory were: first, his warnings about the 'irrelevant notion of mind' (P.o.M. 4) or an 'undue admixture of psychology' (P.o.M. 53) – although of course, naïvely (whence the need for the warnings), the mental phenomena of logical activity strike us first. Secondly, the famous analogy of (I.M.P. 2):

> Just as the easiest bodies to see are those that are neither very near nor very far, neither very small nor very great, so the easiest conceptions to grasp are those that are neither very complex nor very simple.

In the context 'simple' is used in a *logical* sense; but the remark applies also to space or matter when 'simple' is used in a *physical* sense; evidently it is intended generally as an introduction to 'high' theory.

Both these points are in sharp contrast to the style of his analyses of social and political problems, for example, in N.P. concerning politically important motives. Certainly, there is no guarantee that these problems lend themselves to high theory at all. Even so, Russell's analyses do nothing, in conflict with the requirement of philosophic contemplation (P.P. 243), to stop 'the world [from becoming] definite, finite, obvious'. Besides, like everybody else, Russell was quite ready to apply his 'logical' maxims to economic life; to accept that this is dominated by rational self-interest, yet knowing perfectly well that, individually, businessmen are as lazy, vain and generally irrational as the rest of us. (Presumably their irrational actions cancel out.)

The second example does not involve delicate moral issues. The subtitle of H.W.P. reads: [Philosophy] and its Connection with Political and Social Circumstances. True, Russell interprets 'social' in a rather broad sense, for example, in his analysis of Nietzsche's views on etiquette (H.W.P. 767); but in the discussion of the philosophical works of Frege or of himself there is simply no trace at all of any connexion with social circumstances. Yet, in the ordinary sense of 'philosophic contemplation' and particularly in the sense of P.P. 244, one should look at oneself from outside. Now it so happens that the matter of artificial languages, a principal topic of P.M., has traditionally been regarded as a political issue, at least in Romantic and nationalist political philosophy. This was mentioned on p. [57] in connexion with the conservative de Maistre and the progressive Condillac; but also, back in the *Theaetetus* (184c), Plato has Socrates connect formal precision with lack of breeding. Evidently, the conservative view was that there is a universal human capacity for acquiring formal languages, but that only people of the same (proper) background are capable of free and easy intellectual intercourse. In modern jargon, formalization or mechanization would be needed not only for communicating masses of information, but simply for communicating information to the masses. From this point of view formalist philosophy suits the outsiders as, according to some Marxists, idealist philosophy suited the ruling classes. P.M. shows how unexpectedly far the – accepted – universal capacity for acquiring formal language goes, and may be thought to weaken the conservative case.

It is of course a fact that the century of democracy is also the century of formalization to which P.M. contributed so much. But this fact, and the connexion it may suggest, did not have an important place in Russell's view of things. In short, whatever its practical merits the view was often – to quote again from P.P. 243 – characteristically, *un*contemplative, 'unfamiliar possibilities [being] contemptuously rejected'.

Russell's Picture of America

It remains to mention Russell's view of ordinary life around him. Probably, his encounter with America is as representative as any other part of his long, active and varied life. On the personal side, he returned there repeatedly in the first half of this century, worked there as already mentioned in part I, and both his first and last wives were Americans. Also, for anyone interested in the liberal ideas of the last century, America is simply bound to be fascinating. Although it is unfashionable to say so, these ideas – as originally conceived – have been followed there to an incomparably higher degree than elsewhere. Some highly uniform societies have been more democratic, for example, in ancient Greece (if the slaves are not counted) or modern Sweden (where legal discrimination on religious grounds till the middle of this century may have encouraged homogeneity). But, for good or ill, America has provided incomparably more opportunity for the (instant) use of native talents and for social mobility than any other country with a similar population mixture; for groups of widely different background or none at all as it were: chasing opportunities, many practically lost their mother tongue altogether. It would, perhaps, be too much to expect that this social mobility would benefit only people of exceptional refinement and sensibility or that it was likely to create social conventions (on speech and manners) which work smoothly and naturally.

Russell's America consisted mainly of university society; at both ends of the scale (Harvard and midcentury UCLA), and figures on its borders such as the self-made millionaire Dr Barnes, a patron of the arts and humanities, who battled with Russell over Pithergawras (A_2 338). This society has changed since Russell's days, particularly after the first Sputnik. But as far as his times are concerned, the picture created by Russell in his autobiography is certainly quite true. The picture is produced by a series of concrete episodes; several of them are gems, for example (A_1 325–327). The short description of the bullying President of UCLA (A_2 333) conveys much of the atmosphere, since made familiar by McCarthy (1952), the famous novel about administrators at a minor American university. The comparison between the reactions to policemen of his young son and of university professors accused of speeding (A_3 13) is, or should be, a classic.

As already mentioned, Russell's picture of his times in America is true; both perceptive and very amusing. What is striking is that the picture includes very little reflection about the overt facts, little connexion with general views which he expresses so to speak abstractly. Specifically, he said quite explicitly (A_3 329) that 'institutions mould character'. His picture of the characters he met in America does not include any reflection on how they were 'moulded' by the social institutions of the country. (Yet most of the concrete episodes merely illustrate the surely obvious consequences of the social mobility of American society mentioned already.) Nor does he speak of the inherent difficulties when academics who are accustomed to judge cases become university administrators whose business it is to settle cases. The difficulties were compounded at the end of the thirties by the fact that many distinguished exiles had jobs below their academic standing at American universities. This put the administrators in a false position. Russell mentions that some of these administrators were pompous bullies; but not the temptation – in their position – to stand on their dignity. They did so in the style they had learnt at (American) public schools or, perhaps, from Hollywood films. Since Russell does not mention these things, his picture also leaves out the remarkable qualities of those characters who lived under the same institutions but did not offend his aesthetic sensibilities.

For present conceptions, Russell's view of America is narrow, especially if – as seems appropriate – one thinks of other great writers with high ideals. Thus, Solzhenitsyn (1968a) and (1968b) presents public prosecutors and commissars as 'moulded' by institutions, caught up in them. This then leaves room for real moral freaks, good or bad, as in the portrait of Stalin in Solzhenitsyn (1968a). Russell's view doesn't.

On the other hand, present views on social matters are probably narrower than Russell's – which he called his 'social vision' (A_3 330). He saw 'in imagination the society . . . where individuals grow freely, and where hate and greed and envy die because there is nothing to nourish them'. There is little in his autobiography to make his vision concrete. He does not seem to have been particularly romantic about humanity-in-the-raw; in A_1 240, 244 and especially in P.D. 214 where he criticizes Tolstoy for his saintly picture of Russian peasants. Yet however unconvincing it may be (at least for those of us who do not know these peasants), this picture makes Tolstoy's social vision quite concrete, since the vision is practically realized already.

There is much more to convey what Russell called his 'personal vision', above all the description of his relation with Joseph Conrad (A_1 320–324), obviously – for Russell – a kind of paradigm for the possibilities of human relationships. There is deep admiring affection and, in particular, there is no trace of contempt for any aspect of the other person. And other episodes and letters in the autobiography suggest that, all through his life, Russell was linked to several people by similar, so to speak, chemical bonds. These bonds seem to have developed freely and naturally without the caution or cunning calculation which are sometimes said to be necessary to protect such relations and which were so alien to Russell.

Many people have helped, directly or indirectly, in the preparation of this memoir; in particular, Sir Isaiah Berlin and Mr Kenneth Blackwell of the Bertrand Russell Archives at McMaster University, Hamilton, Ontario in Canada.

Notes

1 The letters A, etc. refer to the bibliography, at the end of this memoir, containing Russell's writings actually quoted here, and the numbers are page numbers. To avoid misunderstanding it should be noted that the pagination of A_1–A_3 differs substantially from the English edition of Russell's autobiography.

2 As so often, defects in terminology reflect a defective analysis of the notion considered; cf. p. [44].
3 These laws can be made quite precise relative to given primitive or atomic predicates. Any formal language is given with a list of such predicates, but not unanalysed ordinary language. Is *male* or (its negation) *female* primitive?
4 The type structure of P.M. is not cumulative, and therefore formally quite different from the modern presentation which is used here.
5 For example, C may be the generalized continuum hypothesis; or the negation of Souslin's hypothesis by Jensen (1972). In contrast we do not know whether Cantor's continuum hypothesis or Souslin's hypothesis is true for the full cumulative hierarchy; nor, equivalently, for $C_{\omega+\omega}$ on p. [43]. In other words our present knowledge of sets is much more efficient when applied to the L_α's than when applied to the C_α's (in terms of which the L_α's are defined).
6 The reader of pp. [45–48] in part II will recall the hazards of such an (inductive) analysis without safeguards against systematic errors and ommissions.

References

Bernard, J. F. 1973. *Talleyrand*. New York.
Cantor, G. 1885. Review of Frege (1884). *Deutsche Literaturzeitung*, 6, 728–729; reprinted on pp. 440–441 of Zermelo (1932).
Cantor, G. 1899. Letter to Dedekind; reprinted on pp. 443–447 of Zermelo (1932).
Crawshay-Williams, R. 1970. *Russell remembered*. London.
Dedekind, R. 1872. *Stetigkeit und irrationale Zahlen*. Braunschweig.
Dedekind, R. 1888. *Was sind und was sollen die Zahlen*. Braunschweig.
Descartes, R. 1637. *Discours de la méthode*. Leyden.
Frege, G. 1879. *Begriffsschrift*. Halle a/S.
Frege, G. 1884. *Grundlagen der Arithmetik*. Breslau.
Frege, G. 1893. *Grundgesetze der Arithmetik*. Jena.
Getty, P. J. 1963. *My life and fortunes*. New York.
Jensen, R. B. 1972. The fine structure of L. *Annals of Mathematical Logid*. 4, 229–308.
Hermann, I. 1949. Denkpsychologische Betrachtungen im Gebiete der mathematischen Mengenlehre. *Schweiz. Z. Psychologie*, 8, 189–231.
Holmberg, M. A. (ed.) 1951. *Les prix Nobel en 1950*. Stockholm.
Hume, D. 1777. *An enquiry concerning the principles of morals*. London.
McCarthy, M. T. 1952. *The groves of Academe*. New York.
Maistre, J. de 1821. *Les soirées de Saint-Pétersbourg ou entretiens sur le gouvernement temporel de la providence: suivis d'un Traité sur les sacrifices*. Paris.
Musil, R. 1930. *Der Mann ohne Eigenschaften*. Berlin.
Nkrumah, K. 1970. *Consciencism* (rev. edn). London and New York.
Rokeach, M. 1964. *The three Christs of Ypsilanti; a psychological study*. New York.
Schilpp, P. A. (ed.) 1944. *The philosophy of Bertrand Russell*. Evanston and Chicago.
Solzhenitsyn, A. I. 1968a. *The first circle*. London.
Solzhenitsyn, A. I. 1968b. *The cancer ward*. London.
Sturm, C. 1835. Mémoire sur la résolution des équations numériques. *Mémoires présentés par divers savants étrangers à l'Académie Royale des Sciences de l'Institut de France, Sciences Mathématiques et Physiques*, 6.
Watling, J. 1970. *Bertrand Russell*. Edinburgh.
Zermelo, E. 1930. Über Grenzzahlen und Mengenbereiche. *Fund. Math.* 16, 29–47.
Zermelo, E. (ed.) 1932. *Georg Cantor: Gesammelte Abhandlungen*. Berlin.

Bibliography

A fuller bibliography is to be found on pp. 111–115 of Watling (1970).

A_1–A_3 *The autobiography of Bertrand Russell*, 1872–1914, 1914–1944, 1944–1968, Atlantic Monthly Press, 1967, 1968, 1969 resp. *N.B.* – Page numbers quoted in the memoir refer to the hard cover edition.

D.T.   On some difficulties in the theory of transfinite numbers and order types. *Proc. Lond. Math. Soc.* (2) 4, 29–53 (1906).

H.W.P.   *A history of western philosophy.* New York, 1945.

I.M.P.   *Introduction to mathematical philosophy.* London, 1919.

M.D.   My mental development, pp. 1–20 in Schilpp (1944).

N.P.   What desires are politically important? Nobel lecture 11 December 1950, pp. 259–270 of Holmberg (1951).

O.D.   On denoting, *Mind*, 14, 479–493 (1905).

P.D.   *My philosophical development.* New York, 1959.

P.L.   *A critical exposition of the philosophy of Leibniz.* Cambridge, 1900.

P.M.   *Principia mathematica*, vol. 1. (with A. N. Whitehead), Cambridge, 1910.

P.o.M.   *The principles of mathematics.* London, 1903.

P.P.   *The problems of philosophy.* London, 1921.

4

Bertrand Russell as a Philosopher

A. J. Ayer

I. Russell's Approach to Philosophy

The popular conception of a philosopher as one who combines universal learning with the direction of human conduct was more nearly satisfied by Bertrand Russell than by any other philosopher of our time. Other philosophers, though not many in this country, have taken an active part in public life, but none of these matches Russell in the width of his interest in the natural and social sciences or in the range of the contributions which he made to philosophy itself. He himself, no doubt with good reason, attached the greatest value to the work which he did on mathematical logic, both in its philosophical and technical aspects, but the interest which he also paid to the theory of knowledge, to the philosophy of mind, to the philosophy of science, and to metaphysics in the form of ontology was comparably rewarding. In all these domains, Russell's work has had a very great influence upon his contemporaries, from the beginning of the century up to the present day. In the English-speaking world at least, there is no one, with the possible exception of his pupil Ludwig Wittgenstein, who has done so much in this century, not only to advance the discussion of particular philosophical problems, but to fashion the way in which philosophy is practised.

As he relates in his autobiography, Russell was led to take an interest in philosophy by his desire to find some good reason for believing in the truth of mathematics. Already at the age of eleven, when he had been introduced by his brother to Euclidean geometry, he had objected to having to take the axioms on trust. He eventually agreed to accept them, only because his brother assured him that they could not make any progress otherwise, but he did not give up his belief that the propositions of geometry, and indeed those of any other branch of mathematics, needed some ulterior justification. For a time, he was attracted to John Stuart Mill's view that mathematical propositions are empirical generalizations, which are induct-ively justified by the number and variety of the observations that conform to them, but this conflicted with the belief, which he was unwilling to relinquish, that mathematical propositions are necessarily true. Taking the necessity of the propositions of formal logic to be relatively unprob-lematic, he chose rather to try to justify mathematics by showing it to be derivable from logic. This enterprise, in which he had been anticipated by Gottlob Frege, required, first, the discovery of a method of defining the fundamental concepts of mathematics in purely logical terms, and sec-ondly, the elaboration of a system of logic which would be sufficiently rich for the propositions of mathematics to be deducible from it. The first of these tasks was carried out, among other things, in *The Principles of Mathematics*, which Russell published in 1903, when he was just over thirty years of age, and the second, in which he had the assistance of Alfred North Whitehead, in the three monumental volumes of *Principia Mathe-matica*, which appeared between 1910 and 1913.

How far Russell and Whitehead succeeded in their attempt to reduce mathematics to logic is a question into which I shall not enter here. That there has been a junction of mathematics with logic is not disputable, but whether this is to be regarded as an annexation of mathematics by logic or of logic by mathematics depends very largely on the status which one assigns to set-theory. The point which I wish to make here is that both Russell's belief that the propositions of mathematics stand in need of justification and his method of justifying them, by reducing them to pro-positions which apparently belong to another domain, are distinctive of his whole approach to philosophy. He was a consistent sceptic, in the sense of holding that all our accepted beliefs are open to question; he conceived it to be the business of philosophy to try to set these doubts at rest, and for reasons which I shall presently give, he thought that the best way of setting them at rest was to reduce the propositions on which they bore to proposi-tions which themselves were not doubtful to the same degree.

In most cases, the reason why Russell thought that the truth of a given class of propositions was open to doubt was that they referred to a type of entity of whose existence one could not be certain. He came to believe that the acceptance of any proposition, which was not simply a minuting of one's own current experience, was the outcome of some form of inference, but thought it important to distinguish between inferences which remained at the same level, in the sense that the entities which were referred to in the conclusion were of the same sort as those which already figured in the premisses, and inferences in which there was a transition to a different level. Inferences of the second type were more hazardous, just because of the possibility that the additional entities which were introduced in their conclusions did not in fact exist. Russell himself made this point very clearly in relation to his attempt to reduce numbers to classes.

Two equally numerous collections [he said] appear to have something in common: this something is supposed to be their cardinal number. But so long as the cardinal number is inferred from the collections, not constructed in terms of them, its existence must remain in doubt, unless in view of a metaphysical postulate *ad hoc*. By defining the cardinal number of a given collection as the class of all equally numerous collections, we avoid the necessity of the metaphysical postulate, and thereby remove a needless doubt from the philosophy of arithmetic.[1]

Russell referred to this as an application of what he called 'the supreme maxim in scientific philosophizing': 'Wherever possible, logical constructions are to be substituted for inferred entities.'[2] An object was said by him to be a logical construction or, as he sometimes preferred to put it, a logical fiction, when the propositions in which it figures can be analysed in such a way that in the propositions which result from the analysis the object no longer appears as a subject of reference. Thus, classes were treated by Russell as logical fictions on the ground that the propositions in which we refer to classes can be satisfactorily replaced by propositions in which we refer not to classes but to propositional functions. Points and instants are logical fictions because the demands which we make of them are equally well satisfied by suitably ordered sets of volumes or events. The self is a logical fiction in the sense that it is nothing apart from the events which constitute its biography. In this case, the effect of adopting Russell's maxim is that we discover the principle according to which different states are to be assigned to the same self, not in fastening upon some further entity, a spiritual substance, to which they bear a common relation, but rather in drawing attention to some special relations which they bear to one another.

This last example shows that when Russell spoke of an object as a logical fiction, he did not mean to imply that it was imaginary or non-existent. To say that Plato and Socrates are logical fictions is not to class them with fictitious entities, like Theseus or Hercules. Similarly, in the period during which Russell held that physical objects were logical constructions, he did not wish to suggest that they were unreal in the way that gorgons are unreal. What he meant rather was that they are not resistant to analysis; when they are subjected to it, they dissolve into something else. Logical fictions do indeed exist, but only in virtue of the existence of the elements out of which they are constructed. As Russell put it, they are not part of the ultimate furniture of the world.

This raises the question how we are to determine what ultimately exists. Russell employed two criteria which he handled in such a way that they led somewhat circuitously to the same result. The first criterion, as I have already indicated, is epistemological. The basic entities are those of whose existence we can be the most certain. We shall see later on that Russell interpreted this criterion in a liberal fashion, allowing it to cover not just the hardest of data, which were, in his view, the feelings, images, and sense-impressions that one is currently having, but also data of this class which one remembers having had, data which are or have been presented to others, and even merely possible sense-impressions to which he gave the name of sensibilia. His reason for this liberality was that it is the least that is consistent with the possibility of constructing anything worth having: his apology for it was that the entities which he postulated were not of a different order from those which are primitively given. Even so, we shall also see that he ended by finding this basis too narrow. In the picture of the world at which he eventually arrived the main elements are not even of the order of hard data, at least in any straightforward sense, but events not directly accessible to observation, in which our belief is founded on a hazardous process of inference.

The second criterion is logical. It requires that the basic entities be simple, both in the sense of being individuals, as opposed to classes, and in the sense that they be capable of being denoted by what Russell called logically proper names. To explain how this second condition operates it will be necessary to say something about Russell's theory of descriptions.

II. The Theory of Descriptions and The Theory of Types

The problems which led Russell to formulate his theory of descriptions were connected with his assumption that the meaning of a name is to be identified with the object which the name denotes. The question whether a sign is a name is thereby linked with the question whether there is an object for which it stands. In what may be called his Platonic period, which covers the publication of *The Principles of Mathematics*, Russell was extremely liberal in his provision of objects. Anything that could be mentioned was said by him to be a term; any term could be the logical subject of a proposition; and anything that could be the logical subject of a proposition could be named. It followed that the range of objects which it was possible to name was not limited to things which actually existed at particular places and times: it extended also to abstract entities of all sorts, to non-existent things like Pegasus or the present King of France, even to logically impossible objects like the round square or the greatest prime number. Such things might not exist in space and time; but the mere fact that they could be significantly referred to was taken to imply that they had some form of being.

Russell did not long remain satisfied with this position. Not only did it exhibit what he called 'a failure of that feeling for reality which ought to be preserved even in the most abstract studies',[3] but it raised difficulties which it had not the resources to meet. For example, if denoting phrases like 'the author of *Waverley*' function as names, and if the meaning of a name is identical with the object which it denotes, it will follow that what is meant by saying that Scott was the author of *Waverley* is simply that Scott was Scott. But, as Russell pointed out, it is clear that when George IV wanted to know whether Scott was the author of *Waverley*, he was not expressing an interest in the law of identity. Again, if the phrase 'the present King of France' denotes a term, and if the law of excluded middle holds, one or other of the two propositions 'The present King of France is bald' and 'The present King of France is not bald' must be true. Yet if one were to enumerate all the things that are bald and all the things that are not bald, one would not find the present King of France on either list. Russell remarked characteristically that 'Hegelians, who love a synthesis, will probably conclude that he wears a wig'.[4] On this view, there is a difficulty even in saying that there is no such person as the present King of France, since it would appear that the term must have some form of being for the denial of its existence to be intelligible. The problem, in Russell's words, is 'How can a non-entity be the subject of a proposition?'[5]

These difficulties are inter-connected. They all arise from the combination of two assumptions: first, that denoting phrases like 'the present King of France' and 'the author of *Waverley*' function as names, and, secondly, that a name has no meaning unless there is some object which it denotes. In order to meet them, therefore, Russell had to abandon at least one of these assumptions, and he chose to abandon the first. His theory of descriptions is designed to show that expressions which are classifiable as definite or indefinite descriptions are not used as names, in that it is not necessary for them to denote anything, in order to have a meaning. Or rather, since Russell came to the conclusion that expressions of this kind have no meaning in isolation, his point is better put by saying that it is not necessary for them to denote anything in order to contribute what they do to the meaning of the sentences into which they enter. Russelll characterized these expressions as 'incomplete symbols', by which he meant not only that they were not required to denote anything, but also that they were not resistant to analysis. The theory of descriptions was intended to show that descriptive phrases satisfied these two conditions.

The method by which this is achieved is very simple. It depends on the assumption that in all cases in which a predicate is attributed to a subject, or two or more subjects are said to stand in some relation, that is to say, in all cases except those in which the existence of a subject is simply asserted or denied, the use of a description carries the covert assertion that there exists an object which answers to it. The procedure is then simply to make this covert assertion explicit. The elimination of descriptive phrases, their representation as incomplete symbols, is achieved by expanding them into existential statements and construing these existential statements as asserting that something, or in the case of definite descriptive phrases, just one thing, has the property which is contained in the description. So in the simplest version of the theory, which is set out in *Principia Mathematica*, a sentence like 'Scott is the author of *Waverley*' is expanded into 'There is an *x*, such that *x* wrote *Waverley*, such that for all *y*, if *y* wrote *Waverley*, *y* is identical with *x*, and such that *x* is identical with Scott'. Similarly, 'The present King of France is bald' becomes 'There is an *x*, such that *x* now reigns over France, such that for all *y*, if *y* now reigns over France, *y* is identical with *x*, and such that *x* is bald'. The question how a non-entity can be the subject of a proposition is circumvented by changing the subject. The denoting phrase is transformed into an existential statement which in this case happens to be false.

Once this procedure is understood, it can be seen to be applicable not only to phrases which are explicitly of the form 'a so-and-so' or 'the so-and-so' but to any nominative sign which carries some connotation. The connotation of the sign is taken away from it and turned into a propositional function: when an object is found which satisfies the function, the same treatment is applied so that the original function is augmented by another predicate, and so the process continues until we get to the point where the subject of all these predicates is either referred to indefinitely by means of the existential quantifier or named by a sign which has no connotation at all. It follows that the only function which is left for a name to fulfil is that of being purely demonstrative. In his more popular expositions of his theory, Russell did sometimes write as if he took ordinary proper names like 'Scott' really to be names, but since he held, in my view rightly, that such proper names do have some connotation, his more consistent view was that they are implicit descriptions. Like ordinary descriptions, they can be used significantly even though the objects to which they purport to refer do not exist. On the other hand, it is a necessary condition for anything to be what Russell called a logically proper name that its significant use guarantees the existence of the object which it is intended to denote. Since the only signs which satisfied this condition, in Russell's view, were those that refer to present sensory or introspective data, it is here that he achieved the fusion of his two criteria, the logical and the epistemological, for determining what there ultimately is.

The theory of descriptions, which was at first received very favourably, has more recently met with the objection that it does not give an accurate account of the way in which definite descriptive phrases are actually used. Thus, it has been suggested that such phrases are normally understood not as covertly asserting but rather as pre-supposing the existence of the object to which they are intended to refer, with the result that in the cases where the reference fails, the propositions which the descriptive phrases help to express should be said not to be false but to be lacking in truth value. It has also been remarked that very often the sentences in which we intend to pick out some object by the use of a descriptive phrase are not amenable to Russell's treatment, as they stand. When we say 'The baby is crying' or 'The kettle is boiling' we do not mean to imply that there is only one baby or one kettle in the universe. The pin-pointing of the object to which we are referring is supposed to be effected by the context. But if we have to insert into a sentence of this sort some predicate which the object in question uniquely satisfies, the mere fact that there may be several different predicates which serve this purpose makes it at least very doubtful whether the proposition at which we arrive as the result of the analysis can be logically equivalent to that which was expressed by the sentence with which we began.

These objections would be serious if the theory of descriptions were intended to provide exact translations of the sentence on which it operates. But in fact, though Russell himself may not have been wholly clear about this, what the theory supplies is not a rule of translation but a technique of paraphrase. Its method is to make explicit the information which is implictly contained in the use of proper names or left to be picked up from the context. It is true that the assumption from which the theory started, that the meaning of a name is to be identified with the object which the names denotes, is itself mistaken. But curiously this mistake, so far from invalidating the theory, turns to its advantage. For as a result of laying upon names a condition which the signs that are ordinarily counted as names do not satisfy, Russell arrived at what may well be the correct conclusion that names in their ordinary employment are dispensable. The thesis that all the work that is done by singular terms can equally well be done by purely general predicates is indeed contestable, but it is in any case important to distinguish between the two functions that names commonly perform, that of indicating objects, and that of holding predicates together. In the theory of descriptions, these two functions are dissociated, the work of reference being performed by purely demonstrative signs, and the work of holding predicates together by quantified variables. Since purely demonstrative signs, if they are needed at all, can be embedded in predicates, only the use of quantified variables remains to mark the subject–predicate distinction. So if, as has been suggested,[6] variables themselves can be replaced by combinatorial operators, the old distinction between subjects and predicates disappears. All that may possibly have to remain in its place is the distinction between demonstrative and descriptive signs.

Since the distinction between subject and predicate corresponds, in one of its aspects, to that between substance and attribute, it was quite in accordance with his theory of descriptions that Russell eventually came to the conclusion that substances could be represented as groups of compresent qualities. This theory was developed by him in two of his later works, *An Inquiry into Meaning and Truth*, which was published in 1940, and *Human Knowledge: Its Scope and Limits*, which appeared in 1948, when Russell was seventy-six years of age. An interesting feature of it is that it again marks a point at which his philosophy of logic is connected with his theory of knowledge. The elimination of substance, though consonant with the theory of descriptions, is not demanded by it. Russell might have been content to allow his quantified variables to refer indefinitely to what he called bare particulars, these being in effect the Lockean substances to which his analysis had pared objects down. If he took the further step of reducing these particulars to their qualities, it was because he shared Berkeley's distaste for the admission of what Locke could only describe as 'A something, I know not what'. Once again he sought to dispense with an unnecessary entity, not just from a liking for economy, but rather to avoid the danger of postulating what did not exist.

An important historical effect of the theory of descriptions was to bring into currency the distinction between the grammatical form of a sentence and what Russell called its logical form. This distinction is not an altogether clear one, since the notion of logical form is itself not wholly clear. There was a tendency on Russell's part to believe that facts had a logical form which sentences could copy: the logical form which underlay the grammatical form of an indicative sentence was then identified with the logical form of the actual or possible fact which would verify what the sentence expressed. This would seem, however, to be putting the cart before the horse, since it is difficult to see what means there could be of determining the logical forms of facts other than through the grammatical forms of the sentences which are used to state them. It is a matter of deciding on other grounds which forms of sentences convey their information most perspicuously. Nevertheless, the distinction between grammatical and logical form has proved fruitful in drawing attention to the dangers of our being misled by grammatical appearances. We are not to assume, because the word 'exists' is a grammatical predicate, that existence is a property of what is denoted by the grammatical subject. The fact that 'to know' is an active verb should not deceive us into thinking that knowing is a mental act. The general point which emerges is that sentences which superficially happen to have the same structure may be transformable in very different ways.

A similar influence has been exerted by Russell's theory of types. This theory was devised to deal with an antinomy in the theory of classes, which for a long time impeded the progress of *Principia Mathematica*. The antinomy arises when one predicates of a class that it is or is not a member of itself. At first sight, this may seem legitimate: for example, it seems reasonable to say, on the one hand, that the class of things which can be counted is itself something that can be counted, and, on the other, that the class of men is not itself a man. In this way we appear to obtain two classes of classes: the class of classes which are members of themselves and the class of classes which are not members of themselves. But now if we ask with respect to this second class of classes whether or not it is a member of itself, we get the contradictory answer that if it is, it is not and if it is not, it is.

Russell's solution of this paradox depends on the principle that the meaning of a propositional function is not specified until one specifies the range of objects which are candidates for satisfying it. From this it follows that these candidates cannot meaningfully include anything which is defined in terms of the function itself. The result is that propositional functions, and correspondingly propositions, are arranged in a hierarchy. At the lowest level we have functions which range only over individuals, then come functions which range over functions of the first order, then functions which range over functions of the second order, and so forth. The system has ramifications into which I shall not here enter but the main idea is simple. Objects which are candidates for satisfying functions of the same order are said to constitute a type, and the rule is that what can be said, truly or falsely, about objects of one type cannot meaningfully be said about objects of a different type. Consequently, to say of the class of classes which are not members of themselves that it either is, or is not, a member of itself is neither true nor false, but meaningless.

Russell applies the same principle to the solution of other logical antinomies and also to that of semantic antinomies like the paradox of the liar in which a proposition is made to say of itself that it is false, with the result that if it is true, it is false and if it is false, it is true. The theory of types eliminates the paradox by ruling that a proposition of which truth or falsehood is predicated must be of a lower order than the proposition by which the predication is made. Consequently, a proposition cannot meaningfully predicate truth or falsehood of itself.

But while the theory of types achieves its purpose, it is arguable that it is too stringent. One difficulty which troubled Russell is that it is sometimes necessary in mathematics to express propositions about all the classes that are composed of objects of any one logical type. But then the obstacle arises that, in the ramified theory, the functions which a given object is capable of satisfying may not themselves be all of the same type, and while there is no objection to our asserting severally of a set of functions of different types that they are satisfied by the same object, we violate the theory when we try to attribute to the object the property of satisfying the totality of these functions: for according to the theory, no such totality can meaningfully be said to exist. Russell met this difficulty by assuming the so-called Axiom of Reducibility. He said that two functions were formally equivalent when they were satisfied by the same objects; and he called a function predicative when it did not involve reference to any collection of functions. Then the Axiom of Reducibility is that with regard to any function F which can take a given object A as argument, there is some predicative function, also having A among its arguments, which is formally equivalent to F. This does, indeed, meet the difficulty but it remains open to question whether the Axiom of Reducibility is a logical truth.

A simpler reason for thinking that the theory of types may be too stringent is that very often we do seem able to speak in the same way significantly about objects of different types. For instance, we can count objects at different levels, yet we do not think that numerical expressions have a different meaning according as they are applied to classes which differ in the type of their membership. Russell's answer was that in such a case the expressions do have a different meaning. Expressions which seem to be applicable to objects of different types were said by him to be systematically ambiguous. It was because the ambiguity is systematic that it escaped our notice. The fact is, however, that were it not for the theory of types, we should have no reason for saying in these cases that there was any ambiguity.

In the face of such difficulties, many logicians have preferred to dispense with the theory of types and try to find some other way of dealing with the paradoxes which it was designed to meet. For instance, there are those who hold that the class-paradox can be avoided by depriving it of its subject: they maintain that there is just no class of classes which are not members of themselves. But, whatever its status within logic, the theory has, as I said, had a very strong secondary influence. By lending support to the view that sentences to which there is no obvious objection on the score of grammar or vocabulary may even so be meaningless, it encouraged the Logical Positivists in their attack on metaphysics, and it also helped to make philosophers alive to the possibility of what Professor Ryle has called category mistakes, which consist in ascribing to objects, or events or processes, or whatever it may be, properties which are not appropriate to their type, as when dispositions are confused with occurrences, tasks with achievements, or classes with their members. My own view is that there has been a tendency to exaggerate the extent to which philosophical puzzles arise out of category mistakes, but this is not to deny the fruitfulness of the concept in the cases where it does apply.

III. Russell's Theories of Knowledge

I said earlier that one of the criteria which Russell used for determining what there ultimately is was that of accessibility to knowledge. He took as basic the entities of whose existence and properties we could be the most nearly certain, and these, following the classical tradition of British empiricism, he identified with the immediate data of inner and outer sense. In his book *The Problems of Philosophy*, which was published in 1912, he used the term 'sense-data' to designate 'the things that are immediately known in sensation',[7] and made a point of distinguishing sense-data both from physical objects on the one hand and from sensations on the other, a sensation being, in his view, a mental act which had a sense-datum for its object. Since he saw no reason why the objects of mental acts should themselves be in the mind, he concluded that it was not logically impossible that sense-data should exist independently of being sensed. If he nevertheless believed that they did not so exist, it was because he took them to be causally dependent on the bodily state of the percipient. It was also on empirical grounds that he took sense-data to be private entities. This would seem in any case to follow from the assumption that they are causally dependent upon the bodily state of the percipient, but, in regard at least to visual data, Russell used the further argument that the differences in perspective, which he supposed to arise from the fact that no two observers could simultaneously occupy the same spatial position, made it very improbable that the sense-data which they respectively sensed would ever be qualitatively identical.

In *The Analysis of Mind*, which was published in 1921, Russell gave up his belief in the existence of mental acts. This was partly because he had come to believe that the self which was supposed to perform these acts was a logical fiction, and partly because he had decided that no such things were empirically detectable. Since he no longer believed that there were sensations, as he had previously conceived of them, the idea of there being objects of sensations also had to go, and to this extent he also gave up his belief in the existence of sense-data. But although, in his book *My Philosophical Development*, which appeared in 1959, he spoke of himself as having 'emphatically abandoned'[8] sense-data at this time, the change in his view is much less radical than this would suggest. He did stop using the term 'sense-datum' but he continued to speak of percepts, to which he attributed the same properties as he had attributed to sense-data except that of being correlative to sensory acts.

In any case, the question which chiefly interested him was not how sense-data, or percepts, are related to the persons who experience them but how they are related to the physical objects which we think that we perceive; and on this question he consistently took the view that physical objects are not directly perceived. Here again he follows the classical empiricist tradition in relying on what is known as the argument from illusion. In *The Problems of Philosophy*, he concentrated mainly on the fact that the appearances of physical objects vary under different conditions, which he interpreted as showing that none of them can be identified with the real properties of the objects in question: but in his later writings he attached greater importance to the causal dependence of these appearances upon the environment and upon the character of our nervous systems. Thus, he was used to remarking that the fact that light takes time to travel shows that when we look at an object like the sun we do not see it in the state in which it currently is but only, at best, in the state in which it was several minutes ago. But his main argument went deeper. He maintained that since the perceptible properties, such as size and shape and colour, which we attribute to physical objects, appear to us as they do partly because of the states of our nervous systems, we have no good reason to believe that the objects possess these properties in the literal way in which they are thought to by common sense. If the attitude of common sense is represented by naïve realism, the theory that we directly perceive physical objects much as they really are, then Russell's opinion of common sense was that it conflicted with science: and in such a contest he thought that science ought to be held victorious. As he put it in *An Inquiry into Meaning and Truth* in a formulation which greatly impressed Einstein: 'Naïve realism leads to physics, and physics, if true, shows that naïve realism is false. Therefore, naïve realism, if true, is false: therefore it is false.'[9]

Whether such arguments do prove that we directly perceive sense-data, or percepts, as opposed to physical objects, is open to doubt. The fact that a curtain may appear a different colour to different observers or to the same observer under different conditions does indeed show that our selection of one particular colour as the real colour of the curtain is to some extent arbitrary, but it hardly seems to warrant the conclusion that what one sees is not the curtain but something else. The fact that light from a distant star may take years to reach us does refute the naïve assumption that we see the star as a contemporary physical object but again does not seem sufficient to prove that we see some contemporary object which is not the star. The causal argument is indeed more power-ful. If we make it a necessary condition for a property to be intrinsic to an object that it can be adequately defined without reference to the effects of the object upon an observer, then I think that a good case can be made for saying that physical objects are not intrinsically coloured, though whether this entitles us to say that they are not 'really' coloured will still be debatable. Even so, it does not obviously follow that the colour which we attribute to a physical object is a property of something else, a sense-datum or a percept. If we are going to draw any such conclusion from Russell's arguments we shall have to make two further assumptions: first, that when we perceive a physical object otherwise than as it really is, there is something we can be said to perceive directly, which really has the properties that the physical object only appears to us to have; and secondly, that what we directly perceive, in this sense, is the same, whether the perception of the physical object is veridical or delusive. Russell took these assumptions for granted, but they are not generally thought to be self-evident; indeed, most contemporary philosphers reject them.

My own view, for which I have argued elsewhere,[10] is that something like Russell's position can be reached more satisfactorily by another method. The first step is to remark that there is a sense in which our ordinary judgements of perception go beyond the evidence on which they are based: for instance, when I identify the object in front of me as a table, I am attributing to it many properties which are not vouchsafed by anything in the content of my present visual experience. The second step is to assume the possibility of formulating propositions which simply monitor the evidence without going beyond it. I call such propositions experiential propositions and claim that they are perceptually basic, in the sense that no ordinary judgement of perception can be true unless some experiential proposition is true. In accordance with Russell's later views, I conceive of the objects which figure in the propositions as complexes of qualities rather than particulars in which the qualities inhere. An important further point is that they are not private entities. At this primitive level, where neither physical objects or persons have yet been introduced, the question whether these sensory elements are public or private, physical or mental, does not significantly arise.

If we grant Russell this much of his starting point, then the next question which we have to consider is whether our primitive data are, as he put it, 'signs of the existence of something else, which we can call the physical object'.[11] The answer which he gave in *The Problems of Philosphy* was that we have a good if not conclusive reason for thinking that they are. The reason is that the postulation of physical objects as external causes of sense-data accounts for the character of the data in a way that is not matched by any other hypothesis. Russell did not then think that we could discover anything about the intrinsic properties of physical objects, but did think it reasonable to infer that they are spatio-temporally ordered in a way that corresponds to the ordering of sense-data.

The postulation of physical objects as unobserved causes was at variance with Russell's maxim that wherever possible logical constructions are to be substituted for inferred entities, and in his book *Our Knowledge of the External World as a Field for Scientific Method in Philosophy*, which was published in 1914, and in two essays, written in 1914 and 1915, which were reprinted in the collection entitled *Mysticism and Logic*, he sought to exhibit physical objects as logical constructions. It was for this purpose that he introduced the concept of a 'sensibile' with the explanation that sensibilia are objects of 'the same metaphysical and physical status as sense-data'.[12] Having, as I think mistakenly, assumed that sense-data had to be located in private spaces, on the ground that there could be no spatial relations between the data which were experienced by different observers, Russell took the same to be true of sensibilia. He then gave a technical meaning to the word 'perspective' which was such that two particulars, whether sense-data or sensibilia, were said to belong to the same perspective if and only if they occurred simultaneously in the same private space.

The theory which Russell developed with these materials has some affinity with Leibniz's monodology. He treated each perspective as a point in what he called 'perspective-space', which, being a three-dimensional arrangement of three-dimensional perspectives, was itself a space of six dimensions. The physical objects which had their location in perspective-space were identified with the classes of their actual and possible appearances. To illustrate how appearances were sorted, Russell used the example of a penny which figures in a number of different perspectives. All the perspectives in which the appearances of the penny are of exactly the same shape are to be collected and put on a straight line in the order of their size. In this way we obtain a number of different series in each of which a limit will be reached at the point 'where (as we say) the penny is so near the eye that if it were any nearer it could not be seen'.[13] If we now imagine all these series to be prolonged, so as to form lines of perspectives continuing 'beyond' the penny, the perspective in which all the lines meet can be defined as 'the place where the penny is'.[14]

Russell then drew a distinction between the place *at* which and the place *from* which a sense-datum or a sensibile appears. The place at which it appears is the place where the thing is of which it is an element. The place from which it appears is the perspective to which it belongs. This enabled him to define 'here' as 'the place in perspective-space which is occupied by our private world', a place which in perspective-space 'may be part of the place where our head is'[15] and it also afforded him a means of discriminating the various distances from which a thing may be perceived, and of distinguishing changes in the objects from changes in the environment or in the state of the observer.

This theory is highly ingenious, but seems to me to fail on the count of circularity. The difficulty is that if the physical object is to be constructed out of its appearances, it cannot itself be used to collect them. The different appearances of the penny, in Russell's example, have first to be associated purely on the basis of their qualities. But since different pennies may look very much alike, and since they may also be perceived against very similar backgrounds, the only way in which we can make sure of associating just those sensibilia that belong to the same penny is by situating them in wider concepts. We have to take account of perspectives which are adjacent to those in which they occur. But then we are faced with the difficulty that perspectives which contain only sensibilia as opposed to sense-data are not actually perceived; and there seems to be no way of determining when two unperceived perspectives are adjacent without already assuming the perspective-space which we are trying to construct.

Another serious difficulty is that the method by which Russell ordered the elements of his converging series is not adequate for the purpose. He relied on the assumption that the apparent size of an object varies continuously with the distance and its apparent shape with the angle from which the object is viewed. But, in view of the principle of constancy, this is psychologically false. The assumption might be upheld, if apparent shapes and sizes were determined physiologically, but to do this would again be to bring in physical objects before we had constructed them.

The main source of these difficulties, in my view, is Russell's mistaken assumption that his sensory elements are located in private spaces. But for this assumption, there would be no need for the complicated ordering of so many perspectives. As I have argued elsewhere,[16] we can obtain the equivalent of Russell's sensibilia merely by projecting spatial and temporal relations beyond the sense-fields in which they are originally given. Because of the fact that similar percepts are usually obtainable at the meeting point of similar sensory routes, we are able to postulate the existence at these points of what I call standardized percepts. We can then proceed inductively to locate such percepts in positions which we have not actually traversed. In this way we obtain a skeleton of the physical world of common sense which we can further articulate by various processes of correlation. It is true that this method will not enable us to achieve Russell's goal of exhibiting physical objects as logical constructions out of sensibilia. We shall not be able to translate propositions which refer to physical objects into propositions which refer only to percepts. We shall, however, be able to show how our belief in the physical world of common sense is constituted as a theory with respect to a primary system of percepts, and how this system in its turn is theoretically based on the data which figure in our experiential propositions, all without the introduction of any higher-level entities. And this I believe to be the most that is feasible.

Russell carried his reductionism to its furthest point in his book *The Analysis of Mind*, which was published in 1921. Largely following William James, he there maintained that both mind and matter were logical constructions out of primitive elements which were themselves neither mental or physical. Mind and matter were differentiated by the fact that certain elements such as images and feelings entered only into the constitution of minds, and also by the operation of different causal laws. Thus the same percepts when correlated according to the laws of physics constituted physical objects and when correlated according to the laws of psychology helped to constitute minds. In their mental aspect, these elements engaged, among other things, in what Russell called 'mnemic causation', a kind of action at a distance by which experienced data produced subsequent memory images. On the view which he there took, but later became dissatisfied with, that causation is just invariable sequence, there is no theoretical objection to such action at a distance, but Russell ceased to believe in it on the ground of its being inconsistent with the principle, which he adopted in *Human Knowledge*, that events which enter into causal chains are spatio-temporally continuous. He remained faithful to the view that minds are logical constructions, without, however, anywhere giving a precise account of the relations which have to hold between different elements for them to be constituents of the same mind, and he continued to hold, as he put it in the collection of essays entitled *Portraits from Memory*, which he published in 1956, that 'An event is not rendered either mental or material by any intrinsic quality but only by its causal relations.'[17] It is, however, to be noted, first, that this is inconsistent with his earlier view that images and feelings are intrinsically mental and, secondly, that his final reason for the assimilation of mental and physical events is not that they are both constructed out of the same elements but rather that what are called mental events are identical with physical states of the brain.

This is in line with Russell's abandonment, in his later works, of the view that physical objects are logical constructions, in favour of his earlier view that they are inferred entities. In his book, *The Analysis of Matter*, which was published in 1927, there are passages which suggest that he still wanted to identify physical objects with groups of percepts, but more often he took it to follow from the causal theory of perception, which he held to be scientifically established, that we have no knowledge of the intrinsic properties of physical objects or any direct acquaintance with physical space, though he held that we could legitimately infer that it had some structural correspondence with perceptual space. Another conclusion which he drew from the causal theory of perception was that everything that we perceive is inside our own heads. This does indeed sound very paradoxical, but a case can be made for it if one accepts Russell's distinction between perceptual and physical space. For what it then comes to is the reasonable enough decision to identify the physical location of percepts with that of their immediate physical cause. The difficulty is rather that the underlying distinction is hard to accept. Neither is it clear what reasons Russell thought he had for taking the further step of identifying percepts with the events in the brain which are ordinarily thought to cause them.

The view that physical objects are known to us only by inference, as the external causes of our percepts, with the corollary that we can know something of their intrinsic properties, was fairly consistently maintained by Russell in *Human Knowledge* and other later works. One obvious difficulty with any theory of this kind is to see how we can be justified in inferring that any such external objects exist at all. We may, indeed, be entitled to postulate unobservable entities, so long as the hypotheses into which they enter have consequences which can be empirically tested, but it seems to me that a more serious problem is created when these unobservable objects are held to be located in an unobservable space. Not only is it not clear to me what justification there could be for believing in the existence of an unobservable space, but I am not even sure that I find the concept of such a thing intelligible.

A further objection is that the causal theory of perception on which Russell relied itself seems to require that physical objects be located in perceptual space. When my seeing the table in front of me is explained in terms of the passage of light-rays from the table to my eye, the assumption is surely that the table is there when I see it. It is true that we sometimes distinguish between the place where a physical object really is and the place where it appears to be, but the calculations which enable us to make such distinctions are themselves based on the assumption that other objects are where they appear to be. It is only because we start by equating the physical position of things around us with the observed positions of standardized percepts that our more sophisticated methods of locating more distant objects can lead to verifiable results.

This does not mean that we are driven back to naïve realism. Even if we do not accept Russell's distinction between physical and perceptual space, it still remains open to us to regard physical objects as really possessing only those structural properties that physicists ascribe to them. We are not even deterred from regarding percepts as being private to the percipient. Having developed the common-sense conception of the physical world as a theoretical system with respect to sensory qualities, we can interpret into the system the elements on which it is founded. The physical object is set against the percepts from which it was abstracted and made causally responsible for them. The relatively constant perceptual qualities which are attributed to it come to be contrasted with the fluctuating impressions which different observers have of it, and the impressions assigned to the observers. At a still more sophisticated level, we can replace the common-sense physical object by the scientific skeleton on which the causal processes of perception are taken to depend. In this way I believe that a fusion of Russell's theories may lead us to the truth.

IV. Morals and Politics

Of the seventy-one books and pamphlets that Russell published in the course of his life, only about twenty could properly be classified as works of academic philosophy. The rest of them cover a very wide range, including as they do autobiographical writings, biographical writings, books of travel, books on education, books on religion, works of history, popularizations of science, and even two volumes of short stories; but the largest single class consists of works on social questions and on politics. From these works it is apparent, as it clearly was to anyone who knew him, that Russell held very strong moral convictions, but he was not very greatly concerned with ethical theory. Apart from an early essay on 'The Elements of Ethics', which was written about 1910 and included in his *Philosophical Essays*, his main contribution to the subject is to be found in his book on *Human Society in Ethics and Politics*, of which the ethical part was mainly written in 1945–6, although the book was not published until 1954.

The position which Russell took in the earlier essay owed almost everything to his friend G. E. Moore whose *Principia Ethica* had appeared in 1903. Like Moore he held that good is an indefinable non-natural quality, the presence of which is discoverable by intuition, that the objectively right action is the one, out of all the actions open to the agent, that will have the best consequences, in the sense that it will lead to the greatest favourable, or least unfavourable, ratio of good to evil, and that the action which one ought to do is that which appears most likely to have the best consequences. The only point on which he differed from Moore was in holding that the exercise of free-will, which is implied by attributions of moral responsibility, is not only not at variance with determinism but positively requires it. It is, he argued, only because volitions have causes that moral considerations can be brought to bear upon people's conduct. Russell's view of free-will was similar to Locke's in that it disregarded the question whether and in what sense it is possible for us to will anything other than we do. Like Locke, he took it to be enough that our actions should be causally dependent on our choices, no matter how these might be caused.

In *Human Society in Ethics and Politics* Russell took the same view of free-will and he continued to hold that one ought to do the action which will probably have the best consequences, but for the rest he forsook Moore for Hume. He still found no logical flaw in the doctrine that we can know by intuition what is right or good, but objected to it that since people's intuitions conflict it reduced ethical controversy to a mere 'clash of rival dogmas'.[18] Moreover, the fact that the things to which we are inclined to attach intrinsic value are all things which are desired or enjoyed suggested to him that good might after all be definable 'in terms of desire or pleasure or both'.[19]

The definition which he proposed along these lines was that 'An occurrence is "good" when it satisfies desire.'[20] In another passage, however, he suggested that 'Effects which lead to approval are defined as "good" and those leading to disapproval as "bad".'[21] These definitions can perhaps be reconciled by making the assumption that the effects which lead to approval are those which are thought likely to satisfy desire. This leaves it uncertain whether in calling something good I am to be understood as saying just that I approve of it, or that it is an object of general approval, and if it is just a question of my own approval, whether this is on the grounds of its satisfying my own desire or of its giving general satisfaction. Russell did not explicitly distinguish between these possibilities, but in the main he seems to have held that in calling something good I am stating, or perhaps just expressing, my own approval of it, on the ground that its existence is or would be found generally satisfying. Right actions then will be those that, on the available evidence, are likely to have better effects in this sense than any other actions which are possible in the circumstances.

This comes close to utilitarianism, the main difference being that Russell did not fall into the error of assuming that all desire is for pleasure. He was therefore able to admit that 'some pleasures seem to be inherently preferable to others',[22] without giving up his principle that all forms of satisfaction are equally valuable in themselves. At this point, however, there was some discrepancy between his theory and his application of it. In practice, he tended to look upon cruelty as inherently evil, independently of the satisfaction or dissatisfaction that it might cause, and he also attached an independent value to justice, freedom, and the pursuit of truth.

The value which Russell attached to freedom comes out clearly in his political writings. His concern with politics became increasingly practical, but he took a strong interest in political theory. Himself an aristocrat, he thought that a good case could be made for an aristocratic form of government in societies where the material conditions were such that the enjoyment of wealth and leisure was possible only for a small minority. In societies in which it was economically possible for nearly everyone to enjoy a reasonably high standard of living he thought that the principle of justice favoured democracy. He said that although democracy did not ensure good government, it did prevent certain evils, the chief of these being the possession by an incompetent or unjust government of a permanent tenure of power. Russell was consistently in favour of the devolution of power and disliked and distrusted the aggrandizement of the modern state. This was one of the reasons for his hostility to Soviet Communism, as expressed in his book *The Theory and Practice of Bolshevism*, the outcome of a visit which he paid to Russia as early as 1919. If he seemed to become a little more sympathetic to the Soviet Union towards the end of his life, it was only because he had then become convinced that the politics of the American government represented the greater threat to peace.

Russell's desire to diminish rather than increase the power of the state set him apart from the ordinary run of socialists. He was, however, at one with them in wishing to limit the possession and use of private property, in seeing no justification for inherited wealth, and in being opposed to the private ownership of big businesses or of land. In his books, *Principles of Social Reconstruction* and *Roads to Freedom*, which were published in 1916 and 1918 respectively, he displayed a certain sympathy for anarchism, but declared himself more in favour of Guild Socialism, a system which provided for workers' control of industry and for the establishment of two Parliaments, one a federation of trades unions and the other a Parliament of consumers, elected on a constituency basis, with a joint committee of the two acting as the sovereign body. Russell himself added the original proposals that 'a certain small income, sufficient for necessaries, should be secured to all, whether they work or not',[23] that the expense of children should be borne wholly by the community, provided that their parents, whether married or not, were known to be 'physically and mentally sound in all ways likely to affect the children'[24] and that 'a woman who abandons wage-earning for motherhood ought to receive from the state as nearly as possible what she would have received if she had not had children'.[25] He did not discuss how these measures could be afforded.

In his later political writings, though he continued to seek means of curbing the power of the state, Russell was more concerned with the relations between states than with questions of internal organization. Regarding nationalism as 'the most dangerous vice of our time'[26] he thought it likely to lead to a third world war which the use of atomic weapons would render far more terrible than any suffering that the human race had previously known. The only assurance that he could find against the continuing threat of such a disaster was the institution of a world government which would have the monopoly of armed force. While it was obviously better that such a government be constituted by international agreement, Russell thought it more likely to come about 'through the superior power of some one nation or group of nations'.[27] It was for this reason, since it was essential to his argument that the change be peaceful, that he advocated unilateral disarmament. The difficulty was that it was no more probable that a world government would come about peacefully in this fashion than through international agreement. One cannot but admire the passion which Russell brought to the discussion of this question, and the concern for humanity which inspired him; but in his treatment of it he seems both to have over-estimated the likelihood of global nuclear war and correspondingly under-estimated the merits of the traditional policy of maintaining a balance of power.

Russell's writings on political and social questions do not have the depth of his contributions to the theory of knowledge or the philosophy of logic, but they express the moral outlook of a humane and enlightened man and they add to the lucidity which was characteristic of all his work a special touch of elegance and wit. His style contains echoes of Voltaire, to whom he was pleased to be compared, and of Hume with whom he had the greatest philosophical affinity. Like Hume, he could be careless in matters of detail, especially in his later work. After the years of labour which he expended on *Principia Mathematica*, he became impatient with minutiae. The hostility which he displayed to the linguistic philosophy which became fashionable in England in the nineteen-fifties was partly directed against the minuteness of its approach, partly also against its assumption that philosophy could afford to be indifferent to the natural sciences. In an age when philosophical criticism increasingly fettered speculation, his strength lay in the sweep and fertility of his ideas. He was very much a hare and not a tortoise: but it is not the most probable of fables in which the hare does not win the race.

Notes

1 *Mysticism and Logic*, p. 156.
2 Ibid., p. 155.
3 *Introduction to Mathematical Philosophy*, p. 165.

4 'On Denoting', *Logic and Knowledge*, p. 48.
5 Ibid.
6 Cf. W. V. Quine, 'Variables Explained Away', *Selected Logical Papers.*
7 *The Problems of Philosophy*, p. 12.
8 *My Philosophical Development*, p. 245.
9 *An Inquiry into Meaning and Truth*, p. 126.
10 See *The Origins of Pragmatism*, pp. 303–21, and 'Has Austin Refuted the Sense-datum Theory?' in *Metaphysics and Common Sense.*
11 *The Problems of Philosophy*, p. 20.
12 *Mysticism and Logic*, p. 148.
13 Ibid., p. 162.
14 Ibid.
15 *Our Knowledge of the External World*, p. 92.
16 See *The Origins of Pragmatism*, pp. 239–41 and 322–3, and *Russell and Moore*, p. 65.
17 *Portraits from Memory*, p. 152.
18 *Human Society in Ethics and Politics*, p. 131.
19 Ibid., p. 113.
20 Ibid., p. 55.
21 Ibid., p. 116.
22 Ibid., p. 117.
23 *Roads to Freedom*, p. 119.
24 *Principles of Social Reconstruction*, p. 185.
25 Ibid., p. 184.
26 *Education and the Social Order*, p. 138.
27 *New Hope for a Changing World*, p. 77.

5

Russell's Philosophy

A Study of its Development

Alan Wood

Bertrand Russell is a philosopher without a philosophy. The same point might be made by saying that he is a philosopher of all the philosophies.

There is hardly any philosophical viewpoint of importance today which cannot be found reflected in his writings at some period.

Whitehead once described Russell as a Platonic dialogue in himself.[1] Lytton Strachey compared Russell's mind to a circular saw.[2] The metaphor is particularly apt. The teeth on opposite sides of a circular saw move in opposite directions; in fact the teeth are moving in every different direction at once. But the saw itself cuts straight forward.

In spite of all the apparently conflicting statements to be found in the total of Russell's philosophical writings, in spite of the number of cases where he champions different opinions at different times, there is throughout a consistency of purpose and direction, and a consistency of method.

'I wanted certainty', Russell wrote in retrospect, 'in the kind of way in which people want religious faith.'[3] I believe the underlying purpose behind all Russell's work was an almost religious passion for some truth that was more than human, independent of the minds of men, and even of the existence of men. It is well to be brought face to face, at the start, with one of the problems of conflicting quotations which faces any student of Russell. For we can also quote him as calling on us, in the context of a popular essay, 'to recognize that the non-human world is unworthy of worship'.

We are discussing here a matter of motive. I can therefore only appeal to evidence of the strength of Russell's feelings to support my contention that, while seeing two sides to the question, his overriding motive was yearning for absolutely certain impersonal knowledge.

We can cite, for instance, the way he would speak of Kant's allegation of a subjective element in mathematics: the tone of his voice can only be described as one of disgust, like a Fundamentalist confronted with the suggestion that Moses had made up the Ten Commandments himself. 'Kant made me *sick*.'[4]

There was his contempt for 'the grovelling microscopic vision of those philosophers whose serious attention is confined to this petty planet and the grovelling animalcules that crawl upon its surface'. There was his complaint of 'cosmic impiety' against Dewey.[5] In later years, there were his criticisms of some Oxford philosophers for being too much concerned with 'the different ways in which silly people can say silly things',[6] and not with trying to understand the world.

The view I am advocating provides the reconciliation of the apparent contradiction that he could have a passion for mathematics and also a sympathetic understanding of mysticism; the attraction of both was that they aimed at truths independent of passing human experience.

But the strongest evidence is to be found in his letters. For instance, he wrote in 1918: 'I *must*, before I die, find *some* way to say the essential thing that is in me, that I have never said yet – a thing that is not love or hate or pity or scorn, but the very breath of life, fierce and coming from far away, bringing into human life the vastness and the fearful passionless force of non-human things . . .'[7]

I take, therefore, the following passage for my main text:

> When I was young I hoped to find religious satisfaction in philosophy; even after I had abandoned Hegel, the eternal Platonic world gave me something non-human to admire . . . I thought of mathematics with reverence . . . .
>
> I have always ardently desired to find some justification for the emotions inspired by certain things that seemed to stand outside human life and to deserve feelings of awe . . . the starry heavens . . . the vastness of the scientific universe . . . the edifice of impersonal truth which, like that of mathematics, does not merely describe the world that happens to exist.
>
> Those who attempt to make a religion of humanism, which recognizes nothing greater than man, do not satisfy my emotions. And yet I am unable to believe that, in the world as known, there is anything that I can value outside human beings. . . . Impersonal non-human truth appears to be a delusion.
>
> And so my intellect goes with the humanists, though my emotions violently rebel.[8]

This conflict is the main connecting thread in the exposition of the development of Russell's philosophy which follows.

One might sum up his public career as a philosopher, briefly and crudely, as: From Kant to Kant.[9] In *The Foundations of Geometry*, published in 1897, he wrote that his viewpoint 'can be obtained by a certain limitation and interpretation of Kant's classic arguments'.[10] In *Human Knowledge*, published in 1948, he recurred to ideas and nomenclature with a Kantian affinity. But he was still glad to be able to claim that the synthetic *a priori* of *Human Knowledge* was not so subjective as Kant: just as he was not so subjective as Kant in *The Foundations of Geometry*.[11] Russell's intellectual life was devoted to three main quests. He sought impersonal objective truth successively in Religion, Mathematics, and Science.

Not in philosophy.[12] In his heart he usually thought of philosophy as an inferior pursuit compared with mathematics and science. One of the most often repeated notes in his writings is the continued gibery at 'the philosophers' for being too lazy to undertake the study of mathematics, or too stupid to understand it.'[13] He expressed regret more than once (for instance, to Beatrice Webb in 1936) that he had not been a scientist instead of a philosopher.[14]

The key to understanding Russell's philosophy is that it was essentially a by-product. To treat it as though it were an end in itself, though a natural enough mistake for philosophers to make, is liable to render it meaningless. But in fact there is a sense in which *any* worthwhile philosophy is a by-product. As Russell himself wrote, 'A philosophy which is to have any value should be built upon a wide and firm foundation of knowledge that is not specifically philosophical.'[15]

Russell's primary objects were to establish the truth of religion, the truth of mathematics, and the truth of science. He himself stated this explicitly in the case of religion and mathematics. 'I hoped to find religious satisfaction in philosophy . . .'[16]

'I came to philosophy through mathematics, or rather through the wish to find some reason to believe in the truth of mathematics.'[17]

With science the feeling was perhaps not quite so strong: after all, science merely deals with 'the world that happens to exist'. But Professor Weitz, one of the ablest of commentators on Russell, declares that 'Russell's primary interest, it seems to me, has been the attempt to justify science'.[18] In a sense, therefore, it could be said that Russell's career was a threefold failure.

(a) He not only had to abandon religion, but objective ethical knowledge as well. (b) He was not fully satisfied with the system of *Principia Mathematica*, and Wittgenstein convinced him – or almost convinced him – that in any case mathematical knowledge was only tautological.[19] (c) His defence of scientific knowledge in *Human Knowledge* was not in accordance with the kind of standards he had hoped to satisfy earlier.[20]

All philosophers are failures. But Russell was one of the few with enough integrity to admit it. Therein lies his supreme importance. One might write of him, as he himself wrote in praise of Kant, that:

'A candid philosopher should acknowledge that he is not very likely to have arrived at ultimate truth, but, in view of the incurable tendency to discipleship in human nature, he will be thought to have done so unless he makes his failures very evident. The duty of making this evident was one which Kant's candour led him to perform better than most other philosophers.' His philosophical ideas were the by-products of his quests for certain knowledge, and these quests ended in failure. How then could his failures prove so fruitful? Broadly speaking, this came about in two different ways.

(a) It is a solution to a philosophical problem to show that it has no solution: just as it was an advance in mathematics when Lindemann showed that it is impossible to square the circle.

(b) In his quests Russell developed a distinctive philosophical method which added to knowledge, even though it could not confer certainty. 'Every truly philosophical problem', he said, 'is a problem of analysis; and in problems of analysis the best method is that which sets out from results and arrives at the premisses.'[21]

To put it crudely, Russell saw the role of a philosopher as analogous to that of a detective in a detective story; he had to start from results, and work backwards by analysing the evidence. (The extent to which the crudity of this analogy is misleading will emerge later.)

It is perhaps unfortunate that attention has usually been focused on what was only the first part of Russell's description, as given above, of his philosophical procedure. The emphasis has been placed on his methods of 'analysis', and in fact no better single word could be chosen; but 'analysis' has now been used and abused with so many different meanings that it has become almost meaningless. I think it possible that the idea of starting from results and arriving at premisses is prior to that of 'analysis'; and it gives a more fundamental picture of the underlying unity of Russell's work. He started from results and arrived at premisses in *The Principles of Mathematics*. He did exactly the same thing, over forty years later, in *Human Knowledge*, where his main argument for his 'Postulates' of Scientific Inference was the same as his defence of the Axiom of Reducibility in *Principia Mathematica*.[22] His work on epistemology was not a kind of subsidiary supplement to his work on mathematical philosophy. It came from the same workshop and was made with the same tools.

He said: 'The inferring of premisses from consequences is the essence of induction; thus the method in investigating the principles of mathematics is really an inductive method, and is substantially the same as the method of discovering general laws in any other sciences.'

He wrote in 1924 that, both in pure mathematics and in any science arranged as a deductive system; 'Some of the premisses are much less obvious than some of their consequences, and are believed chiefly because of their consequences.'[23]

Why did Russell adopt this philosophical method? Why did he want to find the premisses for a given body of knowledge? Because at first he hoped that, by going far enough back, he could arrive at premisses which were absolutely certain. Why should he want to reduce the number of premises to the fewest possible? One reason was to reduce the risk of error: hence Occam's Razor. What was the purpose of analysis? To increase knowledge. Russell's philosophical method would never, I believe, have been developed if he had not at first been inspired by the hope of arriving at knowledge which was certain. Had he realized from the start that certainty was unattainable, he might have abandoned philosophy and devoted himself to economics, or history. His work is thus a classic example of what can be achieved as a result of attempting the impossible.

Certain consequences follow from Russell's view that the proper philosophical procedure is not deductive, from premises to conclusions, but exactly the reverse.

The only decisive weapon in philosophical controversy is the *reductio ad absurdum*; the premises reached can be shown to lead to contradictions. True, in philosophy it is possible to *disprove* something, but never possible to *prove* anything. Thus: 'Philosophical argument, strictly speaking, consists mainly of an endeavour to cause the reader to perceive what has been perceived by the author. The argument, in short, is not of the nature of proof, but of exhortation.'[24]

The way to clarify controversial questions is by 'a more careful scrutiny of the premises that are apt to be employed unconsciously, and a more prolonged attention to fundamentals'. After that a philosophical argument can only take the form of saying, 'Look, can't you see what I see?' (These are not Russell's words.) A philosophical advance consists in suddenly seeing a new way of looking at something.

Philosophical advances are achieved by analysis, together with something which Russell refers to variously as (a) 'insight',[25] (b) 'intuition',[26] (c) 'instinct',[27] (d) 'vision'.[28]

And though he often stressed the fallibility of 'insight' and 'instinct' into what we believe obvious, he recognized that in the last resort our instinctive belief could only be rejected because it conflicted with another instinctive belief. The best aim philosophy could hope to achieve was, (1) to arrange our instinctive beliefs in a kind of hierarchy from more to less certain; (2) to arrive at a system of beliefs which was internally consistent.[29]

These views of Russell on philosophy are worth stressing. Because he wrote at times as though he rigidly excluded appeals to 'intuition' and 'instinct' (and many other things) from his philosophy, this did not mean that he did not realize their importance. There are many things excluded from his philosophy, to which critics point as evidence of a lack of 'profundity', which are to be found in his way of *doing* philosophy. (And to be found in what he did in other fields.)

The fact that philosophical argument consists of 'exhortation' accounts for much of the informal flavour of his writing, and the use of different popular illustrations of his ideas, in which critics can find contradictions. It is as though Russell were saying 'if *that* way of putting it won't convince you, perhaps *this* will'.[30]

Since Russell reached the above views on philosophy over fifty years ago, there has been time for them to be forgotten, and they have been presented again in recent years as though they were new discoveries due to Wittgenstein and his school. (For instance, Dr Waismann in *Contemporary British Philosophy*: 'There is a notion that philosophical questions can be settled by argument, and conclusively if one only knew how to set about it. . . . I incline to come to a new and somewhat shocking conclusion: that the thing cannot be done. No philosopher has ever proved anything . . . [because] philosophical arguments are not deductive.')[31]

I have referred above to Occam's Razor as a part of Russell's philosophical method inspired by his passion for certain knowledge. This was how Russell himself justified its use. ('That is the advantage of Occam's Razor, that it diminishes your risk of error.')[32] But much more was involved than this; and we must beware of Russell's habit of describing his own work in terms of belittlement.

What he would not say about himself he said about Einstein. He gave a better clue to his real feelings when he wrote that the Theory of Relativity 'is possessed by that sort of grandeur that is felt in vast results achieved with the very minimum of material'.

Occam's Razor is not just a kind of philosophical economy campaign; that is like describing a sculptor as a man who gets rid of unnecessary chips of marble. It is not, as suggested by Wittgenstein, a rule of symbolism. It is not even merely a rule for securing a greater chance of accuracy in philosophical calculations. Russell's use of Occam's Razor was not only a means to an end but part of something which was a motive in itself; a passion which had almost as much force in Russell's mind as his passion for impersonal truth.

It is a passion known to every writer who whittles away unnecessary words from his manuscript, and to every mathematician and scientist in the search for the most elegant proofs and most general laws. It is easier to give illustrations of it than to attempt to define or explain it.[33]

Russell wrote in 1906 that, when choosing among the different alternative systems of primitive propositions for mathematical logic, 'that one is to be preferred, *aesthetically*, in which the primitive propositions are fewest and most general; exactly as the Law of Gravitation is to be preferred to Kepler's three Laws' (my italics).[34] He recalled that he had 'a sense almost of intoxication' when he first studied Newton's deduction of Kepler's Second Law from the Law of Gravitation.[35] He told of his delight when he discovered for himself, as a boy, the formula for the sum of an arithmetic progression, and his delight in such a concise formula as $e^{i\pi} = -1$. In such instances he gave a much truer picture than when he wrote, for example, that the justification for the utmost generalization in mathematics was not

to 'waste our time' proving in a particular case what can be proved generally.[36]

What is involved might variously be described as love of aesthetic elegance, love of unity, love of system, or profundity. (In the only sense of the word 'profundity' which I think has any meaning.) It was a passion partly connected with, and partly at variance with, his passion for impersonal and certain truth. And it proved just as impossible to attain.

In an early article he described how, in the greatest mathematical works, 'unity and inevitability are felt as in the unfolding of a drama . . . The love of system, of interconnection . . . is perhaps the inmost essence of the intellectual impulse'.[37] He was later forced to the conclusion that the love of system was the greatest barrier to honest thinking in philosophy; just as he decided that 'the demand for certainty is one which is natural to man, but is nevertheless an intellectual vice'.[38]

He put his conclusions in their most extreme form when he wrote in 1931:

> Academic philosophers, ever since the time of Parmenides, have believed that the world is a unity . . . . The most fundamental of my intellectual beliefs is that this is rubbish. I think the universe is all spots and jumps, without unity, without continuity, without coherence or orderliness or any of the other properties that governesses love. Indeed, there is little but prejudice and habit to be said for the view that there is a world at all . . . .[39]

> The external world may be an illusion, but if it exists, it consists of events, short, small and haphazard. Order, unity, and continuity are human inventions, just as truly as are catalogues and encyclopaedias.[40]

To appreciate the force of such a passage, it must not be regarded as simply a sweeping attack on most 'academic philosophers'. It was an attack on a position which Russell held himself; and one which he always, in a sense, wanted to hold as intellectually possible.

It may now be easier to understand why Russell's writings are so complex, subtle and intricate, and why Whitehead called him a Platonic dialogue in himself. In fact there is no great philosopher since Plato whose ideas are harder to sum up in a short space. His philosophy was a battleground on which he fought a losing battle against himself; sometimes going one way, sometimes another; and he covered the whole field before reaching conclusions usually diametrically opposed to those which he had hoped for.

It is very difficult to sum up the main point at issue, between Russell and his earliest philosophical opponent, without making it appear that both sides were, in a sense, right. But I think the fundamental point at issue, in Russell's controversy with Bradley over internal relations, was some sort of assumption, on Bradley's part, that an entity *must* have the relations which it has. Perhaps we can best sum up Russell's dilemma by saying that for the most part he *wanted* to believe in a Law of Sufficient Reason; his intellectual integrity made him reject it; and he was therefore left with the problem of explaining how scientific knowledge could be possible.

Paradoxically enough, the very clarity of Russell's usual style has obscured the continual subtlety and originality of his arguments. The polemic overstatements and sweeping epigrams which anyone can understand have been quoted again and again; the books where he is painfully working his way from one position to another, or arguing with himself, often remain unread. According to a modern commentator of some repute, Russell 'even on the most difficult topics is always simple, easy'; from which it would seem a fair deduction that the commentator in question has never read *The Principles of Mathematics*, nor even *Human Knowledge*.

As Russell himself said in criticism of Santayana, a smooth literary form is rarely compatible with original ideas, which are more likely to be marked – at least in their first expression – by 'uncouth jargon'. Russell himself kept remarkably free from 'uncouth jargon'; but his philosophy was far from 'simple'.[41] It is right that any study of a philosopher should be prefaced by a statement of the author's own views, so that the reader can allow for any unconscious bias.

By temperament I am a mystic Bergsonian; I cannot be satisfied with the static analytic approach of Russell. In fact my main aim, in studying his philosophy, was to find some way of getting round his conclusions; but in this, so far, I have been completely unsuccessful; and I do not believe that anyone else has produced any answer to his philosophy which can be accepted with intellectual integrity.

As I have said, it is hard to be sure about exactly what point is at issue between Russell and the monists. Russell could hardly quarrel with Bradley's statement that 'Since what I start with in fact is this, and what analysis leaves to me instead is that – I therefore cannot but reject, at least in part, the result of analysis.'[42] To the question 'Does analysis mean falsification?' I believe the only correct answer is 'Yes, if you don't know what you are doing.' A physicist is obviously wrong if he thinks that, after carrying out the hydrolysis of water, he can still get a cooling drink from the products of his analysis; but the fact remains that analysis is the proper method of increasing our knowledge of water. A physiologist who dissects a living body cannot expect to be able to put the body together again, or (I believe) to discover what makes the body live and breathe. But most major advances in medicine have come from accepting the materialistic view of the human body as a working hypothesis; even though some doctors in recent years have tended to go astray through regarding the materialistic view as sufficient in itself. In the same way, I believe that Russell was right, as a method of increasing knowledge, in pushing the philosophy of analysis as far as it will go; in his case he came up against its furthest present-day limits, and could not really feel satisfied with his conclusions, when he came to ethical theory.

The philosopher has the choice today of advancing precise thinking as far as possible, while recognizing spheres remaining separate outside it, or else attempting a grand synthesis in which his emotions and his mystic yearnings are brought in to muddle up his thinking. Russell followed in the first course.

In short, I believe that analysis is abundantly justified as a method, but can be misleading if it comes to be regarded as a metaphysic. There are hints in Russell's writings that he himself may have felt this: for instance (my italics): 'Speaking generally, scientific progress has been made by analysis and *artificial* isolation.'[43]

In at least one passage he emphasized the distinction I have in mind between a metaphysic and a method. He wrote of Meinong (in 1904): 'Although empiricism as a philosophy does not appear to be tenable, there is an empirical method of investigating, which should be applied in every subject-matter.'

Notes

1 Conversation between Whitehead and B.R., reported to Alan Wood.
2 Lytton Strachey to Virginia Woolf, May 27, 1919.
3 'Reflections on My Eightieth Birthday', in *Portraits from Memory.*
4 B.R. in conversation with Alan Wood.
5 *History of Western Philosophy*, page 856.
6 Review of Urmson's *Philosophical Analysis* in *The Hibbert Journal*, July 1956. cf. 'The Cult of "Common Usage",' in *Portraits from Memory.*
7 Letter from B.R. to Constance Malleson.
8 'My Mental Development' in *The Philosophy of Bertrand Russell* (Evanston and Cambridge, 1944).
9 I cannot subscribe to this formula. My final views are less Kantian than Alan Wood supposes. I will mention two points. First: though the external world is probably not quite like the world of perception, it is connected with the world of perception by correlations, which are impossible in a philosophy which regards time and space as subjective. Second: the principles of non-deductive inference which I advocate are not put forward as certain or *a priori*, but as scientific hypotheses. – B.R.
10 *Foundations of Geometry*, page 179.
11 B.R. to Alan Wood.
12 For one thing, he never made up his mind exactly what he meant by philosophy.
13 For example, in *Principles of Mathematics* (*passim*), *Mysticism and Logic*, page 80, *Introduction to Mathematical Philosophy*, page 11, and *Sceptical Essays*, page 72.
14 Letter to Beatrice Webb.
15 Review of Urmson's *Philosophical Analysis* in *The Hibbert Journal*, July, 1956.
16 *Philosophy of Bertrand Russell* ('My Mental Development').

17 'Logical Atomism' in *Contemporary British Philosophy*, Vol. I (ed. J. H. Muirhead: Allen and Unwin, London).

18 *Philosophy of Bertrand Russell*, page 102.

19 'Reflections on My Eightieth Birthday' in *Portraits from Memory*.

20 *Introduction to Mathematical Philosophy*, page 71.

21 'Philosophical Importance of Mathematical Logic' (*Monist*, October 1913); cf. *Our Knowledge of the External World*, page 211.

22 Vol. I, page 59.

23 *Logic and Knowledge*, page 325; cf. *Human Knowledge*.

24 Russell prefaced these remarks, in *The Principles of Mathematics*, by saying they arose from the consideration of mathematical philosophy, and were 'not necessarily' applicable to other branches of philosophy. In view of the underlying unity of his philosophical method, referred to earlier, I do not think this qualification is now necessary (pages 129, 130).

25 *Principles of Mathematics*, page 129; cf. *Our Knowledge of the External World*.

26 *Our Knowledge of the External World*, page 31; cf. *Philosophy of Leibniz*, page 171.

27 Letter from B.R. to F. H. Bradley.

28 *Our Knowledge of the External World*, page 241.

29 *Problems of Philosophy*.

30 Perhaps it is of interest to note that A. D. Lindsay made a similar remark about Kant.

31 Vol. III, page 471.

32 'Philosophy of Logical Atomism' (*Logic and Knowledge*).

33 cf. *Mysticism and Logic*, page 70.

34 *Philosophy of Leibniz*, page 8.

35 *On Education*, page 203.

36 *Introduction to Mathematical Philosophy*, pages 197–8.

37 *Mysticism and Logic*, page 66; cf. *Our Knowledge of the External World*, page 238.

38 *Unpopular Essays*, page 42.

39 *The Scientific Outlook*, page 98.

40 Ibid., page 101.

41 B.R. on George Santayana.

42 F. H. Bradley, *Philosophy of Logic*, page 693.

43 *Human Knowledge*, page 49.

6

The Early Wittgenstein and the Middle Russell*

Kenneth Blackwell

The early relationship of Ludwig Wittgenstein and Bertrand Russell was, perhaps in part because of its intensity, one of the most fruitful in the history of philosophy. To understand the relationship fully requires that attention be paid to both its philosophical and biographical aspects. Yet those who write about a man's philosophy and those who write his life usually fail to integrate the philosophical studies or the life (as the case may be) into their own works. The biography of Russell by Ronald W. Clark has, to cite an example on one side, drawn the criticism that its philosophy is there in isolation, "like a remote and unimportant country shown in an inset in a map."[1] Perhaps the biographer would answer that philosophical commentators are guilty of a similar fault, namely, that of generally ignoring the life when critical events in a man's philosophical development are under examination. Many books on Wittgenstein, for instance, devote their first chapter to his life and then confine themselves to his philosophy. I have found the biographical and the philosophical approaches not only inseparable but rewarding.

Much of our knowledge of the personal side of the relationship of Wittgenstein and Russell has only recently come to light, but no treatise has yet been written on the philosophical side. There doubtless will be, for there is room for a substantial volume to trace the interactions in logic and epistemology of these two philosophers of the century. Such a volume would not be grounded in history and biography, but rather in philosophy. Its theme could be the tensions inherent in an epistemology based upon the doctrine of acquaintance. Both Russell and the early Wittgenstein held such an epistemology, and the latter's first work, *Tractatus Logico-Philosophicus*, is (roughly) an account of the world as assumed by this epistemology, but notably lacking in explicit assumptions to that effect. The last book Wittgenstein more or less completed, *Philosophical Investigations*, is an attack on that account and on that epistemology. This is why I think Russell was so notoriously hostile to it, and cast upon the memory of its author the most wounding aspersion he could think of: that in that work Wittgenstein "seems to have grown tired of serious thinking and to have invented a doctrine which would make such an activity unnecessary."[2] Turning to Russell's side of the relationship, we find a history of alterations in his theory of belief due both to Wittgenstein's direct criticisms of it and to various indirect criticisms suggested by Wittgenstein's philosophy of logic (especially with regard to logical constants and forms). In addition, certain technical improvements in *Principia Mathematica* seem due to Wittgenstein, as well as the view that mathematics is wholly tautological (a view which, as Russell put it, "Wittgenstein has sometimes seemed to teach").[3] There is also Russell's own confession – which itself has to be studied and verified – that he "went too far in agreeing with" the early Wittgenstein[4] and that (by implication) his own later work in philosophy repudiates some of the earlier Wittgensteinian influences.

It is insufficiently realized that the personal contacts between Wittgenstein and Russell were not confined to the years up to 1922, when the English translation of the *Tractatus* was published and Russell indicates that Wittgenstein desired to see no more of him.[5] The contacts resumed after Wittgenstein returned to Cambridge in 1929, and seem to have been neither unfriendly nor divest of philosophical discussion. See, for example, Russell's report in 1930 to the Council of Trinity College on *Philosophical Remarks*,[6] or Wittgenstein's letter of (presumably) November 1935, when he wished to attend Russell's paper on "The Limits of Empiricism."[7] As far as I can discover, the personal relationship did not again deteriorate until about the time of Russell's return to Trinity College in 1944. About this time there is the story that

> Someone was inclined to defend Russell's writings on marriage, sex, and "free love": Wittgenstein interposed by saying: "If a person tells me he has been to the worst of places I have no right to judge him, but if he tells me it was his superior wisdom that enabled him to go there, then I know that he is a fraud."[8]

Then there are Wittgenstein's remarks that, at a certain meeting of the Moral Sciences Club, Russell was "most disagreeable. Glib and superficial, though, as always, *astonishingly* quick";[9] that "Russell isn't going to kill himself doing philosophy now."[10] There is the incident (which exists in rumour if not in fact) which might be called the "poker–Popper" incident.[11] And after Wittgenstein's death in 1951, there are Russell's diatribes against "the cult of common usage." He even revised the summation of his account of Wittgenstein in the manuscript of his autobiography. As published, it reads: "In spite of such slight foibles, however, he was an impressive human being." In the original version of 1931, which was retained until about 1966, Russell wrote: "In spite of such slight foibles, however, I consider him about the most impressive human being I have ever known."[12] Let us therefore turn from the much less interesting (and less edifying) relationship of the middle and late Wittgenstein and the late and *very* late Russell, to the period in which the middle-aged Russell encountered the youthful Wittgenstein.

The period we are about to examine, namely 1911 to 1914, used to be very little known, even after the publication of Russell's autobiography. I used to think of it principally in terms of his affair with Lady Ottoline Morrell and numerous addresses to the Aristotelian Society. Now, however, with the availability at McMaster University and the University of Texas of the enormous correspondence of Russell with Lady Ottoline, we know much more. Since they could not meet very often, letters were their chief means of communication, and both were indefatigable correspondents. Russell once told Lady Ottoline he could easily write all day long to her (letter #52, p/3 May 1911). One biographer devotes 100 pages out of 650 to these years. The image of these years is now somewhat altered. True, there is still the affair with Lady Ottoline, now in daily detail, but the period is also represented in my mind by various writing projects of Russell's which failed, and by the ubiquitous presence of Wittgenstein. From Wittgenstein's side, it is a great help that we now have the *Letters to Russell, Keynes and Moore*, superbly dated, translated and annotated, and we are now much more certain of the circumstances of the composition of Wittgenstein's first surviving substantial work, "Notes on Logic," and the order to be assigned the two surviving versions of the text.[13] There is also a surviving insubstantial work, the review of Peter Coffey's *The Science of Logic*, which appeared in the *Cambridge Review* for 6 March 1913.[14] And there are the extracts from David Pinsent's diary, which are available in Trinity College Library. I have seen only the entries used by von Hayek in his aborted "Sketch of a Biography of Ludwig Wittgenstein," of which he sent a carbon copy to Russell. Of a strictly philosophical nature, the chief document to surface in recent years is Russell's unfinished book on theory of knowledge. This manuscript is a real missing link. A reviewer of *Notebooks, 1914–1916* remarked that "if Wittgenstein at this time shared Russell's general conception of the nature of philosophy, it is also clear that he was reacting sharply to a number of specific views, either held by Russell at about 1913 or else attributed to him."[15] The implication is that these specific views do not appear in any of Russell's published writings. The unpublished manuscript on theory of knowledge was written in 1913, and it provides a bridge between the views Russell expressed in *The Problems of Philosophy*, which was written in July 1911, and those in *Our Knowledge of the External World* (1914) and the lectures on "The Philosophy of Logical Atomism" (1918). From this plethora of material I shall first trace the personal relationship which evolved, because it was important for the philosophy, and then examine a critical event in the philosophical relationship. I believe the two aspects are inseparable in understanding Russell's abandonment of the theory of knowledge manuscript, in particular his "paralysis"[16] over Wittgenstein's criticism of that work.

Wittgenstein and Russell were twenty-two and thirty-nine, respectively, when they first met. The date was 18 October 1911, and the Michaelmas term of the second year of Russell's five-year Cambridge lectureship was a week old. Wittgenstein had apparently been advised by Frege to study with Russell,[17] though he does not seem to have told Russell so, and Russell consistently says in his writings on Wittgenstein that "He asked people at Manchester (so he told me) whether there was such a subject [as the principles of mathematics], and whether anyone worked at it. They told him that there was such a subject and that he could find out more about it by coming to me at Cambridge . . ."[18] It would be useful for disentangling the separate influences of Frege and Russell if we knew which came first. Both influences seem to have begun before the personal relationships developed. Russell, in the article just quoted from, states Wittgenstein "did not, I think, know Frege personally at that time, but he read him and greatly admired him."[19] But although an awareness of the Fregean background is very important to an understanding of the *Tractatus*,[20] the Russellian background seems equally important. Wittgenstein was reading Russell as early as 1909, when he proposed a solution to Russell's contradiction in a letter to Philip Jourdain.[21] The first meeting between Wittgenstein and Russell began auspiciously enough. Russell reported to Lady Ottoline that his new student had "acquired, by himself, a passion for the philosophy of mathematics, and has now come to Cambridge on purpose to hear me" (#225, p/18 Oct. 1911). Wittgenstein refused to speak German on that occasion, although his English was not good. Apparently, the same day, after Russell's lecture, he came back with him to his rooms and "argued till dinner-time." Russell's impression after one day was a definite one: Wittgenstein was "obstinate and perverse, but I think not stupid"; but he threatened to be an infliction (#227, p/19 Oct. 1911).

The memories of his first term remained sharp with Russell, and several of his customary anecdotes about Wittgenstein date from this time. There is the one about Wittgenstein refusing to admit there was not a hippopotamus in the room, in the face of Russell's refutation of his theory that "nothing empirical is knowable" (#241, p/2 Nov. 1911). (In the retelling, forty years later, the non-existent animal became a rhinoceros.[22]) A few days after this incident we get a slight elaboration of Wittgenstein's theory: he "was refusing to admit the existence of anything except asserted propositions" (#247, p/7 Nov. 1911), or maintaining that "there is nothing in the world except asserted propositions" (#254, p/13 Nov. 1911). Can we not see connections between this remark and *Tractatus*, 2.04: "The totality of existent atomic facts is the world"? On the other hand, it contradicts a statement in "Notes on Logic" that "There are only unasserted propositions" (Summary, p. 5). To Russell's discredit as a teacher on this occasion, he told Wittgenstein "it was too large a theme"; his theme remained large and it remained the same. For a short time Russell was disappointed in Wittgenstein: "He is armour-plated against all assaults of reasoning"; "it is really rather a waste of time talking with him" (#259, p/15 ?Nov. 1911). But this impression did not last. By the end of the term Russell reported he was getting to like the man who had turned out to be, as he said, Austrian, literary, pleasant-mannered, and probably very intelligent (#271, p/29 Nov. 1911). The most important of the anecdotes concerns the occasion on which Wittgenstein was hesitating between philosophy and aviation, and asked Russell for advice. The date was 27 November 1911 (#268); Russell later recorded only that this occurred "at the end of his first term."[23] When Wittgenstein brought the piece of writing Russell requested he do over the Christmas vacation, Lady Ottoline was told it was "very good, much better than my English pupils do. I shall certainly encourage him. Perhaps he will do great things." But he had a reservation: "On the other hand I think it very likely he will get tired of philosophy" (#320, p/23 Jan. 1912). The anecdote about Wittgenstein being the only one in Moore's class who looked puzzled dates from Wittgenstein's second term (see #368, p/5 March 1912).

In his obituary notice, Russell recalled that Wittgenstein "made very rapid progress in mathematical logic, and soon knew all that I had to teach."[24] Probably this happened within a year. Indeed, Wittgenstein must already have been advanced in the subject. On 26 January 1912, he proposed to Russell "a definition of logical *form*" (#325). This, unfortunately, is the last time in the letters to Lady Ottoline that Russell identifies Wittgenstein's philosophical views. His explanation of this view is not revealing – he added only that it was "opposed to logical *matter*." I do not know how Russell conceived of "logical form" as distinct from "logical matter" here, unless he regarded the logical constants as the matter of logic. Although Lady Ottoline had studied logic under the neo-Hegelian David G. Ritchie at St Andrews University back in 1897,[25] it would not have been symbolic logic that she studied. It is a pity for our knowledge of this period that she did not have a better grounding. At any rate, Wittgenstein does not seem, by this date, to have developed his fundamental view that "logical form" cannot be described but only shown, or he would not have attempted a definition of "logical form." Subsequent references to philosophy and logic in the correspondence are merely tantalizing. On 27 February 1912, Wittgenstein "brought a very good original suggestion, which I think is right, on an important point in logic" (#360). A few weeks later, Russell and Wittgenstein "had a close equal passionate discussion of the most difficult point in mathematical philosophy . . . He has suggested several new ideas which I think valuable" (#388, p/17 March

1912). A month later, Russell told Lady Ottoline that he had "got a number of new technical ideas from [Wittgenstein] which I think are quite sound and important" (#422, p/23 April 1912). I cannot determine what these "new technical ideas" were, but "the most difficult point in mathematical philosophy" might concern the concept of "logical form," or, as S. T. Sommerville has suggested,[26] the theory of types. Later in the year the point (whatever it was) much exercised Russell in trying to write a paper on "What is Logic?" Near the end of 1912 Wittgenstein was reported to be making "great progress" with what Russell termed "his logical problems" (#615 [Oct. 1912]).

Let us now pay greater attention to the personal relationship, which was developing as fast as Wittgenstein's philosophical ideas. One of the factors in forming the relationship was that Russell saw Wittgenstein as the perfect student. Already by March 1912 Russell had said, "Yes, Wittgenstein has been a great event in my life – whatever may come of him" (#397 [late March 1912]). Yet his impact on Russell had just begun. Russell came to see Wittgenstein as embodying (the Platonic image is appropriate at this stage in Russell's philosophy) the ideal philosophic nature. The qualities of this nature were a strong impulse to analysis, titanic energy, unswerving devotion to work and to truth, contempt for traditional patterns of thought, an ironic wit, utter unconcern with ordinary standards of success (such as getting one's degree), etc. Here are some of Russell's descriptions:

He has the theoretical passion *very* strongly – it is a rare passion and one is glad to find it. He doesn't want to prove this or that, but to find out how things really are . . . something about him makes him a hero.

(#373, p/8 March 1912)

No one could be more sincere than Wittgenstein, or more destitute of the false politeness that interferes with truth; but he lets his feelings and affections appear, and it warms one's heart.

(#375, p/10 March 1912)

[C. D.] Broad is . . . the most *reliable* pupil I have had – practically certain to do a good deal of useful but not brilliant work; whereas Wittgenstein . . . is full of boiling passion which may drive him any-where. [Unquestionably a virtue to Russell's romantic mind.]

(#384, p/15 March 1912)

He has the intellectual passion in the highest degree; it makes me love him. His disposition is that of an artist, intuitive and moody . . . he has just the sort of rage when he can't understand things that I have.

(#385, 16 March 1912)

He is the ideal pupil – he gives passionate admiration with vehement and very intelligent dissent . . . He spoke with intense feeling about the *beauty* of the big book [i.e. *Principia*], said he found it like music. He is not a flatterer, but a man of transparent and absolute sincerity . . . He is far more terrible with Christians than I am.

(#388, p/17 March 1912)

I saw a good deal of Wittgenstein this afternoon – he wears well. He is quite as good as I thought. I find him strangely exciting. He lives in the same kind of intense excitement as I do, hardly able to sit still or read a book. He was talking about Beethoven – how a friend described going to Beethoven's door and hearing him "cursing, howling and singing" over his new fugue; after a whole hour Beethoven at last came to the door, looking as if he had been fighting the devil, and having eaten nothing for 36 hours because his cook and parlour-maid had been away from his rage. That's the sort of man to be.

Wittgenstein brought me the most lovely roses today. He is a treasure . . . I shan't feel the subject neglected by my abandoning it, as long as he takes it up. I thought he would have smashed all the furniture in my room today, he got so excited. He asked me how Whitehead and I were going to end our big book, and I said we should have no concluding remarks, but just stop with whatever formula happened to come last. He seemed surprised at first, and then saw that was right. It seems to me the beauty of the book would be spoilt if it contained a single word that could possibly be spared. I argued about Matter with him. He thinks it a trivial problem. He admits that if there is no Matter then no one exists but himself, but he says that doesn't hurt, since physics and astronomy and all the other sciences could still be interpreted so as to be true. – Yes, I think my daily round here *is* useful – Wittgenstein alone would have made it so.

(#422, p/23 April 1912)

Wittgenstein's mature philosophic style is recognizable in the early period – just as is his style in domestic furnishings. His style in both these disparate areas has the quality of shunning all ornamentation.[27] Russell tried to change the philosophic style.

I told him he ought not simply to *state* what he thinks true, but to give arguments for it, but he said arguments spoil its beauty, and that he would feel as if he was dirtying a flower with muddy hands. He *does* appeal to me – the artist in intellect is so very rare. I told him I hadn't the heart to say anything against that, and that he had better acquire a slave to state the arguments.

(Between #467 and #468 [27 May 1912])

Russell told Wittgenstein that he would not get a degree "unless he learnt to write imperfect things – this all made him more and more furious" (#566 [Sept. 1912]). As for furniture, Wittgenstein lectured Russell on how it should be made: ornamentation should be abolished where it is not part of the construction. Not surprisingly, he had a very difficult time finding anything simple enough either in Cambridge or London.

It was also in mid-1912 that the pair began ethical discussions. Wittgenstein suddenly said one day how he admired the text "what shall it profit a man if he gain the whole world and lose his own soul," and remarked "how few there are who don't lose their own soul." Russell said "it depended on having a large purpose that one is true to." Wittgenstein replied character-istically that "he thought it depended more on suffering and the power to endure it." Russell was surprised by this discussion (#472, p/30 May 1912). Another ethical discussion drew the comment from Russell that "His out-look is very free; principles and such things seem to him nonsense, because his impulses are strong and never shameful" (#475, p/1 June 1912). Only idealized characters *never* have "shameful" impulses; this was not an occasion on which Russell demonstrated insight into human nature. Wittgenstein, if not before, put him right on this matter in a letter of 3 March 1914, in which he asserted that his life was "*FULL* of the ugliest and pettiest thoughts and acts imaginable."[28] Apparently Russell still had not, at this point, realized Wittgenstein thought this way about himself. In addition to discussions of meta-ethics, they also discussed normative value judgments. I shall come to certain of these soon.

One of the foregoing extracts indicates that Russell was interested at this time (April 1912) in problems connected with knowledge of the material world. In fact, he was committed to delivering a paper on the subject at Cardiff. The paper was duly delivered in May. It was then thoroughly revised (the manuscript is in the Russell Archives), and Russell hoped it would be published in the *Monist*, which had earlier in 1912 published his paper on "The Philosophy of Bergson."[29] Wittgenstein had by now begun making criticisms of Russell's work, but had liked the peroration of the Bergson paper; however, he did not like this sort of thing "unadulterated," as in "The Free Man's Worship" (#387, p/16 March 1912). Then he objected to the last chapter of *The Problems of Philosophy*, on "The Value of Philosophy." One must not *say* that philosophy has value. As Russell reported his view, "people who like philosophy will pursue it, and others won't, and there is an end of it" (#388, p/17 March 1912; see also #387, p/ 16 March 1912). At first Wittgenstein told Russell that "On Matter" was the best thing he had done – but he had only read the beginning and end. Then he decided he did not like the rest of the paper – "but only," Russell thought, "because of disagreement, not because of its being badly done" (#460, 22 May 1912; 467, 26 May 1912). Yet even after the thorough revisions, Russell did not publish the paper.

This was also for Russell a time of failures in writing projects of a more literary nature. He was always sensitive to criticism from those whose judgment he admired, and because of these failures he was especially susceptible to such criticism. In the summer of 1911, after writing *The Problems of Philosophy*, he had gone on to produce a book-length manuscript on his philosophy of religion, known as "Prisons." Only some outlines and a summary chapter are extant. I shall return to the summary chapter, which was published as "The Essence of Religion." There was also an autobiography, written about April 1912, of which no trace remains. Then came an autobiographical novella, "The Perplexities of John Forstice," written in June 1912 but published posthumously (in Russell's *Collected Stories*) because he was never quite satisfied with it. Only the last could have been influenced by Wittgenstein, and then only with respect to its being withheld from publication; there is, in fact, no evidence that he did influence it. "The Essence of Religion" appeared in the October 1912 issue of the *Hibbert Journal*, and it set out the foundations of Russell's normative ethic. It deals Spinozistically with such concepts as "freedom from the finite self,"[30] and Platonistically with three elements in Christianity "which it is desirable to preserve if possible: worship, acquiescence, and love."[31] The language is the language of incarnation. The highest wisdom is to be free of the free man's last prison: "the insistent demand that our ideals shall be already realized in the world." One October afternoon Russell was interrupted in composing a letter to Lady Ottoline: "Here is Wittgenstein just arrived, frightfully pained by my Hibbert article which he evidently *detests*. I must stop because of him" (#597 [Oct. 1912]). A few days later we learn why Wittgenstein detested the article. "He felt I had been a traitor to the gospel of exactness, and wantonly used words vaguely; also that such things are too intimate for print. I minded very much, because I half agree with him" (#600, p/11 Oct. 1912). Two days later, Russell returned to the subject. "Wittgenstein's criticisms disturbed me profoundly. He was so unhappy, so gentle, so wounded in his wish to think well of me" (#602, p/13 Oct. 1912). The same day he told Lady Ottoline that his mind was full of the paper on "What is Logic?" He thought it might be really important. But Wittgenstein had been with him "arguing logic – it *is* difficult, but I feel I must have another go at it." The next day he reported that he could not get on with "What is Logic?" and felt strongly inclined to leave it to Wittgenstein (#603, p/14 Oct. 1912).

Among Russell's papers is a five-page manuscript entitled "What is Logic?" It is not a real paper, only a point-by-point summary of the problems such a paper might discuss. "Logic" is defined as "the study of the forms of complexes." Russell first considers "complex" as a primitive idea, or indefinable. Then he tries "form." He lists the symbols of various atomic forms. He specifically excludes judgment from consideration, and so does not list a form for judgment. He shows that, to avoid an infinite regress, the form of a complex must not be considered a constituent of the complex. (Otherwise a form of the new complex composed of the original constituents plus the original form would be required, and so on). Wittgenstein's letters to Russell in the next few months show him hard at work on what he calls "the complex problem" and the theory of symbolism. We learn that in December 1912 Wittgenstein discussed with Frege what he called "our Theory of Symbolism" (meaning Russell's and his), and in a letter of January 1913 explained what the theory amounted to. It amounted to the view that "there cannot be different types of things," and that a proper theory of symbolism must render any theory of types "superfluous." In the form of the statement "Socrates is mortal," the variables for "Socrates" and "mortality" must be of different kinds.[32] If they are, they will not be substituted for the wrong way around. It was a letter like this, and the discussions which must have ensued afterwards, which could have led to Russell's statement, in introducing the *Tractatus*, that "In the part of [Wittgenstein's] theory which deals with Symbolism he is concerned with the conditions which would have to be fulfilled by a logically perfect language." We shall see that allegations of imperfect symbolism have been brought against the theory of judgment Russell was soon to develop. It is undeniable, however, that both men were concerned with developing an ideal notation – though that is not to conclude (least of all from the sentence just quoted from the Introduction to the *Tractatus*) that Russell considered that to be Wittgenstein's *only* concern.[33]

By the winter of 1912–13, then, Russell seems to have bequeathed the problems of philosophical logic to Wittgenstein. He more than once remarked to Lady Ottoline that Wittgenstein could soon take his place at Cambridge (#678, p/21 Jan. 1913). Indeed, Wittgenstein was to be a member of a school Russell dreamt of founding, Wittgenstein's qualification being that he was the ideal mathematical philosopher. We find the following reverie in a letter of December 1912:

I believe a certain sort of mathematicians have far more philosophical capacity than most of the people who take up philosophy. Hitherto the people attracted to philosophy have been mostly those who loved the big generalizations, which are all wrong, so that few people with exact minds have taken up the subject. It has long been one of my dreams to found a great school of mathematically-trained philosophers, but I don't know whether I shall ever get it accomplished. I had hopes of [H. T. J.] Norton, but he has not the physique. Broad is all right, but has no fundamental originality. Wittgenstein of course is exactly my dream. But I should like to make mathematics the ordinary training for a philosopher – I am sure it ought to be. That would require a tremendous propaganda of the sort that moves educational bodies; and I am afraid vested interests would always be too strong. However, when I am too old for original work I dare say I shall take it up.

(#663, 29 Dec. 1912)

Russell founded no such school, but he never tired of making the point that philosophers ought to come to philosophy with a scientific background. By this time one has the feeling that Russell, while not exactly having surrendered his judgment to Wittgenstein's, had convinced himself that his student was closer to his philosophic ideal than he was himself. Take, for example, the degree of devotion to serious matters. There is the priceless incident of North Whitehead's boat race, which Russell and Wittgenstein went to watch. After the race, Wittgenstein

suddenly stood still and explained that the way we had spent the afternoon was so vile that we ought not to live, or at least he ought not, that nothing is tolerable except producing great works or enjoying those of others, that he has accomplished nothing and never will, etc. – all this with a force that nearly knocks one down. He makes me feel like a bleating lambkin.

(#629, p/9 Nov. 1912)

I think Russell had decided by this time that his teaching of Wittgenstein was finished, his main job now being that of guiding Wittgenstein's work and keeping him stable. ("He is a great task but quite worth it," he told Lady Ottoline [#646, p/30 Nov. 1912].) For in logical matters Wittgenstein had now, it appears, learned all that Russell considered he had to teach.

We could expect to hear of criticisms from Wittgenstein of *Principia Mathematica*, and we do catch echoes of discussions on that subject. All three volumes had appeared by April 1913. In the late summer of 1913 Pinsent recorded in his diary that the first volume will have to be rewritten and Wittgenstein will write the first eleven chapters.[34] Russell had already said as much to Lady Ottoline six months before. On 23 February, he told her: "Wittgenstein has persuaded me that the early proofs of Principia Mathematica are very inexact"; adding, "fortunately it is his business to put them right, not mine" (#707). In the same letter Russell mentioned he "could have written a book with the store of ideas I have already, but now I have a higher standard of exactness." The higher standard of exactness was, I infer, due to Wittgenstein's influence. Yet it is worth noting that at this time Wittgenstein published his review of Coffey. The logical points made in the review are not original to Wittgenstein, but rather associated with Russell and the school to which he belonged. Wittgenstein began the points with a complaint indicative of the mathematical logician's concern with clarity:

Mr Coffey, like many logicians, draws a great advantage from an unclear way of expressing himself; for if you cannot tell whether he means to say "Yes" or "No", it is difficult to argue against him. However, even through his foggy expression, many grave mistakes can be recognized clearly enough; and I propose to give a list of some of the most striking ones . . . [35]

I do not mean to deny Wittgenstein's fundamental originality, however. Pinsent, who polished Wittgenstein's own rough translation of this review from the German original, recorded a few days before he worked on the translation that Russell had just acquiesced without a murmur in a new discovery of Wittgenstein's.[36] But it is now time for us to consider the book Russell might have written with the store of ideas he said he already had.

During the Christmas vacation of 1912 Russell had retreated to a small village to work on "matter." Whitehead, he said, was already at work on the mathematical end, and he was working on the psychological end (#662, 28 Dec. 1912). Several brief manuscripts on the subject are extant, and these lines from one of them describe the crux of the problem:

Physics exhibits sensations as functions of physical objects.
But epistemology demands that physical objects should be exhibited as functions of sensations.
Thus we have to solve the equations giving sensations in terms of physical objects, so as to make them give physical objects in terms of sensations.
That is all.[37]

At the same time Russell began to think about the two lecture courses he had agreed to give at Harvard a year hence, and the series of public lectures for the Lowell Institute he was to give at the same time. The public lectures, published as *Our Knowledge of the External World*, were initially planned to cover a very different topic, variously called "the search for wisdom" or "the search for insight" (#737, p/8 April 1913). (This topic was rejected by President Lowell because of the religious implications Russell would draw.[38]) After sketching an outline for the original topic he turned to the course on theory of knowledge. "For a long time," he told Lady Ottoline, "I have planned a book on theory of knowledge, then I thought I could do Matter first, but now I see that even apart from having to lecture, theory of knowledge must come first" (#750, n.d.). Apparently Russell kept the plans for this book from Wittgenstein. By now (April 1913), Russell was writing:

I find I no longer ever talk to him about *my* work, but only about his. When there are no clear arguments, but only inconclusive considerations to be balanced, or unsatisfactory points of view to be set against each other, he is no good; and he treats infant theories with a ferocity which they can only endure when they are grown up. The result is that I become completely reserved, even about work.

(#753, p/23 April 1913)

However, if Russell was reserved about philosophical and logical matters, he was not when it came to "improving" Wittgenstein. Here is a report of one struggle to improve him:

I had a terrific contest with Wittgenstein late last night, because I told him it would do him good to read French prose, and that he was in danger of being narrow and uncivilized. He raged and stormed, and I irritated him more and more by merely smiling. We made it up in the end, but he remained quite unconvinced. The things I say to him are just the things you would say to me if you were not afraid of the avalanche they would produce – and his avalanche is just what mine would be! I feel his lack of civilization and suffer from it – it is odd how little music does to civilize people – it is too apart, too passionate, and too remote from words. He has not a sufficiently wide curiosity or a sufficient wish for a broad survey of the world. It won't spoil his work on logic, but it will make him always a very narrow specialist, and rather too much the champion of a party – that is, when judged by the highest standards.

(#717, p/6 March 1913)

Whether or not Wittgenstein became, in some sense, too much the champion of a party, the charge of being always a very narrow specialist does not stick. Or perhaps it does, in the sense that *all* his writings are philosophical, whereas Russell wrote on history, science, politics, love, and much else.

I am not going to describe in detail the composition of the unfinished book on theory of knowledge, or the evidence for identifying the missing first six chapters with articles by Russell which appeared quarterly in the *Monist* from 1914 to 1915. A full account, with a reconstruction of the table of contents, has been given elsewhere.[39] The title for this untitled manuscript may as well be "Theory of Knowledge." From a reference within the manuscript, it can be seen that Russell at least placed it within the class of books bearing that name,[40] and he preferred that term to "epistemology." It is the cessation of work on "Theory of Knowledge" which constitutes the critical event in the early philosophical relationship of Russell and Wittgenstein.

"Theory of Knowledge" was to have two major sections, an "analytic" section and a "constructive" section. The analytic section was divided into three parts: acquaintance, judgment, and inference. The latter two parts were also called "atomic propositional thought" and "molecular propositional thought," respectively. Only the first two parts of the analytic section were written. The constructive section, if we have correctly identified the outline of it, was to conclude with "matter." To construct matter logically, Russell planned to move from knowledge of logic to knowledge of sense (including time and space), and thence to knowledge of science. In the final part, the problem was so to state the existence of certain sense-data and certain principles of inference that science would follow. Matter, causality, and induction could all then be dealt with. Clearly Russell had a large book in mind – in fact, his first large book since completing his share of *Principia* three years earlier. We may presume that, after a decade on *Principia*, Russell felt rather disoriented without another large project on hand. So for this reason, and because of the literary and philosophical failures I have mentioned, he became very much involved emotionally when he began "Theory of Knowledge." I believe he hoped (though he did not say so) that it would do for epistemology what *Principia* had done for logic and mathematics. In short, while eschewing axioms and symbolic demonstration, he hoped to erect an unimpeachable system, which would function deductively, demonstrating our knowledge of the external world. It was to be a far grander effort than the book of this title written partly in despair and with drastically pruned ambitions a few months later.[41]

Russell began "Theory of Knowledge" on 7 May 1913. A few days later Wittgenstein appeared on the scene. He gave Russell a climbing rose in a pot (he was fond of giving him flowers), but "was shocked to hear I am writing on Theory of Knowledge – he thinks it will be like the shilling shocker [i.e. *The Problems of Philosophy*], which he hates. *He* is a tyrant if you like" (#775, p/13 May 1913). After the first six chapters were written, Wittgenstein came to Russell "with a refutation of the theory of judgment which I used to hold. He was right, but I think the correction required is not very serious. I shall have to make up my mind within a week, as I shall soon reach judgment" (#782, p/21 May 1913). Russell was now writing on acquaintance with universals – predicates and relations, and logical data such as logical constants and forms ("which is difficult," he confessed [#784, p/23 May 1913]). "I shall come to more interesting things soon, when I get on to judgment" (#783, p/22 May 1913).

When he began judgment, Russell "got a new way of dividing the subject – *quite* new, and much more searching than the traditional divisions . . . any number of really important new ideas came to me" (#785, 24 May 1913). Then, after "trying to understand what is meant by understanding a sentence or statement" (#786, p/25 May 1913), Russell had another visit from Wittgenstein. He was probably half-way into Part II, Chapter II, entitled "Analysis and Synthesis." He had written more than 225 pages. He told Lady Ottoline:

we were both cross from the heat – I showed him a crucial part of what I have been writing. He said it was all wrong, not realizing the difficulties – that he had tried my view and knew it wouldn't work. I couldn't understand his objection – in fact he was very inarticulate – but I feel in my bones that he must be right, and that he has seen something I have missed. If I could see it too I shouldn't mind, but as it is, it is worrying, and has rather destroyed the pleasure in my writing – I can only go on with what I see, and yet I feel it is probably all wrong, and that Wittgenstein will think me a dishonest scoundrel for going on with it. Well well – it is the younger generation knocking at the door – I must make room for him when I can, or I shall become an incubus.

(#787, p/28 May 1913)

Russell carried on writing, but without enthusiasm. One difficulty derived from trying to take account of Wittgenstein's criticisms, which had "to do with problems I want to leave to him" (#792, p/28? May 1913). Russell was also worried by "the difficulty of not stealing his ideas – there is really more merit in raising a good problem than in solving it," he said (#793, p/1 June 1913). Wittgenstein chose this susceptible moment to attack Russell personally.

He came analysing all that goes wrong between him and me, and I told him I thought it was only nerves on both sides and everything was all right at bottom. Then he said he never knew whether I was speaking the truth or being polite, so I got vexed and refused to say another word. He went on and on and on.

(#798, p/5 June 1913)

After further difficulties, however, the two men were reconciled. Russell finished Part II of Section A on 6 June, and decided to leave Part III and the whole of Section B until later. In thirty-one days – all during the Cambridge Easter term – he had written 350 pages; but as the sheer quantity of output failed to sustain Russell, we need not be overly impressed by it. He judged that "the best thing in my writing on theory of knowledge is the map of the country – that was already partially in the shilling book. It is very new, I think, and much more according to the natural division of the subject." The rest of the book could be corrected at leisure (#806, p/12 June 1913). This was wishful thinking, which Russell must have realized. Indeed, at this point he felt ready for suicide. Wittgenstein wrote to him on 27 July that he was "very sorry to hear that my objection to your theory of judgment paralyzes you. I think it can only be removed by a correct theory of propositions."[42] Russell went on to have a wretched summer. It was compounded by difficulties with Lady Ottoline, and led even to his praying in a cathedral while touring in Italy.[43] Wittgenstein on the other hand, had a productive summer, resulting in his "Notes on Logic."

It is worth noting that Russell's honesty triumphed in the end, since that is what worried him most about the event. It is admirable that his desire for the respect of his philosophic ideal (a mirror-image of his own self-respect) weighed more heavily with him than the investment of energy and several years' thought in "Theory of Knowledge." It reminds one of Frege's admission that Russell's discovery of his contradiction "has shaken the basis on which I intended to build arithmetic." Russell called Frege's dedication to truth on this occasion an act "of integrity and grace." It cannot be said that Russell "responded [like Frege] with intellectual pleasure clearly submerging any feelings of personal disappointment."[44] Nevertheless the fundamental integrity was there. The admission of failure was made only to Lady Ottoline, it appears. He told her Wittgenstein's attack on his work made a large part of the book he intended to write impossible for years to come (#811, p/20 June 1913). Three years later he confessed it was "an event of first-rate importance in my life."[45] Russell did not, however, forgo the opportunity to publish what he still thought correct of the first part of "Theory of Knowledge," and thus we have the six *Monist* articles of 1914–15.[46]

The place of "Theory of Knowledge" in the development of Russell's epistemology raises several historical questions. Wittgenstein knew *The Problems of Philosophy*. In this book Russell had elaborated his theory of knowledge by acquaintance. In it he had also elaborated the theory of judgment published earlier in the Introduction to *Principia Mathematica* and the final essay of *Philosophical Essays* (1910). In *The Problems of Philosophy* he had promoted the concept of the "sense" of the subordinate relation in belief statements to being a characteristic of the multiple judging relation. In this way he had hoped the propositional ordering of the constituents of belief would be less objectionably effected. But Russell was in difficulty in other areas, notably the ontological one. His philosophy at this time was strongly Platonistic: he thought he had to admit that relations have being, and the case for qualities appeared almost as strong.[47] A year of Wittgenstein's impact later, in "What is Logic?" he added the logical form of the proposition believed to the belief complex. In "Theory of Knowledge," as we shall see, he was strongly tempted to say that we have acquaintance with logical forms, as well as with logical constants. The historical questions which puzzle one are these:

1 What was the "map" of theory of knowledge which Russell said he had acquired while writing *The Problems of Philosophy*?
2 What could Wittgenstein's "refutation" of Russell's former theory of judgment have been?

3 What was the non-serious correction Russell thought his new theory of judgment required before he could begin writing it out?

4 What was the new way of dividing the subject of judgment which he arrived at when he began writing out the new theory?

5 What was Wittgenstein's criticism of the book, and was it identical with the objection to Russell's theory of judgment which "paralyzed" him when Wittgenstein put it in a letter?

6 Was this objection the only objection Wittgenstein raised to "Theory of Knowledge," and could it have been serious enough to cause Russell the despair which resulted in the abandonment of the manuscript and the publication of only the first six chapters? (There were three more chapters before the part on judgment – all on acquaintance with universals.)

Answers to the first four questions seem possible from a study of the documents. For instance, the "map" of theory of knowledge may well have been its division into knowledge of things and knowledge of truths, with the subdivision of knowledge of things into knowledge by acquaintance and by description.[48] But it is the last two questions which are by far the most interesting, and they are both philosophical and biographical. We want to know why Russell stopped writing his book, and whether Wittgenstein's criticism, as we have it, was the sole motive force. What exactly was the objection from Wittgenstein? We know what it was verbally – at least we think we do, although it was made in a letter after the second visit, and Russell had already admitted failure in letters to Lady Ottoline. The objection as given in Wittgenstein's letter of *circa* 14 June 1913, is in this passage:

> I can now express my objection to your theory of judgment exactly: I believe it is obvious that, from the proposition "A judges that (say) a is in the Relation R to b", if correctly analysed, the proposition "aRb. v. ~aRb" must follow directly *without the use of any other premiss.* This condition is not fulfilled by your theory.[49]

One of the chapters Wittgenstein must have seen is Chapter IX of Part I, "Logical Data." This chapter, which is very short, concerns acquaintance with logical constants and logical forms. One commentator has traced Wittgenstein's denial in the *Tractatus* that these phrases denote objects of any kind whatsoever back through the *Notebooks* and to the early letters to Russell. I quote:

> The supposed logical constants, then, whose existence Wittgenstein was concerned to deny were not only the supposed references of words like 'and', 'or', 'not', etc.; nor these together with the supposed referents of the words 'some', 'all' and 'is identical with' – though these (truth

functions, generality, and identity) did in time become the three ranges of so-called logical constants that he thought he had to deal with. Originally the notion covered much more: all the forms of propositions – the general notion of predicate, the general notion of dual relation, triple relation, and any other forms there might be of whatever complexity and level had been supposed to be logical objects, and Wittgenstein was denying them that status.[50]

This critic goes on to locate the object of Wittgenstein's denial in the chapter on "Logical Data." A second commentator has singled out this chapter, noting that the concept of acquaintance with logical forms and constants does not reappear in "The Philosophy of Logical Atomism" and drawing the inference that Wittgenstein's criticism was the cause.[51] When we examine that chapter, we find that Russell, while still Platonistic, is altogether tentative about the ontological status of logical objects. Although he concludes that "acquaintance with logical form . . . is a primitive constituent of our experience," he adds the rider, "whatever its ultimate analysis be."[52] And earlier in the chapter we can see more clearly that Russell was unsettled about the ultimate analysis. He wrote:

> It would seem that logical objects cannot be regarded as "entities", and that, therefore, what we shall call "acquaintance" with them cannot really be a dual relation. The difficulties which result are very formidable, but their solution must be sought in logic.
>
> (MS, p. 181).

Russell had temporarily ceased doing fundamental work in logic at this time, and there is here a markedly less confident note than is exhibited in his pre-Wittgenstein article of 1911, "The Philosophical Importance of Mathematical Logic," in the passages dealing with logical objects.[53] Again, later in the chapter, Russell wrote: "'Logical constants,' which might seem to be entities occurring in logical propositions, are really concerned with pure *form*, and are not actually constituents of the propositions in the verbal expression of which their names occur" (MS, p. 182). Is this the abolition of "logical matter," about which Russell wrote Lady Ottoline in 1912? And again, "the form is not a 'thing,' not another constituent along with the objects that were previously related in that form" (MS, p. 183). There are other, similar reservations. I think it is primarily this topic which comprised the problems Russell wished to leave to Wittgenstein, and on which there was the worry of "the difficulty of not stealing his ideas." It correlates well with a letter of October 1913 to Lady Ottoline. Russell remarked to her that "Theory of Knowledge" "goes to pieces when it touches Wittgenstein's problems" (#900, p/24 Oct. 1913). Indeed, in saying that logical constants are really concerned with pure form, it looks as though Russell was already borrowing from Wittgenstein. For in *Our Knowledge of the External World* he credits the same point to "unpublished work by my friend Ludwig Wittgenstein."[54]

Part II of "Theory of Knowledge" concerns "atomic propositional thought." Part III was to concern "molecular propositional thought"; that is, inference. The doctrine of acquaintance with logical data was to be employed in this part. In an outline Russell wrote:

> *Observe.* A Judgment requires acquaintance with *one* form of atomic complex. An inferential consciousness requires acquaintance with such terms as *or* and *not*, i.e. with a form of complex in which propositions are constituents.[55]

Thus the inventory of logical forms was to be even further enlarged to include forms of arguments.

What was new in the chapter on "The Understanding of Propositions," to which Wittgenstein surely presented the objection which was called "paralyzing?" (Incidentally, one distinguished critic, in his review of the *Notebooks*, where the letter was first printed, could not take the paralysis seriously. He wrote: "His old teacher must have been teasing him to elicit from Wittgenstein in his letter of 22.7.13 the sober 'I am very sorry to hear that my objection to your theory of judgment paralyzes you.' "[56]) What was new in the theory was the introduction of the logical form of propositions expressing attitudes – such as judging or believing, doubting, and understanding – towards other propositions. This development of Russell's theory of judgment from that presented in *The Problems of Philosophy* is just what another distinguished critic had once noted was lacking (in the published accounts, of course). At least this is what I think the following statement means: "Russell's theory would . . . require different relations of judging (differing as to number and the logical types of the terms between which they hold) for every different logical form of sentences expressing judgments."[57] Russell offered the following symbol for the logical form of someone's judgment that A is similar to B:

$$J (S, A, B, \text{similarity}, xRy).$$

I have great difficulty in deciding whether Russell originated this analysis. There is nothing, so far as I can see, indicating that credit belongs to Wittgenstein. But on the other hand, Russell twice in the next few years credited him for the discovery of what in 1918 he called "a new beast for our zoo" (adding "nothing that occurs in space is of the same form as belief").[58] In 1914, in the *Monist* version of Chapter IV of "Theory of Knowledge," he put it more fully:

It can be shown that a judgment, and generally all thought whose expression involves *propositions*, must be a fact of a different logical form from any of the series: subject–predicate facts, dual relations, triple relations, etc. In this way, a difficult and interesting problem of pure logic arises, namely a problem of enlarging the inventory of logical forms so as to include forms appropriate to the facts of epistemology.

Russell added in a footnote that he had come to know this through unpublished work of his friend Mr Ludwig Wittgenstein.[59] Yet we cannot credit Wittgenstein for the analysis of the form "J (S, A, B, similarity, *x*R*y*)," because it was surely just such an analysis that he objected to. Perhaps, then, the credit is for an analysis of judgment into a different form, say the form "J (S, *p*)," expressing that there is a relation of judgment between a subject S and a proposition *p*. At least this fits the demand of "Notes on Logic" that "a proposition itself must occur in the statement that it is judged."[60] But to distinguish this form from that of an old theory of Russell's, the concept of the "bipolarity" of "*p*" must be added.

"Notes on Logic" are the only document we can turn to for an elaboration of Wittgenstein's objection to Russell's theory of judgment. The "Notes" were composed in September and early October 1913. They contain several passages critical of Russell's theory of judgment. I quote from the earlier version:

When we say A judges that etc., then we have to mention a whole proposition which A judges. It will not do either to mention only its constituents, or its constituents and form, but not in the proper order. This shows that a proposition itself must occur in the statement that it is judged . . .

(Summary, p. 2)

The proper theory of judgment must make it impossible to judge nonsense. [Repeated at *Tractatus*, 5.5422.]

(Summary, p. 5)

Every right theory of judgment must make it impossible for me to judge that this table penholders the book. Russell's theory does not satisfy this requirement.

(3rd MS, p. 15)

There is no thing which is the form of a proposition, and no name which is the name of a form. Accordingly we can also not say that a relation which in certain cases holds between things holds sometimes between forms and things. This goes against Russell's theory of judgment.

(4th MS, p. 19)

[I]t seems that we shall only be able to express the proposition "A believes p" correctly by the *ab*-notation; say by making "A" having a relation to the poles "a" and "b" of a–p–b.

(4th MS, p. 21)

So Wittgenstein thought Russell's analysis of the judging event into constituents and form did not allow for the integrity of the proposition judged; and further, that inappropriate substitutions could be made in Russell's formula. His example, "this table penholders the book," is not, however, a happy one. "Penholders" is not a relation, although Russell's formula calls for a relation between the two other terms in a judgment of the form "*a*R*b*." It is a mystery why Wittgenstein thought Russell's formula could yield "this table penholders the book." A superior example of nonsense has been suggested. In this example, a genuine relation is substituted, but a relation which is inappropriate to the objects it purportedly relates. For example, Russell's formula might yield the judgment that "2 loves 7"[61] or "the knife is the square root of the fork."[62] But I do not think that this objection would have been sufficient to "paralyze" Russell. One is not paralyzed until one is unable to move in any direction, and it must first be shown that in Russell's philosophy all avenues were closed. I think we must credit the judging person with a certain amount of selectivity when it comes, under Russell's analysis, to putting terms and relations together. No person would in fact try to make this sort of nonsensical judgment. Yet the crucial chapter does show Russell struggling with other difficulties in forming coherent propositions from his heaps of constituents, all of which leaves me convinced that Russell's philosophical susceptibility to Wittgenstein's paralytic sting lies in this chapter.

In "The Philosophy of Logical Atomism" Russell made much more of the subordinate verb in a judgment. He also made much less of the multiple relation the subject has to the constituents and form of his judgment. It is in this area that Wittgenstein's objection may have had its paralyzing effect. But I put this forward only as a suggestion, for there are passages in "Notes on Logic" which tend to make one think otherwise.

In the passages I quoted from the "Notes," the emphasis is on there being a complete, significant proposition that is judged. Criticism is directed against Russell's analysis into constituents and form, as if from these elements one could never be certain that a powerful multiple judging relation could assemble a significant proposition. This is surely the thrust of Wittgenstein's objection that the proposition "aRb. v. ~aRb" must follow from the proposition "A judges that (say) a is in the Relation R to b." Since 1907 Russell had ceased to believe in propositions as entities.[63] His stock example of a false proposition was: "Charles I died in his bed,"[64] and he refused to admit there was an objective falsehood corresponding to this proposition. The correct explanation of error, he thought, must lie in the judging relation relating the elements of a judgment in a way that they are not, in fact, related – the elements of a judgment being identical with the elements of the fact it is hoped to state. Wittgenstein, in "Notes on Logic," gives ample evidence of believing in the analysis of propositions into constituents and forms. Yet in mid-1913 he was telling Russell that his similar analysis would not put the analysed judgment back together again. In reply, Russell could not revert to his pre-1907 theory that a judgment consists of a person in a judging relation to a complete propositional entity. He could neither opt for his old theory nor see his way to improving the new theory. Thus, I suggest, he was paralyzed. As he told Lady Ottoline: "[Wittgenstein] has seen something I have missed." The chapter on "The Understanding of Propositions," like that on "Logical Data," shows him to be worried by difficulties on all sides; Wittgenstein's criticism, which is admittedly difficult to fathom, seems to have pushed Russell over the brink into rejection of work he was less than confident of even before the criticism. The solution to the problem of Russell's paralysis will, however, not become clear until it is shown how Wittgenstein managed to retain a Russellian analysis of propositions while insisting that only a complete proposition can be the object of judgment.[65]

There is among Russell's papers an undated document, called "Props," which seems to be an attempt to take Wittgenstein's objection into account. The document also grapples with Wittgenstein's new theory of the bipolarity of propositions. This theory was contained in the remark from "Notes on Logic" about "'A' having a relation to the poles 'a' and 'b' of a–p–b." But the document is very obscure, and I shall pass it by with the note that it almost certainly dates from these months, since the first page is written on the verso of a rejected draft of page 197 of "Theory of Knowledge."

By the time of "Notes Dictated to Moore" in April 1914[66] Wittgenstein had another criticism to make of the Russellian theory of judgment. He repeated the criticism in the *Tractatus*. The criticism treats propositions like "A believes that p" as truth-functional, as of the form "'p' says p" (*Tractatus*, 5.542). This analysis dispenses with the subject and correlates the constituents of the proposition with the constituents of the fact it is about. Russell was much attracted to the theory and in 1925 devoted to it Appendix C of the second edition of *Principia Mathematica*; but its attraction was rendered possible for him only by his own abandonment of the subject in 1919.[67] If Wittgenstein had come up with this view in 1913, Russell would not likely have been affected by it. So much for Russell's paralysis.

The story of how "Notes on Logic" came to be written is fairly well known, but I can provide some fresh details of Russell's reaction to

Wittgenstein's first substantial piece of work. Russell was happy that at last his star pupil was producing written work. On first hearing of it he told Lady Ottoline: "[Wittgenstein] has done extraordinarily good work, and has I think practically solved the problems he was working at. You can hardly believe what a load this lifts off my spirits – it makes me feel almost young and gay" (#858, p/29 Aug. 1913). A little later, after Wittgenstein had read him bits of the work he had done, Russell remarked that he thought "it is as good as anything that has ever been done on logic" (#883, p/4 Oct. 1913). When it came actually to composing the "Notes," there were great difficulties. "[Wittgenstein's] artistic conscience got in the way, and because he couldn't do it perfectly he couldn't do it at all" (#891, p/9 Oct. 1913); but by trying different methods Russell finally dragged it out of him, as he said, "with pincers." Russell was by now quite over the failure of "Theory of Knowledge," and took pride in making the work of his "ideal pupil" known. "Wittgenstein makes me feel it is worth while I should exist, because no one else could understand him or make the world understand him," he wrote in the letter just cited. Bradley's *Essays in Truth and Reality* appeared in January 1914, and it contained a criticism of Russell's theory of judgment as published in *The Problems of Philosophy* and elsewhere. Russell wrote to Bradley: "Chiefly through the work of an Austrian pupil of mine, I seem now to see answers about unities; but the subject is so difficult and fundamental that I still hesitate."[68] (The term "unities" appears to be synonymous with "complexes" – in this context, "judgments," as the mind was thought to unify the constituents of judgment into a judgment.) The reason we have "Notes on Logic" in the form in which it was published in the *Notebooks* is that Russell wanted to use it, as he said, "for lecturing on logic at Harvard" (#997, p/28 Feb. 1914). Still unable, presumably, to accept Wittgenstein's style of exposition, Russell translated and classified the remarks Wittgenstein had given him. At Harvard Russell was recollected by one observer to have been "enthusiastic" about Wittgenstein, passing around "samples from his papers"[69] and, in the words of a second observer, "telling his class about Wittgenstein's genius, and his original ideas."[70] For the next ten years Russell continued the practice of referring, whenever appropriate, to Wittgenstein's unpublished work and, after it was published, to the *Tractatus*.

There is a final episode in the relationship of the early Wittgenstein and the middle Russell – an episode I wish we knew more about. At the beginning of 1914 Wittgenstein wrote Russell at least three letters. The first is full of the usual sort of introspective news and moral advice Russell was accustomed to from that source. The second extant letter refers to a quarrel they had presumably just had. Upon receiving the letter Russell informed Lady Ottoline of Wittgenstein's declaration that he and I are so dissimilar that it is useless to attempt friendship, and he will never write to me or see me again. I dare say his mood will change after a while. I find I don't care on his account, but only for the sake of logic. And yet I believe I do really care too much to look at it. It is my fault – I have been too sharp with him.

(#990, p/19 Feb. 1914)

In the third extant letter Wittgenstein's mood did change. He agreed that they might resume discussing their work, but they must never talk about anything involving their value judgments. That was because neither could ever be honest about his value judgments without hurting the other. There must be a letter missing between the first and second extant letters, and I do not wish to guess at what brought on the crisis, or why Russell might have been "too sharp" with him. The crisis is extraordinary, if we consider it without the benefit of hindsight knowledge of Wittgenstein's character. It is evident that for two full years Russell and Wittgenstein enjoyed a relationship that was extremely fruitful for their shared interests, and it is also evident that there was not only great respect but great affection on both sides. And now Wittgenstein wished to end it because it rankled him that he and Russell could not be perfectly open with one another and did not share the same values on all important questions. With hindsight, however, the break is not surprising and indeed seems inevitable.

The early relationship was terminated by the First World War. Russell remained dedicated to getting Wittgenstein's work published, but their relationship was never again a fruitful one. The early relationship saw Wittgenstein learn all that Russell had to teach him in logic and in much of philosophy, and Russell not only kept him fairly stable but encouraged him to communicate his work. It appears that a study of the "Theory of Knowledge" manuscript would show the *Tractatus* to be far more directed against Russell's philosophy than has been supposed.[71] Russell learned – at the peak of his accomplishments in logic – that he must have even higher standards, and that much of what he had derived as philosophically important from mathematical logic was questionable. In particular, the concept of logical form, on which he had worked for many years, turned out to be a very elusive concept indeed. He also found that the work he had set out to do in theory of knowledge was impossible for him for years to come.

In the conflict of these two lives there is much high feeling, mystery and drama. There is much good philosophy. And there are many problems for the philosophical historian and biographer to solve. At one time Wittgenstein gave Russell the lives of several great composers to read, and Russell read them. Wittgenstein was pleased, for, he said, "These are the actual sons of God."[72] It has been a privilege to indulge with you my fascination with the lives and thoughts of two more actual sons of God.

Notes

* I am indebted in this essay in various ways to Michael Radner, Evan Simpson, Irving Copi, Albert Shalom (for inviting me to read a draft to his *Tractatus* seminar at McMaster), Stefan Andersson, Nicholas Griffin (for discussions based on his paper, "Russell's Multiple Relation Theory of Judgment"), Elizabeth Ramsden Eames, and John G. Slater. Quotations from unpublished letters and manuscripts by Bertrand Russell are © Res-Lib Ltd., 1981, and are included with the permission of McMaster University and also (in the case of his letters to Lady Ottoline Morrell) the Humanities Research Center, the University of Texas at Austin, and (in the case of manuscripts) the Bertrand Russell Estate. References to Russell's letters to Lady Ottoline are given in the text in the form of a number followed by a date; "p/" before the date stands for "postmarked."

1 D. F. Pears, "Russell's Life" [review of R. W. Clark, *The Life of Bertrand Russell*], *New Review*, 2 (Dec. 1975), 63–6 (at 65). What Pears actually says is: "the work of a philosopher is too much part of his life to be included in his biography like a remote and unimportant country shown in an inset in a map."

2 *My Philosophical Development* (London: Allen & Unwin, 1959), p. 217.

3 *My Own Philosophy* (Hamilton, Ont.: McMaster University Library Press, 1972), p. 4. Written in 1946. The next year Russell instructed his publisher to alter a statement in the "Introduction to the Second Edition" of *The Principles of Mathematics*, p. ix, line 9. The statement had read: "In order that a proposition may belong to mathematics it must have a further property: according to Wittgenstein it must be 'tautological,' and according to Carnap it must be 'analytic.'" Russell instructed his publisher to alter "Wittgenstein" to "some" (letter to Sir Stanley Unwin, 17 July 1947).

4 *My Philosophical Development*, p. 112.

5 *Autobiography*, II (London: Allen & Unwin, 1968), 100–1.

6 Ibid., 199–200.

7 In L. Wittgenstein, *Letters to Russell, Keynes and Moore*, ed. G. H. von Wright (Oxford: Blackwell, 1974). Wittgenstein did attend the paper, and later wrote on its subject. See his "Cause and Effect: Intuitive Awareness," ed. Rush Rhees and trans. Peter Winch, *Philosophia*, 6 (1976), 391–408 (preceded by the German text).

8 M. O'C. Drury, *The Danger of Words* (London: Routledge & Kegan Paul, 1973), p. xiii.

9 *Letters to Russell, Keynes and Moore*, p. 186.

10 Norman Malcolm, *Ludwig Wittgenstein: A Memoir*, 2nd edn (London: Oxford University Press, 1966), p. 68.

11 See Ronald W. Clark, *The Life of Bertrand Russell* (London: Cape/Weidenfeld & Nicolson, 1975), p. 494, and Karl Popper, "Autobiography," *The Philosophy of Karl Popper*, ed. P. A. Schilpp (La Salle, Ill.: Open Court, 1974), I, 97–8. Peter Geach and Casimer Lewy were at the meeting and deny the incident happened.

12 *Autobiography*, II, 101; "My First Fifty Years," typescript, Bertrand Russell Archives, p. 143, and "printer's copy" (which was withdrawn), p. 502.

13 See B. F. McGuinness, "Bertrand Russell and Ludwig Wittgenstein's 'Notes on Logic,'" *Revue Internationale de Philosophie*, 26 (1972), 444–60.

14 Reprinted in Eric Homberger *et al.*, eds., *The Cambridge Mind* (London: Cape, 1970).

15 Max Black, *Mind*, 73 (1964), 134.

16 See Wittgenstein's letter to Russell of 22 July 1913 (*Letters to Russell, Keynes and Moore*, p. 24).

17 According to von Wright's "Biographical Sketch," in Malcolm, p. 5.

18 "Ludwig Wittgenstein," *Mind*, 60 (1951), 297. Cf. *Autobiography*, II, 98; *Portraits from Memory, and Other Essays* (London: Allen & Unwin, 1956), p. 23.

19 *Mind*, 60 (1951), p. 298.

20 Michael Dummett, *Frege: Philosophy of Language* (London: Duckworth, 1973), p. 662.

21 Jourdain noted in his correspondence book on 20 April 1909 that Russell had "said that the views I gave in reply to Wittgenstein (who had 'solved' Russell's contradiction) agree with his own" (p. 205). Original at Mittag-Leffler Institut, Djursholm, Sweden. I. Grattan-Guinness drew my attention to this. See his *Dear Russell – Dear Jourdain: A Commentary on Russell's Logic, Based on His Correspondence with Philip Jourdain* (London: Duckworth, 1977 [i.e. 1978]), pp. 114–15.

22 *Mind*, 60 (1951), 297. Russell here restated the theory as "that all existential statements are meaningless."

23 *Autobiography*, II, 99.

24 *Mind*, 60 (1951), 298.

25 *The Early Memoirs of Lady Ottoline Morrell*, ed. R. Gathorne-Hardy (London: Faber & Faber, 1963), p. 102. For Ritchie, see David G. Ritchie, *Philosophical Studies*, ed. with a memoir by Robert Latta (London: Macmillan, 1905).

26 In his dissertation, "Types, Categories, and Significance" (unpubl. Ph.D. dissertation, McMaster University, 1979), Appendix A.

27 See Allan Janik and Stephen Toulmin, *Wittgenstein's Vienna* (New York: Simon & Schuster, 1973), pp. 93, 204–5.

28 *Letters to Russell, Keynes and Moore*, p. 53. My quotation contains a correction of the original translation. The correction is the addition of the phrase "and acts" and is due to David Bell in his review of the *Letters* in *Russell: The Journal of the Bertrand Russell Archives*, no. 15 (Autumn 1974), 26–8.

29 Read to The Heretics at Cambridge on 11 March 1912; *Monist*, 22 (July 1912), 321–47.

30 See John King-Farlow, "Self-Enlargement and Union: Neglected Passages of Russell and Famous Ones of Proust," *Theoria to Theory*, II (1977), 105–15.

31 "The Essence of Religion," in R. E. Egner and L. E. Denonn, eds., *The Basic Writings of Bertrand Russell* (London: Allen & Unwin, 1961), p. 568. For a discussion – especially of the Platonistic elements – see Ronald Jager, "Russell and Religion," in J. E. Thomas and K. Blackwell, eds., *Russell in Review* (Toronto: Samuel Stevens Hakkert, 1976).

32 For a discussion of this point a couple of years later in Wittgenstein's development, see McGuinness, "The *Grundgedanke* of the *Tractatus*," in Godfrey Vesey, ed., *Understanding Wittgenstein* (London: Macmillan, 1974), p. 56.

33 See M. Teresa Iglesias, "Russell's Introduction to Wittgenstein's *Tractatus*," *Russell*, nos 25–8 (1977), 21–38 (esp. 29, 38).

34 Quoted by von Hayek, p. 18.

35 *The Cambridge Mind*, p. 128.

36 Quoted by von Hayek, pp. 16–17.

37 "Matter" (1913), unpublished manuscript, Russell Archives, p. 9.

38 A. Lawrence Lowell to Russell, 6 June 1913.

39 By Elizabeth Ramsden Eames and myself, "Russell's Unpublished Book on Theory of Knowledge," *Russell*, no. 19 (Autumn 1975), 3–14, 18, and in her Introduction to *Theory of Knowledge: the 1913 Manuscript, The Collected Papers of Bertrand Russell*, vol. VII (London: Allen & Unwin, 1984).

40 Blackwell and Eames, p. 4.

41 For a revision of Russell's account of how he wrote this book, see my "Our Knowledge of *Our Knowledge,*" *Russell,* no. 12 (Winter 1973–4), 11–13.

42 *Letters to Russell, Keynes and Moore,* p. 24.

43 See the long letter quoted by Clark, pp. 209–10 (#850, p/19 Aug. 1913).

44 Frege to Russell, 22 June 1902, and Russell to Jean van Heijenoort, 23 November 1962, in van Heijenoort, ed., *From Frege to Gödel* (Cambridge, Mass.: Harvard University Press, 1967), p. 127.

45 *Autobiography,* II, 57 (dated only [1916]).

46 Russell took steps to publish the six chapters within three weeks of putting "Theory of Knowledge" aside. See Blackwell and Eames, pp. 11–12.

47 *The Problems of Philosophy* (London: Williams & Norgate [1912]), ch. 9.

48 Ibid., ch. 5, "Knowledge by Acquaintance and Knowledge by Description." I owe this suggestion to John G. Slater.

49 *Letters to Russell, Keynes and Moore,* p. 23.

50 McGuinness, "The *Grundgedanke* of the *Tractatus,*" pp. 50–1.

51 Pears, "Russell's Life" p. 65.

52 "Theory of Knowledge," unpublished manuscript, Russell Archives, p. 186.

53 *Revue de Métaphysique et de Morale,* 19 (May 1911), 281–91; trans. into English by P. E. B. Jourdain, *Monist* 23 (Oct. 1913), 481–93; reprinted (and mistitled) in Russell, *Essays in Analysis,* ed. Douglas Lackey (London: Allen & Unwin, 1973).

54 *Our Knowledge of the External World* (London and Chicago: Open Court, 1914), p. 208.

55 "Atomic Propositional Thought," n.d. file 210.06556–F1.

56 Irving Copi, *Journal of Philosophy,* 60 (1963), 766.

57 Peter Geach, *Mental Acts* (London: Routledge & Kegan Paul [1957]), p. 49.

58 "The Philosophy of Logical Atomism," in R. C. Marsh, ed., *Logic and Knowledge* (London: Allen & Unwin, 1956), p. 226.

59 "Definitions and Methodological Principles in Theory of Knowledge," *Monist,* 24 (Oct. 1914), 584.

60 "Notes on Logic," earlier version, Russell Archives, Summary, p. 2. The earlier version has now replaced the later version in Wittgenstein's *Notebooks 1914–1916,* 2nd edn, edited by G. E. M. Anscombe and G. H. von Wright (Oxford: Blackwell, 1979).

61 Black, *A Companion to Wittgenstein's Tractatus* (Ithaca: Cornell University Press, 1964), p. 301.

62 Pears, *Bertrand Russell and the British Tradition in Philosophy,* 2nd edn (London: Collins/Fontana, 1972), p. 217.

63 See Section III of "On the Nature of Truth," *Proceedings of the Aristotelian Society,* n.s. 7 (1907), 44–9. This section was not included when the other sections were reprinted as "The Monistic Theory of Truth" in *Philosophical Essays* (1910).

64 "On the Nature of Truth and Falsehood," *Philosophical Essays* (London: Longmans, Green, 1910), p. 173; "Theory of Knowledge," MS, p. 200.

65 In addition to those already mentioned, there are the following published commentaries on Wittgenstein's criticism of Russell's theory of judgment: G. E. M. Anscombe, *An Introduction to Wittgenstein's Tractatus,* 3rd edn (London: Hutchinson, 1967), pp. 45–6; J. Griffin, *Wittgenstein's Logical Atomism* (Oxford: Blackwell, 1964), pp. 113–14; P. M. S. Hacker, *Insight and Illusion: Wittgenstein on Philosophy and the Metaphysics of Experience* (Oxford: Clarendon Press, 1972), pp. 60–1; A. J. P. Kenny, *Wittgenstein* (London: Allen Lane The Penguin Press, 1973), p. 101; Guy Stock, "Wittgenstein on Russell's

Theory of Judgment," in Vesey, ed., *Understanding Wittgenstein*, pp. 62–75. Pears has the benefit of using the manuscript of "Theory of Knowledge" in "The Relation between Wittgenstein's Picture Theory of Propositions and Russell's Theories of Judgment," *Philosophical Review*, 86 (April 1977), 177–96, and in "Wittgenstein's Picture Theory and Russell's *Theory of Knowledge*," in *Wittgenstein and the Vienna Circle and Critical Rationalism: Proceedings of the Third International Wittgenstein Symposium*, ed. H. Berghel, A. Hübner and E. Köhler (Vienna: Hölder–Pichler–Tempsky, 1979), pp. 101–7. See also the bibliography in Nicholas Griffin's unpublished paper, "Russell's Multiple Relation Theory of Judgment," and his "Russell on the Nature of Logic," *Synthese*, 45 (September 1980), 117–88 (esp. 170–80).

66 Appendix II, *Notebooks, 1914–1916*, p. 118. (Pointed out by Hacker, p. 61n.)

67 It should be noted that he did so before receiving the typescript of the *Tractatus* (in June or July 1919). Russell abandoned the subject in "On Propositions: What They Are and How They Mean" (*Aristotelian Society Supp.*, Vol. 2 [1919], 1–43), and he had finished a first draft of this paper by early March 1919 (see Russell to Constance Malleson, 4 March 1919). The paper was not, however, delivered until 11 July 1919.

68 F. H. Bradley, "A Discussion of Some Problems in Connexion with Mr Russell's Doctrine," *Essays in Truth and Reality* (Oxford: Clarendon Press, 1914), pp. 293–309. Russell to Bradley, 30 Jan. 1914, Merton College Library, Oxford (copy at McMaster).

69 Harry T. Costello, "Logic in 1914 and Now," *Journal of Philosophy*, 54 (25 April 1957), 246.

70 Victor F. Lenzen, "Bertrand Russell at Harvard, 1914," *Russell*, no. 3 (Autumn 1971), 5.

71 Even the *Tractatus*'s mysticism may be related to Russell's thinking on the subject. For an examination of the affinities, see B. F. McGuinness, "The Mysticism of the *Tractatus*," *Philosophical Review*, 75 (1966), 305–28.

72 Wittgenstein to Russell, 16 Aug. 1912 (*Letters to Russell, Keynes and Moore*, p. 15).

7

Russell's Dismissal from Trinity

A Study in High Table Politics

Paul Delany

Russell's dismissal from Trinity College in 1916 has now passed into legend as one of the most notorious infringements of academic freedom since Socrates was given hemlock. Our knowledge of this episode has come largely from one source, G. H. Hardy's *Bertrand Russell and Trinity: a College Controversy of the Last War.*[1] Recently, the Bertrand Russell Archives acquired new evidence on the struggle behind the scenes at Trinity over Russell's dismissal.[2] This material does not challenge the fundamentals of Hardy's narrative, but it makes possible a less reticent account of the affair with much new information about two key participants: Hardy himself and A. N. Whitehead.

To read *Bertrand Russell and Trinity* well, one must know how to read between the lines. Hardy was Russell's most active and dedicated supporter in 1916, but not at all his most visible one. In 1919 he again promoted Russell's reinstatement, and in 1941, when he wrote his pamphlet, he was organizing a third campaign to get Russell back. Each time, Hardy knew that the best way to succeed was to keep several arm's lengths between himself and his candidate. In writing about the events of 1916–19 he preserved a scrupulously cool tone, he defined the struggle as primarily one between youth and age, and he said practically nothing about Russell's current battles. Russell had been dismissed from the City College of New York in 1940 for 'immorality', before he ever met a class. He then accepted a lecturing position from the eccentric Albert Barnes, but by early 1941 he had quarrelled with his employer and was homesick for England. Hardy's pamphlet was part of a broad campaign of wirepulling that culminated in the offer to Russell of a Trinity Fellowship in the autumn of 1943. Russell came back – to the rooms previously occupied by Newton – and remained a Fellow of Trinity for the rest of his life. He had gone there to sit a scholarship examination in December 1889, so his connection with Trinity lasted eighty years. Like many of his relationships, this one fluctuated between times of passionate devotion and times when both parties were thoroughly exasperated with each other. But 1916 was clearly the stormiest year of all.

I

On 5 June 1916 Russell was convicted for writing a pamphlet 'likely to prejudice the recruiting and discipline of his Majesty's forces', and sentenced to a fine of £100 plus £10 costs. An appeal against the conviction failed on 29 June. The Council of Trinity, the governing board of the College, were required by the statutes to meet if a Fellow was convicted 'of a crime of whatever nature or description'. On Tuesday 11 July they met to decide what to do about Russell. The Council were empowered (but not obliged) to expel delinquent Fellows by a vote of seven members, of whom the Master had to be one, out of thirteen. The eleven who attended voted unanimously to remove Russell from his lectureship. A substantial minority wanted even stronger action, presumably the formal removal of Russell's name from the College books.[3]

The Master was H. Montagu Butler: eighty-three years old, former Dean of Gloucester, former Chairman of the Church of England Purity Society, father of three sons in the army, and an Apostle. 'I never discharged a more painful public duty', he would write, 'than in taking action against B. Russell, and I was never more clear as to the necessity in the interests of the College.'[4] Butler had been Senior Classic at Trinity in 1855, and Headmaster of Harrow at the age of twenty-six. He was appointed Master of Trinity in 1886 by the Prime Minister, Lord Salisbury, the Mastership being in the gift of the Crown. The revised statutes of 1882 had deleted the requirement that the Master be in Orders of the Church of England, but Salisbury chose not to break precedent by appointing a layman. There was some dislike of the appointment, partly because Butler was an outsider (many Fellows would have preferred Henry Sidgwick), and partly because he was a cleric.

Although two clerical Fellows (F. R. Tennant and F. A. Simpson) supported Russell, there can be little doubt that the rest of the clerical party – six or seven Fellows, of whom two were on the Council – disliked Russell and were glad to get rid of him.[5] The Master was a 'muscular Christian' of the classic Victorian type: a fervent Imperialist, an opponent of Home Rule, and a firm supporter of the war. He had arranged for troops to be billeted in the College, for Nevile's Court to be made into a hospital, and for officers to dine in Hall – where champagne would be served when one of them left for the front. Butler also preached regularly to the troops, with emphasis on the moral temptations that awaited them in France.

Butler had not been a dominant Master – in fact, he was famous for sleeping through meetings – and before 1914 the younger Fellows seem to have treated him with amused tolerance. But when the war began Russell came to feel that Butler and a cabal of his jingoistic supporters had desecrated the College. Russell's complaints to Lady Ottoline Morrell suggest that he had not hesitated to let his enemies know what he thought of them:

> The melancholy of this place now-a-days is beyond endurance – the Colleges are dead, except for a few Indians and a few pale pacifists and bloodthirsty old men hobbling along victorious in the absence of youth. Soldiers are billeted in the courts and drill on the grass; bellicose parsons preach to them in stentorian tones from the steps of the Hall . . . . No one thinks about learning or feels it of any importance . . . I am *intensely* disliked by the older dons, and still more by their wives, who think I should not mind if they were raped. It is the young who like me.[6]

Clearly, Russell was a thorn in the side of the ruling group at Trinity. But when the Council acted against him he must also have taken it as a bitterly personal rejection, for among the eleven who voted him out there were five Apostles: the Master, Henry Jackson, Rev. V. H. Stanton, J. D. Duff and J. McT. E. McTaggart. All were older than Russell, and elected at a time when the Society's prevailing tone had been more conventional. Still, to be 'hounded out of Trinity' (in D. H. Lawrence's phrase) by so many of his brother Apostles must have been a final turn of the knife for Russell. Outside the Council three other Fellows were Apostles: James Ward, G. H. Hardy and A. N. Whitehead. The first two were staunch supporters of Russell, but Whitehead, as we shall see, effectively sided with the Council; so that the final roster was two loyal Apostles and six who favoured his dismissal.

This split within the Society was invisible to outsiders, since Apostles were sworn to keep the very existence of their group secret.[7] They were a closed elite whose chief concern – effectively its only concern – was the personal relations between its members. Nor would it be far off the mark to describe the Fellows of Trinity in similar terms. From the beginning Russell's fate was largely determined by how much the Fellows liked or disliked him as a person, and they were free to act on their feelings because both sides agreed to fight out the affair behind the walls of the College. When Russell was denied his appointment to CCNY the case was taken up by the courts, the AAUP, the Mayor of New York, and many other parties. But in 1916 almost everyone took it for granted that all jurisdiction in the affair lay with the Council of Trinity. Russell himself would have relished a public battle over the issue of academic freedom; but his supporters judged that such a fight would defeat their principal aim, which was to get Russell back. In the long run, what counted for them was 'the interest of the College'. The reputation of Trinity as a seat of learning had been wounded, and the only thing that could heal it was Russell's return. It was not a question of the rights of the faculty *vis-à-vis* the administration, since Trinity, like the rest of the Oxford and Cambridge colleges, considered itself to be a self-governing body of Fellows. The Russell dismissal was a family quarrel and neither side was eager to have neighbours peering over the fence.

None the less, several of the younger Fellows, such as Hardy, J. E. Littlewood and Donald Robertson, were 'incoherent with fury' over the ejection of Russell, and eager to do something about it.[8] Hardy had not believed that the Council would go so far as to dismiss Russell, but he had already decided on the right response if they did: a vote of censure by the Fellows, as soon as the war was over, leading to the Council's resignation. When the axe fell, he proposed this strategy to Russell. The decision could not be reversed until after the war, but there should be an immediate 'memorial' – a manifesto putting the Council on notice that they were going to be called to account when the time was ripe.[9]

Hardy felt the strongest personal loyalty to Russell, and he was the only one of the 'angry young Fellows' who was regularly present at Trinity. Soon after the war began, Russell had already marked him down as a key ally:

> he is prepared to give all his leisure to work for peace. And as almost all his pupils here have gone to the front he has a great deal of leisure. . . . He has absolutely first-rate ability, not only as a mathematician, but as an organizer, intriguer, and wire-puller. He loves hidden power, and suffers from his life not being sufficiently exciting and dangerous. If the Government tried threatening him with the police, his eye would gleam and he would feel he was getting some fun at last. I have always thought him utterly heartless, but I think perhaps I was wrong.[10]

Russell's flagrant opposition to the war set off a struggle within Trinity that Hardy was still waging a quarter of a century later with his pamphlet about the events of 1914–19. When the Council acted against Russell in July 1916 Hardy knew that he had no chance of rallying the moderate Fellows against the dismissal, since he wore mufti and was known as a prominent supporter of the Union of Democratic Control.[11] He needed a 'heavyweight' to spearhead the protest, and his first choice was Russell's distinguished collaborator on *Principia Mathematica*. Although Whitehead had left Cambridge in 1910 and was teaching at the University of London, he was still a Fellow of Trinity and a formidable committee-man.[12]

> assuming Whitehead to be sound, he ought to take the lead and leave the pacificist gang to do the clerical work. And I shd be guided by him. For my own part I shd be in favour of giving the widest publicity to the whole business.

> How much it matters to you I don't know and you may well be sick of
> the College. But even if you welcomed it, the College cannot allow Parry
> and Co to make it publicly obscene in this sort of way. As for that ghastly
> shit McTaggart, he shd be cursed and Robeyised – but I doubt if he'd feel
> even that now.[13]

Henry John Roby had been elected an Apostle in 1855; he resigned in the
same year and was ritually cursed for his defection. All five Apostles on the
Council could be condemned for betraying their 'brother', but McTaggart
was the closest to Russell in age and had served, for a while, as his
philosophical mentor.

If McTaggart was the Society's Cassius, Hardy soon found that Whitehead was warming up for the role of Brutus:

> I saw Whitehead: he is no good. He was exceedingly long-winded and
> apologetic: he is going to circulate his own views at length. I'm not
> blaming him – his views are what they are, just like yours, and it's an
> awkward pinch for him and we parted quite good friends. He quite
> understood that he would be impossible as captain.[14]

Russell had flatly disagreed with both the Whiteheads over the war from
the beginning, but for two years now they had tried to keep their friendship going on a strained, one might even say schizophrenic basis. The
Whiteheads kept sending Russell messages of concern and affection, such
as one from Alfred wishing him 'Good luck . . . in every way' on the eve of
his trial.[15] Yet neither of the two men could refrain from scratching on old
wounds. When Russell asked Whitehead to help him protest against the
treatment of conscientious objectors, he got a reply in the style of Horatio
Bottomley: 'I am not greatly impressed by men who ask me to be shocked
that they are going to prison, while ten thousand men are daily being
carried to field hospitals, women and children have been raped and mutil-
ated, and whole populations are living in agony. Frankly, the outcry is
contemptible.'[16] Throughout the Russell affair, the Whiteheads were driven
half frantic by concern for their sons. The elder, North, had already
enlisted at the time of Russell's dismissal; the younger, Eric, was seventeen
and would be taken in a year.

It was an explosive situation, and neither Russell nor Whitehead was
fully conscious of the complex feelings both of them had about the war.[17]
The closeness of their friendship somehow drove them on to repeat their
verbal stabs. So, by a kind of fatal necessity, Russell went as soon as he
could to seek help from the Whiteheads over his dismissal. Mrs Whitehead
was 'furious with Trinity', he reported to Ottoline; 'he began by being, but
went down and talked the matter over and came to the conclusion that the
Council were not to blame'.[18] Whitehead had jumped in with both feet; by

the time Russell came to see him, on 14 July, he had already gone up to Cambridge to confer with the Council and nearly completed an eight-page pamphlet giving a formal statement of his views.[19]

The dismissal seems to have strained Whitehead's nerves to the breaking-point, for his pamphlet is painfully incoherent and uncertain. He points out that a Conservative peer (Lord Parmoor) and the Archbishop of Canterbury have publicly corroborated Russell's two main points: that conscientious objectors have been mistreated in military prison, and that they should remain under civil jurisdiction even after being sentenced. So why should Russell be punished for saying the same things as Lord Parmoor and the Archbishop?

> For the moment the equities of individual cases are subordinate to the safety of the State and of the cause for which our men are dying. Our statesmen have characterised it as the cause of freedom, of justice, and of civilization; and that is the thought which sustains us as in our minds we follow the fate of our boys.
>
> I make no criticism on the College Council for their action. Their minute, removing Mr. Russell from his lectureship, is on the face of it a support of the State in its decision as to the civil discipline necessary in the immediate present (p. 7).

Whitehead's reasoning seems to have been as follows: Lord Parmoor and the Archbishop had said the same things, but they had not said them 'heedlessly', as Russell had. When people set out to stir up trouble in time of war, the State could repress them in the name of collective self-preservation. And if the State had acted rightly, then the Council of Trinity could not be blamed for backing it up.

At the same time, Whitehead felt, the Council should preserve 'a just appreciation . . . of the future obligations of the College' (*ibid.*). He said nothing more definite about the Council's duties before bringing his pamphlet to an obscurely portentous conclusion: 'The existing Master and Fellows of Trinity have in their hands issues, which for succeeding generations, greedy of knowledge of these great times, will affect the honour of England, the good faith of its professions of motive, and the fame of its Seats of Learning' (p. 8). What this meant was that the Council was right to dismiss Russell, but should reinstate him after the war. If they refused to do so, they would show that they had acted more from malice than from public-spiritedness, and would then go down in history as wrong.[20]

Whitehead wanted to show formal loyalty to Russell, as his old friend and intellectual collaborator, but his basic allegiance was to the Council. Over the years, Russell's sharp tongue in debate and his general bumptiousness had left many scars. Of the three major philosophers who were his contemporaries in the Society, McTaggart was his avowed enemy, Whitehead was disaffected and G. E. Moore, for all his dislike of the jingoes, would do nothing to help Russell in his troubles with Trinity.[21]

II

With Whitehead out of the picture, Hardy then wrote to F. M. Cornford asking him to be the official sponsor of the protest. It was essential, he told Cornford, that the campaign be led by Fellows who had taken commissions, since 'those of us who are not respectable should make use of the respectability of those who are'.[22] But Hardy was constantly active behind the scenes, and in his pamphlet of 1942 he was simply not telling the truth when he claimed that he 'did not take any part in the actual quarrel, except to sign the protest at the time'.[23]

Why did Hardy pick Cornford as Russell's standard-bearer? Although he was over forty and had a child, Cornford had been an early volunteer. In 1916 he was serving as a rifle instructor, but he still had a home in Cambridge and kept up his College ties. He had supported Hardy in November 1915 when the Council banned a meeting of the Union of Democratic Control that had been announced for Littlewood's rooms in Trinity. After the dismissal, Cornford told Russell that 'the Council has disgraced us', and that the older dons were 'in various stages of insanity'.[24] He could be relied on to take a firm moral stand, but in a way that would not offend his more warlike colleagues. He had published a widely admired book on Thucydides, and had married into the Cambridge 'aristocracy': his wife, Frances, was the daughter of Francis Darwin (a Fellow of Christ's) and the granddaughter of Charles Darwin.

For all his anger, Hardy was keeping his eye on the long-term goal of getting Russell reinstated as a member in good standing of the College; and the banning of the UDC meeting had shown that in any immediate showdown over Russell's dismissal he was bound to lose. The issue needed to be kept alive, and quietly nourished. Cornford seemed the ideal agent for such delicate work, for in 1908 he had published a satirical pamphlet on academic politics that had become an instant classic: *Microcosmographia Academica: Being a Guide for the Young Academic Politician*.[25] However, Cornford's treatise was a spoof on the entrenched inertia of academe – the rule that 'nothing is ever done until every one is convinced that it ought to be done, and has been convinced for so long that it is now time to do something else'.[26] The Russell case was a notable exception to this rule. An inner group of academics, whose average age was nearly sixty, had swiftly and boldly removed an enemy from the College. Faced with a *fait accompli* by the 'old men in a hurry' of the Council, Cornford and his allies were knocked off balance. He agreed that there should be a protest; but it was now the Long Vacation, when little could be done at Cambridge, and nothing could be done quickly. He sent out a round of letters to possible supporters, trying to muster a counter-offensive for the autumn.

One person capable of decisive reaction was Russell himself; but he too vacillated. Much as he despised the Council's decision, he also found it a relief, and felt little urgency about getting it reversed. Since his intense and short-lived friendship with D. H. Lawrence in 1915 he had been feeling emotionally stifled by Cambridge, and attracted by Lawrence's urging that he should 'retire out of the herd and then fire bombs into it'.[27] In July 1916 he was exhilarated by the rousing welcome given him by the miners of South Wales, on his speaking-tour for the No-Conscription Fellowship. He told Ottoline that he wanted to become a completely different kind of teacher:

Probably *for me* it is a good thing, though it is sad that Trinity should do it. It decides the issue. I will make myself a teacher of all the working-men who are hungry for intellectual food – there are many throughout the country – I am always coming across them. I am amazed at the number of them at my meetings who have read my *Problems of Philosophy*. I foresee a great and splendid life in that sort of thing – dealing with political ideas, but keeping out of actual politics. And I want to enlist all the teachers and men of education who will have been turned out for being C.O.s. There are numbers of them. Think of building up a new free education not under the State! There are infinite possibilities – finance is the only difficulty, but not an insuperable one. I could give heart and brain and life to that. . . . I am delighted at the way the question of Cambridge has been solved. I hope the Council will be made to feel that they have acted unworthily. I feel quite impersonal about it, as I am glad to have my own course decided for me. Every bit of persecution is useful – it makes people see that no good comes out of war.[28]

The court order to sell Russell's goods to pay the £110 fine was to be carried out on 26 July. Philip Morrell generously offered to raise enough money from supporters to pay £125 for the first item auctioned and thus discharge the fine. But Russell was eager to make a clean break by clearing out all his household goods:

I have too many possessions, and I shall be glad to be rid of some – I hated the thought of my flat [in London] being sold up, but I don't mind about Trinity at all. . . . I think perhaps it would be best that my Cambridge furniture should actually be sold. . . . I shall never go back to Trinity, so it doesn't matter offending them past forgiveness.[29]

After the first lot, Russell withdrew his library from the auction; then everything else in his rooms was sold off for thirty pounds, from rugs to teacups.[30] A bare fortnight after his dismissal he had evacuated his base at Cambridge and plunged back into his hectic life in London. Apart from his work for the No-Conscription Fellowship, he was running two major love-affairs – with Ottoline and with Vivienne Eliot – and would soon add a third, with Lady Constance Malleson.[31] Why should he haunt Trinity in some faint hope of being reinstated when he would have wanted, in any case, to do a minimum of teaching until the end of the war? The place had no appeal for him any more, what with the bloodthirsty old dons, the five Apostles who had voted to dismiss him, and for good measure the failure of Whitehead to lift more than a finger to help.

III

Cornford went softly with Russell's defence. By temperament he preferred the path of conciliation and gentle pressure (the opposite of the man he represented). His advisers on the form of a protest were Hardy, Ward, Simpson, and Whitehead; this informal steering committee thus had two members who favoured strong action – Hardy and Ward – and three 'minimalists'. Indeed, Whitehead's support was so minimal as to be almost invisible:

> At present I feel that we should recognize the supreme crisis in the State as giving honest and substantial grounds for the Council's action. But the whole circumstances are such that if they do not rectify the matter after the war, a scandalous injustice will have been perpetrated – much to our discredit. My hope is that they, of their own motion, will so act – especially if the generality of the fellows, in ways which seem to them appropriate, let the Council know that this is their expectation.
>
> If the Council will act, I hope that there will be no College Meeting to deal with the question. We can discuss till doomsday how big the greatest crisis in the world's history is, and what is the greatest amount of national discipline which authorities are justified in imposing. The trouble is that our pacifists refuse to recognize any crisis except an inexplicable desire on the part of men of all nations to kill each other.
>
> Of course, if the Council will not act, we must have a meeting and express our minds as to the injustic perpetrated, and the discredit which they will have brought on us. . . . But this is after the war, and I have great hopes of the Council.[32]

The hard-core protesters like Hardy felt mistrust and even contempt for Whitehead, but continued to court him because his prestige made him an essential name to have on their side. The 'moderates', on the other hand, accepted Simpson's strategy: to avoid any 'definite alignment of forces', because if the 'neutrals' were not prodded too hard now they would come down on the right side once the war was over. Simpson himself almost threw in his hand at the start when Russell, in a calculated gesture of contempt, wrote to the Head Porter directing him to take his name off the College books. The protest would now get so few signatures, Simpson thought, that it might be best to abandon it.[33] It is not clear why Russell's gesture should be considered so shocking, given what the College had done to him; but three years later A. E. Housman brought it up when he was sent another petition for Russell's reinstatement: 'what prevents me from signing your letter is Russell's taking his name off the books of the College. After that piece of petulance he ought not even to want to come back.'[34] Cornford persuaded Simpson, at least, to overlook Russell's action, and a petition finally went out early in October 1916.

The protest drafted by Cornford and Simpson could scarcely have been milder:

> The undersigned Fellows of the College, while not proposing to take any action in the matter during the war, desire to place it on record that they are not satisfied with the action of the College in depriving Mr. Russell of his lectureship.

This did nothing more than put the Council on notice that some of the Fellows might, at some future time, do something on Russell's behalf. Several of Russell's supporters were dismayed that the protest was so late and so feeble. One of these was Eric Neville, who had been a student of Russell's in 1910. 'I am sorry', he told Cornford, 'the list is not to be made as public as the action which it condemns; will you gain any signatures by privacy, and even if you do, would not the credit of the College be restored further by a small list published than by a large list seen only by those who could predict its composition?' Neville suggested putting out a 'minority report' that publicly condemned the Council's action as 'petty, impertinent, and unpatriotic'.[35] Probably eight or ten Fellows would have signed such a protest (out of about sixty); but in the end everyone agreed to keep their quarrel within the walls of Trinity.

The person most responsible for keeping the protest private was Hardy. Once Cornford had drafted the memorial, Hardy wrote to Russell about it:

> I wish you would tell me your *considered* view (if you are clear what it is yourself) about Trinity. You see there are two rival opinions. *I* think (with James Ward) that the Council are really malignant and obstinate – that, even after the war, they will be so still: and that the only thing to do is to fight and try to break them. For I imagine it to be certain that you would not come back, at any rate, unless asked to do so by a *repentant* College. And, taking that as so, it seems merely silly to try to avoid a row.

The other view is that, as soon as the war is over, the Council will bow gracefully to opinion in the hope of perpetuating their beneficent rule. This is the Whitehead–Harrison–Simpson line. Cornford, of course, is out of touch with local opinion now, and seems to incline to whichever side has talked to him last. What they are after, naturally, is a rather colourless manifesto to attract doubtful signatures. Of course, to some extent, it is funk, and the hope of not compromising themselves: but not entirely.[36]

Russell's reply did not provide much guidance, except on the issue of whether to have a row:

I agree with your view as to the Council, but I think that after the war it ought to be possible to elect a Council which would take a different view. I see no object whatever in trying to avoid a row. The Whitehead–Harrison–Simpson line does not seem to me any use. I cannot the least tell what I, personally, shall wish to do when the war is over, but I think it unlikely that I can ever again endure the stuffiness of a high table, even if it could endure me, with all the cold draughts that I should let in.[37]

What seems to have finally tipped the balance was Hardy's expectations from the 'service vote'. He was convinced that after the war the Fellows who had done military service (about a third of the College) would gain the moral initiative and could dictate a settlement. In the meantime, however, anyone in uniform would find it extremely awkward to appear as a public supporter of Russell. A year later, the Siegfried Sassoon affair made it clear that pacifists and soldiers simply would not be allowed to act in unison. The best Russell could expect from the average serving officer was summed up in a letter from the trenches by C. N. S. Woolf, Leonard Woolf's younger brother. He would sign the protest, he told Cornford, provided it remained secret and nothing was done about it until after the war. But he was not signing out of any solidarity with the Russell who had been convicted under the Defence of the Realm Act:

I entirely disagree with everything I have heard of Russell's opinions about the war and I entirely disagree with the whole movement he is mixed up with. I think the whole movement very pernicious. In war there are only two things to do – in my opinion – fight or keep quiet: if people want to talk or write or protest, let them do it when the fighting's over.
. . . I'm *not* protesting against any action that may have been taken against Russell except that of the College Council. I object to that because I consider it no business of the Council to punish Russell in this matter. Trinity is a home of learning – nothing else – and we don't show our patriotism by driving out of it a scholar like Russell. If he is a

bad citizen, as I and many of us think, it cannot alter the fact that he is a very great scholar. The State is quite capable of punishing him, if it wants to; Trinity has got to keep learning going till after the war – not an easy job, I should imagine. The State – and rightly I think, will look after Russell's and other people's anti-war views; the College Council, I'm sure, needn't fear these views are going to enter into the next volume of *Principia Mathematica*.[38]

C. E. Stuart and G. B. Tatham, also infantry officers, refused to be drawn in so far. Stuart said he was very sorry for Russell's misfortunes, and admired him more than ever; but he didn't know enough about the affair to condemn the Council. Tatham merely said he was glad to have nothing to do with it all. All three – Woolf, Stuart and Tatham – were killed at the front. Woolf's letter so impressed Cornford that he sent it to R. D. Hicks, one of the elderly jingoes, in the hope of getting him to sign the memorial. Hicks retorted that 'the salutary prejudice called our country' prevented him wanting even to discuss the issues. Russell had been guilty of a long string of offences, and patriots were right to 'fight honestly and stoutly against him'. Russell and Whitehead, he felt, were being disingenuous in trying to crawl under the skirts of the Archbishop of Canterbury. 'Is it honest of such men', Hicks concluded, 'to take advantage for their own ends of a religious sentiment which they really despise? Some will unkindly call it a dirty trick.'[39] E. D. Adrian signed out of admiration for Russell's scholarship, but noted that he would like to kick the bottom of Mr Everett (the pacifist whose treatment had been the original *casus belli*). Another signer, for reasons not recorded, was Captain J. R. M. Butler, the son and future biographer of the Master.

The Cornford correspondence confirms the political truism that people take sides for all kinds of reasons, and that academics can provide even more odd and diverse grounds for belief than the man in the street. But in the end, the decision for the Fellows of Trinity was a simple one: to sign the memorial, or not sign it. Whitehead, perhaps the most self-divided of them all, added to his signature the odd note: 'Unless the Council proposes to offer to Mr. Russell a suitable academic post'. His covering letter to Cornford leaves the issue unclear, but everything else in the correspondence argues that he expected this post to be withheld until *after* the war:

I enclose my signature, with a note appended. Of course, even if the Council act as suggested, they will have been unnecessarily clumsy in their action – first dismissing and then reconstructing a modified post, *e.g.* a research post with occasional lectures. But I should not say (in that case) that I wanted to put my opinion on permanent record. Everyone has had to take action, or make speech, under stress and pressure, and should not be criticized too closely. For example, Bertie has said things

about the young men who went to war which have hurt us bitterly – and
has published them in America – So remembering that where action is
concerned, very little can escape criticism, I am anxious simply for
substantial justice, and the substantial good name of the College as
regards its respect for learning.[40]

Cornford sent the memorial to Council on 17 January 1917, with twenty-
two signatures. A few more might still trickle in; but six months had now
passed since Russell's dismissal, there was no chance of getting a majority
of the Fellows to sign, and even those who had signed were not ready for
further action. The Council received the submission and naturally did
nothing. Probably they assumed that the dissidents, having fired off their
popgun, would sheepishly disperse and be heard from no more. Russell had
sold his furniture and gone, and there was no reason to expect him back.

IV

In January 1917 Whitehead threatened a complete break with Russell, by
refusing further collaboration on philosophical projects, and by challen-
ging him to do something about the deportation of French and Belgian
workers to Germany.[41] Evelyn again tried to heal the breach, telling Russell
that Whitehead was angry because their pacifist friends had neglected her
during her recent illness:

> We are all suffering from conscientious motives, you would be the last to
> deny that our share of it is a very heavy one – the irritation you feel in
> Alfred is not against *you*, he does not like your views, you do not like his,
> the irritation does not spring from the divergence, Alfred is *the* most
> liberal minded person I have ever met. . . . [H]e resents the way in which
> I have been treated at a time of acute suffering, when owing to illness,
> and inability to go out during many months, these same intimate friends
> have been unable to spare an hour to come and cheer my loneliness by
> kind friendship . . . [42]

In March 1918 the Whiteheads' son Eric was killed in action, at the age of
nineteen; a month later, Russell went to jail for his continuing anti-war
activities. Before going, he sent a letter of condolence that softened
Whitehead's heart. He promised to visit Russell in Brixton Prison (which
he did regularly), and ended 'Goodbye, old fellow, and good luck to you
during the next trying few months. Yours affectionately, Alfred.'[43] Russell
had been deeply fond of Eric, and probably assumed that by sharing
Whitehead's grief, and paying the price of his own beliefs, he had done
more than enough to restore the friendship. If so, he was quite wrong.

A few days after the 11 November Armistice, Hardy asked Cornford to lead another assault on the Council:

My own attitude is

(a) the question must and will be raised, so soon as there is a full High Table again

(b) if it can be raised in as conciliatory a way, and by as moderate people as possible (provided always what is proposed is enough to satisfy a man of Russell's eminence and pride) so much the better – people of my way of thinking will not want to wreck things by violence

but (c) if the 'reasonable' people – of whom I regard you as the natural leader – do not, within reasonable time, show definite signs of action, then the unreconcileable element will get out of hand – I mean people like Littlewood, Donald Robertson, Winstanley, and myself: –

and (d) that will mean that the present condition of suspicion and quarrel will be prolonged indefinitely, and a very serious handicap to all efforts of the College to get itself straight again.

It seems to me that what wd not be enough is that the College authorities shd be willing to say 'now it's all over, we forgive you'. Russell is not a schoolboy to shake hands after a flogging. What is wanted is some definite expression of *regret* – nothing unnecessarily violent or provocative, but a clear reversal.

E.g. (I only state this as an illustration) I think everyone would regard as sufficient a motion passed by a College meeting 'that the meeting regrets Mr. R.'s removal from his lectureship in 1916, and requests the Council to take the steps necessary for his reinstatement'.

Something on those lines wd, I should think, command the assent of all signatories of your memorial.[44]

Hardy was proposing that a meeting of the whole College should pass a vote of censure on the Council, at which point those members of Council who had voted to dismiss Russell would have been morally obliged to resign. Before bringing on such a showdown, Cornford consulted Whitehead, probably because he thought him the best 'litmus test' of where opinion in the College was likely to settle. The response showed that Whitehead's position was harder now than it had been in 1916:

The subject of B. R.'s relations to Trinity is difficult and painful. I will express my views to you categorically and without expressions of personal feeling.

(1) The governing factor in the situation is the second offence and conviction, which is ignored both in Hardy's letter and yours. Here B. R. was seriously in the wrong.

(2) Public feeling is strong on this point. The immediate restoration of

B. R. to his position in Trinity, which necessarily recalls influences other than those of the public lecturer on philosophic studies, is impossible, unless we are prepared to ruin the college.

(3) For the immediate future the best prospect is that a lectureship can be provided for him in some other university and College, where his immediate activities would naturally be in connection with his more formal duties of teaching. Steps are being taken in this direction. Perhaps you know about them. Gilbert Murray is the promoter and he could inform you as to their chances of success.

(4) It seems to me to be a plain duty for you to take an early opportunity of talking the matter over with the Master.

(5) As the question of appointments is outside the competence of the College Meeting, it seems that motions commenting on appointments or dismissals, or urging appointments of particular men, should be out of order.

(6) I hope that I have misunderstood paragraph (d) in G. H. H.'s letter. As fellows we are both governors and servants of the college. In our former capacity we must give our opponents credit for a sense of duty, however mistaken, and as servants we must loyally work under the conditions laid down by the constituted authorities. I do not understand the reference to 'suspicion and quarrel'. Such suggestions of consequences can have no place in our determination of college policy. . . .

It is a great thing that the horrors of the last four years are over. But nothing can put back those we have lost, or lighten the pain. . . . [45]

Cornford now faded out of the picture. His wife had suffered a nervous breakdown, and he did not have the stomach for another round of academic guerrilla warfare. But Hardy was nothing if not persistent and kept on lobbying within the College. As the months passed, he came to realize that if he wanted to get Russell back he would have to play a less aggressive hand. By late summer of 1919 another memorial was launched under the sponsorship of H. A. Hollond, offering terms that were scrupulously neutral. If the Council agreed to take Russell back, they would not have to admit any guilt for his dismissal. Some of Russell's supporters considered this a whitewash and refused to sign the memorial. Hardy wrote to him and said that it was 'hardly conceivable' that Whitehead would refuse to sign such a watered-down protest, 'though, after [the] preface to his book, I can believe anything almost of him'.[46]

The book was *An Enquiry Concerning the Principles of Natural Knowledge*, published in September 1919 and dedicated to Eric: 'The music of his life was without discord, perfect in its beauty'. In the Preface Whitehead had acknowledged his indebtedness to Russell, but also to a group of others that included McTaggart; he observed that they were all, 'amid their divergencies of opinion, . . . united in the candid zeal of their quest for truth'. It was a classic proof of Evelyn Whitehead's claim that her husband was the most liberal-minded person she had ever met. Unfortunately, Whitehead's liberalism was of a kind that allowed him to forget that McTaggart had ruthlessly denied Russell the opportunity to seek truth within the precincts of Trinity College. Nor did Whitehead's principles allow him to sign Hollond's request that the Council should now forgive, forget, and take Russell back:

> I have read over your draft letter to the Master many times, and wish that I could make up my mind to sign it. But I cannot in honesty do so, although I agree with almost every word of what you make the signatories say. My difficulty is that there is another side which is ignored. It is a side which is naturally underestimated by those members of the Society with whose approval the draft letter has been circulated – a body of men with an honourable record of active service during the war. I mean the point of view of those who saw their children go into the furnace, and who now live on the memory of the high ideals which led to that sacrifice. It is expressed with pathetic obviousness daily in the 'In Memoriam' columns of the *Times*.
>
> I am well aware of the immense sympathy which Russell feels for the heroism and the loss. But most unfortunately his public utterances did not adequately express his full feelings. His pointed literary style, and a natural irritation at the mixed phenomena which all mass action must exhibit, led to articles in America and England with stinging phrases belittling the motives of the sacrifice and calculated to delay the marshalling of the forces of industry or national action which might have led to an earlier decision. As a result I cannot estimate the force of antagonism which might be aroused by his immediate reinstatement. The feeling is so deep that the mention of his name raises a storm of protest. Accordingly – since, apart from Russell's opinions, this situation has arisen from his own unguarded expression of them – I cannot take the very strong step of urging the Council to proceed to his immediate reinstatement. Time should be given. I cannot say how long: it depends upon the course of events in the near future. I look on this hasty action as ill-judged and as in effect delaying the issue which we must all desire. But in questions where such primal feelings are aroused there can be only one sedative, and that is Time.[47]

Two months later, when it was clear that the Council was going to be forced to reinstate Russell, Whitehead decided at the last minute to sign the memorial after all. He told Hollond,

> [T]he 'simplest course', is for me to sign and to send you a covering letter (enclosed) to send in with it. I feel a most distressing difficulty over the

whole matter. Owing to the fact that some of Russell's activites appear to me to have been indefensible, I cannot take the line that justice must be done, though the heavens fall. Accordingly it is a question of letting feeling subside, of wiping a sponge over the past, of ceasing to judge each other's actions, of recognising that Bertie is a dear fellow and a great man, and of getting him back when it can be done with reasonable safety to the College.[48]

Hardy gave Russell a cynical report of this change of heart: 'I did succeed in getting W. in the end: I wrote a letter which went almost to the point of offensiveness, as a gamble, and it came off.'[49] Having been thus pressured into standing up for Russell, Whitehead characteristically sent in a covering letter that told the Council he was doing his utmost to support *them!*[50] One suspects that the die-hards on the Council, as they faced defeat, were less than grateful for Whitehead's sentiments.

And so the rift within Trinity was covered over, if not healed. The settlement was an exact restoration of the pre-war status quo: Russell was not offered a Fellowship, but a modest lectureship like the one he had before, and with a modest salary of 250 guineas per annum. The deal was made grudgingly and secretly, and it left untouched the real and great issue, of academic freedom. All that could be said for it was that it allowed the Fellows of Trinity to restore their collegiality and carry on their traditional work, no longer fretted by 'suspicion and quarrel'. The war had passed through the quadrangles and gone; now the academics made their treaty – one which, unlike Versailles, pretended as far as possible that the war had never happened.

Notes

1 Privately printed by Cambridge University Press, 1942; reissued in facsimile by Cambridge, 1970, with a Foreword by C. D. Broad. A typescript of Hardy's pamphlet in the Russell Archives has significant differences from the published version; see particularly n. 47 below. Additional material on Russell's dismissal may be found in Ronald W. Clark, *The Life of Bertrand Russell* (London: Jonathan Cape and Weidenfeld & Nicholson, 1975), and in Jo Vellacott, *Bertrand Russell and the Pacifists in the First World War* (New York: St. Martin's Press, 1980). For permission to quote from unpublished letters I am indebted to Mrs T. North Whitehead and to the London Mathematical Society (for G. H. Hardy).

2 Donation by Christopher Cornford of papers belonging to his father, F. M. Cornford. See *Russell*, n.s. 5 (Winter 1985): 98.

3 This would have taken away Russell's right to use the Senior Combination Room or dine at High Table. Ward to Cornford, 26 July 1916. (Unless otherwise noted, all documents, or copies thereof, cited are in the Russell Archives; file numbers are given in parentheses. Documents belonging to the Cornford acquisition, such as this one, are in file REC. ACQ. 912.)

4 Quoted in J. R. M. Butler, *Henry Montagu Butler: Master of Trinity College Cambridge* (London: Longmans, Green, 1925), p. 216.

5 Hardy considered the Rev. R. StJ. Parry, who was on the Council, to be the ringleader of the attack on Russell.

6 Russell to Morrell, #1,361 and 1,383, 19 March and [12?] May 1916 (Morrell Papers, Harry Ransom Humanities Research Center, University of Texas at Austin).

7 Hardy, naturally, says nothing about the Society in *Bertrand Russell and Trinity*.

8 Russell to Morrell, # 1,389, Saturday afternoon [?15 July 1916].

9 Hardy to Russell, early July 1916.

10 Russell to Morrell, #1,110, [18 Sept. 1914].

11 He had in fact volunteered for military service, but had been turned down on medical grounds.

12 Victor Lowe, *Alfred North Whitehead, the Man and His Work*, Vol. I: *1861–1910* (Baltimore and London: Johns Hopkins University Press, 1985), p. 317.

13 Hardy to Russell, *c.* 12 July 1916.

14 Hardy to Russell, *c.* 14 July 1916.

15 Whitehead to Russell, 4 June 1916.

16 Whitehead to Russell, 16 April 1916. In *To the Master and Fellows* (p. 4), Whitehead notes that he 'unfortunately' destroyed Russell's appeal. The opinions quoted here should be compared with what Whitehead *says* his opinions were on the issue (*ibid.*, pp. 4–6).

17 See, for example, D. H. Lawrence's famous attack on Russell for 'satisfying in an indirect, false way your lust to jab and strike' (*The Letters of D. H. Lawrence*, Vol. II, ed. G. Zytaruk and J. Boulton [Cambridge: Cambridge University Press, 1981], p. 392). It should be noted that we cannot know the exact degree to which Russell personally provoked Whitehead, since his letters to him were destroyed (at Whitehead's direction) by Evelyn Whitehead; but Russell's published writings on the war were infuriating enough.

18 Russell to Morrell, #1,391, [17?] July 1916. On the day Russell came to London from South Wales he saw his lawyer, the Whiteheads, and the T. S. Eliots, and attended a No-Conscription Fellowship committee meeting.

19 Reproduced complete in *Russell*, n.s. 6 (1986), pp. 62–70.

20 This interpretation is supported by Whitehead's letter to Cornford of 1 August 1916 (REC. ACQ. 912).

21 Moore, a university lecturer, was not a Fellow of Trinity; but he had rooms in the College – of which he was a former Prize Fellow – and dined in Hall. He made a public protest against the banning of the UDC meeting in Littlewood's rooms, but faded into the woodwork when Russell's dismissal came up. See Paul Levy, *Moore: G. E. Moore and the Cambridge Apostles* (London: Weidenfeld & Nicolson, 1979), Chap. 10.

22 Hardy to Cornford, [14? July 1916] (REC. ACQ. 912).

23 *Bertrand Russell and Trinity*, p. 2.

24 Quoted in *The Autobiography of Bertrand Russell, 1914–1944* (London: Allen & Unwin, 1968), p. 69 (original letter in RA).

25 Reprinted: New York: Barnes & Noble, 1966.

26 *Microcosmographia*, p. 10.

27 *The Letters of D. H. Lawrence*, II: 546. See also my *D. H. Lawrence's Nightmare: the Writer and His Circle in the Years of the Great War* (New York: Basic Books, 1978), Chap. III, *passim*.

28 Russell to Morrell, #1,389 and 1,390, [15? and 19? July 1916].

29 Russell to Morrell, #1,391, [17? July 1916]. Russell proposed that he should pay

the fine himself from the proceeds of the auction, and the money collected by Philip Morrell should go to the NCE. Cornford and Hardy were among the fund's subscribers.

30 The bill of sale is in RA 710.110337.
31 Russell met Lady Constance on 31 July; they became lovers in late September.
32 Whitehead to Cornford, 1 Aug. 1916 (REC. ACQ. 912).
33 Simpson to Cornford, Thursday, [14? Sept.], and Sunday [24 Sept.? 1916] (REC. ACQ. 912). Russell wrote to the porter around mid-September.
34 *Bertrand Russell and Trinity*, p. 54.
35 Neville to Cornford, 16 Oct. 1916 (REC. ACQ. 912). E. W. Barnes and C. D. Broad also wanted a stronger protest.
36 Hardy to Russell, 19 Sept. [1916].
37 Russell to Hardy, 25 Sept. 1916.
38 Woolf to Cornford, 19 Nov. 1916 (REC. ACQ. 912).
39 Hicks to Cornford, 29 Nov. 1916 (REC. ACQ. 912).
40 Whitehead to Cornford, 18 Oct. 1916 (REC. ACQ. 912). Whitehead was referring to passages of this sort: 'There is a wild beast slumbering in almost every man, but civilized men know that it must not be allowed to awake . . . War is perpetrating this moral murder in the souls of vast millions of combatants; every day men are passing over to the dominion of the brute by acts which kill what is best within them. Yet, still our newspapers, parsons, and professors prate of the ennobling influence of war' (Russell, 'The Danger to Civilization', *The Open Court*, 30 [March 1916]: 174; reprinted in his *Justice in Wartime* [Chicago: Open Court, 1916]).
41 For details see Clark, p. 318.
42 Evelyn Whitehead to Russell, 10 Jan. 1917.
43 Whitehead to Russell, 1 April 1918.
44 Hardy to Cornford, *c.* 18 Nov. 1918 (REC. ACQ. 912).
45 Whitehead to Cornford, 27 Nov. 1918 (REC. ACQ. 912).
46 Hardy to Russell, early Sept.? 1919 (REC. ACQ. 912).
47 Whitehead to Hollond, 24 Sept. 1919. This letter, and the one that follows, is taken from a typescript of Hardy's *Bertrand Russell and Trinity* in the Russell Archives (file 710.050781). In this manuscript Hardy says that the letters are included in an appendix; in the printed version he describes them as 'too long, and perhaps too personal, to quote' (p. 55). Probably Whitehead had refused his permission.
48 Whitehead to Hollond, 24 Nov. 1919.
49 Hardy to Russell, 30 Nov. 1919.
50 'I am however now convinced that the balance of feeling in the College is such that the reinstatement of Mr. Russell at a reasonably early date is the wiser course for the responsible governing authorities of the college. Accordingly I feel that it will be convenient for the Council and will strengthen their hands to have a plain list of the fellows who are prepared to support them in that course, for the reasons urged in the memorial' (Whitehead to Hollond, 24 Nov. 1919 [Trinity College Library]; copy in RA, REC. ACQ. 403).

8

A Chair of Indecency

Barry Feinberg and Ronald Kasrils

A New York Appointment

The College of the City of New York was a municipal-run institution controlled by the government of New York City. A series of procedural steps were therefore required before Russell's appointment could be officially finalised. Russell received a letter from Nelson Mead, the college's acting president, informing him that the Administrative Committee of City College had unanimously approved his appointment and, subject to one final step of ratification, that it would commence from February 1941. The body responsible for approving all appointments was the Board of Higher Education of the City of New York, which controlled the four tax-supported colleges of the city. At its meeting of 26 February, the Board unanimously approved the Russell appointment. As a result, Ordway Tead, Chairman of the Board of Higher Education, informed Russell on 29 February:

> It is with a deep sense of privilege that I take this opportunity of notifying you of your appointment as Professor of Philosophy at City College for the period 1 February 1941 to 30 June 1942. . . . I know that your acceptance of this appointment will add luster to the name and achievements of the department and the college, and that it will deepen and extend the interest of the college in the philosophic bases of human living.

Russell's appointment was to carry a salary of $8,000 per annum and the faculty of the college were delighted that he would soon be joining them. One of the first letters of congratulation was from Philip Wiener on behalf of the college's Philosophy Department,[1] which had originally recommended him for the post:

As Secretary of the new Philosophy Department, severed from the Psychology Department as of 1 March 1940, may I transmit the felicitations of our department as well as of our colleagues in other departments on your appointment to the head of Professorship of the Department of Philosophy. . . . We look forward toward your coming East with a great deal of pleasure.

Russell was pleased to be going to City College as it had a liberal reputation, and a record of fostering the education of the lower classes and immigrant groups. However, he was well aware of the problems such institutions faced in maintaining a liberal position. According to Russell:

The College of the City of New York was an institution run by the City government. Those who attended it were practically all Catholics or Jews; but to the indignation of the former, practically all the scholarships went to the latter. The government of New York City was virtually a satellite of the Vatican, but the professors of City College strove ardently to keep up some semblance of academic freedom. It was no doubt in pursuit of this aim that they had recommended me.[2]

The Board of Higher Education, too, was considered for the first time in years a liberal body – moreover the mayor of New York, Fiorello La Guardia, had won office on a platform of reform aimed against city corruption. The new Board of Higher Education was seen as one of the challenges to the Tammany Hall politicians whose administrations had preceded La Guardia's.

In spite of Russell's insight into the American educational system, and his concern for academic freedom, he could not have anticipated the stormy events which were to follow. Reaction to the appointment was swift and aggressive; Russell's writings on religion and morality provided the focal point of an attack launched by his old adversary, Bishop Manning,[3] and other opponents of liberalism. It was alleged that Russell was morally unfit for a public teaching position and this created an opportunity for assailing the Board, and questioning its competence and autonomous right to make the appointment. The conservative New York *Sun* carried an editorial denouncing the Board's decision, and on 1 March, the New York press published an open letter from Bishop Manning which was an embittered outburst against Russell and the Board of Higher Education. Basing his harangue on misapplied quotations from Russell's writings, the Bishop depicted Russell as a polluter of public morals, and saw the appointment as a threat to religious life. Manning protested:

Can any of us wish our young people to accept these teachings as decent, true, or worthy of respect? What is to be said of colleges and universities which hold up before our youth as a responsible teacher of philosophy and as an example of light and leading a man who is a recognised propagandist against both religion and morality, and who specifically defends adultery. . . . Can anyone who cares for the welfare of our country be willing to see such teaching disseminated. . . . How is it that the College of the City of New York makes such an appointment as this?[4]

Bishop Manning's views received far wider attention and support than had been the case in 1929. This reflected the hardening of reaction, and the political polarisation in America, in the years immediately preceding the war; and it vindicated Russell's belief that a militaristic policy would require an assault on liberalism in America. Bishop Manning's attack has been described by Professor Paul Edwards, in his account of these events, as: "The signal for a campaign of vilification and intimidation unequaled in American history since the days of Jefferson and Thomas Paine."[5]

Edwards goes on to demonstrate the extent of bigoted reaction:

The ecclesiastical journals, the Hearst Press, and just about every Democratic politician joined the chorus of defamation. Russell's appointment, said the *Tablet*, came as a "brutal, insulting shock to old New Yorkers, and all real Americans." Demanding that the appointment be revoked, it editorially described Russell as a "professor of paganism," as "the philosophical anarchist and moral nihilist of Great Britain . . . whose defense of adultery became so obnoxious that one of his 'friends' is reported to have thrashed him." The Jesuit weekly, *America*, referred to Russell as "a desiccated, divorced and decadent advocate of sexual promiscuity . . . who is now indoctrinating the students at the University of California."[6]

While letters from outraged citizens and priests venting their moral indignation over Russell's appointment filled the press columns, there were other pressures mounting. The clamour was enjoined by ultra right-wing sects, pro-Nazi propagandists, and various Catholic groups sympathetic to fascism. The Knights of Columbus saw the appointment as symbolic of a rising tide of liberalism. The Chairman of the Catholic Affairs Committee of the New York State Council of the organisation described Russell as "an articulate spearhead of the radical, atheistic and anti-religious elements of our time" and denounced the appointment as "a disgrace to our city."[7]

The Board of Education was under great pressure to rescind the appointment. Charles H. Tuttle, one of its members, persuaded the Board to reconsider Russell's appointment, in the light of the public outcry against it. In effect this was a call for Russell's dismissal. Tuttle stated that he was "unaware of Earl Russell's views on religion and morality at the time the appointment was under consideration."[8] Tuttle was a leading lay member of Manning's diocese.

The Board announced, on 7 March, a bare week after Manning's onslaught, that the whole question would be reviewed at its next meeting on 18 March. Meanwhile, Russell, the figure at the center of the storm, was 3,000 miles away, quietly attending to his duties in Los Angeles. He relied on newspaper reports and occasional communications from City College for information on the controversy. Both the Board and the college were determined to handle the situation with academic restraint, and were concerned not to involve Russell too deeply in the affair.

The first official reaction from the administration of the college was a statement by President Mead that Russell was appointed to teach mathematics and logic and not morals and religion. They apparently hoped to ride out the storm and it appears that the strength of the campaign, and the extent of its co-ordination, were seriously underestimated. On 9 March, Philip Wiener wrote to Russell for brief descriptions of his courses for inclusion in the college catalogue which was soon going to press. The concluding paragraph of this letter gives little idea of the ferocity of the battle raging in New York or of the ruthlessness of the antagonists:

> You may have noticed in the newspapers that your appointment has already begun to have an educational effect. Despite the clamor of certain groups, whose opposition was to be expected, there is clearly no danger of a reversal of the Board's decision.

However, the City College students, the very people Bishop Manning sought to protect, were fully aware of the dangerous implications caused by the witch-hunt against Russell, and pointed out that in essence the attack was part of a process undermining academic freedom. The student council of the college issued a press statement on 9 March and sent a copy to Russell:

> The appointment of Bertrand Russell to the staff of City College has brought forth much discussion in the press and has evoked statements from various organisations and individuals. We do not wish to enter any controversy on Professor Russell's views on morals and religion; we feel that he is entitled to his own personal views.
>
> Professor Russell has been appointed to the staff of City College to teach mathematics and logic. With an international reputation, he is eminently qualified to teach these subjects. He has been lecturing at the University of California and has been appointed Visiting Professor at Harvard University before he comes to City College in February 1941.

The student body, as well as the faculty, are of the opinion that the addition of Professor Russell to the faculty cannot but help to raise the academic prestige and national standing of our college. . . .

By refusing to yield to the pressure being brought to bear, and by standing firm on the appointment of Professor Russell, the Board of Higher Education will be saving City College an academic black eye and doing its duty to the community in the highest sense. . . .

City College has long been subject to attack from various sources seeking to modify or destroy our free higher education; the attack on Bertrand Russell is but another manifestation of this tendency.

Russell thanked the students for their statement and wrote in reply:

I am very happy to have the support of the student council in the fight. Old York was the first place where Christianity was the State religion, and it was there that Constantine assumed the purple. Perhaps New York will be the last place to have this honour.[9]

One of the first major organisations to come to the defence of Russell's appointment was the Committee for Cultural Freedom. On 5 March they confirmed this in a letter to the Board of Higher Education and followed up with a letter published in the New York *Herald Tribune* of 9 March. The letter was signed by Sidney Hook, Chairman of their executive committee:

The hue and cry which has recently been raised in some quarters over the appointment of Bertrand Russell . . . carries with it a serious attack on hard-won principles of academic and cultural freedom. The ultimate implications of the organised campaign against Mr Russell's appointment menace the integrity of our intellectual life, which consists in the free and open consideration of alternatives honestly held and scientifically reasoned. . . .

To censor Mr Russell's intellectual activity, because some of his views on matters not germane to his chief theoretical interest are objectionable to some members of the community, clearly contravenes the Statement on Academic Freedom and Tenure adopted both by the American Association of University Professors and the Association of American Colleges.

Following the Board of Higher Education's announcement that it would rediscuss Russell's appointment, the campaign to intimidate the Board was stepped up. Inevitably, the "communist" smear was applied by the Hearst Press. By lifting convenient quotes from *Practice and Theory of Bolshevism*, Hearst's *Journal-American* referred to Russell as a spokesman for communism and demanded an investigation of the Board of Higher Education.

Appeals by obscure religious sects and defenders of public virtue, such as the Sons of Xavier, the St Joan of Arc Holy Name Society, and the Empire State Sons of the American Revolution appeared regularly in the press. These called for the dismissal of Russell and those members of the Board who stood firm on the appointment.

According to Russell, "priests lectured the police, who were practically all Irish Catholics, on my responsibility for the local criminals."[10] Paul Edwards elaborates on this in his account of the controversy:

> Speaking at the annual communion breakfast of the Holy Name Society of the New York Police Department, Monsignor Francis W. Walsh recalled to the assembled policemen that they had, on occasion, learnt the full meaning of the so-called "matrimonial triangle" by finding one corner of the triangle in a pool of blood, "I dare say, therefore," he continued, "that you will join me in demanding that any professor guilty of teaching or writing ideas which will multiply the stages upon which these tragedies are set shall not be countenanced in this city and shall receive no support from its taxpayers."[11]

The appeal to protect the taxpayers' money was a recurrent theme in the attacks on the Board, and was volubly taken up as the key issue by the Tammany office-holders who were constantly harassing the La Guardia administration. Most of these Democratic officials had connections with the groups calling for Russell's blood, and on 15 March the City Council passed a resolution by sixteen votes to five calling upon the Board of Higher Education to revoke the Russell appointment. The warning was strategically timed three days before the Board was due to re-convene.

During this period, Russell's supporters were by no means inactive, even though they could not hope to match the powerful resources of their opponents. Not surprisingly, the universities and learned associations were the first to raise their voices in defence of the City College appointment. The Committee for Cultural Freedom and the American Civil Liberties Union, together with the City College Philosophy Department, were instrumental in organising support from the country's leading scholars and academics. It was clear that a determined struggle had to be waged to encourage the Board to stand by its original decision. City College was by no means immune to the tremendous pressure generated by Bishop Manning's attack, and it is to the credit of the Philosophy Department that they remained unanimous in their will to continue the fight. Dr Y. H. Krikorian, Chairman of the Philosophy Department, gave some idea of the spirit prevailing in his department, when he wrote to Russell on 13 March:

> The members of the Department of Philosophy are very glad that you have accepted their invitation. We are all looking forth for your coming.

We are quite sure that the attempt to obstruct your coming will fail. President Mead has received hundreds of letters from distinguished philosophers and scholars protesting the possible revocation of your appointment. . . . We enjoy the fight, for it is for a philosopher we all admire, and for a cause we all like.

One aspect of the agitation against Russell was the fact that he was not an American national. His detractors seized on this point to claim that as an alien he was legally barred from teaching at a New York State college. In order to counter this technical objection, Russell was advised by City College to indicate his intention to apply for citizenship. Russell was not in favour of the suggestion and wired Acting President Mead on 12 March:

> In other circumstances I might have applied for American citizenship but cannot contemplate doing so in deference to an illiberal and nationalistic law unworthy of a great democracy. Sure you will agree that such laws hamper intellectual intercourse and co-operation between nations and should not be deferred to.

However, after consulting its lawyers, City College was confident that the objection to Russell on grounds of citizenship was without merit, "since there is a law adopted in 1938 which permits the Board of Higher Education to waive the requirement." This information was conveyed to Russell by Professor Daniel Bronstein of the Philosophy Department on 15 March. Bronstein also indicated that the controversy was causing a certain amount of embarrassment at the college; not the least of which arose out of Russell's objection to applying for American citizenship:

> The annoyance your case is now causing some people at City College is of no moment. I think you are aware of the fact that the idea of your appointment originated in the Philosophy Department and that you have our unanimous support. Nor do we agree with Acting President Mead's statement to the press that "you were invited to teach courses in logic and mathematics, and not to express your personal views on other questions. . . ." I have heard that you sent a telegram to Acting President Mead in which you say that you will not become an American citizen and in which you make not altogether complimentary remarks about the United States. I hope my information is not accurate since such statements are, of course, not calculated to help our case, and may alienate members of the Board who otherwise would support you. If you can find it consistent with the canons of scientific method to refrain at this time from making predictions about your own future intentions with regard to citizenship . . . it would greatly strengthen our case.

As a consequence of Bronstein's letter, Russell wrote to Mead explaining in more detail his attitude to the citizenship issue:

> I understand with regret that my telegram to you about question of citizenship gave unintended impression of criticism of United States. I am living here and seeking employment because I wished my children to grow up in a country which appeared to me to be the hope of the world. But on hearing that my appointment might possibly be rescinded technically on grounds of nationality I thought, and still think, that this issue is even more important than that of religious opinions. The growth of national barriers is the greatest source of evil in the modern world. My objection to applying now for American citizenship is not an objection to American citizenship but an inability to concede that the race or nationality to which a human being happens to belong is of any importance. If I were in England I should oppose with all my energy any proposal that professors from America or any other country should be asked to become British subjects.[12]

Meanwhile, the Philosophy Department had issued a press statement on 13 March, in which it declared that its recommendation of Russell to the City College post was "a judgment which has the endorsement of hundreds of philosophers including heads of philosophy departments throughout the country." The statement continued:

> Professor Russell's work in logic has not merely become a classic, but has actually initiated a new era in the development of that science. His writings on the philosophy of the sciences are of major importance. His ethical writings, which have been so violently attacked in the last fortnight, are the fearless attempts of a critically minded philosopher to formulate principles of conduct conducive to human welfare. Disagreement with his specific suggestions for the reconstruction of institutions or personal morals should not lead one to belittle the morally constructive character of his ideas.
>
> Any revocation of Professor Russell's appointment would lead to the inquisition by laymen into all sorts of personal views held by a prospective teacher instead of the considered judgment of his professional colleagues who are better qualified to know his competence. A college should encourage open consideration of alternatives, honestly held and scientifically reasoned. In the interplay of reasoned opinions, not in the imposition of the dogmas of any specific group, lies the promise of higher education.
>
> The attack on Professor Russell's appointment is fundamentally an attack upon the liberal democratic tradition, upon which the institutions of our country are founded. On this issue there can be no retreat.

The department took the initiative in requisitioning signatures from their colleagues throughout the country to attach to a statement addressed to the Board of Higher Education:

We, members of the American Philosophical Association and teachers of Philosophy in American educational institutions, regard Professor Bertrand Russell as one of the outstanding philosophers of our time, and while not all of us share his personal views on theism and marriage, we consider that these views in no way disqualify him from teaching college students. Indeed, any revocation of his appointment because of his personal opinions would be a calamitous setback to that freedom of thought and discussion which has been the basis of democratic education.

The Committee for Cultural Freedom contacted Presidents Hutchins and Sproul of Chicago and California, asking them for statements on Russell's record at their universities. Both could confirm that Russell had not spent his time corrupting the young and gave favourable reports which the committee released to the press on 14 March. The committee next drew up a letter which was signed by seventeen prominent professors at Columbia, Harvard, Johns Hopkins, Cornell and New York University, and the president of Brooklyn College. On 16 March, the letter was sent to *The New York Times*, the *Herald Tribune* and to Mayor La Guardia, who was contriving to remain silent on the issue. The letter warned that as a consequence of the campaign against Russell, "no American college or university is safe from inquisitional control by the enemies of free inquiry." The seventeen signatories defended Russell's appointment and declared:

To receive instruction from a man of Bertrand Russell's intellectual caliber is a rare privilege for students anywhere. . . . His critics should meet him in the open and fair field of intellectual discussion and scientific analysis. They have no right to silence him by preventing him from teaching. . . . This issue is so fundamental that it cannot be compromised without imperiling the whole structure of intellectual freedom upon which American university life rests.

The Russell affair had become a *cause célèbre* amongst the most distinguished intellects of the day, including Albert Einstein, Alfred North Whitehead, Oswald Veblen, Harlow Shapley, Edward Kasner and John Dewey, who played an important part in the campaign. In a communication to Morris Raphael Cohen, Professor Emeritus of Philosophy at City College, whose retirement had occasioned the invitation to Russell, Einstein stated:

Great spirits have always found violent opposition from mediocrities. The latter cannot understand it when a man does not thoughtlessly submit to hereditary prejudices but honestly and courageously uses his intelligence.[13]

Einstein was so moved by the persecution of Russell that he penned the following poem:

It keeps repeating itself
In this world, so fine and honest;
The Parson alarms the populace,
The genius is executed.[14]

Fellow English expatriates, Charles Chaplin, Aldous Huxley, G. E. Moore and Alfred North Whitehead, informed Russell of their sympathy and support. Not all religious spokesmen agreed with Bishop Manning's denunciation of Russell. The more enlightened religious leaders supported the Board's appointment of Russell, and among them were Rabbi Jonah B. Wise, Professor J. S. Bixler of Harvard Divinity School, Professor E. S. Brightman, the Director of the National Council on Religion and Education, the Reverend Robert G. Andrus, Counsellor to Protestant students at Columbia University, and the Reverend John Haynes Holmes. Bishop Manning's right to speak for the Episcopal Church was challenged by a fellow clergyman, the Reverend Guy Emery Shipler, who pointed out in the *New Republic*:

Bishop Manning has been given no authority to represent the Protestant Episcopal Church in such controversies. . . . He has every right to speak for himself; he has no right to speak either for his own diocese or for the national Church. . . . It is unfortunate that the public is under the illusion that every time a bishop . . . bursts into print with a point of view stemming from the Dark Ages he represents the Protestant Episcopal Church.[15]

Explaining Manning's alignment with the Catholic agitation against Russell, Shipler stated:

It is not so well known, outside the Episcopal Church, that Bishop Manning is an Anglo-Catholic, that is, one of the comparatively small group in the Episcopal Church whose theological concepts and whose concepts in the field of "morals" – speaking technically – are essentially identical with the official standards of the Roman Catholic Church.[16]

Warder Norton, of W. W. Norton, the man who had published most of Russell's books in America since 1927, including many of the texts under attack, organised a group of nine major publishers to issue a press statement characterising Russell's appointment as reflecting the greatest credit on the Board of Higher Education. The statement, by way of a publisher's manifesto, appeared on the front page of *The New York Times* on 18 March 1940, and averred:

> We do not necessarily subscribe personally to all the views expressed by those whose books we publish, but we welcome great minds to our lists, particularly now at a time when brute force and ignorance have gained such ascendancy over reason and intellect in many parts of the world. We think it more important than ever to honor intellectual superiority whenever the opportunity presents itself.

The New York *Post* was one of the city newspapers most favourably disposed to the Russell cause, and, as the date for the Board's next meeting drew near, requested a statement from Russell on his "position in the matter." Russell wired the New York *Post*:

> My position is quite simple. I have been offered and have accepted an appointment as Professor of Philosophy. Neither my views on religion and morality nor those of Bishop Manning are relevant. To prohibit any man from teaching a subject which he is competent to teach because of his religion, race or nationality is of course a familiar proceeding in despotic countries, but the attempt to do so here seems inconsistent with American traditions and professions of free speech and civil liberties.
>
> I realise that this illiberal action comes from a small but powerful minority and I am glad to find it so widely and emphatically resisted.[17]

The *Nation* of 16 March carried an editorial which succinctly recounted the unfolding of the controversy and the reason for the attack on the Board:

> Tennessee is far from being the only place in the country where ignorance makes a monkey of education. Hillbillies from Morningside Heights, led by His Most Worshipful Eminence Bishop Manning, and bigots from the backwoods of Brooklyn, mobilised by the Hearst Press, have raised a hue and cry against Bertrand Russell. In the world of education and enlightenment, Mr Russell is a distinguished philosopher, mathematician, and logician, but there must be several hundred thousand New Yorkers who now believe that he is a confirmed lecher, an advocate of adultery, and a believer in the nationalisation of women. . . . The Hearst Press, scenting its favorite journalistic combination, sex and

subversion, leaped to the fray. The Knights of Columbus girded on their armor. Behind the uproar is the fact that for the first time in years New York City has a liberal Board of Higher Education. We hope it will repudiate in no uncertain terms an attack which, if successful, would be a serious blow to academic freedom, not only in New York City but throughout the country.

In the few days prior to the Board of Higher Education's meeting, the campaign for and against Russell intensified. On 14 March, over 2,000 students and faculty members filled the Great Hall at City College to attend a rally called by the Student Union protesting at the attempts to rescind Russell's appointment. From California, Russell wired a message to the meeting: "Most grateful for your support against clerical interference with academic freedom."

Addressing the rally, Morris Raphael Cohen, declared that if the campaign to debar Russell succeeded, "the fair name of our city will suffer as did Athens for condemning Socrates as a corrupter of its youth or Tennessee for finding Scopes guilty of teaching evolution."[18]

The strong sentiment for Russell amongst the students was indicated by the numerous letters they sent to him. William Swirsky, who worked on the College's undergraduate newspaper, the *Campus*, wrote:

> The exaltation I enjoyed upon learning you were coming to teach at my college was as boundless as my sorrow intense when I read and heard the scurrilous attacks on your character . . . of the 6,000 students at the branch [of the college] with which you will be connected, not more than twenty-five have evinced any dissatisfaction whatever with your appointment. . . . As Professor Krikorian said: "his presence within the very walls of our college would be electrifying." If there is anything my paper, the students or the faculty (100 per cent behind your appointment) can do to help you, please let me know.[19]

Swirsky closed his letter: "with deep envy of the students who have enjoyed your classes in California and terror that the Board of Higher Education may kowtow to the reactionary but bombastic elements of our city."

From Bernard Goltz, a member of the Student Council, Russell received the following expression of hope:

> I write this letter on the eve of the meeting of the Board of Higher Education called to reconsider your appointment to the Philosophy Department of C.C.N.Y. If the question of your appointment had been left to the student body, I am positive that there would be no question as to the outcome. The student body is almost unanimously united in supporting the appointment. It is unfortunate that the

politicians on the B.H.E. could not resist the pressure placed on them by the bigots and Grundies of our city. . . .

I do not know what the decision of the Board will be. But it is my sincere hope that they will not deprive the students at the college of the benefit of your great learning.[20]

In sharp contrast to the dignified campaign waged on behalf of Russell, those who opposed his appointment became even more frenzied in their efforts to intimidate the Board. They, too, held a mass rally at which leading city politicians whipped the audience into a state of near-hysteria. Councilman Charles E. Keegan described Russell as a "dog" and declaimed: "If we had an adequate system of immigration, that bum could not land within a thousand miles."[21] The Registrar of New York County, Miss Martha Byrnes, recommended that Russell be "tarred and feathered and driven out of the country."[22] George V. Harvey, President of the Borough of Queens, threatened the closure of the municipal college by depriving them of their 1941 budget allocation of $7,500,000 if the Board persisted with Russell's appointment. Reminding the Board of its obligations, he said: "The colleges would either be godly colleges, American colleges, or they would be closed."[23]

The Board of Higher Education met on 18 March and continued its deliberations well into the night. After intensive debate in which every factor involved was thoroughly considered, the motion brought by Charles Tuttle to rescind the appointment of Russell was defeated by eleven votes to seven. So crucial had the issues become that several Board members made statements defending their voting position. They requested that these be recorded in the minutes of the meeting.[24] Of those who changed their minds, William P. Larkin, the seconder of Tuttle's motion, echoed the objections that had been hurled at the Board from press and pulpit:

I am opposed to him [Russell] because he is a recognised propagandist against both religion and morality who not only condones, but puts a halo around violation of one of God's fundamental commandments, and advocates a code of morals which self-respecting pagans would repudiate. If appointed, under the shibboleth of "freedom of speech" and "academic freedom" atheism and the ethics of the barnyard would inevitably be preached to the children and youth of New York. I am opposed to an alien propagandist being given the right to use public classrooms to destroy time-honored beliefs of this country and its citizens.[25]

Larkin concluded: "It is absolutely unthinkable that the Board of Higher Education would turn over the Chair of Philosophy with all its potentialities for good or evil to the most outspoken foe of religion in the world today."

Among others casting their votes against Russell were Albert Weiss and Ernest Seelman. Weiss explained:

> I voted in the Administrative Committee as well as on the Board for Mr Russell. I have come to the conclusion I cannot subject the children of our great city to the teaching of the sex philosophy of Mr Russell. I have therefore changed the vote.[26]

Ernest Seelman voted for reconsideration: "because I do not believe it is necessary to appoint a man of such questionable views, which have so offended the religious and moral beliefs of a great portion of our community."[27]

It is clear that the campaign to intimidate members of the Board had been partially successful. Speaking as one of those who had not been swayed, Dr Joseph J. Klein declared:

> Aside from every other consideration urged on us so eloquently tonight, I wish to say that I resent the effort of rabbi, priest, or minister, through organised pressure and otherwise, to attempt to influence my official conduct as a member of this public Board . . . organised religion should be told, in unmistakable terms, that it must not attempt to intrude in matters of public education.[28]

The campaign on Russell's behalf had undoubtedly impressed some of the Board members. Lauson H. Stone, who voted with the majority, drew attention to:

> the numerous communications received from individuals of note and from organisations in academic fields [which] make it perfectly clear that to rescind the appointment of Mr Russell because of his personal views would create an issue involving fundamental educational principles of far greater importance than Mr Russell himself.[29]

Another Board member who voted for Russell was Joseph Schlossberg, the General-Secretary of the Amalgamated Clothing Workers of America, who wrote to Russell: "It does not happen often that one is both right and in the majority. My voting for you as Professor in City College has placed me in this privileged position. I am looking forward to the pleasure of meeting you here."[30]

After the meeting, Ordway Tead, the chairman, made the following statement on behalf of the Board:

> The appointment of Professor Bertrand Russell as Professor of Philosophy was made by unanimous vote of the City College Administrative

Committee and the Board of Higher Education. At the time of his appointment, the majority of the Board were fully acquainted with the eminent scholastic position of Professor Russell as embodied in his philosophical and mathematical writings. Professor Russell is one of the two or three most outstanding living mathematical philosophers, with over thirty books to his credit, of which only three or four have been popular treatments of current problems.

Since coming to this country, he has been for nearly a year at Chicago University, and President Hutchins assures us that Professor Russell made an important contribution there. From there he went to the University of California, and President Sproul writes that he has been "a most valuable colleague." At the College of the City of New York, Professor Russell will teach logic, the philosophy of mathematics, and the philosophy of science. He brings to this position the reputation of a world-renowned scholar now rounding out a distinguished career.[31]

The battle, however, was not over. Charles Tuttle sounded an ominous note when, as spokesman for the anti-Russell faction, he said: "The issue now passes from the Board of Higher Education to the public. Particularly in view of the close vote, public opinion will control in the end."[32]

Immediately after the decision became known, leading faculty members of the Philosophy Department at City College telegraphed Russell the news. Russell wired back: "Many thanks for telegram. I am delighted both on public and personal grounds and very grateful for your splendid support. Samson Agonistes 1268–76[33] for deliverer read deliverers."[34]

With the *sang-froid* he had displayed throughout this period, Russell commented to the Los Angeles *Daily News* of 19 March: "I would like to lecture in New York, but it is for them to decide. I can't imagine why there should be such a fuss. I believe I was hired to teach philosophy and logic, not morality."

For the first time since the onset of the controversy, he issued a statement, reported in *The New York Times* of 21 March, and given wide coverage in the national press, defending his views:

I am, of course, delighted by this victory both on public and private grounds. I came to live in this country because I believed America to be the hope of the world and because I wished my three children to grow up in a land of liberal thought and hope for the future and not in Europe, where all that I care for most seems likely to perish.

It was distressing to meet in the metropolis of the world's greatest democracy an attempt to establish an inquisition over teachers and a rigorous censorship over students.

As to "free love," I am far from advocating promiscuity either among students or elsewhere, but I do think that young people should be allowed, if they wish, to live together in unions which may or may not develop into permanent marriage. This would, in fact, diminish promiscuity.

It is ridiculous to say that I advocate infidelity in marriage, on the contrary, I think that fidelity in marriage is highly desirable.

Grateful to the City College students for their support, Russell wrote to William Swirsky of the *Campus*:

I am very glad indeed that the students do not share Bishop Manning's views about me; if they did it would be necessary to despair of the young. It is comforting that the Board of Higher Education decided in my favour, but I doubt whether the fight is at an end. I am afraid that if and when I take up my duties at City College you will all be disappointed to find me a very mild and inoffensive person, totally destitute of horns and hoofs.[35]

Russell also wrote to Warder Norton, thanking him for the publishers' statement which he had contributed to the controversy. Russell added:

I am very much impressed by the courage of the Board of Higher Education in upholding my appointment. I did not think that they would do so. It still seems to me probable that my enemies will find some way of ousting me; if necessary, by some change in the law. But it is a grand fight and I seem to have recovered with radicals the ground that I had lost by disliking Stalin.[36]

Norton queried whether Russell had not felt inclined to dismiss the affair with "one of your good cracks" which elicited the following comment:

I have not felt tempted to indulge in quips, as the matter was obviously too serious. I should have liked to suggest that no one should be allowed to be a bishop until a Board of Logicians had passed upon his logic, but I am afraid the popular appeal of logic is insufficient.

Complimenting the Philosophy Department, Russell in a letter to Dr Krikorian stated:

I am very much impressed by the campaign that my partisans conducted. Obscurantists are always organised, but the friends of freedom, by their very nature, tend not to be. It is obvious that but for a great deal of hard work by the members of the Department of Philosophy, the issue would not have been what it was. I find it hard to believe that the other side will accept defeat, and I am waiting to see what their next move will be.[37]

The Chair of Indecency

At the very moment when Board Member C. Tuttle was blandly declaring that the Russell controversy would be settled by the public, manoeuvres were being completed to challenge the Board's decision in the courts. On the day after the Board meeting, an order was sought in the State Supreme Court directing the Board of Higher Education as respondent, "to rescind and revoke the said appointment of the said Dr Bertrand Russell."[38] The suit was brought, not against Russell, but against the Municipality of New York as the governing authority of the Board of Higher Education. This was presumably the way "public opinion" was to be consulted.

The papers of the petitioner, Mrs Jean Kay, a taxpayer, living in Brooklyn, and of her attorney, Joseph Goldstein, had already been drawn up on 18 March, in anticipation of the boardroom defeat. Mrs Kay was in no way connected with City College. Her children did not attend the college and when approached by the press neither she nor her legal representative would reveal the source of their funds. Her petition initially alleged that Russell's appointment was illegal and improper on two grounds: that as an alien he could not be legally employed under the State Education Law; and that his teachings were sexually immoral and "constitute a danger and a menace to the health, morals and welfare of the students who attend the College of the City of New York." She feared the students "may follow and make practical application and carry out the teachings of the said Dr Bertrand Russell on sex relationship." According to Mrs Kay, the practical application of Russell's philosophy would "result in violations of laws and statutes of the State of New York."[39]

The supporting affidavit of Joseph Goldstein,[40] an ex-magistrate under the previous Tammany administration, was a masterpiece of character assassination. Goldstein asserted that Russell "has exhibited practically all his life marked eccentricities and mental quirks, and his conduct throughout his life has been queer and unusual." The fact that Russell had been married three times was used to illustrate this claim. Goldstein went on to allege that Russell had:

> conducted a school in England, where he taught that children need not respect their parents. He also conducted a nudist school for both sexes of all ages, children, adolescents and adults. He participated in this nudist colony and went about naked in the company of persons of both sexes who were exhibiting themselves naked in public.

Among Russell's many eccentricities, Goldstein explained, was his "malicious libel" against the United States expeditionary forces in England, for which offence he served a six-month prison term in 1918. Russell's "peculiar tactics, mannerisms, eccentricities and queer conduct," Goldstein pleaded, "are sufficient grounds for an examination by a competent alienist as to his mental condition." Reviewing Russell's "philosophy," Goldstein quoted from *Marriage and Morals, Education and the Good Life, Education and the Modern World*, and *What I Believe*, and submitted the four volumes to the court as exhibits. Goldstein claimed that Russell's moral depravity had been sufficiently demonstrated and that his writings exposed him before the entire world "as a person entirely bereft of moral fiber." The conclusion was inevitable. Goldstein maintained that:

> he is lecherous, salacious, libidinous, lustful, venerous, erotomaniac, aphrodisiac, atheistic, irreverent, narrow-minded, bigoted, and untruthful; that he is not a Philosopher in the accepted meaning of the word; that he is not a lover of wisdom; that he is not a searcher after wisdom; that he is not an explorer of that universal science which aims at an explanation of all the phenomena of the universe by ultimate causes; that in the opinion of your deponent and multitudes of other persons he is a sophist; that he practices sophism; that by cunning contrivances, tricks and devices and by mere quibbling, he puts forth fallacious arguments and arguments that are not supported by sound reasoning; and he draws inferences which are not justly deduced from a sound premise; that all his alleged doctrines which he calls philosophy are just cheap, tawdry, worn-out, patched up fetishes and propositions, devised for the purpose of misleading the people.[41]

Goldstein closed his brief with the contention that it was not academic freedom Russell sought "but license to teach and be the purveyor of filth, obscenity, salaciousness and blasphemy."

The press reported these dramatic developments with alacrity, quoting extensively from Goldstein's affidavit. Defence of the action was undertaken by the City Corporation, acting on behalf of the Board of Higher Education. Russell was kept in touch with the proceedings by the City College Philosophy Department, but only saw copies of the relevant documents after the court hearing.

Argument on Mrs Kay's petition was heard before Justice John E. McGeehan of the Supreme Court on 27 March. McGeehan was an Irish Catholic sponsored by Tammany Hall and had "distinguished himself by trying to have a portrait of Martin Luther removed from a court-house mural illustrating legal history."[42]

The Board's case was greatly weakened by its legal adviser's decision not to contest the attacks on Russell's character and writings. Their defence was limited to the technical point concerning Russell's citizenship. The assistant corporation counsel, Nicholas Bucci, merely argued that the requirements of the education law as to the employment of American citizens were limited to pre-university teaching and was therefore not binding on the Board of Higher Education. Neither did the defence deal with a third ground of complaint instituted into the proceedings, which charged that the Board had not subjected Russell to a legally required civil service examination to determine "merit and fitness."

Throughout the proceedings, Justice McGeehan showed the keenest interest in the evidence on Russell's "moral fitness," and it was on Russell's character and writings that Attorney Goldstein and the counsel he briefed, William S. Bennet, concentrated their main line of fire. As counsel Bennet prepared to address the court on Russell's writings, he first of all found it necessary to apologise: "I am confident that your Honor wishes me to omit the salacious portions of his teachings, as far as possible." To which McGeehan replied: "Not that it would offend me because I have heard nearly everything that the human ear could have heard in my short and checkered career [*sic*]."[43] McGeehan clearly expected the worst.

Bennet summarised for the court the immoral nature of Russell's writings and personal life. He then turned to Russell's imprisonment during the First World War for stating that the American army was accustomed to the role of strike-breaking, and, in an angry denunciation declared of Russell:

> It is a lie, a vicious, nasty lie that Russell knew was a lie when he said it, an insult to every American soldier and to every American citizen, and it is against the public policy of the State . . . to employ in its schools or in civil office or any other place a man who in a time when we were fighting for a principle vilified the army of the United States and lied about it. It is the most disgraceful, shocking attempt to appoint a person to the public schools which has ever taken place in the State of New York.[44]

Supplementing his affidavit, Goldstein elaborated for the court his evidence on Russell's "nudist colony" in England, again alleging that Russell "paraded himself nude, together with his wife, in public." Goldstein concluded:

> The spectacle, your Honor, of our citizens contributing to pay him $8,000 a year to bring his filthy ideas into our colleges is repugnant, and I don't believe it requires too much argument that such a man should not be permitted to be a teacher in school. . . . Furthermore, this old man who is about 70 years of age has gone in for salacious poetry, and we fear he might teach that to the children . . . in his philosophy he quotes, for instance, with approval, such poetry as this:
>
> > "Do not mock me in thy bed
> > While these cold nights freeze me dead."[45]

Have we got to pay him $8,000 a year to have such philosophy taught in our schools? I have also adverted in my affidavit and I believe it is borne out by proof that he winks at homo-sexualism; I say, I will go further, that he approves of it.[46]

Reserving his decision, Judge McGeehan adjourned the court so he could read the books presented in evidence, and remarked: "If I find that these books sustain the allegations of the petition I will give the Appellate Division and the Court of Appeals something to think about."[47]

Three organisations were represented at the hearing and were permitted to file briefs as friends of the court – the American Civil Liberties Union, the National Lawyers Guild, and the New York College Teachers' Union. These parties all supported the Board. They contended that the appointment was lawful, that citizenship was not an issue, and that the appointment should not be disturbed because it would be an interference with academic freedom. The brief submitted by the National Lawyers Guild pointed out:

Dr Russell is said to hold certain views on religion, morality and sex. None of these views is either revolutionary or new. Some of them were advocated by Judge Lindsey twenty years ago. The college libraries are well stocked with Dr Russell's books, and no epidemic of immorality has resulted, as far as the public is aware.

The attorney representing the American Civil Liberties Union was Osmond K. Fraenkel. He attended the argument before Justice McGeehan and reported to the Civil Liberties Union on 27 March:

In my opinion the case was very badly handled by the corporation counsel's office. For this I do not blame Mr Bucci, the assistant in charge, who is a very able lawyer. I can only suppose that he acted under instruction. The reason for my criticism is this: The Board put in no answer but made a motion to dismiss, thus giving the judge an opportunity to write an opinion denouncing Bertrand Russell for the charges as made in the petition. Moreover, the Board argued only the technical question concerning the application of the citizenship requirement. No attempt was made to show the extent to which the Board of Higher Education, in its recent session, took into consideration the various criticisms which had been made of Mr Russell or to argue the legal point that its decision on that subject was not subject to review in the courts. . . . It seems to me that it might be desirable to have Mr Russell represented by counsel of his own choosing so that some control over the outcome of the case could be exercised independent of the Corporation Counsel's office. If that is to be done at all, it has to be done very promptly.

The Director of the American Civil Liberties Union, Roger N. Baldwin, wrote to Russell on 29 March, enclosing a copy of Fraenkel's letter, and stated:

> Because we consider the action against the Board of Higher Education a direct threat to academic freedom, we are vitally interested in the successful defense of the case. If you contemplate having a New York attorney appear in this case for you, we shall be glad to co-operate in every way.

Justice McGeehan announced his verdict on 30 March. In a lengthy judgement[48] he revoked the Board's appointment of Russell, on all three grounds contested by the petitioner. He agreed that the citizenship requirement was a valid complaint; he upheld the contention that the Board's failure to test Russell's "merit and fitness" was a sufficient cause to sustain the petition; he found, as the "most compelling" ground of all, that Russell was morally unfit for the position. In assessing Russell's moral character, McGeehan sustained the view that "Mr Russell has taught in his books immoral and salacious doctrines." He proceeded to describe the appointment as "an insult to the people of the City of New York," and accused the Board of Higher Education of "establishing a chair of indecency" at City College. By their selection of Russell, the judge declared, the Board had "acted arbitrarily, capriciously and in direct violation of the public health, safety and morals of the people."

To those who claimed that academic freedom was under attack, the judge pontificated:

> While this court would not interfere with any action of the Board so far as a pure question of "valid" academic freedom is concerned, it will not tolerate academic freedom being used as a cloak to promote the popularisation in the minds of adolescents of acts forbidden by the penal law.

So enraged was the judge by Russell's "moral character" that he passed the opinion that Russell would be denied American citizenship if he ever applied for it. McGeehan later remarked that he "had to take a bath" after reading one of Russell's books, and was of the view that Russell wanted "to make strumpets out of all our girls."[49] John Dewey expressed the doubt that the judge had ever read the books at all, and the *New Republic* stated that the judgement must have been "produced at superhuman speed if the Justice actually wrote it after all the evidence was in."[50]

There was jubilation among those who had crusaded for Russell's removal. The New York *Sun* proclaimed:

Mrs Kay carried the day!

After millions of bitter words had been exchanged between those who assailed the appointment of Bertrand Russell as Professor of Philosophy at City College because of the "advocacy of immorality" contained in his writings, and those who insisted that barring him from the post would be "a blow to academic freedom," Supreme Court Justice John E. McGeehan yesterday granted the Brooklyn housewife's petition for an order revoking Russell's appointment and discharging him from the position.

Unless the ruling is upset by a higher court – and a number of legal observers insist that it is not likely to be – Professor Russell will be among those absent from the faculty of City College for all time.[51]

Judge McGeehan received lavish praise from the Jesuit weekly, *America*, which described him as "a virile and staunch American" who was "a pure and honorable jurist and . . . rates among the best as an authority on law."[52] The *Tablet* declared that the decision "carries a note of simplicity and sincerity that immediately wins acclaim."[53]

Upon hearing of the decision, Russell described McGeehan as "a very ignorant fellow". He added: "As an Irish Catholic, his views were perhaps prejudiced, but he had no right to make such a statement from the Bench."[54]

Speaking to newsmen who had descended on his doorstep, Russell remarked:

I am not as interested in sex as is Bishop Manning, who is greatly concerned with it. Sex is only a small part of what I have written. Bishop Manning and his supporters have noticed only this part. They don't notice that almost all of my writing has been on other subjects.[55]

Of the charges that were brought against him, Russell said: "Precisely the same accusations were brought against Socrates – atheism and corrupting the young." Russell added: "Any person who expresses an opinion without regard to its popularity expects to get in trouble – and I don't like to hold my tongue about important affairs."[56] However, he sounded a warning: "All this fuss frightens me. It makes me fear that within a few years, all the intellect of America will be in concentration camps."[57] In an interview given to a Los Angeles newspaper on his attitude to Christianity, Russell stated.

The Bible provides texts for many different moods. The good Christians who are attacking me so savagely in New York seem to prefer: "Thou shalt not commit adultery," "There shall be weeping and gnashing of teeth," "Let Him be crucified," and so on.

My grandmother gave me, when I was a child, a Bible in which she had written her favorite texts, and to these I have added some of my own. I suggest them as required reading for Episcopal Bishop William T. Manning who stands in the front rank of my accusers. They are:
"Thou shalt not follow a multitude into evil."
"Thou shalt love thy neighbour as thyself. . . . "
"Blessed are ye when men shall revile you and persecute you and shall say all manner of evil things against you falsely for my sake. Rejoice and be exceedingly glad for great is your reward in heaven. For so persecuted they the prophets which were before you."[58]

Prior to McGeehan's judgement, Russell had issued a statement, on 28 March, expressing his reaction to Mrs Kay's and Attorney Goldstein's pleas in court. Russell had declared:

I have hitherto kept an almost unbroken silence in the controversy concerning my appointment to City College, and I could not admit that my opinions were relevant. But when grossly untrue statements as to my actions are made in court I feel that I must give them the lie.

I never conducted a nudist colony in England. Neither my wife nor I ever paraded nude in public. I never went in for salacious poetry.

Such assertions are deliberate falsehoods which must be known to those who make them to have no foundation in fact. I should be glad of an opportunity to deny them on oath.[59]

An anonymous correspondent from Newark, New Jersey, wrote to Russell indicating the fierce hatred that had been aroused against him:

Just whom did you think you were fooling when you had those hypocritically posed "family man" pictures taken for the newspapers? Can your diseased brain have reached such an advanced stage of senility as to imagine for a moment that you would impress anyone? You poor old fool!

Even your publicly proved degeneracy cannot overshadow your vileness in posing for these pictures and trying to hide behind the innocence of your unfortunate children. Shame on you! Every decent man and woman in the country loathes you for this vile action of yours more than your other failings, which, after all, you inherited honestly enough from your decadent family tree. As for your questions and concern regarding Church and State connections in this country – just what concern has anything in this country got to do with you? Any time you don't like American doings, go back to your native England (if you can!) and your stuttering King, who is an excellent example of British degenerate royalty – with its ancestry of barmaids, and pantrymen!

Or did I hear someone say you were thrown out of that country of liberal degeneracy, because you out-did the royal family. HAW!

Yours
Pimp-Hater

P.S. – I notice you refer to some American judge as an "ignorant fellow." If you are such a shining light, just why are you looking for a new appointment at this late date in your life? Have you been smelling up the California countryside too strongly?[60]

Russell agreed with the American Civil Liberties Union proposal that he should contest the court decision, and Osmond Fraenkel was engaged to lodge an appeal on his behalf. The first opportunity Russell had of studying the case against his appointment was when Fraenkel sent him copies of Mrs Kay's petition and Goldstein's affidavit. Russell provided Fraenkel with information relevant to the issues raised by these documents. Concerning Mrs Kay's allegations, Russell wrote to him on 4 April:

the petition is based on a misunderstanding of the word "philosophy" (which I know is often taken by ignorant people to mean theories for the conduct of practical life). . . . The books and opinions mentioned are no part of my philosophy and cannot be correctly described as philosophy at all. Those of my books mentioned in the petition are on the subject of sociology, which I have never taught in any school or college and will not teach at C.C.N.Y.

Russell listed for Fraenkel's information those of his books which dealt with philosophy and logic and suggested that they be produced in court. He gave details of his *curriculum vitae* and suggested that "these facts might be useful in dealing with the proposal of a competitive examination, which would in fact be rather difficult. The only competent examiner would be Dr Whitehead, who would be disqualified as a collaborator."

Regarding Goldstein's affidavit, Russell informed Fraenkel:

I have never kept a nudist colony. The school which I kept for some time for little children in England could not be so described. The children bathed naked. Otherwise they often played in hot weather wearing little or nothing, as nearly all children do nowadays. They were all under the age of 12.

I have never myself appeared naked in public. I believe "parade" was the word used. This accusation is equally false with regard to my wife. . . .

The salacious poetry charge is totally unfounded . . . I have never written a word of poetry in my life. I read a great deal of poetry, both alone and aloud to my family, but none of it salacious, and at Chicago I used to read poetry aloud with my students. But I cannot suppose the charge to be based on knowledge of this custom.

Fraenkel proposed to counter Goldstein's summations of Russell's writings by comparing them to the books themselves. In a letter of 9 April, Russell approved of this plan and stated: "I should like emphasis to be laid on the distinction between advocating and not punishing such practices as infantile masturbation." Russell indicated his willingness "to submit to examination by a number of eminent alienists, if this would do anything to discredit Goldstein's outrageous affidavit." He went on to add: "I understand from Mr Baldwin that you intend to defend me without charge. I appreciate deeply the generous and liberal spirit which you show in this."

Judge McGeehan's decision was greeted by an outcry of nationwide proportion, led by Russell's supporters. With the battle now revolving around the Courts of Appeal, the campaign to reinstate Russell became dependent upon the Board of Higher Education being allowed to make an effective appeal. The case had become a rallying point for liberal opinion throughout the country, and in order to co-ordinate protest action and raise funds for the appeal, a Bertrand Russell–Academic Freedom Committee was formed. The Committee represented many shades of opinion, with Professor Montague of Columbia University acting as chairman, and a host of college presidents as sponsors, including Sproul and Hutchins. On the executive committee were John Dewey, of the Committee for Cultural Freedom; Dr Franz Boas, the world-famous anthropologist, representing the Committee for Democracy and Intellectual Freedom; Roger Baldwin, of the American Civil Liberties Union; George Countz of the American Federation of Teachers; Morris Ernst, of the National Lawyers Guild; and Arthur O. Lovejoy, of the American Association of University Professors.

The Philosophy Department at City College had already joined with the Committee for Cultural Freedom and the American Civil Liberties Union in issuing a statement, on 31 March, urging the Board of Higher Education to appeal against the McGeehan decision.[61] The joint statement charged that the court decision ignored convincing testimony of Russell's competence as an educator, and accepted "without relevant proof . . . allegations that were false with regard to his moral character and fitness." The statement expressed the fear that the decision had established a "positively dangerous precedent" for appointment and removal of teachers on grounds other than their fitness as educators. Numerous bodies wrote to Mayor La Guardia and Ordway Tead, Chairman of the Board of Higher Education, urging them to fight the McGeehan judgement. The American Students Union pledged "to fight the decision with every resource at our command."[62]

Among the first to speak out on behalf of Russell were his own students at the University of California. Senior students at UCLA issued a statement expressing their confidence in Russell and said:

Far from in any way corrupting the morals of his students, he had, on the contrary, done much to encourage a higher and finer ethical standard by his own personal uprightness, his tolerance, kindliness and complete intellectual honesty.[63]

UCLA faculty members also stood by Russell, and Dr Hans Reichenbach, Professor of Philosophy, spoke for them all when he said:

We all know Professor Russell to be one of the greatest philosophers of our time. He has had great success in his instruction on the U.C.L.A. campus and is well liked by the faculty members. I am astonished at the action taken by the New York Supreme Court.[64]

Russell was particularly happy with the "sympathetic reactions" of his students. "They have been very gracious," he told the press, "and the unanimous sympathy they have given me is heartening." He was also "gratified" by the extensive support he had received from academics, and remarked: "They have lived up to their standards of intellect."[65]

Messages of support from all over America continued to flow into Russell's Los Angeles home. Ohio State University students telegraphed: "Ready to fight this thing for you and with you." Sixty faculty members of Northwestern University, Illinois, pledged "financial aid to defend your rights."

Students at City College were in a state of great agitation. An emergency protest committee was set up to organise student activity, and William Swirsky, who was on the committee, notified Russell:

A student protest demonstration is taking place Friday. . . . Wednesday will see the results of a drive for 5,500 signatures on petitions urging your reinstatement. Every student organisation is aroused and the faculty is thoroughly indignant. We've got to win this fight![66]

The protest meeting at City College was called by the Student Council, and held on 5 April. Students packed the Great Hall as speakers urged the Board of Higher Education to appeal against the court decision, and warned that attempts to ban Russell constituted a flagrant violation of academic freedom. Messages of support received from distinguished figures were read to the meeting. Thomas Mann, who had been invited to address the assembly, wired:

Not yet being a citizen of this country I do not feel justified to be the speaker in this cause which only Americans have to decide, but I feel more than compelled to express my sympathy with the aims of your gathering and with the idea of spiritual freedom. Knowing the technique of its destruction from bitter experience, I can but agree with your endeavour not to tolerate intolerance.[67]

Upton Sinclair, a graduate of City College, wired:

> The judge and the bishop have publicised the fact that England has loaned us one of the most learned and generous men of our time. The advocates of fixed dogmas should not be allowed to rob us of Bertrand Russell's services, nor of our most precious democratic principle, freedom of thought and speech.[68]

A telegram from UCLA students stating: "Your meeting protesting persecution of Bertrand Russell has complete support of U.C.L.A. students who know this great man," received thunderous and sustained applause.

Professor Krikorian wired Russell:

> The student body gave an amazing demonstration in favor of you on Friday. Our morale is high and will fight the case to the bitter end. Both the person involved and the cause have deeply stirred the enlightened groups for academic freedom. Russell Committee to coordinate activity and to be ready for long-drawn fight.[69]

Russell was prepared to travel to New York and speak in public on behalf of the campaign. In view of the legal proceedings, Fraenkel advised him not to make public statements on McGeehan's decision, and the Committee for Cultural Freedom, who were hoping to invite him East, cancelled their plans. The radical American Committee for Democracy and Intellectual Freedom, however, organised a protest rally at Carnegie Hall, on 13 April, which was addressed by Dr Franz Boas, Professor Walter Rautenstrauch, and others.

Commenting on the campaign for academic freedom that had generated behind him, Horace Kallen wrote to Russell: "You seem predestined to carry the flag of free thought against its enemies."[70] Russell replied on 14 April:

> No doubt I ought to consider myself very lucky to be in this privileged position; but it was quite unintentional. I really much prefer abstract work and never expect these fights I find myself in. But the only thing I hate more than fighting is running away.
>
> The terrific movement to support me is personally very gratifying and publicly very encouraging. I have never seen professors so roused or so united.

The moves to reinstate Russell through the Appeal Courts were firmly obstructed. Pressure was directed against the Board of Higher Education to dissuade it from proceeding with an appeal. The Tammany politicans were particularly active in the New York State legislature, which was already on record as holding that "an advocate of barnyard morality is an unfit person to hold an important post in the educational system of our State at the expense of the taxpayers."[71] More ominously, the State legislature adopted the notorious Dunigan Bill which called for a $50,000 witch-hunt into the New York educational system. Speaking for his bill, Senator John J. Dunigan, the minority leader, declared that the investigation was directed principally at the Board of Higher Education.[72] A resolution was adopted by the New York City Council urging the mayor to reconstitute the Board and appoint more "creditable" members. The clerical lobby was equally active, and Lambert Fairchild, of the National Committee for Religious Recovery, denounced those members of the Board who supported Russell as "renegade Jews and renegade Christians."[73] The Board, despite the minority that lined up behind Episcopalian Tuttle, refused to give way and voted to appeal against McGeehan's decision. Mayor La Guardia, with an eye for the Catholic vote, was embarrassed by the confrontation, and manoeuvred to prevent the Board from appealing.

The reactionary drive to eliminate liberal teaching influences from the colleges was aided by Mayor La Guardia's action, of 5 April, when he removed from the 1941 city budget the financial allocation for the post which Russell was to fill. The mayor justified his action by declaring it was "in keeping with the policy to eliminate vacant positions."[74] A few weeks later, the Board of Estimates, the controlling financial body of the city, strengthened the mayor's hand by prohibiting the use of any funds for the employment of Russell. The corporation counsel, appointed by the mayor to handle the Board's legal affairs, in an unprecedented action declined to represent the Board in the matter of their appeal. He strongly urged them against an appeal, which he considered "would be an unfortunate case upon which to base a legal test of the issues," and advised them instead to accept an offer from Mrs Kay's counsel, which in the event of their dropping proceedings, would mean that "no order would be entered against the Board upon Judge McGeehan's decision."[75] The mayor fully supported the corporation counsel, whom he held was the sole authority legally entitled to represent the Board. Russell in a letter to Warder Norton on 27 April 1940 commented: "I shall be curious to know whether La Guardia is able to prevent the B.H.E. from employing Buckner [private counsel]. His moves to prevent a proper trial of the issue are very mean." Flouting the mayor, the Board engaged private counsel to handle their appeal, but after several hearings the Appellate Division of the Supreme Court dismissed the appeal on the ground that the Board had no authority to appoint private counsel.

Russell's appeal fared no better. On 16 April, Justice McGeehan refused to allow Russell to intervene, on the grounds that he had "no legal standing in the proceeding; that he had delayed too long in asserting this right; and that there had been sufficient opportunity for him to answer Mrs Kay's charges at the time of the original hearing."[76] All further attempts to appeal the case in higher quarters failed, and the McGeehan judgement became final. Speaking of the unsatisfactory disposition of the case, Professor Morris Cohen stated: "If this is law, then surely, in the language of Dickens, 'the law is an ass'."[77] John Dewey commented: "As Americans, we can only blush with shame for this scar on our repute for fair play."[78]

The City College controversy was major news in the New York press for several weeks. Most leading New York newspapers took the view that the courts should not interfere with the Board of Higher Education's appointments. The papers most favourably disposed to Russell were the *Post*, the communist party's *Daily Worker*, and the Jewish press. The *Journal-American*, the *Mirror* and the *Sun* were most hostile. The *Herald Tribune* declared that "no friend of civil liberty and academic freedom"[79] could remain indifferent to the Bertrand Russell case. *The New York Times*, while giving the controversy comprehensive coverage, refrained from editorial comment. On 20 April, however, an editorial was published reflecting on the "bitterness of feeling" which the issue had generated. Holding that the original appointment was "impolitic and unwise," *The New York Times* contended that Russell "should have had the wisdom to withdraw from the appointment as soon as its harmful results became evident."

A letter from Russell appeared in *The New York Times* on 26 April 1940:

I hope you will allow me to comment on your references to the controversy originating in my appointment to the College of the City of New York, and particularly on your judgment that I "should have had the wisdom to retire from the appointment as soon as its harmful effects became evident."

In one sense this would have been the wisest course; it would certainly have been more prudent as far as my personal interests are concerned, and a great deal pleasanter. If I had considered only my own interests and inclinations I should have retired at once.

But however wise such action might have been from a personal point of view, it would also, in my judgment, have been cowardly and selfish. A great many people who realised that their own interests and the principles of toleration and free speech were at stake were anxious from the first to continue the controversy. If I had retired I should have robbed them of their *casus belli* and tacitly assented to the proposition of opposition that substantial groups shall be allowed to drive out of public office individuals whose opinions, race or nationality they find repugnant. This to me would appear immoral.

It was my grandfather who brought about the repeal of the English Test and Corporation Acts, which barred from public office anyone not a member of the Church of England, of which he himself was a member, and one of my earliest and most important memories is of a deputation of Methodists and Wesleyans coming to cheer outside his window on the fiftieth anniversay of this repeal, although the largest single group affected was Catholic.

I do not believe that the controversy is harmful on general grounds. It is not controversy and open difference of opinion that endanger democracy. On the contrary, these are its greatest safeguards. It is an essential part of democracy that substantial groups, even majorities, should extend toleration to dissentient groups, however small and however much their sentiments may be outraged.

In a democracy it is necessary that people should learn to endure having their sentiments outraged. Minority groups already endure this, although according to the principles of the founders of the American Constitution they are equally entitled to consideration. If there is 10 per cent of the population of New York that holds opinions similar to mine, then 10 per cent of the teachers in New York should be allowed to hold those opinions. And this should apply to all unusual opinions. If it is once admitted that there are opinions toward which such tolerance need not extend, then the whole basis of toleration is destroyed.

Jews have been driven from Germany, and Catholics most cruelly persecuted because they were repugnant to the substantial part of the community which happened to be in power.

In a somewhat lighter vein, Russell provided a tailpiece to the City College affair in his letter to Warder Norton of 27 April 1940:

Mrs Kay should have a complimentary copy of "Language, Truth and Fact," [*Inquiry into Meaning and Truth*], with the author's thanks for her help in advertising it. Her counsel asserts that I am "aphrodisiac" – evidently he hasn't the vaguest idea what the word means. I should like to think him right on this point.

Notes

1 27 February 1940.
2 B. Russell, *Autobiography* (London, 1968), Vol. II, p. 219 (Boston 1968), p. 334.
3 See B. Feinberg and R. Kasrils, *Bertrand Russell's America, 1895–1945* (New York, 1974), p. 113.
4 Quoted by the American Civil Liberties Union in their pamphlet *The Story of the Bertrand Russell Case* (January 1941), p. 4; and by Paul Edwards in "The Bertrand Russell Case" which appears as an appendix to Russell's *Why I Am*

Not a Christian, and Other Essays (London and Simon & Schuster, New York, 1957), p. 182.

5 Edwards, op. cit., p. 182.

6 Ibid., p. 183.

7 American Civil Liberties Union, op. cit., pp. 4–5.

8 Ibid., p. 5.

9 To Bernard Goltz, Secretary to the Student Council at CCNY, on 22 March 1940; B. Russell, *Autobiography*, Vol. II, p. 227, p. 347.

10 Ibid., p. 219, p. 334.

11 Edwards, op. cit., p. 185.

12 Taken from an undated holograph copy. This communication possibly took the form of an overnight cable.

13 Otto Nathan and Heinz Norden (eds), *Einstein on Peace* (Simon & Schuster, New York, 1960), p. 310; originally published in *The New York Times* (19 March 1940).

14 B. Russell, *Autobiography* (London, 1969), Vol, III, p. 60 (Boston, 1969), pp. 69–70.

15 The *New Republic* (8 April 1940); quoted in John Dewey and Horace M. Kallen (eds), *The Bertrand Russell Case* (Viking Press, New York, 1941), p. 152.

16 Dewey and Kallen, op. cit., p. 153.

17 Taken from an undated holograph copy; the New York *Post*'s cable was dated 13 March 1940.

18 Edwards, op. cit., p. 188.

19 15 March 1940.

20 18 March 1940.

21 Edwards, op. cit., p. 186.

22 Ibid.

23 Ibid.

24 "Minutes of the Meeting of the Board of Higher Education of the City of New York" (18 March 1940), see Supreme Court, New York County, Appellate Division, *Papers on Appeal from Order* in the matter of the application of Jean Kay against the Board of Higher Education of the City of New York.

25 Ibid., pp. 94–6.

26 Ibid., p. 99.

27 Ibid., p. 97.

28 Ibid., p. 93.

29 Ibid., p. 98.

30 29 March 1940.

31 American Civil Liberties Union, op. cit., p. 5.

32 Ibid.

33 "O, how comely it is, and how reviving/To the spirits of just men long oppressed,/When God into the hands of their deliverer/Puts invincible might,/To quell the mighty of the earth, the oppressor,/The brute and boisterous force of violent men,/Hardy and industrious to support/Tyrannic power, but raging to pursue/The righteous, and all such as honour truth!" (Milton).

34 19 March 1940.

35 22 March 1940; B. Russell, *Autobiography*, Vol. II, p. 228; p. 348.

36 Ibid.

37 Ibid.

38 Supreme Court, New York County, Appellate Division, *Papers on Appeal from Order*, in the matter of the application of Jean Kay against the Board of Higher Education of the City of New York, p. 40.

39 Ibid., pp. 35–41.
40 Ibid., pp. 42–50.
41 Ibid., p. 49.
42 John Dewey and Horace M. Kallen, *The Bertrand Russell Case* (Viking Press, New York, 1941), p. 21.
43 Supreme Court, New York County, Appellate Division, op. cit., p. 71.
44 Ibid., pp. 76–7.
45 Quoted by Russell in his *Marriage and Morals* (London, 1929), p. 60 (Horace Liveright, New York, 1929), p. 71, to illustrate the forthright character of Renaissance love poetry.
46 Supreme Court, New York County, Appellate Division, op. cit., pp. 77–8.
47 The New York *Herald Tribune* (28 March 1940).
48 Dewey and Kallen, op. cit., pp. 213–25; see also Supreme Court, New York County, Appellate Division, op. cit., pp. 102–17.
49 The New York *Herald Tribune* ((?) May 1940).
50 P. Edwards, "The Bertrand Russell Case," appendix to Russell's *Why I Am Not a Christian, and Other Essays* (London and New York, Simon & Schuster, 1957), p. 192.
51 The New York *Sun* (31 March 1940).
52 Edwards, op. cit., p. 212.
53 Ibid., p. 213.
54 Undated and unidentified Los Angeles newsclipping.
55 The New York *Herald Tribune* (1 April 1940).
56 Ibid.
57 The *Daily News*, Los Angeles (29 March 1940).
58 Undated and unidentified newsclipping.
59 *The New York Times* (29 March 1940).
60 B. Russell, *Autobiography* (London, 1968), Vol. II, p. 226 (Boston, 1968), pp. 344–5.
61 The New York *Herald Tribune* (1 April 1940).
62 Ibid.
63 Undated and unidentified Los Angeles newsclipping.
64 The Los Angeles *Times* (1 April 1940).
65 Ibid.
66 1 April 1940.
67 The *Beaver* (CCNY student newspaper) (5 April 1940).
68 Sinclair sent a copy of this telegram to Russell on 4 April, with the comment: "I do not know whether you happen to know that C.C.N.Y. is my *alma mater . . .*"
69 8 April 1940.
70 From Kallen's letter of 2 April 1940.
71 A resolution, including this statement, submitted by Senator Phelps, a Manhattan Democrat, was adopted on 25 March 1940.
72 *The New York Times* (26 March 1940); a large-scale investigation into the New York educational system followed.
73 Edwards, op. cit., p. 213.
74 American Civil Liberties Union, *The Story of the Bertrand Russell Case* (January 1941), p. 8.
75 Ibid., pp. 9–10.
76 Ibid., p. 8.
77 Dewey and Kallen, op. cit., p. 143.
78 Ibid., p. 60.
79 Ibid., p. 15.

9

War and Peace in the Nuclear Age

Alan Ryan

From 1945 until his death in 1970, Russell thought, wrote and campaigned endlessly in the hope of bringing sanity and order to world politics and persuading his fellow creatures to turn away from the impending nuclear catastrophe. His career as polemicist, agitator and amateur world states-man fell into three phases. The first was his reaction in the early post-war years to the invention and use of nuclear weapons and his call for a world government which would have a monopoly of such weapons. From the outset he thought Britain should remain a non-nuclear power; and the second stage of his public career came when he took his advocacy of nuclear disarmament for Britain on to the streets with the creation of the Campaign for Nuclear Disarmament in 1958. The last was his increasingly fierce criticism of American foreign policy from 1960 onwards, culminating in his part in the campaign against America's intervention in Vietnam.

The quarter of a century between the end of the war and his death in 1970 saw some striking reversals. Immediately after the war, while America still had a monopoly of nuclear weapons, Russell was ready to see world government instituted by the threat or even by the actuality of a nuclear war. By the time he died, he had long been convinced that the Soviet Union was no threat to world peace and the United States a real menace. It is an intriguing question: what had changed in the interim – Russell, America, or the balance of world power? British readers whose memory stretches back to the 1960s will have a clear picture of Russell addressing large crowds in Trafalgar Square, organizing "sit-down" campaigns and other forms of civil disobedience, getting himself arrested and spending another week in Brixton prison, forty-three years after his first visit. Why was he so com-mitted to British unilateral disarmament that he supported "direct action," such as invading airfields and submarine bases and "sit-down" campaigns in central London, when he did not advocate American unilateralism, and was as ambiguous a "pacifist" in the 1950s as he had been in the 1930s or during the First World War?

In his final decade of active campaigning, Russell was a very public presence; he operated successively through the Pugwash conferences, CND, the Committee of 100, the Bertrand Russell Peace Foundation and its offspring, the War Crimes Tribunal. As a very old man, he worked through a variety of other people, above all his secretary Ralph Schoenman, the young American who largely controlled what the public saw and heard of Russell between 1961 and 1967. Distinguishing Russell's views from those of his helpers and the various groups he worked with becomes more difficult as he becomes more and more the spokesman of a movement. Cynics said at the time that Russell was the captive of his followers and that his role was to sign what Schoenman made up; even before that, they had said that Russell was unduly under the influence of his fourth wife – who was certainly radical in her politics, if not, on the face of it, more so than her notably strong-willed and independent husband.

In the absence of an unvarnished account of Russell's last years by those who worked with him, common sense and caution have to go a long way. Russell maintained to the end that his position had been consistent from 1945, and that although he had followed the practice of governments and businesses in employing spokesmen to state his position, what came out under his name was exactly what he wanted to say.[1] This chapter will broadly confrim that. His views on international affairs were not so very different from what they had been before. The curiously bloodless bloodthirstiness of some of his proposals and the hostility he displayed towards America were not aberrations of extreme old age or thrust upon him by wild young men. His extremist proposals for a world government with a monopoly of destructive power were of a piece with views he had expressed in 1915, and his hostility to America was much like the contempt he displayed in 1918 when he was jailed for it.[2] In the 1920s, as well as in the 1940s and 1950s, he had described America as an illiberal, hysterically anti-communist, lynch-mob-governed, racist slum which ought none the less to take up the reins of world government. His readiness to distinguish so sharply between the benefits of world peace and the squalor of American society and politics was in its own way admirable. We expect a historian to remain appalled at Roman brutality even while admiring the benefits the *pax Romana* brought to the (compulsorily) civilized world; and Russell displayed just this distance when he demanded that the unlovable United States should assume the mantle of world leadership. Even when he lost his temper and said things he regretted afterwards – as when he declared that Harold Macmillan was more wicked than Hitler – he still made sense. What we may more seriously complain of is not the wild ideas foisted on him by his helpers, but that at some times he flatly contradicted himself, and at others was disconcertingly evasive. Whatever the merits of his advocacy of an aggressive American foreign policy in 1945–9, for example, he ought not to have denied having put it forward – especially when he went on almost at once to withdraw the denial too. Nor should he have simultaneously declared that the Russians' overriding duty was to move with extreme caution and that they had every right to put missiles into Cuba if they chose to.

Russell was seventy-three when the war ended, eighty-eight in 1960, and ninety-five at the height of the campaign against the American presence in Vietnam. After 1954 he produced no sustained philosophical work. Although he had been an energetic traveller immediately after the war, he made few foreign trips after the mid-1950s, and after 1956 was increasingly unwilling to leave his home in North Wales; in his late eighties he was increasingly frail and suffered digestive disorders which prevented him going out very much. He was inevitably cut off from much that went on in the outside world. How seriously should we take his last writings on politics: his attacks on America over the war in Vietnam, his denunciation of the Warren Tribunal's inquiry into the assassination of President Kennedy, and so on? One obstacle to taking them seriously is that he did not compose all of them; after 1958 he received endless requests for messages of encouragement, to disarmament meetings, then to anti-Vietnam war meetings. By the mid-1960s messages went out in large numbers, were distributed as news releases, and were inevitably constructed on "boiler plate" principles – the same paragraphs were endlessly re-used in different contexts. Russell justified this by observing, "It is a curious thing that the public utterances of almost all Government officials and important business executives are known to be composed by secretaries or colleagues, and yet this is held unobjectionable. Why should it be considered heinous in an ordinary layman?" This would be fair enough if the only question was whether Russell the campaigner was *responsible* for the campaigns waged in his name. However, nobody expects government press releases to reveal the real thinking of politicians; but we are concerned with what Russell thought, and the fact that these statements offer little evidence of that is a difficulty. Indeed, they can bear rather little intellectual scrutiny. Read in the mass, the products of what one might call "the Schoenman years" are alarming; the proportion of abuse to argument is very high; disputed facts are confidently asserted without any suggestion that they are open to reasonable doubt – Russell rightly insisted that he always cited "sources" but seemed unable to see that it was the reliability of those sources which his critics questioned. Throughout the campaign against the Vietnam war, every horror is explained by conspiracy and malice. America is declared to be a near-fascist state in the hands of mad generals; the Vietnam war is doubly genocidal, setting Negro soldiers and Asians to kill each other; the atrocities which indubitably did mark the war are put down to policy rather than panic. Kennedy was killed by the FBI, or the CIA, or at any rate by their friends.[3] And so on.

Russell got angrier as he got older. With not long to live, he felt that he must make what difference he could, and he became readier to sacrifice both coherence and accuracy to impact. In reply to a critic in *Tribune* who had complained of the "unsociological" quality of Russell's writings on nuclear warfare, he wrote,

> I used to deal with wide sociological questions, for example in *Principles of Social Reconstruction, Roads to Freedom* and *Power*, but the Bikini test of 1 March, 1954 persuaded me that there was no time for long-term solutions and that some more immediate and specific movement was necessary for the preservation of mankind . . . if you saw a man dropping lighted matches on heaps of TNT, you would feel it necessary to stop him without waiting for vast schemes of social reform. And that is the present situation as I see it.

So we cannot be sure when he meant to be taken seriously, or when he was simply happy that his name would help the opponents of American folly and wickedness; letters to friends were notably more cautious and measured than his public blasts against American imperialism. Since he thought the superpowers might blow everything sky-high by mischance or blind stupidity, it was not only old age that made him angry and impatient. As he remarked more than once, there is little point studying logic if nobody survives to understand the results. In that perspective, veracity came a poor second to impact. When the Bertrand Russell Peace Foundation was founded in 1963, its chief asset was his name, and he was ready to lend it to his helpers without overmuch scrutiny of the terms.[4] The reader does not need to be adept in political theory to realize that Russell did not pen everything which went out over his signature – a knowledge of English grammar suffices.

It is not their hostility to America or their extravagance which makes Russell's last writings inauthentic. There is nothing inexplicable in Russell's antipathy to American foreign policy after 1957; it became sharper after the Cuban missile crisis of 1962, but that is not surprising. Nor is the wildness which was always likely to break out in anything he wrote. What is at odds with his earlier views is quite different. When he assails American policy in Vietnam he is sentimental about the Vietcong, who, he claims, are a "non-communist, neutralist, popular front" trying to keep the South Vietnam government to the terms of the Geneva accords of 1954. He asks us to applaud their bravery and to admire their fastidious concern not to injure the civilian population, or to injure only those who have collaborated with the American enemy. This legalism was a characteristic New Left trope, as was the rhetoric of such passages as this: "The people of

Vietnam are heroic, and their struggle is epic; a stirring and permanent reminder of the incredible spirit of which men are capable when they are dedicated to a noble ideal. Let us salute the people of Vietnam."[5] All his life, Russell had been a resolute opponent of the doctrine of "the superior virtue of the oppressed." Then he had written of the delusion that subject peoples were peculiarly admirable, "One by one these various nations rose to independence, and were found to be just like everybody else; but the experience of those already liberated did nothing to destroy the illusion as regards those who were still struggling."[6] He had thought it enough to point to the horrors of war and oppression; he had never thought the victims of oppression were made better by their sufferings, and would have thought their moral merits irrelevant. The belief that the Vietcong were morally special was a piece of New Left sentimentality which one can imagine Schoenman swallowing, but not Russell. Again, Russell attacked American imperialism in flatly Marxist terms that he would formerly have mocked.[7] He had always thought America was an imperialist power which used its military strength to make life easier for big business, but he also thought nations were driven by autonomous ideological forces, too. Powerful states simply wanted to make the world conform to their image, and Marxists looked for economic explanations where none were to be had. Schoenman wrote of Russell's wonderful openness to his young collaborators;[8] judging by his final repudiation of Schoenman, the truth is rather that Russell thought little of Schoenman's intelligence, but was happy to employ his energy and unwilling to waste time on quarrels with his own side.[9] The causes of American intervention mattered less than stopping it.

Twenty years earlier, Russell was one of the first laymen to come to terms with the existence of nuclear weapons. He was one of the few who were wholly at home with the physics of nuclear warfare, and he was an opponent of British nuclear weapons before the British government had seriously thought of producing them. The numerous articles and broadcasts he made in the 1950s advocate world government, appeal for verifiable disarmament, and suggest ways of reducing military tension by diplomatic means; but they also display an unostentatious familiarity with the new technology which would have been astonishing in anyone but the author of *The ABC of Atoms. Has Man a Future?* contains perhaps the clearest couple of paragraphs on the nature of nuclear fusion and fission and on the difference between atomic and hydrogen bombs that anyone ever wrote.[10] One of his first interventions in the nuclear debate came in a speech to the House of Lords on 28 November 1945, in which he appealed for a world government strong enough to contain the new menace. His familiarity with the physics of the bomb did nothing to make him happier about its existence. For one thing, many scientists involved with the bomb had worked on it only because they feared that German scientists must be close to creating a nuclear weapon. Like them, Russell was horrified at its use against Japan – by August 1945 Japan was close to defeat and was known to pose no nuclear threat. A demonstration of the bomb's destructive capabilities would, they thought, have been enough to bring about a Japanese surrender. Its use against undefended cities conjured up visions of future wars in which whole cities were reduced to radio-active ash and their inhabitants annihilated with them or stricken with lingering radiation-induced diseases. Russell's fears were even more vivid than his hearers'. When most laymen had hardly any idea of the nature of the new weapon, Russell could look ahead and see the dangers of more powerful weapons yet, for he understood the implications of the fact that atomic bombs momentarily created temperatures sufficient to launch nuclear fusion, and warned the House of Lords that "some mechanism analogous to the present atomic bomb could be used to set off a much more violent explosion which would be obtained if one could synthesize heavier elements out of hydrogen." That was the recipe for thermonuclear weapons.[11]

Russell was not alone in his fears. Where he was almost isolated was in his insistence that America must use her monopoly of nuclear weapons to create a world government armed with the power to destroy any country which tried to create nuclear weapons of its own. In 1945 the only possible target of this pressure was Stalin's Russia. For the next few years he was ritually denounced by the Soviet press as a mad warmonger, a fact which caused him some amusement in view of the way American newspapers treated him as a raving Red – but he was also treated with some suspicion by his friends on the English Left. Russell proposed that America should lead a confederation which monopolized nuclear weapons and the right to manufacture them, individual nations abandoning that right and reducing their non-nuclear armaments.[12] Once founded, it would have no trouble surviving, for it would possess overwhelming nuclear superiority over any nation tempted to go its own way. Russell accepted that Russia might well refuse to join on any terms; what was to be done about an intransigent Soviet Union? Russell's answers varied in brevity and clarity, but the essence was that the USA should seek a *casus belli* which would allow it to launch a war to end war. "A *casus belli* should not be difficult to find. Either Russia's voluntary adherence or its defeat in war would render the Confederation invincible, since any war that did occur would be quickly ended by a few atomic bombs." This was not quite to embrace pre-emptive nuclear war, but it came close. Later he sometimes expressed regret at having advocated such a policy, but by no means always, and even at the height of his campaign for British unilateral disarmament he was willing to defend his old views as appropriate for their time.[13]

Russell was not a pacifist, because he was a consequentialist. Even the horrors of nuclear war could in principle be outweighed by a good enough outcome. War was almost invariably bad in fact because it set civilization back, aroused the most obscene human passions and was inherently uncontrollable. Most wars were aimed at futile goals such as national glory or the conquest of useless territory. But absolute pacifism was not warranted. "I have repeated *ad nauseam* that I am not a pacifist, that I believe that some wars, a very few, are justified, even necessary." The Second World War was a good war; it would have been better had Hitler been stopped by other means, but Nazi domination would have been vastly worse than the war. Russell observed in October 1945, "I should, for my part, prefer all the chaos and destruction of a war conducted by means of the atomic bomb to the universal domination of a government having the evil characteristics of the Nazis."[14] Was a one-sided nuclear war with Russia a reasonable way of achieving a world without national nuclear armaments? Russell had no doubt that it was. Non-consequentialists might think it was not. There are many good ends we must not achieve by illicit means: the police must not get a murderer to confess by threatening to kill his wife and children, governments must not keep rents down by murdering the occasional landlord, and so on. By analogy, it would be illicit to bomb the Soviet Union into non-nuclear virtue. "Just-war" doctrines which many people, non-Catholic as well as Catholic, find intuitively attractive would condemn it as the murder of innocent Soviet citizens for an uncertain future good. Russell never took such views seriously. Indeed, he was chronically incapable of believing that anyone could. Yet it is not hard to see their appeal. Even if it were true that a pre-emptive war against the Soviet Union would have made the world safer in 1986, most of us would think that it would have been iniquitous to murder large numbers of 1946 Russians to achieve it. *Our* survival is *our* business. There is a large moral gap between thinking that our forebears have left us a dangerous world to cope with and thinking that it would have been quite all right for them to massacre several million people to make life easier for us.

To all this Russell was deaf; nor were his opponents particularly acute in making the point. When critics complained of the inconsistency between his earlier advocacy of American aggressiveness towards Russia and his later defence of an extremely conciliatory policy, they missed the target. He replied, reasonably enough, that only idiots would advocate the same policies in changed conditions.[15] Once Russia had nuclear weapons it was impossible to bully the Soviets into disarmament. On his own terms, Russell was right; altered circumstances are decisive. His critics were prone to believe that they had scored a decisive blow by pointing out that by the early 1950s he no longer held the views he had held in 1945–8; they failed to point out that the earlier policy was intolerable in its own right. Few remarked on the curiously detached way in which Russell discussed a policy which by his own estimate would involve the deaths of up to half a billion people.[16]

Nor did they point out that Russell's advocacy of an aggressive American policy had varied in tone but never in content. The content always included the probability of a war. The tone varied according to whether Russell thought it would be a long war or a short one. It became less optimistic. Initially he thought the war would last a few weeks, reducing Moscow and Leningrad to rubble and bringing the Soviet Union to heel. A look at the map and at the capabilities of American bombers might have made him less sanguine; second thoughts about the bombing campaign against cities like Hamburg might have done the same. As time passed the scenario changed: bombers could not stop the Red Army before it reached the Channel. To win the war, America would have to bomb Europe to bits. Five hundred million dead was a plausible casualty figure and European civilization would be set back by five centuries (by what standards, he did not say); none the less, the war was worth fighting because it would establish world government and save European values.[17] It is an open question whether the claim makes sense, let alone whether it is morally acceptable. We often speculate in an idle way whether the Black Death was an utter disaster or whether it did some good, too; and we ask similar questions of man-made catastrophes such as the Thirty Years War; but Russell's arithmetic was not meant as idle speculation. He thought it the proper basis of foreign and military policy. One may doubt that it is. To claim that "European values" will be preserved by killing half a billion people and setting civilization back half a millennium is somehow absurd. It is like a surgeon offering us an operation in which our vital organs are removed as a prophylactic and telling us it would be a fair price for survival – "Survival as what?" we might well ask.

Russell's later reaction to all this was also odd. Though he had published his views prominently, he claimed that he had lost interest in them once he had changed his mind: as he later wrote, "at the time I gave the advice I gave it so casually without any real hope that it would be followed, that I soon forgot I had given it." Moreover, he seemed to think, even when he published his *Autobiography*, that he had held these views only during 1948 – which is quite false. More than once he denied that he had ever advocated the policy of leaning hard on the Soviet Union at all – then admitted when shown the evidence that it had looked like a good idea at the time and he had simply forgotten doing it.[18] Whether this was old age catching him out, it is hard to say; if it was a deliberate attempt to deceive, it was uncharacteristically cowardly, and inept too, when the printed record was all too easily accessible. It is hard to believe in a lapse of memory, however; he wrote several defences of his position, not just one, and they were spread over three years, not confined to one occasion. He did not write as if he was suggesting something "off the cuff."

Two things about those early post-war years stand out. The first is the ferocity of his hatred of the Soviet Union; he thought no policy too barbarous if Russia was its target. The basis of Russell's hostility to the Soviet Union was very much what it had been twenty-five years earlier when he had written *The Practice and Theory of Bolshevism*, the main change being that he concluded from the Yalta agreement that Stalin had the same territorial ambitions as the tsarist regime a century earlier, and that he was appalled by the behaviour of Soviet troops. This comes out particularly clearly in the article in *Cavalcade* in which he spelled out his policy of creative blackmail for the sake of world government. If world government proved unattainable, the second best was an alliance of western powers under the American nuclear umbrella – in essence, NATO.[19] Russell thought that it was only American nuclear superiority that stopped Stalin pressing on into western Europe and installing universal totalitarianism. Russell's views were not ill-founded. With hindsight, one can see that the Greek Civil War, Tito's escape from Russian hegemony, and the tightening of the Soviet grip on the rest of eastern Europe were episodes in the establishment of the post-war balance of power in Europe. Between 1945 and 1953 they looked like evidence of a settled Soviet ambition for universal political and military domination. For all that, Russell's anti-Russian stance had nothing in common with the hysterical anti-communism of McCarthyite America; it was an old-fashioned liberal hostility to Russian despotism that had led him to oppose the Triple Entente before the First World War and Stalin now.

The other notable feature of Russell's views was his disbelief in sharing nuclear secrets with the Soviet Union as a second best to world government. Others at the time thought that, by sharing nuclear secrets with the Soviets, the USA would calm their anxieties concerning American intentions and allow them to pursue a more relaxed foreign policy. In 1945, Russell was cautious, if not positively hostile. Giving Russia the recipe for an atomic weapon without a *quid pro quo* would not appease Soviet hostility and would amount to arming the enemy. "I am not one of those who favour the unconditional and immediate revelation to Russia of the exact processes by which the bomb is manufactured," he told the House of Lords, "I think it is right that conditions should be attached to that revelation, but I make the proviso that the conditions must be solely those which will facilitate international cooperation; they must have no national object of any kind." In 1946, he wrote in defence of the Baruch Plan, which envisaged "internationalizing" nuclear know-how by creating an international atomic commission which could inspect and supervise the dismantling of atomic weapon piles anywhere in the world. Even then, however, Russell was less interested in the plan itself (which many writers have since criticized as a plan to secure American control of nuclear weapons development by another name) than in the thought that its rejection by the Soviet Union would be evidence of aggressive intent, and the *casus belli* visualized by his policy of creative blackmail.[20] He later claimed that he had advocated an aggressive policy towards the Soviet Union only after the Baruch Plan had been turned down; but his memory again played him false. He had advocated an aggressive policy from the beginning. In his own terms, he need not have apologized. It was at any rate entirely in line with ideas he had held since the 1920s when he had first advocated a *pax Americana*; and, like almost everyone else who had lived through the 1930s and the war, he was affected by the desire not to repeat the errors of the 1930s and appease an unappeasable dictator.

Russell's hostility to Russia made him no less critical of the United States. He made two very successful lecture tours to the USA in 1950 and 1951, interest in his ideas having been aroused by his Nobel Prize. A wild success with his immediate audiences was matched by hostility in the world outside the lecture theatres and university campuses where he spoke. Russell thought, as educated Englishmen are prone to, that Americans suffered from snobbery about money, unwarranted anxiety about sex, and uncontrollable hysteria about socialism and communism; they were gullible, self-righteous and astonishingly ignorant about almost all of America and absolutely all of the rest of the world. Unlike most educated Englishmen, who have no opportunity to ventilate such thoughts, or who keep tactfully quiet if they do, Russell secured his bread and butter – or, rather, secured some jam to put on his bread and butter – by publishing his opinions in any paper or magazine that would take them.[21]

Reactions varied from one issue to another. Liberal East Coast readers enjoyed the splutterings of southern and mid-western fundamentalists when Russell explained why he was not a Christian; but they became tight-lipped when Russell mocked American anti-communism. Russell's views were quite old-fashioned, though he expressed them in inimitably offensive prose. In foreign affairs, great powers should settle non-vital matters as coolly as possible; the distinction between vital and non-vital matters ought to be clear-cut and universally understood and ought to be drawn in a defensive frame of mind; the conduct of international relations ought to be in the hands of professionals who could draw on appropriate expertise. America broke all the rules. The State Department yielded to congressional hysteria and sacked its China experts when they were most needed, and so tied America to Chiang Kai-shek.[22] In the Korean War, the American-led UN forces could and should have held the thirty-eighth parallel and pursued a waiting policy. General MacArthur's pursuit of the North Korean army up to the Chinese border produced the predictable result – Chinese troops and a string of disasters. Russell stood by old-fashioned *Realpolitik*. It was not America's business to save the Russians and the Chinese from communism; the Russians and Chinese had no doubt been ill-advised to install communist governments, but it was up to them to save themselves. It was America's business to draw a clear line beyond which incursions would be resisted – and that was that.

If American foreign policy was inept, American society was becoming increasingly repulsive. Fear of communism threatened colleges and schools as staff were forced to swear loyalty oaths, syllabuses were rewritten to make all forms of socialism seem wicked, and the timidity of the courts meant that teachers whose constitutional rights were threatened stood little chance of resistance.[23] Russell bombarded newspapers and magazines with denunciations of this "reign of terror"; as McCarthyism grew more virulent, so he grew angrier. The trial and execution of Julius and Ethel Rosenberg in 1951 (who may well have been guilty of spying for the Soviet Union, but who did not get an unprejudiced trial and, in less hysterical times, would not have faced treason charges and the death penalty in the first place) made less impact at the time than later; but they confirmed his ill opinion of American justice.[24]

This made little difference to Russell's views on nuclear policy, though it poisoned his opinion of American governments. It was Russia's success in detonating its own atomic bomb in 1949 which changed Russell's views on nuclear policy. It would no longer do to pursue a bold policy, since mutual destruction was the likely outcome. He did not argue for a more pacific foreign policy straight away, and in fact never suggested American renunciation of nuclear weapons; the best American response to Russian nuclear development was further development of its own weapons. Moreover, he initially had no doubt that Britain had to stick with the American alliance, even though he did not wish Britain to become an independent nuclear power – or perhaps even because he did not wish Britain to become an independently armed nuclear power. For all the American silliness about socialism and the ignorance of most Americans about western Europe, America was a broadly liberal, democratic, individualist society of the same cultural stamp.[25] Nor did Russell look on British neutrality as a plausible foreign policy option until much later in the 1950s.

Russell's views changed piecemeal as he came to terms with the full implications of a war fought with hydrogen weapons, and as scientists became increasingly fearful of the effects of testing nuclear weapons in the atmosphere. He later said that although his general perspective on war had not changed – he was still a consequentialist and a rationalist, still not an absolute pacifist – something had altered.[26] The emotional colouring of his ideas had been heightened when he contemplated the full effects of thermonuclear (hydrogen, or fusion) weapons. The prospect of genetic damage reaching into the distant future appalled him, as did the thought that the holocaust might be triggered off by mechanical malfunction, human error or lunacy in high places. Hardly a month went by during the middle and later 1950s without some tale of a near-miss: radar operators were frequently said to have mistaken a flight of geese for incoming missiles, and the story of the rising moon being mistaken for a missile attack was endlessly retold. Russell's imagination was stimulated by all this in a way that even his contemplation of the horrors of bombing in *Which Way to Peace?* had not quite matched.[27] As a mathematician, he was depressed by reflecting that in the long run it was certain that a nuclear war would occur by accident or design; in any week or month, the odds were not very alarming; over the long run it was a racing certainty. He was also struck by a sort of metaphysical horror at the prospect of the total destruction of life on earth. A recent bestselling book suggests[28] that a peculiar horror which many of us feel in the face of nuclear war is the sense that destroying all life and wrecking the entire planet on which everything lives is simply mad. We cannot contemplate it without feeling that our hold on reality is slipping. Russell had always taken refuge in his passion for the sea and the mountains whenever human relationships became unbearable; their detachment consoled him for personal and political disorder. When satellites were invented, he raged against the prospect of embroiling the heavens in our squalid terrestrial squabbles.

> In reading of the plans of militarists, I try very hard to divest myself for the time being of the emotions of horror and disgust. But when I read of the plans to defile the heavens by the petty squabbles of the animated lumps that disgrace a certain planet, I cannot but feel that the men who make these plans are guilty of a certain impiety.

All the same, he always argued that America was right to develop the hydrogen bomb. Russell was sceptical of the value of any nation promising to renounce nuclear weapons, unless the promise could be made to stick by an external sanction. If war broke out, powers with the necessary technology would at once build and use the hydrogen bomb. It was not very sensible of him to denounce the half-loaf of abstention and insist so strenuously on the whole loaf of world government and enforceable disarmament, even though there was something to his claim that only pressures comparable to those which drove nations into nuclear armaments were enough to drive them out again. By 1958 he was less insistent on the whole loaf of world government and was advocating verifiable nuclear disarmament, along with most people in the peace movement. His belief that only world government and overwhelming military power would achieve anything was overtaken by events; technical progress allowed nuclear tests to be detected without on-site inspection, and a ban on atmospheric testing was agreed in 1963. Russell rightly thought that the partial test-ban treaty was a very small advance, and his belief that only pressures as strong as those which drove nations into arming themselves could drive them to disarm had much to be said for it. The fear of accidental war, and repugnance at the thought of poisoning our children, have been powerful forces, but not powerful enough to secure disarmament as opposed to greater caution in armament.[29]

All this was consistent with his belief that nuclear deterrence was a perfectly rational and morally acceptable way to conduct foreign relations.

Russell defended America's decision to develop the hydrogen bomb prim- arily because Russia would certainly try to develop it anyway,[30] and a world in which the Soviet Union had the hydrogen bomb and America did not would be horribly unstable. The point of maximum danger in nuclear strategy is when each side possesses effective first-strike capacity, but inadequate second-strike capacity – that is, in plain language, when each side might gain a victory if it initiated a nuclear attack, but cannot be sure that enough of its weapons would survive an attack on itself to allow it to launch a devastating reprisal. Under these conditions, both sides have an incentive to strike first. What gave Russell nightmares was the thought that a first strike would be less than wholly effective, so ensuring that both sides perished. A Soviet – or an American – lead in the arms race would be dangerous because the lagging side might think that the only way to prevent its rival getting far enough ahead to attack with impunity would be to strike first and cripple its efforts. The full hideousness of such unstable situations lies in the fact that since each side can make the same calculations, both sides know the temptations under which its rival oper- ates and therefore have even more reason to strike first.[31] Until the begin- nings of "de-Stalinization" moreover, Russell continued to think that the Soviet Union was bent on world conquest, from which only the threat of nuclear catastrophe would deter her. Russell's view was wholly plausible, therefore. Mutual deterrence was intrinsically repulsive, but would work so long as both sides were cautious and avoided provocative or ill-thought-out action, and were conscious that a false move meant the end of the world.

This simple view underlay most of Russell's contributions to the nuclear debate of the 1950s. He denounced American and Soviet brinkmanship, appealed for the cessation of weapons testing and encouraged the British to renounce nuclear weapons and support a nuclear-free Europe. There was much to be said for this. It is self-evident that brinkmanship puts up the risk of accidental conflagration; testing weapons in the atmosphere was gratuitous environmental poisoning once the superpowers possessed the means to survive and retaliate for a first strike against themselves; British disarmament made sense as part of a campaign to avoid the "balkaniza- tion" of weapons. Just as the great powers had been pulled into the First World War by the hostilities of the small Balkan countries, Russell feared that America and Russia might be pulled into a nuclear war by the Arab– Israeli conflict, or by the hostilities of India and Pakistan or a local flare-up in Europe; limiting possession of nuclear weapons to the superpowers would reduce such dangers, and since Britain was then the only other nation with nuclear capability, there was a chance that renunciation by Britain might be the start of a non-nuclear club.

Between 1954 and 1964 Russell wrote, broadcast, debated and organized endlessly, both among top scientists through the "Pugwash" conferences and in the hope of reaching a mass audience through the Campaign for

Nuclear Disarmament, the Committee of 100, and finally through the Bertrand Russell Peace Foundation. The essays and lectures of those years (his "books" are no more than essays pulled together) are not intellectually elaborate; at their best they are cool, careful and persuasive. At their worst they are shrill and angry in tone, and hasty in argument. In this, they are very like the hastier and angrier productions of 1914 and 1915. The Russell of 1914 who accused the bishops of supporting the war because they hoped for large dividends on their armaments shares was very like Russell in 1961 accusing Macmillan of being "much more wicked than Hitler." In neither case ought we to take him too literally, nor ignore the small grain of truth embedded in the wild exaggeration. It is true that immersion in money-making dulls our moral sensibilities, and bishops need to remember that as much as anyone; and there are awkward questions to be asked about the ethics of a defence policy based on threatening to incinerate millions of innocent women and children. A government which launched atomic war would kill more innocent victims than Hitler ever killed, which is not a thought to be shrugged off lightly. Traditional just-war doctrines would condemn it as murder on a vast scale, and Russell was not alone in thinking that threatening to commit mass murder is morally dubious.[32] Whether he was the man to say it is another question; unlike theorists of the just war, he did not think that it was wicked to threaten what it would be wicked to do, and his own advocacy of an aggressive policy towards Russia in 1945–9 made him an unconvincing defender of the sanctity of innocent life. But in 1914 he had been an unconvincing superintendent of the moral standards of bishops.

The other similarity between 1914 and 1960 was the violent changes of mood he experienced when he contemplated the vagaries of human nature, and the extreme prognoses he offered for the future. As in 1914, he asked himself whether mankind was hopelessly addicted to violence and self-destruction. Save when feeling particularly depressed, he still answered, No. The world might become paradise or hell according to human choice, and it was up to individuals to decide.[33] It was noticeable that he hardly considered the possibility that things might go on in much the same way, a good deal sub-paradisaical, but a good deal super-infernal, with mankind very much disliking the fact of existence under the nuclear umbrella but learning how to minimize its risks and anxieties and reduce the dangers of catastrophe. One source of heightened gloom was his conviction that states with thermonuclear weapons facing other states in a fixed condition of mutual distrust would want ever more powerful weapons as an end in itself. He sometimes wrote of the invention of the hydrogen bomb as if it had been fuelled by a pure urge for destruction, rather than by the political considerations he had urged at the time.

The A-bomb when it was new had caused a shudder of horror, and had even stimulated suggestions for international control of atomic energy.

But people soon got used to it and came to realize that the harm which it could do was not enough to satisfy mutual ferocity.

The atomic bomb was already adequate to destroy urban populations and wipe out whole cities; but rural populations and peasant societies were not vulnerable to it. So the urge for wholesale annihilation had to be appeased by the H-bomb which would poison with fall-out those whom it did not instantly destroy by heat and blast.[34] Russell's tendency to libel human psychology in this way went oddly with his habit of depicting most of mankind as the long-suffering victims of wicked governments, mad generals and wild ideologues. It co-existed even more awkwardly with an ability to explain in entirely persuasive terms why nuclear scientists had begun by favouring the development of the atomic bomb (a rational fear that Hitler would get it first and would use it without hesitation) and why so many had now turned against it (an equally rational fear that human error would lead to universal self-destruction). The most eminent of the scientists Russell cited was Einstein, the most controversial Robert Oppenheimer, who had led the Manhattan Project to success and had been denounced as a security risk when he turned against the development of the H-bomb. Since his left-wing inclinations had been known since the 1930s, his disgrace was evidently a put-up job.

Russell's account of this in *Has Man a Future?* is an admirably calm review of the various letters, manifestos and meetings that led up to the creation of the Pugwash Conference in 1957 – and the only point at which his calm slips is when he contrasts the rationality of the scientists who managed (though only just) to set aside their political attachments and think of the welfare of the whole human race with the idiocies of Pugwash's critics in the US Congress.[35] Russell's irritation was more than justified. The Pugwash movement was one of the rare occasions when scientists from behind the Iron Curtain were readily able to discuss arms and disarmament with colleagues from the West; but the Senate Internal Security Committee investigating Pugwash in 1960 took that as evidence only that the American scientists present had been hoodwinked or, perhaps, were plotting treason. Twenty-five years on, it is hard to remember that the death of Joseph McCarthy in 1957 had by no means eliminated the obscene phenomenon of McCarthyism from American politics. When Richard Nixon and John F. Kennedy fought for the presidency in 1960, Kennedy's chief charge against Nixon was that he was vice-president in an administration which was (improbably) soft on communism and had allowed the Russians to take the lead in the production of intercontinental ballistic missiles – they hadn't, in fact, even if they had got into space first with the launch of *Sputnik* on 4 October 1957. Similarly, John Foster Dulles, the chief architect of foreign policy under Eisenhower, more than once declared that he was confident of America's ability to win a nuclear war; what he doubted was the nation's ability to win the Cold War. In such an atmosphere, Russell had some grounds for believing that American politics were dominated by madmen.

So by the late 1950s, Russell's position was that the primary duty of a great power such as the United States was to do everything possible to keep down the temperature of international politics. For the first time, he held a genuinely "Voltairean" position, urging everyone to forgo the pleasures of ideological conflict and moral denunciation for the sake of peace. No moral ideal was worth the destruction of civilization. Russell's American critics concluded that he had become an enthusiast for the Soviet Union and had gone soft on communism in his old age. This was quite untrue. He had once more become an unrespectable radical, but he was as hostile to the Soviet Union as ever, and deeply sceptical about communists in the British peace movement. Even when enraged by American obduracy over the terms of a nuclear test-ban treaty, he still insisted that the Soviet Union was primarily to blame for the failure of attempts to ban atmospheric tests – paranoia was built into every Soviet institution and every Russian ruler, and Russian objections to on-site inspection showed as much. He held much the same anti-patriotic views which had so enraged everyone in 1914–15; his stupider critics thought he was pro-German then, and they thought he was pro-Russian now. That was wrong. What he believed was that since the West was not encumbered by the follies of the Soviet system, it could afford to be accommodating in a way the Soviet Union could not – just as the First World War could have been avoided by British concessions which Imperial Germany could not have been expected to make. This was not to side with Russia, merely to recognize Soviet inability to behave sensibly. It raised a question he never quite answered: did not this policy *encourage* Russia to behave badly, in the knowledge that this would induce the West to behave more and more cautiously?[36]

Domestically, Russell knew that the British peace movement contained fellow-travellers. His attitude to them was purely calculating; if their presence threatened the effectiveness of the peace movement or the Campaign for Nuclear Disarmament, then they must be got rid of. The communist Lady Tyrrell wrote inquiring whether it was true that he did not want communists in CND and got a very sharp little note to say she should choose between working for peace and working for Russia; and when he discovered that the World Peace Council was using his name as a respectable cover, he was quick to stop it.[37] Even when CND was at its largest and most welcoming, Russell did not object to its strikingly undemocratic constitution – its executive council was self-appointed and irremovable by the organization's supporters – a feature which appears to have been intended to reduce the risk of a communist takeover. Russell's reactions to changes in the Soviet Union during the 1950s were like most liberals': he welcomed the thaw which set in after the death of Stalin and hoped for rapid liberalization. For a while he thought it was happening, with Soviet scientists joining the Pugwash conferences and Khrushchev himself encouraging the publication of previously illicit works such as the novels of Solzhenitsyn. Still he did not overlook the continued bloody-mindedness of Soviet foreign policy; he was appalled by the invasion of Hungary in 1956 (and one of his last political gestures was to write a savage denunciation of the invasion of Czechoslovakia in 1968); he thought that the belief in the inevitable triumph of communism, which Khrushchev affirmed in the exchange of letters between Russell, Khrushchev and Dulles published in the *New Statesman* in the autumn of 1957, was quite mad; and his own advocacy of a nuclear-free zone in central Europe was coupled with an insistence that Hungary, Poland, Czechoslovakia and the other "satellite" states must be free to choose their own form of government.[38]

The argumentative record from 1954, when he made his famous broadcast on "Man's Peril," to the end of 1960 when he resigned the presidency of CND and embarked on a campaign of direct action and civil disobedience with the Committee of 100, is all of a piece.[39] The only ultimate solution was world government backed by a monopoly of force, implementing a system of legal agreements like those which keep the peace domestically. This ultimate solution would be a long-term prospect and its achievement a very long-drawn-out business. Still, it is the only wholly acceptable solution and we should not rest content with anything less. In the meantime, any government which does not bend all its efforts to securing a reduction of tension is guilty of reckless unconcern for the lives and happiness of mankind. As technology advances, the risks become greater and so does the wickedness of government inaction. The best thing the British government could do under these circumstances was to renounce nuclear weapons and adopt a neutralist foreign policy. This view, advanced from about 1956 onwards, was a real change of heart after Russell's earlier enthusiasm for NATO or an equivalent; Russell did not pause at the position of those unilateralists who hoped to leave nuclear weapons in the hands of the USA and the USSR only, but still envisaged a non-nuclear and conventional role for the other NATO powers. Russell's defence of NATO belonged to the years when he was also advocating a forward policy of pressure on Russia. Now that he was only concerned not to stir up tension, he believed a non-nuclear Britain would do more good as an influential neutral power than as a not very influential non-nuclear member of NATO. He also envisaged neutrality as an element in the creation of a nuclear-free Europe such as was envisaged in the Rapacki Plan, the Polish proposal for dismantling the Warsaw Pact and NATO. Searching for a vehicle for these views, Russell helped to create the Campaign for Nuclear Disarmament.

Russell's reflective thoughts on nuclear disarmament belong to what has usefully been labelled the "pacifist" strain in defence thinking; that is, to the strand of thought which accepts that war may be justified from time to time, but which holds that these occasions are infrequent, and that the best policy for governments to pursue is a cautious and unaggressive one. Once nuclear weapons exist, caution becomes more imperative than ever. This thought readily leads to the view that for any nation other than the super-powers to possess nuclear weapons adds needlessly to the danger of accidental war, without doing anything for the security of their possessor. There are further considerations which press in the direction of unilateralism for a country the size of Britain which is not already locked into a situation like that of the USA and the Soviet Union where a sudden move by either side is perilous, and which does not have the excuse of a country such as Israel which faces enemies who regard themselves as in a state of permanent if not always active war. British dependence on American weapons put Britain at the mercy of American foreign policy; for anyone with Russell's grim view of Eisenhower and Dulles, that was unbearable. Far from being safe under the American nuclear umbrella, Britain had become an "unsinkable aircraft carrier" and therefore a prime target for a Soviet strike. To get out of that situation, nothing would do but unilateral disarmament and neutrality. Russell may also have felt that the permanent confrontation between Russia and the West on the German frontier and in Berlin was so dangerous that it had to be dismantled at all costs. Russell was by no means the only distinguished intellect heading in the same direction; George Kennan, the chief architect of the American policy of containment immediately after the war, had by 1957 turned about and contemplated the dismantling of the two frozen alliances. He may well have had more impact than anyone on Russell's thinking and on the formation of CND.

Was Russell right to argue for unilateralism? It is impossible to say with certainty. It is obviously possible that one effect of British nuclear disarmament would be to make Britain more vulnerable to blackmail by powers with nuclear weapons, notably the Soviet Union, and it is largely on this argument that all British governments have rested their rejection of unilateral nuclear disarmament since 1958. Again, opponents of unilateralism often argue that it would be right to get rid of nuclear weapons but wrong to do so without exacting some reciprocal concessions from other countries, notably the Soviet Union. This was the thought which led Aneurin Bevan to change his mind about Britain's nuclear status; he wanted not to "go naked into the negotiating chamber."

To rebut such arguments is not the work of a moment, nor even of a shelf of books on nuclear strategy. A solid argument for Russell's neutralism was that a Britain which had renounced its imperial pretensions and was intent on avoiding external entanglements would not excite the suspicion of the Soviet Union and would not be vulnerable to blackmail. Russell himself was badly placed to argue this, since he would have had to change his mind about the aggressive intentions of the Soviet Union even more drastically than he did. He would also have had to take a stand on how Britain could square neutrality with a more "European" economic and foreign policy. Unilateralist politics always wavered between an isolationist desire to cut Britain off from global conflicts and a moralizing ambition to lead the rest of western Europe into non-nuclear virtue. Russell was no more decisive than his followers. The best case for Russell is the simplest. The details of unilateralism would doubtless be as complicated as the details of any other defence policy, but the campaign for unilateral disarmament had a simple message – what one might paraphrase as "we want out." By insisting that the only policy prudence and morality dictated was unilateral withdrawal from the nuclear arms race and nuclear-armed alliances, Russell was at least briefly bound to be arguing the right case – if withdrawal was practicable, it was desirable; and if it was not, a pressure group firmly committed to it would restrain governments from adventurism and force them to scrutinize every step of the nuclear path. It was a view which led many sceptics – I was one – into the ranks of CND, and it may well have animated Russell for some of the time. In so far as the world is now marginally less alarming than in 1958, he deserves some share of the credit. He did not have the impact on public opinion that he did without assistance; in the first instance it was the Campaign for Nuclear Disarmament which provided it.

Russell's career in CND was quite brief and often stormy. CND itself emerged in a haphazard way from several different strands of anti-nuclear thinking. One was the Direct Action Comittee under Michael Randle's leadership; this was a pacifist and anarchist movement which Russell did not intellectually agree with, but to which he contributed a few pounds a year, even after he had become President of CND. It was committed to demonstrative protest and civil disobedience. Another strand was Christian pacifist, or Christian "pacificist." Canon Collins was the chairman of Christian Action; he had not been able to persuade Christian Action to back a campaign against British nuclear weapons, but he brought a distinctively Christian contribution to CND. A third element was the National Council for the Abolition of Nuclear Weapons Tests, which had begun life as a Hampstead committee with which Russell had had several exchanges of letters over the previous years. CND was brought into being by a combination of events of which the testing of the British H-bomb in 1957 was probably the most important. The *Autobiography* cites George Kennan's Reith Lectures as an important stimulus, but a Labour Party conference which came very close to renouncing NATO and nuclear weapons, and J. B. Priestley's *New Statesman* article of 2 November 1957 advocating immediate unilateral disarmament, had done much to stir up opinion. Kingsley Martin's recollections of the creation of CND suggest that it was founded to appease the *New Statesman* readers who wrote in to demand that something should be done to follow up Priestley's article. Although he was not a prime mover in its creation, Russell's *New Statesman* correspondence with John Foster Dulles and Nikita Khrushchev in the autumn of 1957 had brought him together with Kingsley Martin, J. B. Priestley and others. Over Christmas 1957 they brought CND into existence, with Russell as President and Collins as Chairman; its public existence was confirmed by a rally in Central Hall, Westminster, in February 1958, and by the first of the Aldermaston marches at Easter. (This one started in London and advanced on the Atomic Weapons Research Establishment at Aldermaston; its successors took the opposite route.) The Aldermaston marches were an idea lifted from the Direct Action movement; they were hugely successful, and enjoyable, occasions.

Russell had a more realistic view of the movement's real influence over the next two years than did the cheerful mob of young people who walked down the Great West Road, slept in school halls over the Easter weekend, and rallied in Trafalgar Square to cheer Russell, Michael Foot, Canon Collins and J. B. Priestley. The campaign's impact on Labour and Conservative politicians was almost negligible; the committed remained committed, to whichever side they belonged. By the time the Labour Party conference in the autumn of 1960 was momentarily converted to unilateralism – or, more exactly, by the time the leadership of the Transport and General Workers' Union had decided to put its block vote behind unilateralism – Russell had despaired of CND. Labour was unlikely to return to power for many years, and the Conservatives were no more likely to espouse neutrality than they had been to vote against going to war in August 1914. In the summer of 1960 Russell and the Reverend Michael Scott laid plans for what became the Committee of 100. The idea was simple, though it is unclear whether it had been floated in discussion in Direct Action for some years already, or whether it was a genuine inspiration of Ralph Schoenman. One hundred people should sign a statement declaring their willingness to break the law in protest against the British government's possession of nuclear weapons.[40] The offences anyone would commit would be minor ones: obstruction, or trespass on military bases. The government would be embarrassed at having to jail or fine respectable people, and the hope was that each person lost to the original hundred by imprisonment would be replaced by another, so stretching the forces of law and order as well as embarrassing them. Russell's correspondence with the original signatories of the manifesto of the Committee of 100 is mildly amusing; he had to spend a good deal of effort reassuring some of his friends that they did not *have* to break the law and persuading others that, if they did, it would be possible to ensure that the time they spent under arrest would not interfere with their careers.

Russell wished to resign the presidency of CND in September 1960; he also wished to speak in favour of direct action at the Trafalgar Square demonstration on 24 September, but he was persuaded that to do so would be disastrous for the defenders of unilateralism at the forthcoming Labour Party conference. Russell's account of all this in his *Autobiography* glosses over a good deal of muddle and acrimony. The backers of the Committee of 100 contrived to make themselves look silly by sending the letter announcing their impending campaign to "someone with a name similar to the intended recipient but with a different address, and, unhappily, entirely different views." This was the conservative journalist and author John Connell (of the *Evening Standard*) who gave the game away to the paper. In spite of everything, a truce was patched up with Canon Collins until the Labour Party conference was over. Then Russell resigned, on bad terms with those he left, and creating a great deal of doubt and confusion among the ordinary members of CND – the majority of whom, however, supported him rather than Canon Collins, whose autocratic outlook on the organization of CND had always riled many of the rank and file. Dissident CND marchers were heard to chant, "Fire the Canon and drop the Bomb," as they marched. It has puzzled many people that Russell went down the path of civil disobedience; he was no Gandhian pacifist and *satyagraha* did not come naturally to him. The best explanation is the one he always gave in interviews and in reply to letters from disheartened members of CND who felt that he had deserted them. Appealing to the Corn Law League and the suffragettes as examples of successful "fanatics" who had not stopped at defying the law, he argued that at a time when newspapers and the mass media were unable to take arguments seriously, dramatic gestures would grab maximum publicity.

Russell's position on civil disobedience was straightforward. He never thought we were obliged to obey governments which were acting stupidly or immorally. Disobedience as such did not pose moral problems; none the less, he had been cautious about issuing a general licence to follow the dictates of conscience, since some people's consciences were quite misguided. He argued along utilitarian lines; for the Committee of 100 it was not a question (as it later was for American soldiers in Vietnam) of a conscientious refusal to obey orders. The question was one of political tactics only. In the 1900s he had taken a squarely tactical view of the suffragettes; when they stirred up public opinion to appreciate their cause, they were justified; when they maddened the public they were foolish. The same was true in the 1960s. Ecstatic supporters such as Ralph Schoenman had wild visions of hundreds of thousands of protesters all joining in mass civil disobedience. Russell knew this was quite mad; there was no chance of assembling a people's army overnight with no organization – and his disciples soon discovered that they could not hire enough buses to transport a couple of hundred protesters to the airbases they hoped to picket, let alone master the logistics of moving an army.[41]

The respectable who complained that he was allowing himself to be used by the fanatical received a sharper brush-off. Past fanaticisms in a good cause had been justified by success; so would this be if it was successful. All he asked was good publicity and maximum embarrassment for the government. He had no enthusiasm for Gandhian campaigns of *passive* resistance such as motivated one wing of Direct Action; he would have accepted armed insurrection as a way of achieving disarmament if there had been any hope of such a thing succeeding. But he knew that the idea of a popular uprising against warfare – which featured in Schoenman's plans – was nonsense. The only question was whether demonstrations, sit-downs, and the activities of "Spies for Peace" (who discovered where the government's wartime communications centres were located and published the information in defiance of the Official Secrets Act) would hasten the arrival of disarmament, neutrality, and an end to testing.

Although Russell himself secured as much publicity as anybody by being charged with incitement after a rally to mark Hiroshima Day in 1961, the campaign did not work. The government was not irredeemably stupid, and although the Committee of 100 gained support whenever the police were ill-tempered and heavy-handed in dragging protesters out of Trafalgar Square and elsewhere, the government's efficient use of the Official Secrets Act to send the most determined Spies for Peace to jail for eighteen months was a decided dampener – such sentences were too long to be a mere irritant to the victims, but not so long as to cause a public outcry.[42] Many of its members made themselves look foolish at the time of the Cuban missile crisis, too. Russell's own attention was being pulled away from British concerns. The signing of the partial test-ban treaty in 1963 persuaded him that governments had woken up to the perils of nuclear war, even if the Cuban missile crisis in October 1962 convinced him that in other respects they were still run by madmen. His attention was now turned outwards; and he embarked on his final career as what I. F. Stone has felicitously christened "World Ombudsman." In September 1963 he established the Bertrand Russell Peace Foundation and announced that he had resigned from the Committee of 100. The Foundation was largely run by Ralph Schoenman until he was swept up in the War Crimes Tribunal, and by a succession of other helpers of whom Christopher Farley was the most important. Until the accession of wealth which was generated in 1967 by the sale of Russell's papers to McMaster University and the publication of his *Autobiography*, it ran on a shoestring or, more accurately, an overdraft and whatever small sums Russell could raise for it. It spawned the Institute for Workers' Control, whose concerns were directly centred on industrial democracy, a juxtaposition which neatly reflected the concerns of the No-Conscription Fellowship half a century before; and it failed to spawn an Atlantic Foundation to study international relations.[43]

The main preoccupation of the Foundation and of Russell himself was the American involvement in Vietnam, but almost any piece of American misbehaviour, internal or external, came under attack. The assassination of President Kennedy in November 1963 and the subsequent commission of inquiry chaired by Chief Justice Earl Warren was one of many occasions when Russell and the Foundation joined in an internal fight, though the Foundation set up a "British Who Killed Kennedy? Committee" to chase that hare. The Warren report was not thought by anyone to be wholly satisfactory; and its more energetic critics denounced it as a cover-up. Russell sided with the critics: the CIA had killed Kennedy because he had savaged them for their bungling of the Bay of Pigs invasion two years before.[44] A year later he joined in the great debate over increasing violence in the Black ghettos. Twenty-five years before, he would have remembered de Tocqueville and thought the rioting a symptom of a revolution of rising expectations; now he claimed that the American government was genocidal, the police pretty much on a par with the camp guards at Auschwitz, and Black rioting a justified response to a campaign of extermination.[45] America received all this with rage and outrage; Russell was interfering where he had no knowledge and no business. Many English readers doubted whether Russell had read, much less written, what he now put his name to; it read like the rantings of the student Left, not like Russell's own immaculate prose. Russell's correspondence would have strengthened their doubts; writing to Jim Boggs, he argued in entirely persuasive terms that the idea of Black insurrection was a suicidal fantasy and that radical reformism was infinitely preferable to revolutionary zealotry. Even then, Russell's demands for the instantaneous restructuring of the American educational and economic systems to accommodate Black grievances were unpersuasive – *how* was any of this to be achieved in what he believed to be a racist state?

There was nothing novel about Russell making wild assertions about American wickedness – on his last visit to the United States in 1951 he had given the impression that he thought every tree in the southern states was hung about with the bodies of lynched Negroes and that any university teacher who defended racial equality would instantly be sacked. At the time the National Association for the Advancement of Colored Peoples was steadily gaining ground in the courts, and three years later won the landmark decision in *Brown* vs *Board of Education of Topeka* which established that segregation was inherently unconstitutional. As always, Russell was not *entirely* wrong; the movement towards racial equality was marked by judicial evasiveness, rioting, police brutality, the murder of civil rights workers, the bombing of churches and the assassination of Black leaders – none of which Americans enjoyed being reminded of by an Englishman. But there was a change of intellectual style. Previously, Russell had held members of governments personally and individually responsible for the misdeeds perpetrated within their jurisdiction, the most striking instance of this being his indictment of Sir Edward Grey.[46] It was not particularly plausible to ascribe so much to the wickedness of individual politicians, but it was at least consistent with his markedly individualist approach to social and political analysis. Now he seemed to have acquired the habit prevalent among the 1960s' radicals of blaming everything on "the system." He could now indict his opponents wholesale and retail, since the fact that President Johnson had not personally ordered the mass murder of Los Angeles Blacks was covered by the self-evident truth that "the system" was racist and murderous and the President the system's servant.[47]

The sceptical Russell, who believed that men did both good and evil by accident and who frequently mastered the temptation to believe in conspiracy, seemed to have vanished entirely, leaving the Russell who saw conspiracy everywhere firmly in command. The sole cause of evil in the world was American imperialism. Whether it was internal American politics, the tangled politics of Greece, the Middle East or whatever else, the hand of the CIA and the dictates of American imperialism were surely there. At times he began to sound like the Ayatollah Khomeini denouncing the "great Satan" – in itself a reason for wondering how much he wrote of all the articles he put his name to. After his death, Christopher Farley told a revealing story about Russell's attitude to every movement he allied himself with. Russell explained that he always felt an outsider; his companions would go on at length about the virtues of pacifism, or the glories of socialism, or the speed with which CND would convert the British people, and a small voice inside Russell's head would always say, "I don't really believe all that." Russell himself confirms this.[48]

We must approach Russell's increasing fear of America's impact on the world cautiously, then. The issue is more complicated still. Russell's hostility to American intervention in Vietnam had two very distinct aspects. The first was his belief that America had become increasingly aggressive and the Soviet Union more defensive and genuinely eager for a quiet existence and some movement towards disarmament; this view was sharpened by the Cuban missile crisis, which Russell saw as essentially caused by American aggression. The second was his belief in the right of Asiatic peoples to self-determination and a guarantee against intervention by colonial powers. The combination made Russell sound like a standard 1960s' "anti-imperialist," and at times led him to present the Vietcong as a band of saints whose patience had finally given out. It is, however, only that sentimentality which is particularly novel and disturbing; his hostility to British and American influence in Asia was genuine and of long standing.

Russell had loathed the British Empire since well before 1914. From the 1920s to the end of the war he had been a staunch defender of Indian independence; he had written angry articles on the Amritsar massacre, on the practice of what was euphemistically termed "rigorous imprisonment," on the 1930s' jailings of Gandhi and Nehru, and on the plethora of arbitrary decrees with which British rule was maintained. He had welcomed the speed with which independence was granted after the war. In all these years he had taken it for granted that one root of colonialism was economic – E. D. Morel, his friend and ally in the Union for Democratic Control, had, after all, made his reputation and earned Russell's admiration for the way he took on the Belgian crown and exposed the brutality of Leopold's exploitation of the Belgian Congo. But Russell was, if anything, more appalled by the tendency of colonial regimes to set up authoritarian police states in the colonies which brutalized national politics as well as the affairs of the colonies themselves.[49]

The only cure was independence; without independence the British would corrupt themselves by running a police state in India. He took it for granted that some Britons would oppose independence because they made money out of the dependent India, and many who had no economic interest would oppose independence because they took pleasure in the vicarious glamour of "their" possessions. Nor did he apply such an analysis to India alone. After his long visit to China in 1921–2, he tried to persuade the British government to channel its share of the Boxer indemnity into Chinese education and away from narrowly selfish schemes; had Ramsay MacDonald's first government remained in power beyond 1924 Russell would have been a member of the Phillimore Committee which considered the disposal of the indemnity – as it was, the Tory government pushed him off the committee which then proceeded to behave as Russell feared it would.[50]

What Russell never put forward in the whole half-century was the doctrine he once mocked as the doctrine of "the superior virtue of the oppressed."[51] This he characterized as the obverse of the usual tendency to think well of ourselves and badly of others. The brutality of the oppressors was sufficient argument against their policies; there was no need to suppose that their victims were particularly attractive, individually or *en masse*, let alone that they had been ennobled by their sufferings. We forbid the police to torture captured burglars because torture is wicked, not because burglars are estimable people; nor do we need sentimental reasons for opposing colonialism. Throughout the 1950s Russell argued as he had for the past four decades: that America would try to preserve her economic advantages he took for granted; what mattered was that it should not threaten the peace. It was brinkmanship rather than imperialism which alarmed him, and it was the self-deception as much as the hypocrisy involved in American alliances with nasty right-wing regimes which received his sardonic analysis. Self-deception and dangerousness ran into each other; Chiang Kai-shek was both a tyrant and an obstacle to peace with communist China; American support for Leon Battista was disgusting rather than dangerous, but when it led to hostility to Castro's socialist revolution, it became dangerous because it invited Soviet competition for influence in the Caribbean. This had European implications. In the early

1950s Russell had had no objections to German rearmament; by 1961 he was ready to assuage Russian fears of a "German finger on the nuclear button" at any price and terrified that the game of "chicken" which Kennedy and Khrushchev were playing over the status of Berlin would erupt into nuclear war.[52]

In the 1950s, as we have seen, Russell thought the Soviet Union would become more liberal; then he realized that change would at best be exceedingly slow. He always agreed that Russia was a nastier place than the United States. Yet after he changed his mind about the possibility of pushing Russia into a more cooperative frame of mind, he became increasingly convinced that it was from America that the threat to peace now emanated. John Foster Dulles's policy of trying to roll back communism was more alarmingly echoed by senior military figures such as Admiral Radford, General Nathan Twining and Air Force General Curtis Le May ("bomber Le May" to both friend and foe) and who would tell anyone who asked that, were it not for pussy-footing politicians, they could bomb the Soviet Union into good behaviour in the course of an afternoon.[53] Russell may have been more easily frightened than the facts warranted, but twenty-five years afterwards the men who gave him sleepless nights still seem pretty alarming.

The Cuban missile crisis, followed by the American build-up of forces in Vietman, convinced him that American foreign policy was too dangerous to be tolerated. The build-up of the Cuban crisis was slow. Throughout 1961 the point of tension was Berlin, where the East German government faced an almost uncontrollable flood of refugees from its oppressiveness (and poverty), and finally took the drastic step of constructing the infamous wall. Another point of tension was Turkey, where the American government had installed Thor ballistic missiles, threatening Moscow from a new direction and at closer range than previous missiles had done – though there is some doubt whether this was any part of American policy, since Kennedy was annoyed to discover their presence there during the missile crisis, having believed that they had been pulled out for the sake of *détente*; and after the crisis was over he was happy to withdraw them as a face-saving gesture to Khrushchev. The Soviet government may have felt that something had to be done to counter these strategic gains; and putting medium-range missiles into Cuba may have looked a cheap way of making up ground. The missiles were on the "wrong" side of the early-warning radar systems, which were largely geared to detecting long-range missiles coming over the North Pole; and, sited only ninety miles from the Florida coast, they were a clear warning to the American government not to do anything rash about Cuba. After the fiasco of the Bay of Pigs invasion in 1961, it was widely expected that the American government would try to avenge itself by full-scale invasion. The Soviet invasion of Afghanistan suggests that this is what the Soviet government would have done, and the Vietnam war suggests it must have been a serious option for Kennedy. In spite of these considerations, the Soviet move was foolish; militarily the missiles were useless since they had too short a range to hit civilian targets in the American north-east, or strategic sites in the mid-west. Their presence was symbolic and irritant.

To install irritants broke all the rules of diplomacy in the nuclear age. Whatever its motivation, it was bound to look like an attempt at unsettling the nuclear balance. It further broke all the rules by reducing both sides' time for manoeuvre during a crisis; the missiles were on indefensible sites, which meant that if they were to be used at all they had to be used as soon as any conflict broke out; but that in turn meant that the American airforce would have to destroy them sooner rather than later. The two things together meant that they were absurdly provocative, the more so when they added nothing to the firepower already possessed by the Soviet submarine missile fleet. No satisfying explanation of what went on inside the Kremlin has ever been given. Kennedy's reactions, on the other hand, have been described over and over again – usually in terms ordinarily reserved for hagiography.[54] In essence, he stuck to one demand: that any missiles already in Cuba should leave and that no new ones should be installed. He declared a blockade of Cuba and announced that the US navy would search Soviet vessels heading for Cuba. Technically, the blockade was a substantial violation of international law and its application to Russian vessels on the high seas could have been taken as an act of war; for two days the world held its breath. Happily nobody made a false move. Kennedy browbeat his admirals into allowing two Soviet vessels through the blockade in order to give Khrushchev plenty of time to reflect; Khrushchev backed away from direct confrontation after extracting an American promise not to invade Cuba, and agreed to withdraw the missiles. Face and lives had both been saved.[55] Though Kennedy has rightly been praised for the coolness with which he handled events, the subsequent history of the Vietnam conflict showed just how difficult it was for a president to keep control of the forces that had already brought him the Bay of Pigs, and that luck as well as good judgement were on his side for once. Nor does the successful resolution of this incident do much to redeem the inept record of American foreign policy before and after 1962.

Russell's view of events was firmly anti-American. He thought the crisis was largely the result of American bullying in Central America – a perfectly sensible long-term view; initially he believed that the missiles were a CIA invention, dreamed up to excuse another attempt to overthrow Castro. In this he was just wrong, though less wrong than the critics who said that it was inconceivable that the CIA would play such a trick on the world at large, let alone attempt to deceive the American government. Russell feared that Kennedy would box himself into a situation where neither he nor Khrushchev could avoid war except by a climb-down, for he saw that

Kennedy would be under tremendous pressure to act tough after the previous year's humiliation. So it was always to Kennedy that he addressed demands for concessions and Kennedy whom he denounced as the likely begetter of World War Three. After the event, he praised Khrushchev, but only because "I feel that support is due to the more pacific party. It is only for this reason that since, though not before, Khrushchev decided not to challenge the blockade, I have thought him more praiseworthy than his opponents." He abused Kennedy as a warmonger, as the man who threatened to blow up the whole world for the sake of American high finance. One cannot but sympathize with Kennedy's retort that Russell's "attention might well be directed to the burglars rather than to those who have caught the burglars." Russell fired off telegrams to U Thant, Macmillan, Kennedy and Khrushchev, and eventually to Castro himself, urging moderation and suggesting the obvious compromise solution of an American pledge of non-invasion in return for the removal of the missiles. Astonishingly, both Khrushchev and Kennedy replied, and the world was treated to the spectacle of the two most powerful men in the world arguing with each other through the sitting room of a ninety-year-old philosopher. Although his aides made any number of exaggerated claims for his influence on events, Russell knew his role in the episode was almost accidental, and that it was the world at large that was being addressed, not he. None the less, he enjoyed the sensation of being at the heart of great events – and engaged in a repeat performance during the Sino-Indian conflict. It was at least flattering that the essential lines of the solution to the conflict were those he had suggested.[56]

The crisis convinced him that America was in the grip of bloodthirsty generals, CIA spies, armaments manufacturers and the peddlers of simple-minded myths. Russell's "statement" on the crisis has rightly been derided as a hysterical and absurdly one-sided outburst: "You are to die," it announced, "not in the course of nature, but within a few weeks, and not you alone, but your family, your friends, and all the inhabitants of Britain, together with many hundreds of millions of innocent people elsewhere. Why? Because rich Americans dislike the Government the Cubans prefer and have used part of their wealth to spread lies about it." There is no reason to doubt Russell's claim that none of this represented any positive enthusiasm for the Soviet cause, and that his only aim was to point out that American bullying of Cuba was on a par with the Soviet domination of Hungary. None the less, continuous high-pitched denunciation aimed only at America hardly made him many friends or converts. It was in this frame of mind that he launched the Bertrand Russell Peace Foundation in September 1963, severed his ties with the anti-nuclear movement in the following spring, and embarked on his final campaign against the war in Vietnam.

Through the Peace Foundation itself he put forward proposals for settling the Middle East crisis, resolving the difficulties of India and Pakistan, and very much more besides. These proposals were carried round the world by Ralph Schoenman, who was uniformly unsuccessful and uniformly disliked, save by Edith Russell and, to a lesser extent, her husband. The campaign which dominated Russell's last years was the struggle against American involvement in Vietnam. Before he died, he had become merely one of innumerable opponents of what had turned into one of the more hideous wars of recent years. A very large minority of all Americans was hostile to the war. Young people felt that the government was at war with them as well as with the Vietcong, and Russell's voice was hardly needed or heeded in the general fury. It ought none the less to be counted in his favour that, whatever the merits and demerits of the way he fought against the war, he was one of the first people to understand what was going on and what it might lead to.[57] In 1963 large parts of the American press were still ready to accept the government line that there were no American troops in Vietnam, or that there were a few who acted as advisers, or that occasionally the advisers were attacked when the Vietcong attacked South Vietnamese troops and had to defend themselves. Russell argued from the start that there was large-scale intervention already, involving American pilots in missions flown by the South Vietnamese airforce, that this intervention was morally and militarily disastrous, that it was bound to increase in scale and to involve America in the cruelties and brutalities of the regime American weapons were propping up. In all of this he was absolutely right. Moreover, his acrimonious contests with American editors and proprietors – notably with *The New York Times* – were marked by the curious fact that Russell's chief source for his accusations of brutality and deception were the newspapers whose editors accused him of everything from senility to rabid communism; how they contrived to print on their news pages accounts of the war which they denied on their editorial pages is one of the small mysteries of journalism. That *The New York Times* later published the *Pentagon Papers* after an epic battle with the government and the courts only adds to the difficulty.[58]

Because Russell was increasingly frail and was protected against the outside world by his various secretaries and helpers, one can only sketch in a general way what he thought about the war. Chiefly he thought that the war was atrocious; in all his writings on the war he dwells almost obsessively on the physical brutalities and horrors of napalm bombing, torture by South Vietnamese troops and police, the self-immolation of Buddhist monks protesting against the Diem regime. Almost everything else was froth. Supporters of the Vietcong, who might have been expected to treat legality as an exploded "bourgeois" notion, expended quantities of ink in arguing that America had violated the 1954 agreement which had been intended to unify North and South Vietnam under a democratically elected government. Russell went along with them, but it is doubtful that he cared about the rights and wrongs of the conflict as a matter of international law, any more than he did about the illegality of Kennedy's blockade of Cuba. To use one of his own images, he felt like a passer-by who sees a large adult beating a small boy with a stick; there's no point in asking how the fight started, the thing is to stop it.[59]

Russell was largely proved right about the atrocities committed during the war – often only after he was dead, when the *Pentagon Papers* revealed the extent to which the military had lied to the US government, and the government had lied to Congress and the American people. On the other hand, the passage of time makes the one-sidedness of his condemnation no more attractive; he was at best evasive on the question of Vietcong terrorism. His view that the oppressed look admirable only until they win would have been sickeningly verified by the Pol Pot regime in Cambodia, and it is hard to imagine which side he would have taken over the subsequent North Vietnamese invasion of Cambodia. One can at least observe that, forty years before, he had pointed out that socialists in power are no less likely than capitalists to be swept away by nationalist passions. That Hanoi and Peking should come to blows would not have surprised him. While the Vietnam war was raging, he was often right on the substance of American misdeeds where he was not right in detail; in 1963, for instance, he accused the American government of supplying lethal defoliants to South Vietnam and was rebuked by Dennis Bloodworth in the *Observer*, who claimed that what had been used was "common weed-killer" – the truth being that the infamous Agent Orange *had* been used as a weedkiller in Nevada (where it had caused sickness in animals and human beings), but was lethal if used in the concentrations and quantities in which it was used in Vietnam.[60] Russell, as ever, gave his critics an excuse to write him off as a raving old man when he accused the American government of deliberate genocide, of encouraging torture, and of creating concentration camps under the guise of the "strategic hamlets" into which the peasants in the countryside were herded to make it easier to protect them from the Vietcong. Even after all the post-mortems, leaked documents and partisan retrospectives, it does not appear that anyone in the Pentagon did want to use South Vietnam as an experimental arena for practising chemical warfare, and there was not much pressure for all-out bombing raids on civilian targets in the north – which were among Russell's accusations. None the less, Russell's view that the war was pointless, atrocious and heading for disaster was quite right. We may flinch at the tone of his appeal to Negro soldiers to desert and join the Vietcong because the war was a racist plot to get poor Blacks and Asians to kill one another; but Blacks and poor Whites were certainly prominent in the army and in the casualty lists, since they were less able to get deferments from the draft than the better-off and more articulate. The simplest case against the war was overwhelming, and Russell was at any rate intermittently sensible enough to stick to the simplest case. The

Diem regime, and its successor under Marshals Ky and Thieu, was tyr-
annical, exploitative and brutal; the American government had made its
usual mistake of thinking anti-communism a proof of moral worth and
popular support. It was bound to find itself enmired in an unwinnable war.
It could not create democracy in Vietnam, but it could undermine it in the
United States.

If that was compelling, the rest was not. Russell's support of the Vietcong was at odds with everything in his career. The decayed condition of
the South Vietnamese government and its armed forces meant that an
American withdrawal was tantamount to a Vietcong victory; whether there
would have been a takeover of the South by Hanoi had the Vietcong won in
the very early 1960s is debatable, but there is no blinking the proposition
that an American defeat meant a communist victory. It was perfectly
possible to accept this without being enthusiastic about the Vietcong; the
British Committee for Peace in Vietnam took the view that the Vietcong
was likely to install a pretty dictatorial regime, but that it would be no
worse than the Diem regime, and that the great thing was to end the civil
war and get foreign troops out. Russell and his allies in the Campaign for
Solidarity with Vietnam mocked this neutralist position, and gave their
enthusiastic backing to the Vietcong, whom they depicted as a purely
indigenous movement of national liberation, with scarcely a communist
in their ranks.[61] This was either disingenuous or self-deceived, or both. It
was also counter-productive; critics thought that if he could believe that, he
could believe anything, and dismissed him as a senile idiot. Even more
oddly, Russell attacked the Soviet Union for excessive timidity in supporting national liberation movements, and demanded Russian intervention on
behalf of the Vietcong, and in support of Cuba, the Angolan independence
movement, and the Palestine Liberation Organization into the bargain.
Russia's chief duty was to send arms and advisers to every anti-American
cause wherever it might be found, and in Vietnam to send in aircraft to
shoot down the American bombers raiding North Vietnam.

This was a complete reversal of everything he had thought, even as
recently as 1962. His view then was that the great powers must above all
else try to keep down the temperature of international relations. He said
during the missile crisis that defending Cuba to the death would be disastrous and praised Khrushchev's statesmanship in backing down gracefully. He had attacked nationalism as a threat to world peace for half a
century and more; now national liberation was the cry of the moment, and
world peace a secondary consideration – no wonder many people find it
hard to believe that Russell was the author of such stuff. Nor is it easy to
suppose that he believed Russia to be a natural ally of national independence. If he did think it, he certainly did not think it for long; in the
summer of 1968, he wrote to President Kosygin pleading that the Soviet
government should leave Czechoslovakia alone, and again in August to

denounce the invasion.[62] What he made of the fact that Cuba and North Vietnam were almost the only countries outside the immediate Soviet orbit to support the invasion, there is no way of knowing. *The New York Times* regularly trotted out the complaint that he had become a communist dupe, dazzled by the flattering attentions of Soviet leaders. The small grain of truth in that is that he was readier than before to believe the worst of American generals, politicians, diplomats and journalists and spent no corresponding effort on denouncing Russian politicians, journalists, generals and diplomats. But soft on communism never was an apt description.[63]

The explanation of Russell's curious shifts in his last years lies perhaps in one thing above all else. Casting his mind back to 1914, he surely felt that the war in Vietnam was proof that western, civilized, rational, liberal, scientific man had reverted to something lower than the beasts. In 1916 angry Englishmen called for bombing raids on German cities in revenge for the Zeppelin attacks on Britain. They knew that they were suggesting something absolutely frightful. Dropping bombs on civilian targets, perhaps killing several dozen women and children, was the act of a barbarian; those who suggested that the British should do such a thing did so in the belief that German "frightfulness" could be deterred only by similar frightfulness on the British side. Fifty years later, scruples seemed to have vanished. The Second World War had acclimatized mankind to high-tech murder, with the fire-bombing of Hamburg and Dresden every bit as obscene as the nuclear bombing of Hiroshima and Nagasaki. To employ the weapons the Americans first handed out to the South Vietnamese and then equipped their own troops with – fragmentation bombs, napalm, bullets with the properties of the outlawed dum-dum – was one more step on the road into the abyss. The gobbledegook in which the American government and military wrapped up the facts of mass murder must have grated all the more hideously on Russell's fastidious ear. At the age of ninety-three or ninety-five, what more could he do than cry out against the horror and lend his prestige and his name to those who seemed most energetic in combating it? Those inclined to sneer would do well to ask themselves how well they have lived up to the injunction not to follow a multitude in doing – or assenting to – evil.

Notes

1 *Autobiography*, pp. 509, 662.
2 *Tribunal*, 3 January 1918 (reprinted in *Autobiography*, pp. 308–10); Alan Ryan, *Bertrand Russell: A Political Life* (New York, 1988), pp. 62–3. *Autobiography*, p. 256.
3 *Autobiography*, p. 662; *Bertrand Russell's America*, II, pp. 274–5; 405; "16 Questions," in *Autobiography*, pp. 699–707.

4 *Tribune*, 15 December 1961, p. 8; *Life*, pp. 803–19 ("Schoenman Memorandum").
5 *War Crimes in Vietnam*, p. 99.
6 *Unpopular Essays*, pp. 80–7.
7 *War Crimes in Vietnam*, pp. 95–8.
8 *Russell: Philosopher of the Century*, "Introduction" – the gushing prose of which is suspiciously like much of *War Crimes in Vietnam* and utterly unlike Russell's.
9 "Memorandum," *Life*, p. 819. The *Autobiography* is kinder, praising his "almost superhuman energy and courageous determination," p. 656.
10 *Has Man a Future?*, pp. 31–2.
11 *Has Man a Future?*, pp. 20–1; *Autobiography*, p. 554.
12 *Bertrand Russell's America*, II, p. 313.
13 *Autobiography*, pp. 508–9; *Bertrand Russell's America*, II, p. 314; *Common Sense and Nuclear Warfare*, pp. 88–90.
14 *Autobiography*, p. 509; *Bertrand Russell's America*, II, p. 312.
15 *Common Sense and Nuclear Warfare*, p. 90.
16 *Bertrand Russell's America*, II, p. 11.
17 Ibid.
18 *New Statesman*, 21 April 1951; *Autobiography*, p. 509; *Common Sense and Nuclear Warfare*, pp. 89–90. Ronald Clark, *Life*, pp. 658–60, is extremely good on this "lapse of memory."
19 *Bertrand Russell's America*, II, p. 314.
20 *Has Man a Future?*, pp. 24–5; *Life*, pp. 652–7.
21 *Bertrand Russell's America*, II, pp. 16–34.
22 Ibid., pp. 37, 43.
23 Ibid., pp. 36ff.
24 *Autobiography*, pp. 574–5.
25 *Bertrand Russell's America*, pp. 13, 324–5.
26 *Autobiography*, p. 555.
27 *Life*, p. 735; *Has Man a Future?*, p. 39.
28 Jonathan Schell, *The Fate of the Earth* (New York, 1982); *Common Sense and Nuclear Warfare*, p. 19.
29 *Common Sense and Nuclear Warfare*, pp. 37–8; *Autobiography*, pp. 578–9.
30 *Autobiography*, pp. 555–6; *Life*, pp. 690–2.
31 *Life*, p. 692.
32 Anthony Kenny, *The Logic of Deterrence* (London, 1985); *Autobiography*, pp. 640–1.
33 *Has Man a Future?*, p. 63.
34 Ibid., p. 31.
35 Ibid., pp. 71–3.
36 *Common Sense and Nuclear Warfare*, pp. 85–8.
37 *Life*, pp. 705–6.
38 *Has Man a Future?*, pp. 125–6.
39 Cf. *Has Man a Future?* and *Common Sense and Nuclear Warfare*.
40 *Life*, pp. 717–18.
41 *Autobiography*, pp. 604–5; *Life*, p. 742.
42 *Life*, pp. 742–3.
43 Ibid., pp. 757ff.
44 *Bertrand Russell's America*, II, pp. 388–9.
45 Ibid., p. 392.
46 *The Entente Policy, Justice in Wartime*, pp. 125ff.
47 *Bertrand Russell's America*, II, p. 392.
48 *Portraits from Memory*, p. 30.

49 Cf. letters to Couturat, in Ryan, *Bertrand Russell*, pp. 29–30.
50 *Autobiography*, pp. 381–3.
51 *Unpopular Essays*, pp. 156ff.
52 *Common Sense and Nuclear Warfare*, p. 30.
53 *Bulletin of the Atomic Scientists*, March 1962, p. 6.
54 Robert Kennedy, *13 Days*, especially pp. 110–25.
55 *Unarmed Victory*, pp. 53ff.
56 *Life*, pp. 744–53; *Unarmed Victory*, p. 59.
57 *Autobiography*, p. 647.
58 C. L. Sulzberger, "Corpse on Horseback," *New York Times*, 4 April 1967; *War Crimes in Vietnam*, pp. 31–9.
59 I owe this recollection to Katharine Tait.
60 *War Crimes in Vietnam*, p. 35; p. 47.
61 Ibid., pp. 66–7, 99–100.
62 *Life*, p. 793.
63 *War Crimes in Vietnam*, pp. 32–3, 38.

10

Portrait of the Philosopher as Father

Katharine Tait

If you have listened to all the talks in this series, you have heard fatherhood discussed from the viewpoint of almost every academic discipline. Now at the end you hear from a non-expert, a 'consumer', if you will, like all the rest of you. And yet not just like all the rest of you, for my father, Bertrand Russell, was not really like anyone else's father. I want to try and tell you what he was like, not as a great philosopher or a political activist, but as a father; and what it was like to be his child.

Before I begin, a word about my method. This is a portrait, not a photograph: it does not claim to be an accurate reproduction, but a picture distilled through the artist's vision. It includes a good deal of background and a good deal of the artist (myself); this last not from vanity, but because what I am and what I think are part of the story of Russell as a father.

The treatment we receive as children largely determines how we behave as parents, whether we copy or reject it. We find ourselves doing what was done to us and expecting what was expected of us; sometimes with horror we hear our parents' voices coming out of our own mouths. But what if we have no parents? How do orphans know how to behave as parents? This must have been a problem for many of you in Germany, as it was for my father. His mother and sister died of diphtheria when he was two, his father when he was four, and his grandfather when he was six. His only brother, seven years older, was sent away to school, leaving Russell alone in a large house with his grandmother, his Aunt Agatha, and an assortment of governesses, tutors and servants. The nearest approach to a father in his life was his Uncle Rollo, who also lived at Pembroke Lodge until he got married. Rollo Russell was a kind and intelligent man and a good story-teller; but he carried the Russell shyness to almost pathological extremes and barely spoke except to children. (Nevertheless, he managed to marry twice.)

My father lived in a hushed household of women devoted to the past. He spent much time alone in the garden imagining the splendour of Pembroke Lodge in his grandfather's time and the lost happiness of his dead parents' home. He seems to have decided very early that he would have children of his own and bring them up more happily and sensibly than he had been raised himself. One can say, of course, that he was trying to make it up to the poor little boy he had been and to show his grandmother how things should really be done, but this is only part of the truth. He could have spent his whole life grieving resentfully over his unhappy childhood, instead of going out to make things better for others. One of the truly great things about my father was that personal grief prompted him to help others rather than to seek sympathy for himself.

He had another motive for having children, equally generous and equally typical of him. He believed profoundly in the power of education to shape character and the power of characters to shape history. He wanted to raise up openminded and courageous human beings who would go out into the world to help others and to fight against the evils he was beginning to perceive in society. His view of the evils of society changed somewhat during his long life and his trust in the efficacy of education diminished, but he never completely lost his hope of reforming the world by changing people's minds.

Though these two ambitions took shape early in my father's life and though he was married at the very young age of twenty-two, it was many years before he had any children through whom to realize them. His first marriage proved childless and his first explorations of the world outside marriage discovered no women eager to have children. Then as now ambitious women did not want to be tied down and women willing to be so tied he did not find interesting. He was getting on for fifty years old when he came to know my mother, a woman he could love who also wanted children. The two of them were equally eager to embark on parenthood, to have children they could both cherish as individuals and train as reformers. They differed, though, in their underlying and not quite conscious motives; his to do better by his children than had been done by him; hers to carry on into another generation the happiness she remembered from her own childhood.

Their first child, John, was born in November 1921 and I just two years later, in December 1923. (Interesting, perhaps, that we were called after our grandparents, John Russell and Kate Stanley. What was my father trying to reproduce?) We lived at first in a flat in London, which I dimly remember: dark woodwork and a bright fire; a big bed with many cushions, on which we were encouraged to jump and play; a child's swing in Battersea Park with my father pushing it. I remember love and laughter and jokes, against a background of order and regularity which was there for our convenience, not for our discipline. All I remember of my father from here is a pervading sense of love and security.

Soon we acquired the house in Cornwall, which I still think of as heaven on earth. Of this I remember much more. A plain house, but sunny and full of bright colours, with a lovely garden and a magnificent view. (My father could not live without a view. It must have made prison very hard for him.) Here also we lived a regular life: work for the adults and lessons for us in the mornings, walks or beaches in the afternoons, tea and bath and reading aloud, followed by bed for us and dinner for the adults. John and I were not, I regret to say, in every respect model children and sometimes we would scurry about the house while the adults were at dinner, until our giggles attracted their attention (as they were meant to do) and we were sternly pointed back to bed by my father.

How well I remember meals in that bright dining room, sitting as the youngest and quietest member at table while my father carved the roast while talking, always talking. I can still see the juices running from the meat under his knife and remember the eagerness with which I awaited my plate. There was only quiet at the table when we had fish. Then my father would take out his glasses, put them on and study his plate with solemnity, making me think there was something wrong with it. But it was only that he couldn't see the bones without his glasses. Fish with bones usually prompted the story of the doctor who got a fishbone stuck in his throat and with his last dying purple breath managed to gasp out 'Glove stretchers!' His wife ran for her glove stretchers, removed the bone just in time, and they lived happily ever after. What are glove stretchers? Your guess is as good as mine. Perhaps they belonged to my father's well brought up Victorian youth.

Of course it rained in Cornwall. It rains a lot there and often there is fog or drizzle or grey sky. But I don't remember that. Only the sunshine and the happiness, and the wind, clear and fresh and exciting. I remember lying under the fragrant hay stooks drying in the fields, watching the little clouds reel through the sky and listening to the larks and the bees. I remember the crunch of sand underfoot, the prickle of barnacled rocks, the chill of the water and the roughness of the waves, which would roll you over and over in their horrible sandy wetness if you were not steady on your feet. The wild blue-green of the sea, the golden gorse, the purple heather, the dry and shining cliff grass – all this seemed as much a part of my father as his white hair, his red face and peeling nose under his panama hat, the long white shirt that protected him from sunburn and the dark pipe moving in his hand as he gestured. It was always moving, for he was always talking, joking, taking it on himself to entertain us all, laughing his loud and sudden laugh as though someone else had made the joke.

Every beach had a little stream, where he taught us to build dams, reinforcing the sand with stones and then waiting for the breathless moment when the trickle over the top became a deluge and the whole structure was destroyed. He taught us to swim and to climb, to float in pools and to breast the waves and to understand the tide and its currents. When the way home from the beach seemed hot and long, he would cheer it with fantastic tales which he made up as he went along; I particularly recall a long serial about a flying post office with wings made of postage stamps. At home in the garden he would throw balls over the roof while John and I rushed round the house to see them come down among the vegetables. My Cornish father was absolute perfection to me, a combination of Father Christmas and the brightest summer sun. I loved him with an intensity I have never known since; he was so wise, so kind, so good, and always the centre of everybody's attention.

Sad that the idyll could not last forever. But there was always the other ambition: to do good to the world by giving us a perfect education, encouraging all that was good in us while discouraging all impulses to laziness, unkindness or deceit. Our parents believed in conditioning. Babies were ethically neutral, they thought, and teaching them right habits from birth would ensure correct behaviour in adult life. 'The right moment to begin the requisite moral training', wrote my father, 'is the moment of birth, because then it can be done without disappointing expectations' (*Education and the Good Life*, New York: Liveright, 1970, p. 90).

I cannot describe my life with my father without getting into educational theory, because so much of what he did with us was determined by his ideas of what ought to be done. The jolly man on the beach was always *thinking*, always pondering what methods to use to bring about the desired results. When I grew up and read his book on education, I understood better what he had been doing in those early years, but I liked it less. He was the kindest man in the world, couldn't bear us to be unhappy, cherished his children every minute, filled our lives with sunshine, and yet . . .

So kind until theory blinded him. In the book on education there is a sad account of John's fear of the dark. According to then current theory this fear was neither innate nor rational; it was usually picked up from some foolish nurse and could therefore be conditioned out of existence. When John showed symptoms of this infection, he was reasoned with gently, persuaded to agree that his fears were foolish, told to lie quiet because nobody would come if he cried again – then left alone in the dark. Do you suppose he stopped being afraid? Our childish fears do not go away because we are told they are foolish; rather we tremble in secret shame until at last we outgrow them. Modern 'scientific' theory combined in my father's mind with memories of his own Spartan upbringing and blinded him to what he was really doing. Certainly John learned that it was useless to cry in the night. But perhaps he also learned that protectors don't come when you need them – a conclusion by no means intended.

What my father *intended* in our education was so often undermined by what he was. He dealt with our rational minds and never realized how much we picked up from tones of voice, gestures, expressions at variance with the spoken words. He meant to encourage us, to expect the best of us, to arrange our lives so that we must acquire good habits, and to fill our minds as full of knowledge as his own. But his secret doubts and inherited negative attitudes were always creeping out round the edges, peeping at us behind his back and assuring us that it was not all such plain sailing. And then besides, he was himself a brilliant man and unaware of the mental limitations of more normal human beings. It was an immense strain understanding all he said, remembering what he told us, struggling with arithmetical and philosophical puzzles. It wasn't meant to be. He was always jolly about it, but you knew he would be disappointed if you couldn't do it, whatever it was. And his mind was like a rapier, sometimes cutting unintentionally. No, it was not an easy life.

We were never supposed to be afraid. Children properly brought up as we were would never be afraid or deceitful or unkind. There would be no need, since no one had taught us to fear and no threatening adult needed to be deceived, or imitated in our dealings with others. We were proud of our father – early on we had a sense that he and we were special – and we did our best to live up to his expectations. But virtuous behaviour never became the automatic response his theories implied. I was always afraid, not always kind and generous and truthful, and I was not cheerful and confident because I always felt I had so many faults to conceal. I felt that, since my father was perfect and his methods of course wise, responsibility for the less than perfect results must lie with ne.

How I loved him in those early years! I cannot describe to you the intensity of my devotion, the way my sun rose and set with him, the source of all joy and wisdom. When he told me that Hungary used to be called Yumyum and they changed it to Hungary because they thought it would be more dignified, I believed him. When he looked out of the window on April Fool's Day and said 'Good gracious, there's an elephant coming up the garden path!' I believed him, although I knew I had been fooled the same way the year before. When he told me the Duke of Wellington had a tail and had a special little hole made in his saddle for it, I believed him. I believed *everything* he said and some things I have never straightened out. Was there a King of Bavaria whose courtiers said he was mad because he bubbled in his soup? Or was that only told to get us to stop doing it?

When he was talking to other adults and I could not understand all he said, I would watch him quietly, devotedly, proud of his wit and brilliance, and yet even then dimly aware of flaws. Perhaps it was his willingness to stretch truth for the sake of a story, for I was passionately honest and accurate – as he had taught me to be. Or was it the uneasy sense that his arguments were not always quite fair, though I could not have said just how? I felt at moments that he was not living up to his own high standards and that troubled me very much. It still does. I still regret the inability of my wonderful father to be what he told me people should be.

When my brother was not quite six years old and I was not quite four, our parents started a school for us. They did not think it would be good for us to grow up without the companionship of other children – my mother because she had enjoyed it herself, my father because he had not – yet they could not find any existing school that met their exacting requirements. No religious indoctrination, of course, no flag-waving patriotism, no corporal punishment, no heavy moral emphasis, absolute freedom of inquiry on all subjects, including sex. There were schools that met these requirements, but most of them did not measure up to the other ones: an orderly, disciplined life, with plenty of outdoor exercise, an academic education that would ask the utmost of both intelligence and memory.

So they started their own school. Twenty-odd young children (the youngest, like me, only about three years old. It seems extraordinary now that this could have been thought good for children of that age, but the emphasis on scientific training led people to believe that experts must be better for children than ignorant parents, however loving.) In any case, there we were, twenty-odd of us in a heavenly rural setting, with the very latest in educational equipment, a group of idealistic young teachers, and two brilliant, dedicated heads.

I have never been able to make up my mind about the school. It did much that they wanted it to do. We spent a great deal of time out of doors in all weathers, climbing trees, exploring, identifying flora and fauna, collecting bones and fossils, simply playing. I remember with pleasure the endless variations of tag and hide and seek we played among the lawns and hedges of the lovely gardens. We had a great deal more freedom than is common and we certainly learned to be independent and self-reliant and ready to question almost anything. We also learned a great deal of history and literature, science, mathematics, and languages – French, German and Russian – as well as how to find out things for ourselves and how to write up what we had found out. I think it is owing to this good beginning that I have never had trouble learning in any other school.

John and I paid a price for this education, though. As heads of the school and teachers in it, our parents had to treat all the children alike. During term-time we could have no special relationship with them. Of course there had always been nannies and governesses in our lives and we were used to being cared for by other people. But our parents had always spent a lot of time with us, always been very close, both from interest and from love. Now they were gone. My shining, laughing, red-faced father was in his study at the top of the tower, writing to make money, worrying about the school, teaching history. When he came down, which was often, he was for everybody – they all wanted to hold his warm dry hand and get close to him, and I had no special claim. It was very hard. Remember I was only four or five years old. I learned then to adore from a distance, unapproaching and unapproachable, and I was never able to unlearn that lesson.

The story of my life with my father is one of ever-increasing separation. This is the normal progress of such relationships, no doubt, but usually the child grows away from the parent. I always felt, on the contrary, that he was moving away from me before I was ready, before I had begun to think of seeking a life of my own. Indeed, what life could I have found more exciting and delightful than the one I had had with him?

After the wrench of the school came my parents' separation, and not too long after that my departure for boarding school. Now there were only school holidays to spend with my father and even these had to be exactly divided up between the two parents, both of whom were living in new homes. It was difficult to feel that we belonged anywhere. Our parents disagreed passionately and profoundly about us. They were still as devoted to us as ever, still as convinced that our education was of crucial importance, but they were no longer in harmony about what was to be done. It was not possible for us to remain neutral. Of course I chose my father, but not without grief. He said things about my mother that seemed unduly harsh and I had to recognize consciously at last that he, the apostle of reason and understanding, the embodiment of kindness, was allowing prejudice to make him unfair.

When I grew older and read some of my father's writings and listened with more understanding to what he said, I saw that he was often unfair. As I had dimly suspected, he did not allow facts to spoil a good story or cripple a good argument. When he thought a cause was right, or a person was wrong, he would let fly with merciless eloquence, indignation and ridicule. Though I generally agreed with him, I often shrank away from his extravagance. A last sad example was his Vietnam War Crimes Tribunal, whose outlandish accusations and tone of shrill indignation caused me acute embarrassment. Yet I had to acknowledge later that in this case almost all he had said had been true. Those terrible things had indeed been done and my good taste was surely a less appropriate response than his wild scolding.

I was always a quiet child, a watcher rather than an actor, and I have been a quiet adult, living a private life far from the pavements of Trafalgar Square. Yet I think perhaps I am more like my father in many ways than like the person he wanted me to be. He wanted us to grow up like his public self: courageous, indignant, ever at work redeeming wrongs. What he got was two people like his private self: shy, burdened with guilt, given to depression, and feeling both useless and worthless. Was this typical Russell character in our genes or did we learn it from our father? Would different children subjected to his methods have turned out closer to his ideal? Why was he, with his awful childhood, more the kind of person he wanted than we, with our ideal one? Genes or methods, take your pick. For myself I can only say that I was always determined to be like my father in every way possible, even to dousing my food with pepper as he did. (Though I gave up that ambition after my first taste.) And I have seen my son model himself on his father in the same way, down to the smallest absurdities of habit. Perhaps love is after all the most effective teacher; but since we do not always understand our children or they us, we cannot be sure what lessons love is teaching them.

I have spoken mostly of my father in the early years of my life because then he was closest and most beautiful. Family complications and the troubles of adolescence cut me off from him as I grew up and my marriage to an American put the Atlantic between us for most of my life. I regret the separation. There was much I could have learned from him, and under-neath our shy skins we loved each other immensely. But it is not easy to be the child of a great man. If we are ever to be more than shadows we must get away, far away, and build our own lives. (In this connection I might add that it is not easy to marry the child of a great man either. My former husband is a man of great intelligence and unusual integrity, but 'he had a hard act to follow', as they say, and in the end we split on the ghost of my father.)

After my father died in 1970 I came to think that I should write a book about him, to tell about the side of him that I had known. It was only as I wrote that I began to see him as a human being, a man with faults and virtues like other men (though better than most), no longer that larger-than-life, utterly charming and cruelly disappointing idol of my early years. I suppose he spoiled me for any other man, but on the whole I think he was worth it.

Select Primary Bibliography

Bertrand Russell authored over 50 books, as well as some 4,300 articles, book chapters, reviews, pamphlets, letters to the editor, press releases and other publications. Russell also authored over 61,000 letters and other documents not originally intended for publication. To date, over 45 anthologies of his writings have also been published.

For a detailed accounting of Russell's published writings, the reader is encouraged to consult *A Bibliography of Bertrand Russell* (London: Routledge, 1994), edited by Kenneth Blackwell and Harry Ruja. It is from this authoritative and comprehensive three-volume work that many of the details of the current bibliography are drawn.

Unlike the Blackwell–Ruja *Bibliography*, this bibliography is not intended to be an exhaustive inventory of Russell's publications. Rather, it is a listing of only his most important and influential English-language writings as they have appeared in book form. The list consists of three categories:

1 monographs and other important and influential books and booklets written by Russell;
2 significant anthologies, which contain many (but not all) of Russell's articles, essays and letters, and
3 Russell's collected papers, as they are appearing in *The Collected Papers of Bertrand Russell*.

1. Important Monographs, Books, and Booklets Written by Russell

(1896) *German Social Democracy*, London: Longmans, Green.
    1. Marx and the Theoretical Basis of Social Democracy; 2. Lassalle; 3. History of German Socialism from the Death of Lassalle to the Passing of the Exceptional Law; 4. The Exceptional Law; 5. The Organization, Agitation, Tactics,

and Programme of Social Democracy Since the Fall of the Socialist Law; 6. The Present Position of Social Democracy.

Appendix: Social Democracy and the Woman Question in Germany, by Alys Russell.

(1897) *An Essay on the Foundations of Geometry*, Cambridge: At the University Press. Introduction: Our Problem Defined by Its Relations to Logic, Psychology and Mathematics; 1. A Short History of Metageometry; 2. Critical Account of Some Previous Philosophical Theories of Geometry; 3. (A) The Axioms of Projective Geometry, (B) The Axioms of Metrical Geometry; 4. Philosophical Consequences.

(1900) *A Critical Exposition of the Philosophy of Leibniz*, Cambridge: At the University Press.

1. Leibniz's Premises; 2. Necessary Propositions and the Law of Contradiction; 3. Contingent Propositions and the Law of Sufficient Reason; 4. The Conception of Substance; 5. The Identity of Indiscernibles and the Law of Continuity: Possibility and Compossibility; 6. Why Did Leibniz Believe in an External World?; 7. The Philosophy of Matter: (a) As the Outcome of the Principles of Dynamics; 8. The Philosophy of Matter: (b) As Explaining Continuity and Extension; 9. The Labyrinth of the Continuum; 10. The Theory of Space and Time and Its Relation to Monadism; 11. The Nature of Monads in General; 12. Soul and Body; 13. Confused and Unconscious Perception; 14. Leibniz's Theory of Knowledge; 15. Proofs of the Existence of God; 16. Leibniz's Ethics.

Appendix: Extracts From Leibniz Classified According to Subjects.

(1903) *The Principles of Mathematics*, Cambridge: At the University Press.

Part I – The Indefinables of Mathematics: 1. Definition of Pure Mathematics; 2. Symbolic Logic; 3. Implication and Formal Implication; 4. Proper Names, Adjectives, and Verbs; 5. Denoting; 6. Classes; 7. Propositional Functions; 8. The Variable; 9. Relations; 10. The Contradiction.

Part II – Number: 11. Definition of Cardinal Numbers; 12. Addition and Multiplication; 13. Finite and Infinite; 14. Theory of Finite Numbers; 15. Addition of Terms and Addition of Classes; 16. Whole and Part; 17. Infinite Wholes; 18. Ratios and Fractions.

Part III – Quantity: 19. The Meaning of Magnitude; 20. The Range of Quantity; 21. Numbers as Expressing Magnitudes: Measurement; 22. Zero; 23. Infinity, the Infinitesimal, and Continuity.

Part IV – Order: 24. The Genesis of Series; 25. The Meaning of Order; 26. Asymmetrical Relations; 27. Difference of Sense and Difference of Sign; 28. On the Difference Between Open and Closed Series; 29. Progressions and Ordinal Numbers; 30. Dedekind's Theory of Number; 31. Distance.

Part V – Infinity and Continuity: 32. The Correlation of Series; 33. Real Numbers; 34. Limits and Irrational Numbers; 35. Cantor's First Definition of Continuity; 36. Ordinal Continuity; 37. Transfinite Cardinals; 38. Transfinite Ordinals; 39. The Infinitesimal Calculus; 40. The Infinitesimal and the Improper Infinite; 41. Philosophical Arguments Concerning the Infinitesimal; 42. The Philosophy of the Continuum; 43. The Philosophy of the Infinite.

Part VI – Space: 44. Dimensions and Complex Numbers; 45. Projective Geometry; 46. Descriptive Geometry; 47. Metrical Geometry; 48. Relation of Metrical to Projective and Descriptive Geometry; 49. Definitions of Various Spaces; 50. The Continuity of Space; 51. Logical Arguments Against Points; 52. Kant's Theory of Space.

Part VII – Matter and Motion: 53. Matter; 54. Motion; 55. Causality;

56. Definition of a Dynamical World; 57. Newton's Laws of Motion; 58. Absolute and Relative Motion; 59. Hertz's Dynamics.

Appendixes: A. The Logical and Arithmetical Doctrines of Frege; B. The Doctrine of Types.

(1910) *Anti-Suffragist Anxieties*, London: The People's Suffrage Federation.

(1910, 1912, 1913) (with Alfred North Whitehead) *Principia Mathematica*, 3 vols, Cambridge: At the University Press. Abridged as *Principia Mathematica to *56*, Cambridge: At the University Press, 1962.

Volume 1.

Introduction: 1. Preliminary Explanations of Ideas and Notations; 2. The Theory of Logical Types; 3. Incomplete Symbols.

Part I – Mathematical Logic: A. The Theory of Deduction; B. Theory of Apparent Variables; C. Classes and Relations; D. Logic of Relations; E. Products and Sums of Classes.

Part II – Prolegomena to Cardinal Arithmetic: A. Unit Classes and Couples; B. Sub-Classes, Sub-Relations, and Relative Types; C. One–Many, Many–One and One–One Relations; D. Selections; E. Inductive Relations.

Volume 2.

Prefatory Statement of Symbolic Conventions.

Part III – Cardinal Arithmetic: A. Definition and Logical Properties of Cardinal Numbers; B. Addition, Multiplication and Exponentiation; C. Finite and Infinite.

Part IV – Relation-Arithmetic: A. Ordinal Similarity and Relation-Numbers; B. Addition of Relations, and the Product of Two Relations; C. The Principle of First Differences, and the Multiplication and Exponentiation of Relations; D. Arithmetic of Relation-Numbers.

Part V – Series: A. General Theory of Series; B. On Sections, Segments, Stretches, and Derivatives; C. On Convergence, and the Limits of Functions.

Volume 3.

Part V – Series (cont.): D. Well-Ordered Series; E. Finite and Infinite Series and Ordinals; F. Compact Series, Rational Series, and Continuous Series.

Part VI – Quantity: A. Generalization of Number; B. Vector-Families; C. Measurement; D. Cyclic Families.

(1912) *The Philosophy of Bergson*, Chicago: The Open Court Publishing Company. 1. The Philosophy of Bergson; 2. On Mr Russell's Reasons for Supposing That Bergson's Philosophy Is Not True, by W. Carr; 3. Mr Wildon Carr's Defence of Bergson.

(1912) *The Problems of Philosophy*, London: Williams and Norgate; New York: Henry Holt and Company.

1. Appearance and Reality; 2. The Existence of Matter; 3. The Nature of Matter; 4. Idealism; 5. Knowledge by Acquaintance and Knowledge by Description; 6. On Induction; 7. On Our Knowledge of General Principles; 8. How *A Priori* Knowledge is Possible; 9. The World of Universals; 10. On Our Knowledge of Universals; 11. On Intuitive Knowledge; 12. Truth and Falsehood; 13. Knowledge, Error, and Probable Opinion; 14. The Limits of Philosophical Knowledge; 15. The Value of Philosophy.

(1914) *Our Knowledge of the External World as a Field for Scientific Method in Philosophy*, Chicago and London: The Open Court Publishing Company.

1. Current Tendencies; 2. Logic as the Essence of Philosophy; 3. On Our Knowledge of the External World; 4. The World of Physics and the World of Sense;

5. The Theory of Continuity; 6. The Problem of Infinity Considered Historically; 7. The Positive Theory of Infinity; 8. On the Notion of Cause, with Applications to the Free-Will Problem.

(1914) *Scientific Method in Philosophy*, Oxford: At the Clarendon Press.

(1915) *Justice in War-Time*, Manchester and London: The National Labour Press.
1. An Appeal to the Intellectuals of Europe; 2. The Ethics of War; 3. War and Non-Resistance; 4. Why Nations Love War; 5. The Future of Anglo-German Rivalry; 6. Is a Permanent Peace Possible?

(1915) *The Policy of the Entente, 1904–14*, Manchester and London: The National Labour Press.

1. Introduction; 2. Morocco; 3. The Anglo-Russian Entente; 4. Persia; 5. What Our Policy Ought to Have Been.

Appendix: A. Press Interpretations of Our Guarantee to Belgium in 1887; B. What Support Did We Offer to France in 1905?

(1916) *Principles of Social Reconstruction*, London: George Allen and Unwin. Repr. as *Why Men Fight*, New York: The Century Company, 1917.
1. The Principle of Growth; 2. The State; 3. War as an Institution; 4. Property; 5. Education; 6. Marriage and the Population Question; 7. Religion and the Churches; 8. What We Can Do.

(1917) *Political Ideals*, New York: The Century Company.
1. Political Ideals; 2. Capitalism and the Wage System; 3. Pitfalls in Socialism; 4. Individual Liberty and Public Control; 5. National Independence and Internationalism.

(1918) *Roads to Freedom*, London: George Allen and Unwin. Repr. as *Proposed Roads to Freedom*, New York: Henry Holt, 1919.
Introduction.

Part I – Historical: 1. Marx and Socialist Doctrine; 2. Bakunin and Anarchism; 3. The Syndicalist Revolt.

Part II – Problems of the Future: 4. Work and Pay; 5. Government and Law; 6. International Relations; 7. Science and Art Under Socialism; 8. The World As It Could Be Made.

(1919) *Introduction to Mathematical Philosophy*, London: George Allen and Unwin; New York: The Macmillan Company.
1. The Series of Natural Numbers; 2. Definition of Number; 3. Finitude and Mathematical Induction; 4. The Definition of Order; 5. Kinds of Relations; 6. Similarity of Relations; 7. Rational, Real, and Complex Numbers; 8. Infinite Cardinal Numbers; 9. Infinite Series and Ordinals; 10. Limits and Continuity; 11. Limits and Continuity of Functions; 12. Selections and the Multiplicative Axiom; 13. The Axiom of Infinity and Logical Types; 14. Incompatibility and the Theory of Deduction; 15. Propositional Functions; 16. Descriptions; 17. Classes; 18. Mathematics and Logic.

(1920) *The Practice and Theory of Bolshevism*, London: George Allen and Unwin. Repr. as *Bolshevism: Practice and Theory*, New York: Harcourt, Brace and Howe, 1920.
Part I – The Present Condition of Russia: 1. What Is Hoped from Bolshevism; 2. General Characteristics; 3. Lenin, Trotsky and Gorky; 4. Art and Education, by Dora Black; 5. Communism and the Soviet Constitution; 6. The Failure of Russian Industry; 7. Daily Life in Moscow; 8. Town and Country; 9. International Policy.

Part II – Bolshevik Theory: 1. The Materialistic Theory of History; 2. Deciding Forces in Politics; 3. Bolshevik Criticism of Democracy; 4. Revolution and

Dictatorship; 5. Mechanism and the Individual; 6. Why Russian Communism has Failed; 7. Conditions for the Success of Communism.

(1921) *The Analysis of Mind*, London: George Allen and Unwin; New York: The Macmillan Company.

1. Recent Criticisms of 'Consciousness'; 2. Instinct and Habit; 3. Desire and Feeling; 4. Influence of Past History on Present Occurrences in Living Organisms; 5. Psychological and Physical Causal Laws; 6. Introspection; 7. The Definition of Perception; 8. Sensations and Images; 9. Memory; 10. Words and Meaning; 11. General Ideas and Thought; 12. Belief; 13. Truth and Falsehood; 14. Emotions and Will; 15. Characteristics of Mental Phenomena.

(1922) *Free Thought and Official Propaganda*, London: Watts and Company; New York: B.W. Huebsch, Inc.

(1922) *The Problem of China*, London: George Allen and Unwin; New York: The Century Company.

1. Questions; 2. China Before the Nineteenth Century; 3. China and the Western Powers; 4. Modern China; 5. Japan Before the Restoration; 6. Modern Japan; 7. Japan and China Before 1914; 8. Japan and China During the War; 9. The Washington Conference; 10. Present Forces and Tendencies in the Far East; 11. Chinese and Western Civilization Contrasted; 12. The Chinese Character; 13. Higher Education in China; 14. Industrialism in China; 15. The Outlook for China.

Appendix.

(1923) *The ABC of Atoms*, London: Kegan Paul, Trench, Trubner; New York: E. P. Dutton.

1. Introductory; 2. The Periodic Law; 3. Electrons and Nuclei; 4. The Hydrogen Spectrum; 5. Possible States of the Hydrogen Atom; 6. The Theory of Quanta; 7. Refinements of the Hydrogen Spectrum; 8. Rings of Electrons; 9. X-Rays; 10. Radio-Activity; 11. The Structure of Nuclei; 12. The New Physics and the Wave-Theory of Light; 13. The New Physics and Relativity.

Appendix: Bohr's Theory of the Hydrogen Spectrum.

(1923) *A Free Man's Worship*, Portland, Maine: Thomas Bird Mosher. Repr. as *What Can A Free Man Worship?*, Girard, Kansas: Haldeman-Julius Publications, 1927.

(1923) (with Dora Winifred Black Russell) *The Prospects of Industrial Civilization*, London: George Allen and Unwin; New York: The Century Company.

Part I: 1. Causes of the Present Chaos; 2. Inherent Tendencies of Industrialism; 3. Industrialism and Private Property; 4. Interactions of Industrialism and Nationalism; 5. The Transition to Internationalism; 6. Socialism in Undeveloped Countries; 7. Socialism in Advanced Countries.

Part II: 8. What Makes a Social System Good or Bad?; 9. Moral Standards and Social Well-Being; 10. The Sources of Power; 11. The Distribution of Power; 12. Education; 13. Economic Organization and Mental Freedom.

(1924) *How to be Free and Happy*, New York: The Rand School of Social Science.

(1924) *Icarus, or the Future of Science*, London: Kegan Paul, Trench, Trubner. Repr. as *The Future of Science*, New York: Philosophical Library, 1959.

1. Introductory; 2. Effects of the Physical Sciences; 3. The Increase of Organization; 4. The Anthropological Sciences; 5. Conclusion.

(1925) *The ABC of Relativity*, London: Kegan Paul, Trench, Trubner; New York: Harper and Brothers.

1. Touch and Sight: the Earth and the Heavens; 2. What Happens and What Is Observed; 3. The Velocity of Light; 4. Clocks and Footrules; 5. Space–Time; 6. The Special Theory of Relativity; 7. Intervals in Space–Time; 8. Einstein's

Law of Gravitation; 9. Proofs of Einstein's Law of Gravitation; 10. Mass, Momentum, Energy, and Action; 11. Is the Universe Finite?; 12. Conventions and Natural Laws; 13. The Abolition of 'Force'; 14. What Is Matter?; 15. Philosophical Consequences.

(1925) *What I Believe*, London: Kegan Paul, Trench, Trubner; New York: E. P. Dutton.

1. Nature and Man; 2. The Good Life; 3. Moral Rules; 4. Salvation, Individual and Social; 5. Science and Happiness.

(1926) *On Education, Especially in Early Childhood*, London: George Allen and Unwin. Repr. as *Education and the Good Life*, New York: Boni and Liveright, 1926. Abridged as *Education of Character*, New York: Philosophical Library, 1961.

Part I – Educational Ideas: 1. Postulates of Modern Educational Theory; 2. The Aims of Education.

Part II – Education and Character: 3. The First Year; 4. Fear; 5. Play and Fancy; 6. Constructiveness; 7. Selfishness and Property; 8. Truthfulness; 9. Punishment; 10. Importance of Other Children; 11. Affection and Sympathy; 12. Sex Education; 13. The Nursery School.

Part III – Intellectual Education: 14. General Principles; 15. The School Curriculum before Fourteen; 16. Last School Years; 17. Day Schools and Boarding Schools; 18. The University; 19. Conclusion.

(1927) *The Analysis of Matter*, London: Kegan Paul, Trench, Trubner; New York: Harcourt, Brace.

1. The Nature of the Problem;

Part I – The Logical Analysis of Physics: 2. Pre-Relativity Physics; 3. Electrons and Protons; 4. The Theory of Quanta; 5. The Special Theory of Relativity; 6. The General Theory of Relativity; 7. The Method of Tensors; 8. Geodesics; 9. Invariants and Their Physical Interpretation; 10. Weyl's Theory; 11. The Principle of Differential Laws; 12. Measurement; 13. Matter and Space; 14. The Abstractness of Physics.

Part II – Physics and Perception: 15. From Primitive Perception to Common Sense; 16. From Common Sense to Physics; 17. What Is an Empirical Science?; 18. Our Knowledge of Particular Matters of Fact; 19. Data, Inferences, Hypotheses, and Theories; 20. The Causal Theory of Perception; 21. Perception and Objectivity; 22. The Belief in General Laws; 23. Substance; 24. Importance of Structure in Scientific Inference; 25. Perception from the Standpoint of Physics; 26. Non-Mental Analogues to Perception.

Part III – The Structure of the Physical World: 27. Particulars and Events; 28. The Construction of Points; 29. Space–Time Order; 30. Causal Lines; 31. Extrinsic Causal Laws; 32. Physical and Perceptual Space–Time; 33. Periodicity and Qualitative Series; 34. Types of Physical Occurrences; 35. Causality and Interval; 36. The Genesis of Space–Time; 37. Physics and Neutral Monism; 38. Summary and Conclusion.

(1927) *An Outline of Philosophy*, London: George Allen and Unwin. Repr. as *Philosophy*, New York: W. W. Norton, 1927.

1. Philosophic Doubts.

Part I – Man from Without: 2. Man and His Environment; 3. The Process of Learning in Animals and Infants; 4. Language; 5. Perception Objectively Regarded; 6. Memory Objectively Regarded; 7. Inference as a Habit; 8. Knowledge Behaviouristically Considered.

Part II – The Physical World: 9. The Structure of the Atom; 10. Relativity; 11. Causal Laws in Physics; 12. Physics and Perception; 13. Physical and

Perceptual Space; 14. Perception and Physical Causal Laws; 15. The Nature of Our Knowledge of Physics.

Part III – Man from Within: 16. Self-Observation; 17. Images; 18. Imagination and Memory; 19. The Introspective Analysis of Perception; 20. Consciousness?; 21. Emotion, Desire, and Will; 22. Ethics.

Part IV – The Universe: 23. Some Great Philosophies of the Past; 24. Truth and Falsehood; 25. The Validity of Inference; 26. Events, Matter, and Mind; 27. Man's Place in the Universe.

(1927) *Why I Am Not a Christian*, London: Watts, New York: The Truth Seeker Company.

(1929?) *Has Religion Made Useful Contributions to Civilization?*, Girard, Kansas: Haldeman-Julius Publications.

(1929) *Marriage and Morals*, London: George Allen and Unwin; New York: Horace Liveright.

1. Introduction; 2. Matrilineal Societies; 3. Patriarchal Systems; 4. Phallic Worship, Asceticism and Sin; 5. Christian Ethics; 6. Romantic Love; 7. The Liberation of Women; 8. The Taboo on Sex Knowledge; 9. The Place of Love in Human Life; 10. Marriage; 11. Prostitution; 12. Trial Marriage; 13. The Family at the Present Day; 14. The Family in Individual Psychology; 15. The Family and the State; 16. Divorce; 17. Population; 18. Eugenics; 19. Sex and Individual Well-Being; 20. The Place of Sex among Human Values; 21. Conclusion.

(1930) *The Conquest of Happiness*, London: George Allen and Unwin; New York: Horace Liveright.

Part I – Causes of Unhappiness: 1. What Makes People Unhappy?; 2. Byronic Unhappiness; 3. Competition; 4. Boredom and Excitement; 5. Fatigue; 6. Envy; 7. The Sense of Sin; 8. Persecution Mania; 9. Fear of Public Opinion.

Part II – Causes of Happiness: 10. Is Happiness Still Possible?; 11. Zest; 12. Affection; 13. The Family; 14. Work; 15. Impersonal Interests; 16. Effort and Resignation; 17. The Happy Man.

(1931) *The Scientific Outlook*, London: George Allen and Unwin; New York: W. W. Norton.

Introduction.

Part I – Scientific Knowledge: 1. Examples of Scientific Method; 2. Characteristics of Scientific Method; 3. Limitations of Scientific Method; 4. Scientific Metaphysics; 5. Science and Religion.

Part II – Scientific Technique: 6. Beginnings of Scientific Technique; 7. Technique in Inanimate Nature; 8. Technique in Biology; 9. Technique in Physiology; 10. Technique in Psychology; 11. Technique in Society.

Part III – The Scientific Society: 12. Artificially Created Societies; 13. The Individual and the Whole; 14. Scientific Government; 15. Education in a Scientific Society; 16. Scientific Reproduction; 17. Science and Values.

(1932) *Education and the Social Order*, London: George Allen and Unwin. Repr. as *Education and the Modern World*, New York: W.W. Norton, 1932.

1. The Individual versus the Citizen; 2. The Negative Theory of Education; 3. Education and Heredity; 4. Emotion and Discipline; 5. Home versus School; 6. Aristocrats, Democrats, and Bureaucrats; 7. The Herd in Education; 8. Religion in Education; 9. Sex in Education; 10. Patriotism in Education; 11. Class-feeling in Education; 12. Competition in Education; 13. Education under Communism; 14. Education and Economics; 15. Propaganda in Education; 16. The Reconciliation of Individuality and Citizenship.

(1934) *Freedom and Organization, 1814–1914*, London: George Allen and Unwin. Repr. as *Freedom versus Organization, 1814–1914*, New York: W. W. Norton,

1934. Repr. in 2 vols as *Legitimacy versus Industrialism, 1814–1848*, London: Unwin Books, 1965, and *Freedom versus Organization, 1776–1914*, London: Unwin Books, 1965.

Part I – The Principle of Legitimacy: 1. Napoleon's Successors; 2. The Congress of Vienna; 3. The Holy Alliance; 4. The Twilight of Metternich.

Part II – The March of Mind: (A) The Social Background: 5. The Aristocracy; 6. Country Life; 7. Industrial Life; (B) The Philosophical Radicals: 8. Malthus; 9. Bentham; 10. James Mill; 11. Ricardo; 12. The Benthamite Doctrine; 13. Democracy in England; 14. Free Trade; (C) Socialism: 15. Owen and Early British Socialism; 16. Early Trade Unionism; 17. Marx and Engels; 18. Dialectical Materialism; 19. The Theory of Surplus Value; 20. The Politics of Marxism.

Part III – Democracy and Plutocracy in America: (A) Democracy in America: 21. Jeffersonian Democracy; 22. The Settlement of the West; 23. Jacksonian Democracy; 24. Slavery and Disunion; 25. Lincoln and National Unity; (B) Competition and Monopoly in America: 26. Competitive Capitalism; 27. The Approach to Monopoly.

Part IV – Nationalism and Imperialism: 28. The Principle of Nationality; 29. Bismarck and German Unity; 30. The Economic Development of the German Empire; 31. Imperialism; 32. The Arbiters of Europe; 33. Conclusion.

(1935) *Religion and Science*, London: Thornton Butterworth; New York: Henry Holt.

1. Grounds of Conflict; 2. The Copernican Revolution; 3. Evolution; 4. Demonology and Medicine; 5. Soul and Body; 6. Determinism; 7. Mysticism; 8. Cosmic Purpose; 9. Science and Ethics; 10. Conclusion.

(1936) *Which Way to Peace?*, London: Michael Joseph.

1. The Imminent Danger of War; 2. The Nature of the Next War; 3. Isolationism; 4. Collective Security; 5. Alliances; 6. The Policy of Expedients; 7. Wars of Principle; 8. Pacifism as a National Policy; 9. Some Warlike Fallacies; 10. Conditions for Permanent Peace; 11. Peace and Current Politics; 12. Individual Pacifism.

(1937) (ed. with Patricia Russell) *The Amberley Papers*, 2 vols, London: L. and Virginia Woolf at the Hogarth Press.

Volume 1.

1. The Stanleys of Alderley; 2. The Russells; 3. Kate Stanley's Childhood and Youth; 4. Amberley's Early Boyhood; 5. Harrow; 6. Edinburgh, Cambridge, and Travels 1860–3; 7. Courtship; 8. Marriage to End of 1865; 9. 1866.

Volume 2.

10. Parliament and America, 1867 and 1868; 11. The South Devon Election; 12. 1869; 13. 1870; 14. 1871; 15. Can War Be Avoided?; 16. Family Controversies; 17. 1872; 18. 1873–4; 19. Death of Kate, Rachel, and Amberley.

(1938) *Power: A New Social Analysis*, London: George Allen and Unwin; New York: W. W. Norton.

1. The Impulse to Power; 2. Leaders and Followers; 3. The Forms of Power; 4. Priestly Power; 5. Kingly Power; 6. Naked Power; 7. Revolutionary Power; 8. Economic Power; 9. Power over Opinion; 10. Creeds as Sources of Power; 11. The Biology of Organizations; 12. Powers and Forms of Governments; 13. Organizations and the Individual; 14. Competition; 15. Power and Moral Codes; 16. Power Philosophies; 17. The Ethics of Power; 18. The Taming of Power.

(1940) *An Inquiry into Meaning and Truth*, London: George Allen and Unwin; New York: W. W. Norton.

Introduction; 1. What Is a Word?; 2. Sentences, Syntax, and Parts of Speech; 3. Sentences Describing Experiences; 4. The Object-Language; 5. Logical Words; 6. Proper Names; 7. Egocentric Particulars; 8. Perception and Knowledge; 9. Epistemological Premises; 10. Basic Propositions; 11. Factual Premises; 12. An Analysis of Problems Concerning Propositions; 13. The Significance of Sentences; 14. Language as Expression; 15. What Sentences 'Indicate'; 16. Truth and Falsehood: Preliminary Discussion; 17. Truth and Experience; 18. General Beliefs; 19. Extensionality and Atomicity; 20. The Law of Excluded Middle; 21. Truth and Verification; 22. Significance and Verifiability; 23. Warranted Assertibility; 24. Analysis; 25. Language and Metaphysics.

(1942) *How to Become a Philosopher . . .*, Girard, Kansas: Haldeman-Julius Publications. Repr. as *The Art of Philosophizing and Other Essays*, New York: Philosophical Library, 1968.

1. How to Become a Philosopher: The Art of Rational Conjecture; 2. How to Become a Logician: The Art of Drawing Inferences; 3. How to Become a Mathematician: The Art of Reckoning.

(1943) *An Outline of Intellectual Rubbish*, Girard, Kansas: Haldeman-Julius Publications.

(1943) *How to Read and Understand History*, Girard, Kansas: Haldeman-Julius Publications.

(1944) *The Value of Free Thought*, Girard, Kansas: Haldeman-Julius Publications.

(1945) *A History of Western Philosophy*, New York: Simon and Schuster; London: George Allen and Unwin, 1946.

Introductory.

Book 1 – Ancient Philosophy:

Part I – The Pre-Socratics: 1. The Rise of Greek Civilization; 2. The Milesian School; 3. Pythagoras; 4. Heraclitus; 5. Parmenides; 6. Empedocles; 7. Athens in Relation to Culture; 8. Anaxagoras; 9. The Atomists; 10. Protagoras.

Part II – Socrates, Plato, and Aristotle: 11. Socrates; 12. The Influence of Sparta; 13. The Sources of Plato's Opinions; 14. Plato's Utopia; 15. The Theory of Ideas; 16. Plato's Theory of Immortality; 17. Plato's Cosmogony; 18. Knowledge and Perception in Plato; 19. Aristotle's Metaphysics; 20. Aristotle's Ethics; 21. Aristotle's Politics; 22. Aristotle's Logic; 23. Aristotle's Physics; 24. Early Greek Mathematics and Astronomy.

Part III – Ancient Philosophy After Aristotle: 25. The Hellenistic World; 26. Cynics and Sceptics; 27. The Epicureans; 28. Stoicism; 29. The Roman Empire in Relation to Culture; 30. Plotinus.

Book 2 – Catholic Philosophy:

Part I – The Fathers: 1. The Religious Development of the Jews; 2. Christianity During the First Four Centuries; 3. Three Doctors of the Church; 4. Saint Augustine's Philosophy and Theology; 5. The Fifth and Sixth Centuries; 6. Saint Benedict and Gregory the Great.

Part II – The Schoolmen: 7. The Papacy in the Dark Ages; 8. John the Scot; 9. Ecclesiastical Reform in the Eleventh Century; 10. Mohammedan Culture and Philosophy; 11. The Twelfth Century; 12. The Thirteenth Century; 13. Saint Thomas Aquinas; 14. Franciscan Schoolmen; 15. The Eclipse of the Papacy.

Book 3 – Modern Philosophy:

Part I – From the Renaissance to Hume: 1. General Characteristics; 2. The Italian Renaissance; 3. Machiavelli; 4. Erasmus and More; 5. The Reformation and Counter-Reformation; 6. The Rise of Science; 7. Francis Bacon; 8. Hobbes's

Leviathan; 9. Descartes; 10. Spinoza; 11. Leibniz; 12. Philosophical Liberalism; 13. Locke's Theory of Knowledge; 14. Locke's Political Philosophy; 15. Locke's Influence; 16. Berkeley; 17. Hume.

Part II – From Rousseau to the Present Day: 18. The Romantic Movement; 19. Rousseau; 20. Kant; 21. Currents of Thought in the Nineteenth Century; 22. Hegel; 23. Byron; 24. Schopenhauer; 25. Nietzsche; 26. The Utilitarians; 27. Karl Marx; 28. Bergson; 29. William James; 30. John Dewey; 31. The Philosophy of Logical Atomism.

(1946) *Ideas That Have Harmed Mankind*, Girard, Kansas: Haldeman-Julius Publications.

(1946) *Ideas That Have Helped Mankind*, Girard, Kansas: Haldeman-Julius Publications.

(1946) *Is Materialism Bankrupt?*, Girard, Kansas: Haldeman-Julius Publications.

(1946) *Physics and Experience*, Cambridge: At the University Press.

(1947) *Philosophy and Politics*, London: Published for the National Book League by The Cambridge University Press.

(1948) *Human Knowledge: Its Scope and Limits*, London: George Allen and Unwin; New York: Simon and Schuster.

Introduction.

Part I – The World of Science: 1. Individual and Social Knowledge; 2. The Universe of Astronomy; 3. The World of Physics; 4. Biological Evolution; 5. The Physiology of Sensation and Volition; 6. The Science of Mind.

Part II – Language: 1. The Uses of Language; 2. Ostensive Definition; 3. Proper Names; 4. Egocentric Particulars; 5. Suspended Reactions: Knowledge and Belief; 6. Sentences; 7. External Reference of Ideas and Beliefs; 8. Truth: Elementary Forms; 9. Logical Words and Falsehood; 10. General Knowledge; 11. Fact, Belief, Truth, and Knowledge.

Part III – Science and Perception: Introduction; 1. Knowledge of Facts and Knowledge of Laws; 2. Solipsism; 3. Probable Inference in Common-Sense Practice; 4. Physics and Experience; 5. Time in Experience; 6. Space in Psychology; 7. Mind and Matter.

Part IV – Scientific Concepts: 1. Interpretation; 2. Minimum Vocabularies; 3. Structure; 4. Structure and Minimum Vocabularies; 5. Time, Public and Private; 6. Space in Classical Physics; 7. Space–Time; 8. The Principle of Individuation; 9. Causal Laws; 10. Space–Time and Causality.

Part V – Probability: Introduction; 1. Kinds of Probability; 2. Mathematical Probability; 3. The Finite-Frequency Theory; 4. The Mises–Reichenbach Theory; 5. Keynes's Theory of Probability; 6. Degrees of Credibility; 7. Probability and Induction.

Part VI – Postulates of Scientific Inference: 1. Kinds of Knowledge; 2. The Role of Induction; 3. The Postulate of Natural Kinds; 4. Knowledge Transcending Experience; 5. Causal Lines; 6. Structure and Causal Lines; 7. Interaction; 8. Analogy; 9. Summary of Postulates; 10. The Limits of Empiricism.

(1949) *Authority and the Individual*, London: George Allen and Unwin; New York: Simon and Schuster.

1. Social Cohesion and Human Nature; 2. Social Cohesion and Government; 3. The Role of Individuality; 4. The Conflict of Technique and Human Nature; 5. Control and Initiative: Their Respective Spheres; 6. Individual and Social Ethics.

(1949) *The Philosophy of Logical Atomism*, Minneapolis, Minnesota: Department of Philosophy, University of Minnesota. Repr. as *Russell's Logical Atomism*, London: Fontana/Collins, 1972.

1. Facts and Propositions; 2. Particulars, Predicates, and Relations; 3. Atomic and Molecular Propositions; 4. Propositions and Facts with More than One Verb; Beliefs, etc.; 5. General Propositions and Existence; 6. Descriptions and Incomplete Symbols; 7. The Theory of Types and Symbolism: Classes; 8. Excursus into Metaphysics: What There Is.

(1951) *The Impact of Science on Society*, New York: Simon and Schuster.
1. Science and Tradition; 2. Effects of Scientific Technique; 3. Science and Values.

(1951) *New Hopes for a Changing World*, London: George Allen and Unwin; New York: Simon and Schuster.
Part I – Man and Nature: 1. Current Perplexities; 2. Three Kinds of Conflict; 3. Mastery over Physical Nature; 4. The Limits of Human Power; 5. Population.
Part II – Man and Man: 6. Social Units; 7. The Size of Social Units; 8. The Rule of Force; 9. Law; 10. Conflicts of Manners of Life; 11. World Government; 12. Racial Antagonism; 13. Creeds and Ideologies; 14. Economic Co-operation and Competition; 15. The Next Half-Century.
Part III – Man and Himself: 16. Ideas Which Have Become Obsolete; 17. Fear; 18. Fortitude; 19. Life Without Fear; 20. The Happy Man; 21. The Happy World.

(1952) *How Near is War?*, London: Derricke Ridgway.

(1952) *What is Freedom?*, London: The Batchwork Press.

(1953) *The Good Citizen's Alphabet*, London: Gaberbocchus Press.

(1953) *Satan in the Suburbs and Other Stories*, London: The Bodley Head.
1. Satan in the Suburbs or Horrors Manufactured Here; 2. The Corsican Ordeal of Miss X; 3. The Infra-Redioscope; 4. The Guardians of Parnassus; 5. Benefit of Clergy.

(1953) *What is Democracy?*, London: The Batchwork Press.

(1954) *History as an Art*, Aldington, Ashford, Kent: The Hand and Flower Press.

(1954) *Human Society in Ethics and Politics*, London: George Allen and Unwin; New York: Simon and Schuster.
Introduction.
Part I – Ethics: 1. Sources of Ethical Beliefs and Feelings; 2. Moral Codes; 3. Morality as a Means; 4. Good and Bad; 5. Partial and General Goods; 6. Moral Obligation; 7. Sin; 8. Ethical Controversy; 9. Is There Ethical Knowledge?; 10. Authority in Ethics; 11. Production and Distribution; 12. Superstitious Ethics; 13. Ethical Sanctions.
Part II – The Conflict of Passions: 1. From Ethics to Politics; 2. Politically Important Desires; 3. Forethought and Skill; 4. Myth and Magic; 5. Cohesion and Rivalry; 6. Scientific Technique and the Future; 7. Will Religious Faith Cure Our Troubles?; 8. Conquest?; 9. Steps Towards a Stable Peace? 10. Prologue or Epilogue?

(1954) *Nightmares of Eminent Persons and Other Stories*, London: The Bodley Head.
1. 'Nightmares of Eminent Persons' Introduction; 2. The Queen of Sheba's Nightmare; 3. Mr Bowdler's Nightmare; 4. The Psychoanalyst's Nightmare; 5. The Metaphysician's Nightmare; 6. The Existentialist's Nightmare; 7. The Mathematician's Nightmare; 8. Stalin's Nightmare; 9. Eisenhower's Nightmare; 10. Dean Acheson's Nightmare; 11. Dr Southport Vulpes's Nightmare; 12. Zahatopolk; 13. Faith and Mountains.

(1955) *John Stuart Mill*, London: Oxford University Press.

(1959) *Common Sense and Nuclear Warfare*, London: George Allen and Unwin.

(1959) *My Philosophical Development*, London: George Allen and Unwin; New York: Simon and Schuster.

1. Introductory Outline; 2. My Present View of the World; 3. First Efforts; 4. Excursion into Idealism; 5. Revolt into Pluralism; 6. Logical Technique in Mathematics; 7. *Principia Mathematica*: Philosophical Aspects; 8. *Principia Mathematica*: Mathematical Aspects; 9. The External World; 10. The Impact of Wittgenstein; 11. Theory of Knowledge; 12. Consciousness and Experience; 13. Language; 14. Universals and Particulars and Names; 15. The Definition of 'Truth'; 16. Non-Demonstrative Inference; 17. The Retreat from Pythagoras; 18. Some Replies to Criticism: (i) Philosophical Analysis; (ii) Logic and Ontology; (iii) Mr Strawson on Referring; (iv) What Is Mind?

Appendix: Russell's Philosophy: A Study of Its Development, by Alan Wood.

(1959) (with Paul Foulkes) *Wisdom of the West*, London: Macdonald.

Prologue; 1. Before Socrates; 2. Athens; 3. Hellenism; 4. Early Christianity; 5. Scholasticism; 6. Rise of Modern Philosophy; 7. British Empiricism; 8. Enlightenment and Romanticism; 9. Utilitarianism and Since; 10. Contemporary; 11. Epilogue.

(1961) *Fact and Fiction*, London: George Allen and Unwin.

Part I – Books That Influenced Me in Youth: 1. The Importance of Shelley; 2. The Romance of Revolt; 3. Revolt in Abstract; 4. Disgust and Its Antidote; 5. An Education in History; 6. The Pursuit of Truth.

Part II – Politics and Education: 1. What Is Freedom?; 2. What Is Democracy?; 3. A Scientist's Plea for Democracy; 4. The Story of Colonization; 5. Pros and Cons of Nationalism; 6. The Reasoning of Europeans; 7. The World I Should Like to Live In; 8. Old and Young Cultures; 9. Education for a Difficult World; 10. University Education.

Part III – Divertissements: 1. Cranks; 2. The Right Will Prevail or the Road to Lhasa; 3. Newly Discovered Maxims of La Rochefoucauld; 4. Nightmares: (i) The Fisherman's Nightmare or *Magna est Veritas*, (ii) The Theologian's Nightmare; 5. Dreams: (i) Jowett, (ii) God, (iii) Henry the Navigator, (iv) Prince Napoleon Louis, (v) The Catalogue; 6. Parables: (i) Planetary Effulgence, (ii) The Misfortune of Being Out-of-Date, (iii) Murderers' Fatherland: A Fable.

Part IV – Peace and War: 1. Psychology and East–West Tension; 2. War and Peace in My Lifetime; 3. The Social Responsibilities of Scientists; 4. Three Essentials for a Stable World; 5. Population Pressure and War; 6. Formal Address to the Congress of the Pugwash Movement in Vienna September 20th, 1958; 7. Address to the C.N.D. Meeting at Manchester, May 1st, 1959; 8. What Neutrals Can Do to Save the World; 9. The Case for British Neutralism; 10. Can War Be Abolished?; 11. Human Life Is in Danger.

(1961) *Has Man a Future?*, London: George Allen and Unwin.

1. Prologue or Epilogue; 2. The Atom Bomb; 3. The H-Bomb; 4. Liberty or Death?; 5. Scientists and the H-Bomb; 6. Long-term Conditions of Human Survival; 7. Why World Government Is Disliked; 8. First Steps Towards Secure Peace; 9. Disarmament; 10. Territorial Problems; 11. A Stable World.

(1963) *Unarmed Victory*, London: George Allen and Unwin and Penguin Books; New York: Simon and Schuster.

1. The International Background; 2. The Cuban Crisis; 3. The Sino-Indian Dispute; 4. Lessons of the Two Crises.

(1965) *On the Philosophy of Science*, Indianapolis, New York, Kansas City: The Bobbs-Merrill Company.

Part I – Formal and Empirical Science: 1. What Is an Empirical Science?; 2. Mathematics and Logic; 3. Interpretation; 4. Minimum Vocabularies.

Part II – Sense Data and the Philosophy of Science: 1. The World of Physics and the World of Sense.

Part III – Physics and Perception: 1. Physics and Experience; 2. Structure; 3. Time and Space; 4. Space–Time; 5. Space–Time and Causality.

Part IV – Psychology: 1. Mental Phenomena.

Part V – Causation and Inference: 1. On the Notion of Cause; 2. Non-Demonstrative Inference.

Part VI – Science and Culture: 1. The Place of Science in a Liberal Education; 2. Science and Human Life.

(1965) (with Russell D. Stetler, Jr) *War and Atrocity in Vietnam*, London: Bertrand Russell Peace Foundation.

(1967) *War Crimes in Vietnam*, London: George Allen and Unwin; New York: Monthly Review Press.

1. The Press and Vietnam; 2. War and Atrocity in Vietnam; 3. Free World Barbarism; 4. Danger in South-East Asia; 5. The Cold War: A New Phase?; 6. The Selection of Targets in China; 7. The Labour Party's Foreign Policy; 8. Peace Through Resistance to US Imperialism; 9. The Only Honourable Policy; 10. Broadcast on National Liberation Front Radio to American Soldiers; 11. Speech to the National Conference of Solidarity; 12. Appeal to the American Conscience.

Postscript: The International War Crimes Tribunal; Appendix: Report From North Vietnam, by Ralph Schoenman.

(1967, 1968, 1969) *The Autobiography of Bertrand Russell*, 3 vols, London: George Allen and Unwin; Boston and Toronto: Little Brown and Company (Vols 1 and 2), New York: Simon and Schuster (Vol. 3).

Volume 1 – 1872–1914.

To Edith; Prologue; 1. Childhood; 2. Adolescence, Appendix: Greek Exercises; 3. Cambridge; 4. Engagement; 5. First Marriage; 6. 'Principia Mathematica'; 7. Cambridge Again.

Volume 2 – 1914–1944.

1. The First War, 'Letters'; 2. Russia; 3. China, 'Letters'; 4. Second Marriage, 'Letters'; 5. Later Years of Telegraph House, 'Letters'; 6. America, 1938–1944, 'Letters'.

Volume 3 – 1944–1967.

1. Return to England; 2. At Home and Abroad, 'Letters'; 3. Trafalgar Square, 'Letters'; 4. The Foundation, 'Letters'.

(1968) *Mr Wilson Speaks 'Frankly and Fearlessly' on Vietnam to Bertrand Russell*, London: Bertrand Russell Peace Foundation.

(1972) *The Life of Bertrand Russell in Pictures and in His Own Words*, ed. by Christopher Farley and David Hodgson, Nottingham: Spokesman Books.

(1972) *My Own Philosophy*, Hamilton, Ontario: McMaster University Library Press.

2. Significant Anthologies of Russell's Writings

(1910) *Philosophical Essays*, London: Longmans, Green.

1. The Elements of Ethics; 2. The Free Man's Worship; 3. The Study of Mathematics; 4. Pragmatism; 5. William James's Conception of Truth; 6. The Monistic Theory of Truth; 7. On the Nature of Truth and Falsehood.

(1918) *Mysticism and Logic and Other Essays*, London and New York: Longmans, Green. Repr. as *A Free Man's Worship and Other Essays*, London: Unwin Paperbacks, 1976.

1. Mysticism and Logic; 2. The Place of Science in a Liberal Education; 3. A Free Man's Worship; 4. The Study of Mathematics; 5. Mathematics and the Metaphysicians; 6. On Scientific Method in Philosophy; 7. The Ultimate Constituents of Matter; 8. The Relation of Sense-Data to Physics; 9. On the Notion of Cause; 10. Knowledge by Acquaintance and Knowledge by Description.

(1927) *Selected Papers of Bertrand Russell*, New York: The Modern Library.
1. Introduction; 2. A Free Man's Worship; 3. Mysticism and Logic; 4. The State; 5. Education; 6. Science and Art under Socialism; 7. The World as It Could Be Made; 8. The Aims of Education; 9. Questions; 10. Chinese and Western Civilizations Contrasted; 11. The Chinese Character; 12. Causes of the Present Chaos; 13. Moral Standards and Social Well-Being; 14. Deciding Forces in Politics; 15. Touch and Sight: the Earth and the Heavens; 16. Current Tendencies; 17. Words and Meaning; 18. Definition of Number.

(1928) *Sceptical Essays*, London: George Allen and Unwin; New York: W. W. Norton.
1. Introduction: On the Value of Scepticism; 2. Dreams and Facts; 3. Is Science Superstitious?; 4. Can Men Be Rational?; 5. Philosophy in the Twentieth Century; 6. Machines and the Emotions; 7. Behaviourism and Values; 8. Eastern and Western Ideals of Happiness; 9. The Harm That Good Men Do; 10. The Recrudescence of Puritanism; 11. The Need for Political Scepticism; 12. Free Thought and Official Propaganda; 13. Freedom in Society; 14. Freedom versus Authority in Education; 15. Psychology and Politics; 16. The Danger of Creed Wars; 17. Some Prospects: Cheerful and Otherwise.

(1935) *In Praise of Idleness*, London: George Allen and Unwin; New York: W. W. Norton.
1. In Praise of Idleness; 2. 'Useless' Knowledge; 3. Architecture and Social Questions; 4. The Modern Midas; 5. The Ancestry of Fascism; 6. Scylla and Charybdis, or Communism and Fascism; 7. The Case for Socialism; 8. Western Civilization; 9. On Youthful Cynicism; 10. Modern Homogeneity; 11. Men *versus* Insects; 12. Education and Discipline; 13. Stoicism and Mental Health; 14. On Comets; 15. What Is the Soul?

(1941) *Let the People Think*, London: Watts and Co. Repr. as *The Will to Doubt*, New York: Philosophical Library, 1958.
1. On the Value of Scepticism; 2. Can Men Be Rational?; 3. Free Thought and Official Propaganda; 4. Is Science Superstitious?; 5. Stoicism and Mental Health; 6. The Ancestry of Fascism; 7. 'Useless' Knowledge; 8. On Youthful Cynicism; 9. Modern Homogeneity; 10. Men *versus* Insects; 11. What is the Soul?; 12. On Comets.

(1946) *Selections from Bertrand Russell*, ed. by V. D. Salgaonkar, Bombay, Calcutta, Madras, London: Macmillan.
1. Introduction: On the Value of Scepticism; 2. In Praise of Idleness; 3. 'Useless' Knowledge; 4. Is Happiness Still Possible?; 5. The World as It Could Be Made; 6. Right Conception of Human Excellence; 7. The University; 8. The Individual versus the Citizen; 9. The Place of Science in a Liberal Education; 10. The Ethics of Power.

(1950) *Unpopular Essays*, London: George Allen and Unwin; New York: Simon and Schuster.
1. Philosophy and Politics; 2. Philosophy for Laymen; 3. The Future of Mankind; 4. Philosophy's Ulterior Motives; 5. The Superior Virtue of the Oppressed; 6. On Being Modern-minded; 7. An Outline of Intellectual Rubbish; 8. The Functions of a Teacher; 9. Ideas That Have Helped Mankind; 10. Ideas That Have Harmed Mankind; 11. Eminent Men I Have Known; 12. Obituary.

(1951) *The Wit and Wisdom of Bertrand Russell*, Boston: The Beacon Press.

1. Art; 2. Behaviorism; 3. Boredom; 4. Character; 5. Communism; 6. Competition; 7. Doubt; 8. Education; 9. Emotions; 10. The Family; 11. Fascism; 12. Fear; 13. Freedom; 14. The Good Life; 15. Happiness; 16. History; 17. Impulse; 18. The Individual; 19. Instinct; 20. Internationalism; 21. Intuition; 22. Language; 23. Leisure; 24. Liberty; 25. Logic; 26. Machines; 27. Morality; 28. Organizations; 29. Patriotism; 30. Philosophy; 31. Politics; 32. Power; 33. Proof; 34. Race; 35. Realism; 36. Reason; 37. Religion; 38. Science; 39. Sex Education; 40. Society; 41. Soviet Russia; 42. The State; 43. War; 44. Western Civilization.

(1952) *Bertrand Russell's Dictionary of Mind, Matter and Morals*, New York: Philosophical Library. Repr. as *Dictionary of Mind, Matter and Morals*, New York: Philosophical Library, n.d. Abridged as *The Wisdom of Bertrand Russell*, New York: Philosophical Library, 1968.

(1955) *Essays*, ed. by Shigeshi Nishimura, Tokyo: Eigo Tsushin Sha.

1. The Road to Happiness; 2. Bernard Shaw, the Admirable Iconoclast; 3. A Scientist's Plea for Democracy; 4. Why Fanaticism Brings Defeat; 5. A Period of Dread and Doubt; 6. H. G. Wells: Liberator of Thought; 7. The Limits of Human Power; 8. Are Human Beings Necessary?

(1956) *Logic and Knowledge: Essays, 1901–1950*, ed. by Robert Charles Marsh, London: George Allen and Unwin; New York: The Macmillan Company.

1. The Logic of Relations; 2. On Denoting; 3. Mathematical Logic as Based on the Theory of Types; 4. On the Relations of Universals and Particulars; 5. On the Nature of Acquaintance; 6. The Philosophy of Logical Atomism; 7. On Propositions: What They Are and How They Mean; 8. Logical Atomism; 9. On Order in Time; 10. Logical Positivism.

(1956) *Portraits From Memory and Other Essays*, London: George Allen and Unwin; New York: Simon and Schuster.

1. Adaptation: An Autobiographical Epitome; 2. Six Autobiographical Talks: (i) Why I Took Philosophy, (ii) Some Philosophical Contacts, (iii) Experiences of a Pacifist in the First World War, (iv) From Logic to Politics, (v) Beliefs: Discarded and Retained, (vi) Hopes: Realized and Disappointed; 3. How to Grow Old; 4. Reflections on My Eightieth Birthday; 5. Portraits From Memory: (i) Some Cambridge Dons of the Nineties, (ii) Some of My Contemporaries at Cambridge, (iii) George Bernard Shaw, (iv) H. G. Wells, (v) Joseph Conrad, (vi) George Santayana, (vii) Alfred North Whitehead, (viii) Sidney and Beatrice Webb, (ix) D. H. Lawrence; 6. Lord John Russell; 7. John Stuart Mill; 8. Mind and Matter; 9. The Cult of 'Common Usage'; 10. Knowledge and Wisdom; 11. A Philosophy for Our Time; 12. A Plea for Clear Thinking; 13. History as an Art; 14. How I Write; 15. The Road to Happiness; 16. Symptoms of Orwell's *1984*; 17. Why I Am Not a Communist; 18. Man's Peril; 19. Steps Towards Peace.

(1957) *Understanding History and Other Essays*, New York: Philosophical Library.

1. How to Read and Understand History; 2. The Value of Free Thought; 3. Mentalism vs Materialism.

(1957) *Why I Am Not a Christian and Other Essays on Religion and Related Subjects*, ed. by Paul Edwards, London: George Allen and Unwin; New York: Simon and Schuster.

1. Why I Am Not a Christian; 2. Has Religion Made Useful Contributions to Civilization?; 3. What I Believe; 4. Do We Survive Death?; 5. Seems, Madam? Nay, It Is; 6. On Catholic and Protestant Skeptics; 7. Life in the Middle Ages; 8. The Fate of Thomas Paine; 9. Nice People; 10. The New Generation; 11. Our Sexual Ethics; 12. Freedom and the Colleges; 13. The Existence of God – a

Debate between Bertrand Russell and Father F. C. Copleston, S. J.; 14. Can Religion Cure Our Troubles?; 15. Religion and Morals.

(1958) *Bertrand Russell's Best: Silhouettes in Satire*, ed. by Robert E. Egner, London: George Allen and Unwin.

1. Psychology; 2. Religion; 3. Sex and Marriage; 4. Education; 5. Politics; 6. Ethics.

(1960) *Bertrand Russell Speaks His Mind*, Cleveland and New York: The World Publishing Company.

1. What is Philosophy?; 2. Religion; 3. War and Pacifism; 4. Communism and Capitalism; 5. Taboo Morality; 6. Power; 7. What is Happiness?; 8. Nationalism; 9. Great Britain; 10. The Role of the Individual; 11. Fanaticism and Tolerance; 12. The H-Bomb; 13. The Possible Future of Mankind.

(1961) *The Basic Writings of Bertrand Russell, 1903–1959*, ed. by Robert E. Egner and Lester E. Denonn, London: George Allen and Unwin; New York: Simon and Schuster.

Part I – Autobiographical Asides: 1. My Religious Reminiscences; 2. My Mental Development; 3. Adaptation: An Autobiographical Epitome; 4. Why I Took to Philosophy.

Part II – The Nobel Prize Winning Man of Letters: 5. How I Write; 6. A Free Man's Worship; 7. An Outline of Intellectual Rubbish; 8. The Metaphysician's Nightmare.

Part III – The Philosopher of Language: 9. Language; 10. Sentences, Syntax and Parts of Speech; 11. The Uses of Language; 12. The Cult of 'Common Usage'.

Part IV – The Logician and Philosopher of Mathematics: 13. Symbolic Logic; 14. On Induction; 15. Preface to *Principia Mathematica*; 16. Introduction to *Principia Mathematica*; 17. Summary of Part III, *Principia Mathematica*; 18. Summary of Part IV, *Principia Mathematica*; 19. Summary of Part V, *Principia Mathematica*; 20. Summary of Part VI, *Principia Mathematica*; 21. Introduction to the Second Edition, *Principia Mathematica*; 22. Mathematics and Logic; 23. The Validity of Inference; 24. Dewey's New *Logic*; 25. John Dewey.

Part V – The Epistemologist: 26. Knowledge by Acquaintance and Knowledge by Description; 27. Theory of Knowledge; 28. Epistemological Premisses.

Part VI – The Metaphysician: 29. Materialism, Past and Present; 30. Language and Metaphysics; 31. The Retreat from Pythagoras.

Part VII – Historian of Philosophy: 32. Philosophy in the Twentieth Century; 33. Aristotle's Logic; 34. St. Thomas Aquinas; 35. Currents of Thought in the Nineteenth Century; 36. The Philosophy of Logical Analysis.

Part VIII – The Psychologist: 37. Psychological and Physical Causal Laws; 38. Truth and Falsehood; 39. Knowledge Behaviouristically Considered.

Part IX – The Moral Philosopher: 40. Styles in Ethics; 41. The Place of Sex among Human Values; 42. Individual and Social Ethics; 43. 'What I Believe'; 44. The Expanding Mental Universe.

Part X – The Philosopher of Education: 45. Education; 46. The Aims of Education; 47. Emotion and Discipline; 48. The Functions of a Teacher.

Part XI – The Philosopher of Politics: 49. The Reconciliation of Individuality and Citizenship; 50. Philosophy and Politics; 51. Politically Important Desires; 52. Why I Am Not a Communist.

Part XII – The Philosopher in the Field of Economics: 53. Property; 54. Dialectical Materialism; 55. The Theory of Surplus Value.

Part XIII – The Philosopher of History: 56. On History; 57. The Materialistic Theory of History; 58. History as an Art.

Part XIV – The Philosopher of Culture: East and West; 59. Chinese and Western Civilization Contrasted; 60. Eastern and Western Ideals of Happiness.

Part XV – The Philosopher of Religion; 61. The Essence of Religion; 62. What is an Agnostic?; 63. Why I Am Not a Christian; 64. Can Religion Cure Our Troubles?

Part XVI – The Philosopher and Expositor of Science; 65. Physics and Neutral Monism; 66. Science and Education; 67. Limitations of Scientific Method; 68. The New Physics and Relativity; 69. Science and Values; 70. Non-Demonstrative Inference.

Part XVII – The Analyst of International Affairs; 71. The Taming of Power; 72. If We are to Survive this Dark Time; 73. What Would Help Mankind Most?; 74. Current Perplexities; 75. World Government; 76. The Next Half-Century; 77. Life without Fear; 78. Science and Human Life; 79. Open Letter to Eisenhower and Khrushchev; 80. Man's Peril; 81. Methods of Settling Disputes in the Nuclear Age.

(1963) *Essays in Skepticism*, New York: Philosophical Library.

1. Man's Record of Beliefs; 2. Intellectual Rubbish; 3. Atheism and Agnosticism; 4. On Being Old.

(1967) *Russell's Peace Appeals*, ed. by Tsutomu Makino and Kazuteru Hitaka, Japan: Eichosha's New Current Books.

1. Message to Japanese Students; 2. An Appeal to the Conscience of Mankind; 3. An Appeal to the American Conscience; 4. My View on the Labour Party's Foreign Policy; 5. The Rise and Fall of CND; 6. Speech at the National Convention of the Vietnam Solidarity Campaign.

(1969) *Dear Bertrand Russell*, ed. by Barry Feinberg and Ronald Kasrils, London: George Allen and Unwin; Boston: Houghton Mifflin.

1. Religion; 2. Peace and Politics; 3. Youth and Old Age; 4. Philosophy; 5. Anekdota.

(1972) *Atheism: Collected Essays, 1943–1949*, New York: Arno Press and the New York Times.

1. Am I an Atheist or an Agnostic?; 2. An Outline of Intellectual Rubbish; 3. Can Men Be Rational?; 4. The Faith of a Rationalist; 5. Ideas That Have Harmed Mankind; 6. Ideas That Have Helped Mankind; 7. On the Value of Scepticism; 8. The Value of Free Thought; 9. What Can A Free Man Worship?

(1972) *The Collected Stories of Bertrand Russell*, ed. by Barry Feinberg, London: George Allen and Unwin; New York: Simon and Schuster.

Part I – Longer Stories: 1. The Perplexities of John Forstice; 2. Satan in the Suburbs; 3. Zahatopolk; 4. Faith and Mountains.

Part II – Short Stories: 5. The Corsican Ordeal of Miss X; 6. The Infra-Redioscope; 7. The Guardians of Parnassus; 8. Benefit of Clergy; 9. The Right Will Prevail or the Road to Lhasa.

Part III – Nightmares: 10. The Queen of Sheba's Nightmare; 11. Mr Bowdler's Nightmare; 12. The Psychoanalyst's Nightmare; 13. The Metaphysician's Nightmare; 14. The Mathematician's Nightmare; 15. The Existentialist's Nightmare; 16. Stalin's Nightmare; 17. Eisenhower's Nightmare; 18. Dean Acheson's Nightmare; 19. Dr Southport Vulpes's Nightmare; 20. The Fisherman's Nightmare; 21. The Theologian's Nightmare.

Part IV – Anecdotes: 22. Family, Friends and Others; 23. Reading History As It Is Never Written.

Part V – Medley: 24. Dreams; 25. Parables; 26. Cranks; 27. The Boston Lady;

28. Children's Stories; 29. Newly Discovered Maxims of La Rochefoucauld; 30. A Liberal Decalogue; 31. 'G' is for Gobbledegook; 32. The Good Citizen's Alphabet and History of the World in Epitome; 33. Auto-Obituary.

(1973) *Essays in Analysis*, ed. by Douglas Lackey, London: George Allen and Unwin.

Part I – Introduction.

Part II – Russell's Critique of Meinong: 1. Meinong's Theory of Complexes and Assumptions; 2. Review of A. Meinong, *Untersuchungen zur Gegenstandstheorie und Psychologie*; 3. Review of A. Meinong, *Über die Stellung der Gegenstandstheorie im System der Wissenschaften*.

Part III – Descriptions and Existence: 4. The Existential Import of Propositions; 5. On Denoting; 6. Mr Strawson on Referring.

Part IV – Classes and the Paradoxes: 7. On Some Difficulties in the Theory of Transfinite Numbers and Order Types; 8. On the Substitutional Theory of Classes and Relations; 9. On 'Insolubilia' and Their Solution by Symbolic Logic; 10. The Theory of Logic Types.

Part V – Philosophy of Logic and Mathematics: 11. The Axiom of Infinity; 12. On the Relation of Mathematics to Logic; 13. The Regressive Method of Discovering the Premisses of Mathematics; 14. The Philosophical Implications [*sic* for 'Importance'] of Mathematical Logic; 15. Is Mathematics Purely Linguistic?

Part VI – Appendix: Four papers by Hugh MacColl.

Part VII – Bibliographies: Two bibliographies by Douglas Lackey and one by Kenneth Blackwell.

(1973, 1983) *Bertrand Russell's America*, ed. by Barry Feinberg and Ronald Kasrils, 2 vols, London: George Allen and Unwin.

Volume 1 – 1896–1945.

Part I: Fourteen chapters, by Barry Feinberg and Ronald Kasrils.

Part II: 1. President Wilson's Statement; 2. America's Entry into the War; 3. Hopes and Fears as Regards America; 4. Impressions of America: Labour and a Third Party; 5. The American Intelligentsia; 6. Is America Becoming Imperialistic?; 7. The New Philosophy of America; 8. Optimistic America; 9. The Cinema as a Moral Influence; 10. Homogeneous America; 11. Thirty Years From Now; 12. The End of Prohibition; 13. On Equality; 14. The Root Causes of the Depression; 15. Can the President Succeed?; 16. On States' Rights; 17. Individual Freedom in England and America; 18. The American Mind; 19. America: The Next World Centre; 20. Democracy and Economics; 21. The Case for U.S. Neutrality; 22. Freedom and the Colleges; 23. Education in America; 24. The Problem of Minorities; 25. Can Americans and Britons Be Friends?; 26. British and American Nationalism; 27. Some Impressions of America.

Volume 2 – 1945–1970.

Part I: Nineteen chapters, by Barry Feinberg and Ronald Kasrils.

Part II: 1. What American [*sic*] Could Do with the Atomic Bomb; 2. The American Mentality; 3. Political and Cultural Influence of the USA; 4. Why America Is Losing Her Allies; 5. Are These Moral Codes Out of Date?; 6. Democracy and the Teachers; 7. The American Way (a Briton Says) Is Dour; 8. Foreword to *Freedom Is as Freedom Does*; 9. Justice or Injustice?; 10. Thermonuclear War: Battle of the Experts; 11. The Imminent Danger of Nuclear War; 12. The Myth of American Freedom; 13. War and Atrocity in Vietnam; 14. Free World Barbarism; 15. The Increase of American Violence;

16. The Negro Rising; 17. Peace Through Resistance to U.S. Imperialism; 18. Broadcast on National Liberation Front Radio to American Soldiers; 19. Introduction to Pamphlet on Black Militancy; 20. The International War Crimes Tribunal and the Nature of the War in Vietnam; 21. The Entire American People Are on Trial.

(1975) *Bertrand Russell: An Introduction*, ed. by Brian Carr, London: George Allen and Unwin.

1. Government and Law; 2. The Taming of Power; 3. Democracy and Scientific Technique; 4. A Liberal Decalogue; 5. *Why I Am Not a Christian*; 6. Christian Ethics; 7. The Case for Pacifism; 8. The Future of Mankind; 9. An Outline of World Government; 10. Why World Government Is Disliked; 11. Appearance and Reality; 12. The Existence of Matter; 13. On Induction.

(1975, 1988) *Mortals and Others*, ed. by Harry Ruja, 2 vols, London: George Allen and Unwin, London: Routledge.

Volume 1.

1. On Jealousy; 2. Sex and Happiness; 3. Tourists: We Lose Our Charm Away From Home; 4. The Menace of Old Age; 5. In Praise of Artificiality; 6. Who May Use Lipstick?; 7. The Lessons of Experience; 8. Hope and Fear; 9. Are Criminals Worse Than Other People?; 10. The Advantages of Cowardice; 11. The Decay of Meditation; 12. Marriage; 13. On Being Good; 14. Who Gets Our Savings?; 15. Children; 16. On Politicians; 17. Keeping Pace?; 18. On Snobbery; 19. Whose Admiration Do You Desire?; 20. On National Greatness; 21. Is the World Going Mad?; 22. Are We Too Passive?; 23. Why We Enjoy Mishaps; 24. Does Education Do Harm?; 25. Are Men of Science Scientific?; 26. Flight From Reality; 27. Illegal?; 28. On Optimism; 29. As Others See Us; 30. Taking Long Views; 31. On Mental Differences Between Boys and Girls; 32. On the Fierceness of Vegetarians; 33. Furniture and the Ego; 34. Why Are We Discontented?; 35. On Locomotion; 36. Of Co-Operation; 37. Our Woman Haters; 38. The Influence of Fathers; 39. On Societies; 40. On Being Edifying; 41. On Sales Resistance; 42. Should Children Be Happy?; 43. Dangers of Feminism; 44. On Expected Emotions; 45. On Modern Uncertainty; 46. On Imitating Heroes; 47. On Vicarious Asceticism; 48. On Labelling People; 49. On Smiling; 50. Do Governments Desire War?; 51. On Corporal Punishment; 52. If Animals Could Talk; 53. On Insularity; 54. On Astrologers; 55. On Protecting Children From Reality; 56. The Decay of Intellectual Standards; 57. Pride in Illness; 58. On Charity; 59. On Reverence; 60. On Proverbs; 61. On Clothes; 62. Should Socialists Smoke Good Cigars?; 63. A Sense of Humour; 64. Love and Money; 65. Interest in Crime; 66. How to Become a Man of Genius; 67. On Old Friends; 68. Success and Failure; 69. On Feeling Ashamed; 70. On Economic Security; 71. On Tact; 72. Changing Fashions in Reserve; 73. On Honour; 74. The Consolations of History; 75. Is Progress Assured?; 76. Right and Might; 77. Prosperity and Public Expenditure; 78. Public and Private Interests.

Volume 2.

1. Christmas at Sea; 2. How People Economise; 3. Do Dogs Think?; 4. How People Take Failure; 5. On Conceit; 6. On Bores; 7. Politics and Sport; 8. On Reticence; 9. The Good Old Days; 10. On Becoming Civilised; 11. On the Art of Persuading; 12. The Prospects of Democracy; 13. The Admiration of Strength; 14. The Triumph of Stupidity; 15. On Utilitarianism; 16. On Race Hatred; 17. The Spirit of Adventure; 18. What Makes People Likeable; 19. On Self-Righteousness; 20. Emotions About Spending Money; 21. The Origin of Victorian Virtue; 22. On Propriety; 23. I Escape from Progress; 24. Experts and

Oligarchs; 25. Fugitive and Cloistered Virtue; 26. On Being Ashamed of Virtue; 27. Men *versus* Insects; 28. The Paralysis of Statesmanship; 29. On Orthodoxies; 30. Means to Ends; 31. Individualist Ethics; 32. The Cult of the Individual; 33. On Being Argumentative; 34. On Mediaevalism; 35. In Praise of Dullness; 36. The End of Pioneering; 37. Combating Cruelty; 38. Can We Think Quickly Enough; 39. On Discipline; 40. Expecting the Millennium; 41. The Churches and War; 42. On Loving Our Neighbours; 43. On Self-Control; 44. Respect for Law; 45. On Euthanasia; 46. On Equality; 47. The Father of the Family; 48. On the Origins of Common Customs; 49. On Transferring One's Anger; 50. On Adult Education; 51. On Curious Beliefs; 52. Competitive Ethics; 53. Is Anybody Normal?; 54. Egoism; 55. Back to Nature?; 56. Parental Affection; 57. Benevolence and Love of Power; 58. Irrational Opinions; 59. Science and Happiness; 60. Social Sciences in Schools; 61. Race and Nationality; 62. The Problem of Leisure; 63. What to Believe; 64. Instinct in Human Beings; 65. Fashions in Virtues; 66. On Comets; 67. Fear and Amusement; 68. On Curious Learning; 69. On Being Important; 70. Censorship by Progressiveness; 71. Protecting the Ego; 72. Climate and Saintliness; 73. Why Travel?; 74. Obscure Fame; 75. Insanity and Insight; 76. On Ceremony; 77. Love of Money; 78. On Specialising; 79. Good Manners and Hypocrisy; 80. On Being Insulting; 81. Vigorous and Feeble Epochs; 82. The Decrease of Knowledge.

(1980) *An Atheist's Bertrand Russell*, Austin, Texas: American Atheist Press.

1. Is Materialism Bankrupt?; 2. Ideas That Have Harmed Mankind; 3. What Is the Soul?; 4. On the Value of Scepticism; 5. Ideas That Have Helped Mankind; 6. The Faith of a Rationalist.

(1986) *Bertrand Russell on God and Religion*, ed. by Al Seckel, Buffalo: Prometheus Books.

Part I: 1. My Religious Reminiscences; 2. First Efforts; 3. Why I Am Not a Christian; 4. What Is an Agnostic?; 5. Am I an Atheist or an Agnostic?; 6. The Faith of a Rationalist.

Part II: 7. The Essence of Religion; 8. Religion and the Churches; 9. A Debate on the Existence of God; 10. What Is the Soul?; 11. Mind and Matter in Modern Science.

Part III: 12. Science and Religion; 13. Cosmic Purpose.

Part IV: 14. An Outline of Intellectual Rubbish; 15. The Value of Free Thought; 16. Sin; 17. Are the World's Troubles Due to Decay of Faith?; 18. Ideas That Have Harmed Mankind; 19. Ideas That Have Helped Mankind.

Part V: 20. Mahatma Gandhi; 21. The Theologian's Nightmare.

(1987) *Bertrand Russell on Ethics, Sex, and Marriage*, ed. by Al Seckel, Buffalo: Prometheus Books.

Part I – Ethics: 1. The Elements of Ethics; 2. Science and Ethics; 3. Power and Ethical Rules; 4. Sources of Ethical Beliefs and Feelings.

Part II – Moral Rules: 5. Is There Ethical Knowledge?; 6. What Makes a Social System Good or Bad?; 7. Moral Standards and Social Well-Being; 8. New Morals for Old; 9. How Will Science Change Morals?; 10. Morality and Instinct; 11. Moral Codes; 12. Taboo Morality; 13. Chinese Morals.

Part III – Sexual Morality: 14. Education Without Sex Taboos; 15. Why a Sexual Ethic Is Necessary; 16. The Place of Sex Among Human Values; 17. Our Sexual Ethics.

Part IV – Marriage and Divorce: 18. Marriage and the Population Question; 19. The Ostrich Code of Morals: Is Companionate Marriage Moral?; 20. My Own View of Marriage; 21. Marriage and Morals; 22. Is Modern Marriage a Failure?; 23. Do I Preach Adultery?; 24. A Liberal View of Divorce.

Part V – Happiness: 25. What Makes People Unhappy?; 26. How to Be Free and Happy.

(1992) *The Selected Letters of Bertrand Russell*, ed. by Nicholas Griffin, Vol. 1, London: Penguin Press.
1. Childhood and Youth (1884–93); 2. Engagement (1893–94); 3. 'A Life of Intellect Tempered by Flippancy' (1895–1901); 4. New Crises (1901–02); 5. 'The Long Task of Thought' (1903–11); 6. New Love (1911–14).

3. The Collected Papers of Bertrand Russell

Volume 1: Cambridge Essays, 1888–99, ed. by Kenneth Blackwell, Andrew Brink, Nicholas Griffin, Richard A. Rempel, and John G. Slater, London, Boston, Sydney: George Allen and Unwin, 1983.
Part I – Adolescent Writings: 1. Greek Exercises; 2. How Far Does a Country's Prosperity Depend on Natural Resources?; 3. Evolution as Affecting Modern Political Science; 4. State-Socialism; 5. The Advantages and Disadvantages of Party Government, and the Conditions Necessary for Its Success; 6. The Language of a Nation Is a Monument to Which Every Forcible Individual in the Course of Ages Has Contributed a Stone; 7. Contentment: Its Good and Bad Points; 8. Destruction Must Precede Construction.
Part II – Later Personal Writings: 9. 'A Locked Diary'; 10. *Die Ehe*; 11. Self-Appreciation.
Part III – Apostolic Essays: 12. Can We Be Statesmen?; 13. Lövborg or Hedda; 14. Cleopatra or Maggie Tulliver; 15. Is Ethics a Branch of Empirical Psychology?; 16. Seems, Madam? Nay, It Is; 17. Was the World Good Before the Sixth Day?
Part IV – Graduate Essays in Epistemology and the History of Philosophy: 18. Paper on Epistemology I; 19. Paper on Epistemology II; 20. Paper on Bacon; 21. Paper on History of Philosophy; 22. Paper on Epistemology III; 23. Paper on DesCartes; 24. A Critical Comparison of the Methods of Bacon, Hobbes and DesCartes; 25. Paper on Bacon; 26. Paper on DesCartes I; 27. Paper on DesCartes II; 28. Paper on Hobbes; 29. On the Distinction Between the Psychological and Metaphysical Points of View.
Part V – Graduate Essays in Ethics: 30. On Pleasure; 31. On the Foundations of Ethics; 32. The Relation of What Ought to Be to What Is, Has Been or Will Be; 33. The Relation of Rule and End; 34. On the Definition of Virtue; 35. The Ethical Bearings of Psychogony; 36. Ethical Axioms; 37. The Free-Will Problem from an Idealist Standpoint; 38. Note on Ethical Theory; 39. Are All Desires Equally Moral?
Part VI – Fellowship and First Professional Papers: 40. Review of Heymans, *Die Gesetze und Elemente des wissenschaftlichen Denkens*; 41. Observations on Space and Geometry; 42. The Logic of Geometry; 43. Review of Lechalas, *Étude sur l'espace et le temps*; 44. The A Priori in Geometry.
Part VII – Political Economy: 45. Note on Economic Theory; 46. German Social Democracy, as a Lesson in Political Tactics; 47. The Uses of Luxury; 48. Mechanical Morals and the Moral of Machinery; 49. Review of Schmöle, *Die Sozialdemokratischen Gewerkschaften in Deutschland seit dem Erlasse des Sozialisten-Gesetzes*.
Appendixes: 1. Outlines and Reports of Lectures; 2. What Shall I Read?
Volume 2: Philosophical Papers, 1896–99, ed. by Nicholas Griffin and Albert C. Lewis, London, Boston, Sydney, Wellington: Unwin Hyman, 1990.

Part I – The Dialectic of the Sciences: 1. Note on the Logic of the Sciences; 2. Various Notes on Mathematical Philosophy; 3. Four Notes on Dynamics; 4. Review of Hannequin, *Essai critique sur l'hypothèse des atomes dans la science contemporaine*; 5. On Some Difficulties of Continuous Quantity; 6. Review of Couturat, *De l'Infini mathématique*; 7. On the Relations of Number and Quantity; 8. The Philosophy of Matter; 9. On the Conception of Matter in Mixed Mathematics; 10. Motion in a Plenum; 11. Why Do We Regard Time, But Not Space, as Necessarily a Plenum?; 12. Review of Love, *Theoretical Mechanics*; 13. On Causality as Used in Dynamics; 14. Review of Goblot, *Essai sur la classification des sciences*; 15. On Quantity and Allied Conceptions; 16. The Classification of Relations; 17. Review of Meinong, *Über die Bedeutung des Weber'schen Gesetzes*.

Part II – An Analysis of Mathematical Reasoning (1898): 18. An Analysis of Mathematical Reasoning Being an Inquiry into the Subject-Matter, the Fundamental Conceptions, and the Necessary Postulates of Mathematics.

Part III – Philosophy of Mathematics (1898–99): 19. On the Principles of Arithmetic; 20. The Fundamental Ideas and Axioms of Mathematics.

Part IV – Geometry (1898–99): 21. On the Constituents of Space and Their Mutual Relations; 22. Are Euclid's Axioms Empirical?; 23. Note on Order; 24. Notes on Geometry; 25. The Axioms of Geometry.

Appendixes: 1. French Texts; 2. Miscellaneous Notes; 3. Extracts from Russell's Mathematical Notebook of 1896; 4. Lost Papers; 5. Versos from Paper 3; 6. Reading Lists for the Philosophy of Dynamics.

Volume 3: Toward the 'Principles of Mathematics', ed. by Gregory H. Moore, London, New York: Routledge, 1993.

Part I – Drafts of *The Principles of Mathematics*: 1. The *Principles of Mathematics*, Draft of 1899–1900; 2. Part I of the *Principles*, Draft of 1901; 3. Plan for Book I: The Variable.

Part II – Absolute Space and Time: 4. Is Position in Time Absolute or Relative?; 5. The Notion of Order and Absolute Position in Space and Time; 6. Is Position in Time and Space Absolute or Relative?

Part III – After Peano: Foundations of Mathematics: 7. On the Notion of Order; 8. The Logic of Relations with Some Applications to the Theory of Series; 9. Recent Italian Work on the Foundations of Mathematics; 10. Recent Work on the Principles of Mathematics; 11. Lecture II. Logic of Propositions; 12. General Theory of Well-Ordered Series; 13. On Finite and Infinite Cardinal Numbers; 14. Continuous Series; 15. On Likeness.

Part IV - Geometry: 16. Note; 17. The Teaching of Euclid; 18. Geometry, Non-Euclidean.

Part V - General Philosophy: 19. Review of Schultz, *Psychologie der Axiome*; 20. Leibniz's Doctrine of Substance as Deduced from His Logic; 21. Review of Boutroux, *L'Imagination et les mathématiques selon Descartes*; 22. Review of Hastie, *Kant's Cosmogony*; 23. Do Psychical States Have Position in Space?

Appendixes: 1. Identity and Diversity; 2. An Assault on Russell's Paradox; 3. Notes on Implication and Classes; 4. French Text of Paper 5; 5. Draft and French Text of Paper 8; 6. Outline of Paper 9; 7. Draft and French Text of Paper 12; 8. French Text of Paper 16; 9. Geometry; 10. Logic and Methodology as a Subject for the B.Sc. Degree; 11. General Theory of Functions.

Volume 4: Foundations of Logic, 1903–05, ed. by Alasdair Urquhart, London, New York: Routledge, 1994.

Part I – Early Foundational Work: 1. Classes; 2. Relations; 3. Functions.

Part II – The Zig-Zag Theory: 4. Outlines of Symbolic Logic; 5. On Functions, Classes and Relations; 6. On Functions; 7. Fundamental Notions; 8. On the Functionality of Denoting Complexes; 9. On the Nature of Functions; 10. On Classes and Relations.

Part III – The Theory of Denoting: 11. On the Meaning and Denotation of Phrases; 12. Dependent Variables and Denotation; 13. Points about Denoting; 14. On Meaning and Denotation; 15. On Fundamentals; 16. On Denoting.

Part IV – Philosophy of Logic and Mathematics: 17. Meinong's Theory of Complexes and Assumptions; 18. The Axiom of Infinity; 19. Non-Euclidean Geometry; 20. The Existential Import of Propositions; 21. The Nature of Truth; 22. Necessity and Possibility; 23. On the Relation of Mathematics to Symbolic Logic.

Part V – Philosophical Reviews: 24. Recent Work on the Philosophy of Leibniz; 25. Review of Couturat, *Opuscules et fragments inédits de Leibniz*; 26. Review of Geissler, *Die Grundsätze und das Wesen des Unendlichen in der Mathematik und Philosophie*; 27. *Principia Ethica*; 28. The Meaning of Good; 29. Review of Delaporte, *Essai philosophique sur les géométries non-euclidiennes*; 30. Review of Hinton, *The Fourth Dimension*; 31. Review of Petronievics, *Principien der Metaphysik*; 32. *Science and Hypothesis*; 33. Review of Poincaré, *Science and Hypothesis*; 34. Review of Meinong and Others, *Untersuchungen zur Gegenstandstheorie und Psychologie*.

Appendixes: 1. Frege on the Contradiction; 2. Comments on Definitions of Philosophical Terms; 3. *Sur la relation des mathématiques à la logistique*.

Volume 6: Logical and Philosophical Papers, 1909–13, ed. by John G. Slater, London, New York: Routledge, 1992.

Part I – Logic and the Philosophy of Mathematics: 1. The Theory of Logical Types; 2. The Philosophical Importance of Mathematical Logic; 3. On the Axioms of the Infinite and the Transfinite; 4. What is Logic?; 5. Reply to Koyré; 6. Review of Reymond; 7. Review of Carus; 8. Review of Mannoury; 9. A Medical Logician.

Part II – The Problem of Matter: 10. On Matter; 11. Nine Short Manuscripts on Matter.

Part III – Metaphysics and Epistemology: 12. On the Nature of Truth and Falsehood; 13. The Basis of Realism; 14. Analytic Realism; 15. Knowledge by Acquaintance and Knowledge by Description; 16. On the Relations of Universals and Particulars; 17. The Nature of Sense-Data: A Reply to Dr Dawes Hicks; 18. On the Notion of Cause.

Part IV – Ethics: 19. The Elements of Ethics; 20. Spinoza.

Part V – Critique of Pragmatism: 21. Pragmatism; 22. The Philosophy of William James; 23. Review of James's *Memories and Studies*; 24. Pragmatism and Logic; 25. Review of James's *Essays in Radical Empiricism*; 26. Review of Boutroux.

Part VI – Critique of the Philosophy of Bergson: 27. The Professor's Guide to Laughter; 28. The Philosophy of Bergson; 29. Metaphysics and Intuition; 30. Mr Wildon Carr's Defence of Bergson.

Part VII – Critique of Idealism: 31. Some Explanations in Reply to Mr Bradley; 32. The Philosophy of Theism; 33. Hegel and Common Sense; 34. The Philosophy of Good Taste; 35. The Twilight of the Absolute; 36. Philosophy Made Orthodox.

Appendixes: 1. F. C. S. Schiller's Replies to Papers 21 and 24; 2. Preface to *Philosophical Essays*; 3. F. H. Bradley's Criticism of Russell and His Reply to Russell; 4. *Sur les axiomes de l'infini et du transfini*; 5. *Le réalisme analytique*; 6. G. Dawes Hicks's 'The Nature of Sense-Data'; 7. Remarks on Opening the

Section; 8. 'Réponse à M. Koyré' and an English Translation of 'Sur les Nombres de M. Russell', by A. Koyré; 9. 'On Mr Russell's Reasons for Supposing that Bergson's Philosophy is Not True', by H. Wildon Carr.

Volume 7: Theory of Knowledge: The 1913 Manuscript, ed. by Elizabeth Ramsden Eames and Kenneth Blackwell, London, Boston, Sydney: George Allen and Unwin, 1984.

Part I – On the Nature of Acquaintance: 1. Preliminary Description of Experience; 2. Neutral Monism; 3. Analysis of Experience; 4. Definitions and Methodological Principles in Theory of Knowledge; 5. Sensation and Imagination; 6. On the Experience of Time; 7. On the Acquaintance Involved in Our Knowledge of Relations; 8. Acquaintance with Predicates; 9. Logical Data.

Part II – Atomic Propositional Thought: 1. The Understanding of Propositions; 2. Analysis and Synthesis; 3. Various Examples of Understanding; 4. Belief, Disbelief, and Doubt; 5. Truth and Falsehood; 6. Self-Evidence; 7. Degrees of Certainty.

Appendixes: A.1 Course Description – Theory of Knowledge; A.2 Course Description – Advanced Logic; A.3 Outline – Theory of Knowledge; A.4 Diagrams – Relation and Judgment; A.5 Outline – Atomic Propositional Thought/Molecular Propositional Thought; A.6 Outline – Molecular Thought; A.7 Outline – Theory of Knowledge Lectures, Part II; B.1 Draft Paper – Props Complex; B.2 Diagrams – Relation and Judgment; C. Reconstructed Table of Contents.

Volume 8: The Philosophy of Logical Atomism and Other Essays, 1914–19, ed. by John G. Slater, London, Boston, Sydney: George Allen and Unwin, 1986.

Part I – Theory of Knowledge and Philosophical Method: 1. The Relation of Sense-Data to Physics; 2. Mysticism and Logic; 3. Preface to Poincaré, *Science and Method*; 4. On Scientific Method in Philosophy; 5. The Ultimate Constituents of Matter; 6. Letter on Sense-Data; 7. Note on C.D. Broad's Article in the July *Mind*.

Part II – Reviews: 8. Competitive Logic; 9. Review of Ruge *et al.*, *Encyclopedia of the Philosophical Sciences*; 10. Mr Balfour's Natural Theology; 11. Idealism on the Defensive; 12. Metaphysics; 13. A Metaphysical Defence of the Soul; 14. Pure Reason at Königsberg; 15. Review of Broad, *Perception, Physics, and Reality*; 16. Professor Dewey's *Essays in Experimental Logic*.

Part III – The Philosophy of Logical Atomism: 17. The Philosophy of Logical Atomism.

Part IV – Towards the Analysis of Mind: 18. Manuscript Notes; 19. On 'Bad Passions'; 20. On Propositions: What They Are and How They Mean.

Appendixes: 1. C. D. Broad's Paper on Phenomenalism; 2. Bertrand Russell's Notes on the New Work He Intends to Undertake; 3. Philosophical Books Read in Prison; 4. Duddington's Letter on Existence.

Volume 9: Essays on Language, Mind and Matter, 1919–26, ed. by John G. Slater, London, Boston, Sydney, Wellington: Unwin Hyman, 1988.

Part I – Philosophy of Mind and Psychology: 1. Analysis of Mind; 2. Miscellaneous Notes; 3. Analysis of Knowing; 4. Points on Memory; 5. Feeble-Minded and Others; 6. What Constitutes Intelligence?; 7. Mr Bertrand Russell's Analysis of Mind; 8. Instinct and the Unconscious; 9. Dr Schiller's Analysis of The Analysis of Mind; 10. Behaviourism; 11. Mind and Matter; 12. Review of C. D. Broad, *The Mind and Its Place in Nature*; 13. Behaviourism and Values.

Part II – Logic, Epistemology and Semantics: 14. Is Logic Deductive?; 15. The Nature of Inference; 16. The Meaning of 'Meaning'; 17. Mathematical Philosophy; 18. Introduction to Wittgenstein's *Tractatus Logico-Philosophicus*;

19. Review of J. M. Keynes, *A Treatise on Probability*; 20. Physics and Perception; 21. The Mastery of Words; 22. The Meaning of Meaning; 23. Vagueness; 24. Truth-Functions and Meaning-Functions; 25. What is Meant by 'A believes p'?; 26. Logical Atomism; 27. Perception; 28. Theory of Knowledge.

Part III – Science, Mathematics and the Philosophy of Science: 29. Einstein's Theory of Gravitation; 30. The Relativity Theory of Gravitation; 31. The Theory of Relativity; 32. Einstein; 33. Philosophical Consequences of Relativity; 34. Relativity, Scientific and Metaphysical; 35. Science and Metaphysics; 36. The New Gravitation; 37. Relativity in Dialogue Form; 38. The Interior of the Atom; 39. The Atom: Its Structure and Its Problems; 40. Atoms in Modern Physics; 41. The Structure of the Atom; 42. Review of C. D. Broad, *Scientific Thought*; 43. The Beginnings of Mathematics; 44. Natural Laws; 45. Leonardo as a Man of Science; 46. The Philosophical Analysis of Matter; 47. Introduction to Vasiliev's *Space Time Motion*; 48. Materialism, Past and Present; 49. Preface to Nicod's *La Géométrie dans le monde sensible*; 50. The Dogmas of Naturalism; 51. Relativity and Religion; 52. Is Science Superstitious?

Part IV – Ethics, Politics and Religion: 53. Philosophers and Rebels; 54. Philosophy and Virtue; 55. Review of Clutton-Brock; 56. The Possibility of Knowledge; 57. Is Knowledge Intuitive?; 58. Is There an Absolute Good?; 59. What is Morality?; 60. Does Ethics Influence Life?; 61. Psychology and Politics; 62. A Russian Communist Philosopher.

Part V – History of Philosophy and Individual Philosophers: 63. The Religion of Neo-Platonism; 64. Philosophy and the Soul; 65. A Microcosm of British Philosophy; 66. Common-Sense Philosophy; 67. Philosophy without Paradox; 68. A Philosophic Realist; 69. The Noble Army of Philosophers; 70. The Wisdom of Our Ancestors; 71. Analytic and Synthetic Philosophers; 72. Philosophic Idealism at Bay; 73. The Christian Warrior; 74. The Aroma of Evanescence; 75. What Constitutes Rationality?; 76. A Synthetic Mind; 77. Mephistopheles and the Brute; 78. A New System of Philosophy; 79. From Comte to Bergson; 80. Lord Balfour on Methodological Doubt; 81. Philosophy in India and China; 82. Early Chinese Philosophy; 83. Philosophy in the Twentieth Century.

Appendixes: 1. 'A New Theory of Measurement'; 2. Two Letters on 'The Mystic Vision'; 3. Syllabuses of Lecture Courses; 4. F. C. S. Schiller's 'Mr Russell's Psychology'.

Volume 10: A Fresh Look at Empiricism, 1927–42, ed. by John G. Slater, London, New York: Routledge, 1996.

Part I – Autobiographical Writings: 1. Things That Have Moulded Me; 2. How I Came By My Creed; 3. My Religious Reminiscences.

Part II – History and Philosophy of Science: 4. Events, Matter, and Mind; 5. Had Newton Never Lived; 6. Einstein; 7. The Future of Science; 8. Physics and Theology; 9. Review of Sir Arthur Eddington, *The Nature of the Physical World*; 10. Review of Sir Arthur Eddington, *The Expanding Universe*; 11. Scientific Certainty and Uncertainty; 12. Review of James Jeans, *The Mysterious Universe*; 13. Determinism and Physics; 14. Philosophy and Common Sense.

Part III – Logic and Probability Theory: 15. Mr F. P. Ramsey on Logical Paradoxes; 16. A Tribute to Morris Raphael Cohen; 17. Probability and Fact; 18. Review of Ramsey, *The Foundations of Mathematics*; 19. Review of Ramsey, *The Foundations of Mathematics*; 20. Congress of Scientific Philosophy; 21. On Order in Time; 22. On the Importance of Logical Form; 23. Dewey's New *Logic*.

Part IV – Educational Theory: 24. How Behaviourists Teach Behaviour; 25. The Application of Science to Education.

Part V – Writings Critical of Religion: 26. Why I Am Not a Christian; 27. Bertrand Russell's Confession of Faith; 28. What Is the Soul?; 29. Why Mr Wood Is Not a Freethinker; 30. Has Religion Made Useful Contributions to Civilization?; 31. Is Religion Desirable?; 32. Morality and Religion; 33. Science and Religion; 34. Need Morals Have a Religious Basis?; 35. The Existence and Nature of God.

Part VI – Epistemology and Metaphysics: 36. Physics and Metaphysics; 37. On the Value of Scepticism; 38. Bertrand Russell Replies; 39. Analysis of Mind; 40. The Decrease of Knowledge; 41. The Social Importance of Culture, On Curious Leaning, and 'Useless Knowledge'; 42. The Limits of Empiricism; 43. Philosophy and Grammar; 44. Philosophy's Ulterior Motives; 45. On Verification; 46. The Relevance of Psychology to Logic; 47. Non-Materialistic Naturalism.

Part VII – Ethics and Politics: 48. How Will Science Change Morals?; 49. Democracy and Emotion; 50. Is There a New Morality?; 51. How Science Has Changed Society; 52. On Utilitarianism; 53. Individualist Ethics; 54. Respect for Law; 55. Competitive Ethics; 56. The Philosophy of Communism; 57. The Ancestry of Fascism; 58. Freedom and Government; 59. On Keeping a Wide Horizon.

Part VIII – History of Philosophy: 60. Philosophy in the Twentieth Century; 61. Plato in Modern Dress; 62. The Philosophy of Santayana; 63. Hegel: *Philosophy of History*; 64. Descartes: *A Discourse on Method*; 65. Benedict de Spinoza: *Ethics*; 66. Lewis Carroll: *Alice in Wonderland*.

Part IX – The 'How-To' Series: 67. How To Become a Philosopher; 68. How To Become a Logician; 69. How To Become a Mathematician.

Appendixes: 1. Syllabus for Lecture Course; 2. 'Achilles and the Tortoise' by F. P. Ramsey; 3. 'Sweet Treasonableness' by S.D. Schmalhausen; 4. 'The Scientific Society' by Bertrand Russell; 5. Report in *Fabian News* of Paper 57; 6. [Manuscript 220.016640]; 7. Two Letters by Hyman Levy; 8. 'The Relevance of Psychology to Logic' by R. B. Braithwaite; 9. John Dewey's Reply to Paper 23; 10. Santayana's Reply to Paper 62; 11. 'A Philosophy for You in These Times'; 12. Notes on Descartes for Paper 64; 13. Notes for Lewis Carroll Broadcast, Paper 66; 14. Nine Manuscripts Preliminary to Paper 42.

Volume 11: Last Philosophical Testament, 1943–68, ed. by John G. Slater, London, New York: Routledge, 1997.

Part I – Autobiographical and Self-Critical Writings: 1. My Mental Development; 2. Reply to Criticisms and Addendum to My 'Reply to Criticisms'; 3. My Own Philosophy; 4. The Faith of a Rationalist; 5. Am I an Atheist or an Agnostic? A Plea for Tolerance in the Face of New Dogmas; 6. Why I Took to Philosophy; 7. Some Philosophical Contacts; 8. Beliefs: Discarded and Retained; 9. My Debt to German Learning.

Part II – Non-Demonstrative Inference: 10. Project of Future Work; 11. Postulates of Scientific Method; 12. Non-Deductive Inference; 13. Postulates of Scientific Inference; 14. Note on Non-Demonstrative Inference and Induction; 15. The Nature and Origin of Scientific Method.

Part III – On Some of His Younger Contemporaries: 16. Logical Positivism; 17. Logical Positivism; 18. Review of A. J. Ayer, *Language, Truth and Logic*; 19. Light versus Heat; 20. Ludwig Wittgenstein.

Part IV – On Some of His Older Contemporaries: 21. Foreword to Feibleman, *Introduction to Peirce's Philosophy*; 22. Whitehead and *Principia Mathematica*; 23. Alfred North Whitehead; 24. A Sage's Table-Talk; 25. Reminiscences of McTaggart; 26. George Santayana; 27. Prof. G. E. Moore/Influence on Lord

Russell; 28. The Influence and Thought of G. E. Moore; 29. Preface to *Le Problème logique de l'induction*, Jean Nicod.

Part V – Metaphysics and Epistemology: 30. Philosophy; 31. Hume; 32. Mind and Matter in Modern Science; 33. The Problem of Universals; 34. Rewards of Philosophy; 35. Mind and Matter; 36. The Principle of Individuation; 37. Perception; 38. Notes on Philosophy.

Part VI – Logic and the Philosophy of Mathematics: 39. Preface to William Kingdon Clifford, *The Common Sense of the Exact Sciences*; 40. Review of Rupert Crawshay-Williams, *The Comforts of Unreason*; 41. William of Occam: Empiricist and Democrat; 42. When Is an Opinion Rational?; 43. Is Mathematics Purely Linguistic?; 44. Mathematical Infinity.

Part VII – Ethics and Politics: 45. The Thinkers Behind Germany's Sins; 46. What Is Democracy?; 47. Philosophy for Laymen; 48. Comments on Articles on Philosophy; 49. A Plea for Clear Thinking; 50. Philosophy and Politics; 51. Review of Amber Blanco White, *Ethics for Unbelievers*; 52. Le Philosophe en temps de crise; 53. Freedom and the Philosopher; 54. Reason and Passion; 55. The Idea of Progress; 56. The Spirit of Inquiry; 57. A Philosophy for Our Time; 58. Knowledge and Wisdom; 59. The Duty of a Philosopher in This Age.

Part VIII – John Stuart Mill: 60. John Stuart Mill and the Idea of Liberty; 61. Mill on Liberty; 62. John Stuart Mill: On Liberty; 63. The Saint of Rationalism; 64. A Good-Hearted Philosopher; 65. Influence of John Stuart Mill; 66. John Stuart Mill; 67. A Discussion on Liberty.

Part IX – Critique of Religion: 68. The Existence of God?; 69. Is There a God?; 70. What is an Agnostic?; 71. Do Science and Religion Conflict?; 72. Preface to *Why I am Not a Christian*.

Part X – Albert Einstein: 73. Einstein and the Theory of Relativity; 74. Man of the Half-Century? I Choose Einstein; 75. Albert Einstein; 76. The Greatness of Albert Einstein; 77. Preface to *Einstein on Peace*; 78. Statement on Einstein; 79. Broadcast Concerning Einstein; 80. Foreword to *The Born–Einstein Letters*.

Part XI – Critique of Ordinary Language Philosophy: 81. The Cult of 'Common Usage'; 82. Philosophical Analysis; 83. Logic and Ontology; 84. Mr Strawson on Referring; 85. What is Mind?; 86. Introduction to Ernest Gellner, *Words and Things*.

Appendixes: 1. 'Philosophy for Lay Students' by W. B. Gallie; 2. Le principe d'individuation; 3. Un Filosofo de Buon Cuore; 4. Foreword to *Logic and Knowledge*; 5. 'Infinity' by E. R. Emmet; 6. [Manuscript RA1 220.016640]; 7. Russell's Notes on Warnock, Strawson, Ryle and Gellner; 8. Russell's Last Philosophical Writing.

Volume 12: Contemplation and Action, 1902–14, ed. by Richard A. Rempel, Andrew Brink, and Margaret Moran, London, Boston, Sydney: George Allen and Unwin, 1985.

Part I – 'Ashes of Dead Hopes': 1. Journal.

Part II – 'Refuge in Pure Contemplation': 2. The Pilgrimage of Life; 3. The Education of the Emotions; 4. The Free Man's Worship; 5. On History; 6. The Study of Mathematics.

Part III – 'Of the Two Natures in Man': 7. Prisons; 8. The Essence of Religion; 9. The Perplexities of John Forstice; 10. Mysticism and Logic.

Part IV – Defence of Free Trade: 11. Literature of the Fiscal Controversy; 12. The Tariff Controversy; 13. Mr Charles Booth on Fiscal Reform; 14. Old and New Protectionism; 15. International Competition; 16. Mr Charles Booth's Proposals for Fiscal Reform; 17. Mr Gerald Balfour on Countervailing Duties.

Part V – Liberalism and Women's Suffrage: 18. On the Democratic Ideal;

19. The Status of Women; 20. The Wimbledon By-Election; 21. After the Second Reading; 22. Mr Asquith's Pronouncement; 23. Liberalism and Women's Suffrage; 24. The Present Situation; 25. Should Suffragists Welcome the People's Suffrage Federation?; 26. Address to the Bedford Liberal Association; 27. Anti-Suffragist Anxieties.

Part VI – Other Edwardian Controversies: 28. Religion and Metaphysics; 29. A History of Free Thought; 30. Freethought, Ancient and Modern; 31. The Development of Morals; 32. Garibaldi's Defence of the Roman Republic; 33. The Politics of a Biologist; 34. Biology and Politics; 35. Memories and Studies; 36. Dramatic and Utilitarian Ethics; 37. The Professor's Guide to Laughter; 38. The Place of Science in a Liberal Education; 39. The Ordination Service; 40. Clio, A Muse.

Appendixes: 1. Press Clippings of Russell's Free Trade Speeches; 2. Comments on Sociological Papers; 3. Press Clippings on the Wimbledon By-Election; 4. Meeting at Cambridge; 5. Deputation to Mr Asquith; 6. A Protest from the Voteless; 7. Women's Suffrage; 8. Persia; 9. Protest Against the Prosecutions; 10. Letters from Professor Gwatkin; 11. *The Harvard Crimson* Interview.

Volume 13: Prophecy and Dissent, 1914–16, ed. by Richard A. Rempel, London, Boston, Sydney, Wellington: Unwin Hyman, 1988.

Part I – 4 August–24 December 1914: 1. Friends of Progress Betrayed; 2. The Rights of the War; 3. Will This War End War? Not Unless the Democracy of Europe Awakens; 4. War: The Cause and the Cure. Rulers Cannot Be Trusted with Peace Negotiations; 5. Our Foreign Office. The Need of Democratic Control; 6. Armaments and National Security; 7. Belgian Professors in Cambridge; 8. Fear As the Ultimate Cause of War; 9. Why Nations Love War; 10. War, the Offspring of Fear; 11. Letter to C. A. Reed; 12. Possible Guarantees of Peace; 13. Peace and Goodwill Shall Yet Reign.

Part II – 1915: 14. The Ethics of War; 15. Can England and Germany Be Reconciled after the War?; 16. The Policy of the Allies; 17. Mr Russell's Reply to His Critics; 18. Is a Permanent Peace Possible?; 19. The Reconciliation Question; 20. A True History of Europe's Last War; 21. Mr Bertrand Russell and the Ethics of War; 22. To Avoid Future Wars; 23. A Notable Gathering; 24. Lord Northcliffe's Triumph; 25. How America Can Help to Bring Peace; 26. The Future of Anglo-German Rivalry; 27. The Philosophy of Pacifism; 28. War and Non-Resistance; 29. On Justice in War-Time. An Appeal to the Intellectuals of Europe; 30. The International Review; 31. The War and Non-Resistance. A Rejoinder to Professor Perry; 32. Edith Cavell; 33. Two Letters; 34. Mr Russell Replies; 35. Review of Gilbert Parker, *The World in the Crucible*; 36. The Unpublished Critique; 37. The Policy of the Entente, 1904–1914: A Reply to Professor Gilbert Murray.

Part III – 1 January–7 December 1916: 38. Syllabuses for Eight Lectures on Principles of Social Reconstruction; 39. Principles of Social Reconstruction; 40. Disintegration and the Principle of Growth; 41. What Is Wanted; 42. Conscription; 43. Mr Russell's Reply; 44. North Staffs' Praise of War; 45. The Danger to Civilization; 46. Principles of Social Reconstruction and Notes for Harvard Lectures; 47. Reply to 'Academicus' on Conscientious Objectors; 48. A Clash of Consciences; 49. Two Years' Hard Labour for Refusing to Disobey the Dictates of Conscience [The Everett Leaflet]; 50. Practical War Economy; 51. Will They Be Shot?; 52. 'Folly, Doctor-Like, Controlling Skill'; 53. The Nature of the State in View of Its External Relations; 54. *Adsum Qui Feci*; 55. Liberty of Conscience; 56. Two Accounts of the Trial; 57. What Bertrand Russell Was Not Allowed to Say; 58. An Appeal on Behalf of Conscientious Objectors; 59. Mr Tennant on the Conscientious Objectors; 60. The Question of the Conscientious Objectors; 61. Why Not Peace Negotiations?; 62. What Are We Fighting For?; 63. The Cardiff Speech; 64. British Politics; 65. Hon. Bertrand Russell Says When Fate of Constantinople Is Settled; 66. The Conscientious Objector; 67. Rex v. Russell; 68. Clifford Allen and Mr Lloyd George; 69. Meeting with General Cockerill; 70. Bertrand Russell and the War Office; 71. The World As It Can Be Made; 72. Foreword to *Political Ideals*; 73. What We Stand For; 74. Mr Russell's Lectures; 75. Mr Bertrand Russell's Case; 76. The N.C.F. and the Political Outlook.

Appendixes: 1. Cambridge Support; 2. Popular Responsibility for War; 3. Cause of Wars; 4. Letter from 36 Sympathizers; 5. Memorandum for Private Deputation to the Prime Minister at the House of Commons; 6. N.C.F. Ideals; 7. Bertrand Russell's Advice; 8. Says War Will Have Bad Effect upon Education; 9. Agenda for Meeting of National Committee of the N.C.F.; 10. Fear Makes War.

Volume 14: Pacifism and Revolution, 1916–18, ed. by Richard A. Rempel, Louis Greenspan, Beryl Haslam, Albert C. Lewis, Mark Lippincott, London, New York: Routledge, 1995.

Part I – Peace Diplomacy and America: 1. The Momentum of War; 2. Letter to President Wilson; 3. Why Do Men Persist in Living?; 4. Two Ideals of Pacifism; 5. The Logic of Armaments; 6. For Conscience Sake; 7. The Pacifist at Large; 8. The Future of The Tribunal; 9. President Wilson's Statement; 10. Why the War Continues; 11. The Prospects of the N.C.F. in the New Year; 12. Prefatory Note.

Part II – The Spectre of Domestic Conscription and the Absolutist Challenge: 13. Universal National Service; 14. The Government and Absolute Exemption; 15. National Service; 16. Liberty and National Service; 17. The Position of the Absolutists; 18. Letters to Home Office Camps; 19. War and Individual Liberty; 20. Saul Among the Prophets (i); 21. Conscientious Objectors.

Part III – Russia Leaves the War: 22. Russian Charter of Freedom; 23. Russia Leads the Way; 24. The Evils of Persecution; 25. The Conscientious Objector: Reply to E. A. Wodehouse; 26. The New Hope; 27. America's Entry into the War.

Part IV – Individual Witness or Collective Action: 28. The Importance of Mental Growth; 29. Should the N.C.F. Abstain from All Political Action?; 30. Home Office Camps and Slacking; 31. Resistance and Service; 32. To the Russian Revolutionaries; 33. The Russian Revolution; 34. Report of Visit to Princetown; 35. How to Destroy Prussian Militarism; 36. The Value of Endurance; 37. Letter of Resignation; 38. Russia and Peace; 39. Absolutist Conscientious Objectors.

Part V – A Summer of Hope: 40. Tribute at Leeds; 41. Lord Derby and Leeds; 42. Conscientious Objectors: Lord Derby and the Absolutists; 43. The Chances of Peace; 44. The Price of Vengeance; 45. The Military Authorities and the Absolutists; 46. Introduction to Clifford Allen's *On Active Service*; 47. Pacifism and Economic Revolution; 48. Leeds Aftermath; 49. The Renewed Ill-Treatment of 'C.O.'s'; 50. A Pacifist Revolution?; 51. Pacifism and Revolution; 52. 'I Appeal unto Caesar'; 53. The Fall of Bethmann-Hollweg; 54. The International Situation; 55. Chancellor and Premier.

Part VI – Political Ideals: 56. Political Ideals; 57. Capitalism and the Wages System; 58. Pitfalls in Socialism; 59. Individual Liberty and Public Control; 60. National Independence and Internationalism.

Part VII – The Coalition's Counter-Offensive Against Dissent: 61. 'Crucify Him! Crucify Him!'; 62. The Russian Revolution and International Relations; 63. C.O. Hunger Strikes; 64. The International Situation: The Pope's Peace Note; 65. Imperialist Anxieties; 66. The N.C.F. Greets the Delegates of Inter-

Allied Socialist Conference; 67. Self-Discipline and Self-Government; 68. Six Months for Spreading Truth; 69. Secret Diplomacy; 70. The Charge of Anarchy; 71. The Kaiser's Reply to the Pope; 72. Is Nationalism Moribund?; 73. Asia and the War; 74. The Times on Revolution; 75. Count Czernin's Speech; 76. A Valuable Suggestion by the Bishop of Exeter; 77. The People and Peace.

Part VIII – The New Dictatorship of Opinion: 78. Saul Among the Prophets (ii); 79. Will Conscription Continue After the War?; 80. The International Outlook (i); 81. A New Tribunal for Gaol Delivery; 82. The New Dictatorship of Opinion; 83. Who Is the British Bolo?; 84. Boloism in Power; 85. The Sanctity of Conscience; 86. Lord Lansdowne's Letter; 87. Military Training in Schools; 88. The Government's 'Concessions'; 89. Freedom or Victory?; 90. International Opinion During 1917; 91. The N.C.F. Christmas Card.

Part IX – Russell Charged: Dissent In Disarray: 92. The German Peace Offer; 93. The Bolsheviks and Mr Lloyd George; 94. Letter to the Morning Post; 95. Draft of Defence; 96. Statements by Bertrand Russell.

Part X – Russell in Prison: 97. Human Character and Social Institutions; 98. Despair in Regard to the World; 99. On a Review of Sassoon; 100. The International Outlook (ii); 101. The Single Tax; 102. For Any One Whom It May Interest; 103. The State God.

Part XI – Epilogue: The Legacies of the Conscientious Objectors: 104. Why Are the C.O.'s Not Released?; 105. What the Conscientious Objector Has Achieved; 106. What the C.O. Stands For.

Appendixes: 1. Joint Advisory Council: A United Policy; 2. The Position in the Home Office Camps; 3. Russia's Charter of Freedom; 4. Guild Socialism and Education; 5. Conscientious Objectors: The 'Absolutists' and the 'Ungenuines'; 6. Resolution on Home Office Camps; 7. Clifford Allen's Defence; 8. Plans for the People's Party; 9. Draft Memorandum to Lloyd George; 10. Question for the House of Commons; 11. Re-organisation of Information Bureau; 12. What We Stand For: Second Manifesto of the No-Conscription Fellowship; 13. Russell's Requests to Brixton Prison Authorities; 14. To All Members of the Fellowship.

Planned and Forthcoming

Volume 5: Philosophical Papers, 1906–08.

Volume 15: Uncertain Roads to Freedom: Russia and China, 1919–22.

Volume 16: Labour and Internationalism, 1922–24.

Volume 17: Behaviourism and Education, 1925–28.

Volume 18: Science, Sex and Society, 1929–32.

Volume 19: Fascism and Other Depression Legacies, 1933–36.

Volume 20: The Man Who Stuck Pins in His Wife, and Other Essays, 1936–39.

Volume 21: The Problems of Democracy, 1940–44.

Volume 22: Civilization and the Bomb, 1944–49.

Volume 23: Respectability – At Last, 1949–53.

Volume 24: Man's Peril, 1954–57.

Volume 25: The Campaign for Nuclear Disarmament, 1958–60.

Volume 26: A New Plan for Peace and Other Essays, 1960–64.

Volume 27: The Vietnam Campaign, 1965–70.

Volume 28: Newly Discovered Papers.

Volume 29: Newly Discovered Papers.

Volume 30: Index.

Select Secondary Bibliography

Bertrand Russell has served as the subject of thousands of books, articles, reviews, commentaries, and other publications. The following bibliography is therefore not intended to be an exhaustive listing of the secondary literature surrounding Russell. Rather, it is meant only to be a listing of the most important and influential English-language writings concerning Russell. The bibliography consists of six categories:

1 books (including monographs, anthologies, and significant booklets or pamphlets) which are in large measure devoted to Russell, his philosophy, or his influence;
2 articles and chapters in books, the main focus of which concerns Russell, or his philosophy, or influence, as well as significant critical notices and major reviews of books authored by Russell;
3 additional important (but usually shorter, often untitled) reviews of books authored by Russell;
4 encyclopedia and dictionary entries devoted to Russell;
5 bibliographies, both of Russell's writings and of the secondary literature surrounding Russell; and
6 internet resources focusing directly on Russell, his work, life, and influence.

This bibliography does not include most newspaper and magazine articles. Nor does it include the many books and articles which mention Russell but which do not discuss his life, philosophy, or influence in significant detail.

1. Books

Aiken, Lillian W. (1963) *Bertrand Russell's Philosophy of Morals*, New York: Humanities.

American Civil Liberties Union (1941) *The Story of the Bertrand Russell Case*, New York: American Civil Liberties Union.

Andersson, Stefan (1994) *In Quest of Certainty*, Stockholm: Almqvist and Wiksell.

Anon. (1962) *Into the Tenth Decade*, London: Malvern Press.

Ayer, Alfred Jules (1972) *Russell*, London: Fontana-Collins.

Bandishte, D.D. (1984) *A Study of the Ethics of Bertrand Russell*, New York: Asia Book Corp.

Barnes, Albert C. (n.d.) *The Case of Bertrand Russell vs Democracy and Education*, Marion, PA.: Albert C. Barnes.

Bell, David R. (1972) *Bertrand Russell*, London: Lutterworth Press.

Bell, John, Julian Cole, Graham Priest, and Alan Slomson (eds) (1973) *The Proceedings of the Bertrand Russell Memorial Logic Conference, Udlum, Denmark, 1971*, Leeds: Bertrand Russell Memorial Logic Conference.

Blackwell, Kenneth (1985) *The Spinozistic Ethics of Bertrand Russell*, London: George Allen and Unwin.

Bowne, G.D. (1966) *The Philosophy of Logic: 1880–1908*, The Hague: Mouton.

Brink, Andrew (1989) *Bertrand Russell, the Psychobiography of a Moralist*, Atlantic Highlands, N.J.: Humanities Press International.

Brown, S. (1978) *Realism and Logical Analysis*, Buckinghamshire: Open University Press.

Burke, Tom (1994) *Dewey's New Logic: A Reply to Russell*, Chicago: University of Chicago Press.

Chisholm, John (1967) *The Theory of Knowledge of Bertrand Russell*, Rome: Catholic Book Agency.

Chomsky, Noam (1971) *Problems of Knowledge and Freedom: The Russell Lectures*, New York: Pantheon.

Church, Alonzo (1966) *Introduction to Mathematical Logic, I*, Princeton, N.J.: Princeton University Press.

Clack, Robert J. (1969) *Bertrand Russell's Philosophy of Language*, The Hague: Nijhoff.

Clark, Cecil Henry Douglas (1958) *Christianity and Bertrand Russell*, London: Lutterworth.

Clark, Ronald William (1975) *The Life of Bertrand Russell*, London: J. Cape.

Clark, Ronald William (1981) *Bertrand Russell and His World*, London: Thames and Hudson.

Cleary, Denis (1961) *The Doctrine of Sensation According to Bertrand Russell*, Rome: Pontiff University Gregor.

Coates, Ken (ed.) (1972) *Essays on Socialist Humanism*, Nottingham: Spokesman Books.

Cocchiarella, Nino B. (1987) *Logical Studies in Early Analytic Philosophy*, Columbus: Ohio State University Press.

Copi, Irving M. (1971) *The Theory of Logical Types*, London: Routledge.

Crawshay-Williams, Rupert (1970) *Russell Remembered*, Oxford: Oxford University Press.

Dejnozka, Jan (1996) *The Ontology of the Analytic Tradition and Its Origins*, Lanham, MD.: Littlefield Adams.

Dewar, Lindsay (1931) *Marriage Without Morals*, London: Society for Promoting Christian Knowledge.

DeWeerd, H.A. (1967) *Lord Russell's War Crimes Tribunal*, Santa Monica: Rand Corporation.

Dewey, John, and Horace M. Kallen (eds) (1941) *The Bertrand Russell Case*, New York: Viking.

Dorward, Alan J. (1951) *Bertrand Russell: A Short Guide to His Philosophy*, London: Longmans, Green.

Duffett, John (ed.) (1968) *Against the Crime of Silence: Proceedings of the Russell International War Crimes Tribunal*, New York: O'Hare.

Duffy, Bruce (1987) *The World As I Found It*, New York: Ticknor and Fields.

Eames, Elizabeth R. (1969) *Bertrand Russell's Theory of Knowledge*, London: George Allen and Unwin.

Eames, Elizabeth R. (1989) *Bertrand Russell's Dialogue with his Contemporaries*, Carbondale: Southern Illinois University Press.

Eisler, Lee (1971) *Morals Without Mystery*, New York: Philosophical Library.

Evans, Gareth (1982) *The Varieties of Reference*, New York: Oxford University Press.

Feinberg, Barry (ed.) (1967) *A Detailed Catalogue of the Archives of Bertrand Russell*, London: Continuum 1 Ltd.

Feinberg, Barry, and Ronald Kasrils (eds) (1969) *Dear Bertrand Russell*, London: George Allen and Unwin.

Feinberg, Barry, and Ronald Kasrils (1973, 1983) *Bertrand Russell's America*, 2 vols, London: George Allen and Unwin.

Fritz, Charles Andrew, Jr (1952) *Bertrand Russell's Construction of the External World*, London: Routledge and Kegan Paul.

Ganapathy, T.N. (1984) *Bertrand Russell's Philosophy of Sense-Data*, Madras: Vivekananda College.

Garciadiego (Dantan), Alejandro Ricardo (1992) *Bertrand Russell and the Origins of the Set-Theoretic "Paradoxes"*, Basle: Birkhaüser Verlag.

Götlind, Erik J.A. (1952) *Bertrand Russell's Theories of Causation*, Uppsala: Almqvist and Wiksells.

Gottschalk, Herbert (1965) *Bertrand Russell: A Life*, London: John Baker.

Grattan-Guinness, I. (1977) *Dear Russell, Dear Jourdain: A Commentary on Russell's Logic, Based on His Correspondence with Philip Jourdain*, New York: Columbia University Press.

Grayling, Anthony (1996) *Bertrand Russell*, London: Oxford University Press.

Greenspan, Louis (1978) *The Incompatible Prophecies: An Essay on Science and Liberty in the Political Writings of Bertrand Russell*, Oakville, Ont.: Mosaic.

Griffin, Nicholas (1991) *Russell's Idealist Apprenticeship*, Oxford: Clarendon.

Hager, Paul J. (1994) *Continuity and Change in the Development of Russell's Philosophy*, Dordrecht: Kluwer.

Hardy, Godfrey H. (1942) *Bertrand Russell and Trinity*, Cambridge: Cambridge University Press, 1970.

Hylton, Peter W. (1990) *Russell, Idealism, and the Emergence of Analytic Philosophy*, Oxford: Clarendon.

Ingram, Kenneth (1928) *The Unreasonableness of Anti-Christianity*, London: Society of SS. Peter and Paul.

Ironside, Philip (1996) *The Social and Political Thought of Bertrand Russell*, London: Cambridge University Press.

Irvine, A.D., and G.A. Wedeking (eds) (1993) *Russell and Analytic Philosophy*, Toronto: University of Toronto Press.

Jackson, Mary Louise (1983) *Style and Rhetoric in Bertrand Russell's Work*, New York: Peter Lang.

Jager, Ronald (1972) *The Development of Bertrand Russell's Philosophy*, London: George Allen and Unwin.

Jourdain, Philip E.B. (1918) *The Philosophy of Mr B*rtr*nd R*ss*ll*, London: George Allen and Unwin.

Julka, K.L. (1977) *The Political Ideas of Bertrand Russell*, Patna: Associated Book Agency.

Kilmister, Clive William (1984) *Russell*, Brighton: Harvester.

Klemke, E.D. (ed.) (1970) *Essays on Bertrand Russell*, Urbana: University of Illinois Press.

Kuntz, Paul Grimley (1986) *Bertrand Russell*, Boston: Twayne.

Lawrence, D.H. (1948) *Letters to Bertrand Russell*, New York: Gotham Book Mart.

Leggett, H.W. (1950) *Bertrand Russell, O.M.*, New York: Philosophical Library.

Lewis, John (1968) *Bertrand Russell: Philosopher and Humanist*, London: Lawrence and Wishart.

Meyer, Samuel (ed.) (1985) *Dewey and Russell: An Exchange*, New York: Philosophical Library.

Monk, Ray (1996) *Bertrand Russell: The Spirit of Solitude*, London: J. Cape.

Monk, Ray, and Anthony Palmer (eds) (1996) *Bertrand Russell and the Origins of Analytical Philosophy*, Bristol: Thoemmes Press.

Montgomery, George Samuel, Jr (1959) *Why Bertrand Russell is not a Christian: An American Opinion*, New York: Dakotan.

Moorehead, Caroline (1992) *Bertrand Russell*, New York: Viking.

Moran, Margaret, and Carl Spadoni (eds) (1984) *Intellect and Social Conscience: Essays on Bertrand Russell's Early Work*, Hamilton: McMaster University Library Press. Preprinted in *Russell*, n.s. 4 (1984), 1–238.

Nakhnikian, George (ed.) (1974) *Bertrand Russell's Philosophy*, London: Duckworth.

Nath, Ramendra (1993) *The Ethical Philosophy of Bertrand Russell*, New York: Vantage.

Oaklander, L. Nathan (1984) *Temporal Relations and Temporal Becoming: A Defense of a Russellian Theory of Time*, Lanham, MD.: University Press of America.

Park, Joe (1963) *Bertrand Russell on Education*, Columbus: Ohio State University Press.

Patterson, Wayne (1993) *Bertrand Russell's Philosophy of Logical Atomism*, New York: Lang.

Pears, David F. (1967) *Bertrand Russell and the British Tradition in Philosophy*, London: Collins.

Pears, David F. (ed.) (1972) *Bertrand Russell: A Collection of Critical Essays*, New York: Doubleday.

Peterson, John (1976) *Realism and Logical Atomism*, Tuscaloosa, ALA.: University of Alabama Press.

Purcell, Victor (Myra Buttle, pseud.) (1960) *Bitches' Brew, or the Plot Against Bertrand Russell*, New York: Watts.

Rao, A.P. (1997) *Understanding Principia and Tractatus: Russell and Wittgenstein Revisited*, San Francisco: International Scholars.

Ready, William (1969) *Necessary Russell*, Toronto: Copp Clark.

Rhees, Rush (ed.) (1981) *Ludwig Wittgenstein: Personal Recollections*, Totowa, N.J.: Rowman Littlefield.

Roberts, George W. (ed.) (1979) *Bertrand Russell Memorial Volume*, London: Allen and Unwin.

Rodríguez-Consuegra, Francisco A. (1991) *The Mathematical Philosophy of Bertrand Russell: Origins and Development*, Basle: Birkhäuser.

Russell, Dora Winifred Black (1977, 1980, 1985) *The Tamarisk Tree*, 3 vols, London: Virago.

Ryan, Alan (1988) *Bertrand Russell: A Political Life*, New York: Hill and Wang.

Sainsbury, Richard Mark (1979) *Russell*, London: Routledge and Kegan Paul.

Savage, C. Wade, and C. Anthony Anderson (eds) (1989) *Rereading Russell: Essays on Bertrand Russell's Metaphysics and Epistemology*, Minneapolis: University of Minnesota Press.

Schilpp, Paul Arthur (ed.) (1944) *The Philosophy of Bertrand Russell*, Chicago: Northwestern University; 3rd edn, New York: Harper and Row, 1963.

Schoenman, Ralph (ed.) (1967) *Bertrand Russell: Philosopher of the Century*, London: Allen and Unwin.

Singh, Amita (1987) *The Political Philosophy of Bertrand Russell*, Delhi: Mittal Publications.

Singh, Surya Nath (1979) *The Educational Philosophy of Bertrand Russell*, Varanasi: Banaras Hindu University Press.

Slater, John G. (1994) *Bertrand Russell*, Bristol: Thoemmes.

Tait, Katharine (1975) *My Father Bertrand Russell*, New York: Harcourt Brace Jovanovich.

Thalheimer, Ross (1931) *A Critical Examination of the Epistemological and Psycho-Physical Doctrines of Bertrand Russell*, Baltimore: Johns Hopkins.

Thomas, J.E., and Kenneth Blackwell (eds) (1976) *Russell in Review*, Toronto: Samuel Stevens, Hakkert and Co.

Trent, Christopher (1966) *The Russells*, London: Muller.

Vellacott, Jo (1980) *Bertrand Russell and the Pacifists in the First World War*, Brighton, Sussex: Harvester Press.

Watling, John (1970) *Bertrand Russell*, Edinburgh: Oliver and Boyd.

Wedgwood, Cicely Veronica (1964) *Mightier Than the Sword*, Philadelphia: Richard West.

Winchester, Ian, and Kenneth Blackwell (eds) (1988) *Antinomies and Paradoxes: Studies in Russell's Early Philosophy*, Hamilton: McMaster University Library Press. Preprinted in *Russell*, n.s. 8 (1988), 1–248.

Wisdom, John (1969) *Logical Constructions*, New York: Random House.

Wittgenstein, Ludwig (1921) *Logisch-philosophische Abhandlung*. Trans. as *Tractatus Logico-Philosophicus*, London: Kegan Paul, Trench, Trubner, 1922.

Wittgenstein, Ludwig (1953) *Philosophical Investigations*, New York: Macmillan.

Wittgenstein, Ludwig (1956) *Remarks on the Foundations of Mathematics*, Oxford: Blackwell.

Wood, Alan (1957) *Bertrand Russell: The Passionate Sceptic*, London: Allen and Unwin.

Wood, G.H. (1928) *Why Mr Bertrand Russell is Not a Christian: An Essay in Controversy*, London: Student Christian Movement.

2. Articles, Chapters in Books, Critical Notices and Major Reviews

Abir-am, P.G. (1996) "Collaborative Couples Who Wanted to Change the World: The Social Policies and Personal Tensions of the Russells, the Myrdals, and the Mead-Batesons", in H.M. Pycior, N.G. Slack, and P.G. Abir-am (eds), *Creative Couples in Science*, New Brunswick, N.J.: Rutgers University Press, 267–281.

Acock, Malcolm (1983) "The Age of the Universe", *Philosophy of Science*, 50, 130–145.

Aiken, Henry David (1946) "Mr Demos and the Dogmatism of Mr Russell", *Journal of Philosophy*, 43, 214–217.

Aldrich, Virgil Charles (1945) "Mr Russell and Dogmatism", *Journal of Philosophy*, 42, 589–607.

Almog, Joseph (1989) "Logic and the World", *Journal of Philosophical Logic*, 18, 197–220.

Alpert, Stephen (1973) "Aesthetics and Logical Atomism", *Russell*, o.s. 10, 12–13.

Ambrose, Alice (1937) "Finitism and *The Limits of Empiricism*", *Mind*, 46, 379–385.

Ambrose, Alice (1979) "Is Philosophy 'An Idleness in Mathematics'?", in Roberts, George W. (ed.), *Bertrand Russell Memorial Volume*, London: Allen and Unwin, 105–127.

Anderson, C. Anthony (1986) "Some Difficulties Concerning Russellian Intensional Logic", *Nous*, 20, 35–43.

Anderson, C. Anthony (1989) "Russell on Order in Time", in Savage, C. Wade, and C. Anthony Anderson (eds), *Rereading Russell: Essays on Bertrand Russell's Metaphysics and Epistemology*, Minneapolis: University of Minnesota Press, 249–263.

Anderson, C. Anthony (1989) "Russellian Intensional Logic", in Almog, Joseph, John Perry, and Howard Wettstein (eds), *Themes From Kaplan*, New York: Oxford University Press, 67–103.

Andersson, Stefan (1993–94) "Religion in the Russell Family", *Russell*, n.s. 13, 117–149.

Anellis, Irving H. (1984) "Russell's Earliest Reactions to Cantorian Set Theory, 1896–1900", *Contemporary Mathematics*, 31, 1–11.

Anellis, Irving H. (1987) "Bertrand Russell's Theory of Numbers, 1896–1898", *Epistemologia*, 10, 303–322.

Anellis, Irving H. (1987) "Russell's Earliest Interpretation of Cantorian Set Theory, 1896–1900", *Philosophia Mathematica*, 2, 1–31.

Anellis, Irving H. (1991) "The First Russell Paradox", in Drucker, Thomas (ed.), *Perspectives on the History of Mathematical Logic*, Basle: Birkhäuser, 33–46.

Anellis, Irving H. (1995) "Peirce Rustled, Russell Pierced: How Charles Peirce and Bertrand Russell Viewed Each Other's Work in Logic, and an Assessment of Russell's Accuracy and Role in the Historiography of Logic", *Modern Logic*, 5, 270–328.

Annan, Noel (1957) "Bertrand Russell", in Lehmann, John, *The Year's Work in Literature 1950*, London: Longmans Green, 12–16.

Anon. (1912) "Religion Without God", *The Nation*, 12 (27 October), 171–172.

Anon. (1940) "The Bertrand Russell Case: the History of a Litigation", *Harvard Law Review*, 53, 1192–1197.

Anon. (1941) "The Bertrand Russell Litigation", *University of Chicago Law Review*, 8, 316–325.

Anon. (1970) "Russell and the Revolutionary", *Observer*, 6 September, 17.

Anon. (1997) "Lasting impressions of Bertie Russell", *Russell*, n.s. 17, 5–10.

Anscombe, G.E.M. (1993) "Russelm or Anselm?", *Philosophical Quarterly*, 43, 500–504.

Armour, Leslie (1979) "Russell, McTaggart, and 'I'", *Idealistic Studies*, 9, 66–76.

Arms, Richard A. (1919) "The Relation of Logic to Mathematics", *Monist*, 29, 146–152.

Armstrong, William M. (1969) "Bertrand Russell Comes to America, 1896", *Studies in History and Society*, 2, 29–39.

Arnstein, Walter L. (1994) "My Interview with Bertrand Russell", *American Scholar*, 63, 123–129.

Atkinson, Charles, and John Hughes (1972) "Russell's Critique of Socialist Theory and Practice", in Coates, Ken (ed.), *Essays on Socialist Humanism*, Nottingham: Spokesman Books, 13–29.

Austin, James W. (1976) "Denoting Phrases and Definite Descriptions", *Southern Journal of Philosophy*, 14, 393–399.

Austin, James W. (1978) "Russell's Cryptic Response to Strawson", *Philosophy and Phenomenological Research*, 38, 531–537.

Avey, Albert E. (1942) "Russell's Quest for Objectivity", *Philosophy and Phenomenological Research*, 2, 376–393.

Avni, Ora (1990) "The First Person", in Avni, Ora, *The Resistance of Reference*, Baltimore: Johns Hopkins University Press, 113–174.

Ayer, Alfred Jules (1938) "On the Scope of Empirical Knowledge", *Erkenntnis*, 7, 267–274.

Ayer, Alfred Jules (1941) "Bertrand Russell on Meaning and Truth", *Nature*, 148, 206–207.

Ayer, Alfred Jules (1967) "An Appraisal of Bertrand Russell's Philosophy", in Schoenman, Ralph (ed.), *Bertrand Russell: Philosopher of the Century*, London: Allen and Unwin, 167–178. Repr. in Pears, David F. (ed.), *Bertrand Russell: A Collection of Critical Essays*, Garden City, New York: Anchor Books, 1972, 6–22.

Ayer, Alfred Jules (1970) "Russell the Philosopher", *New Statesman*, 79 (6 February), 182–183.

Ayer, Alfred Jules (1971) "Bertrand Russell", in Ayer, Alfred Jules, *Russell and Moore: The Analytical Heritage*, Cambridge, Mass.: Harvard University Press, 1–133.

Ayer, Alfred Jules (1976) "Bertrand Russell as a Philosopher", in Thomas, J.E., and Kenneth Blackwell (eds), *Russell in Review*, Toronto: Samuel Stevens, Hakkert and Co., 177–202.

Ayer, Alfred Jules (1990) "Bertrand Russell as a Philosopher", in Ayer, Alfred Jules, *The Meaning of Life*, New York: Scribner, 149–171.

Ayer, Alfred Jules, *et al.* (1988) "The Tenability of Russell's Early Philosophy", *Russell*, n.s. 8, 232–246. Repr. in Winchester, Ian, and Kenneth Blackwell (eds), *Antinomies and Paradoxes: Studies in Russell's Early Philosophy*, Hamilton: McMaster University Library Press, 1988, 232–246.

Bach, Kent (1983) "Russell Was Right (Almost)", *Synthese*, 54, 189–208.

Bach, Kent (1994) "Ramachandran versus Russell", *Analysis*, 54, 183–186.

Bacon, John (1965) "An Alternative Contextual Definition for Descriptions", *Philosophical Studies*, 16, 75–76.

Baillie, James (1997) "Bertrand Russell and Ludwig Wittgenstein: Logical Atomism", in Baillie, James, *Contemporary Analytic Philosophy*, Upper Saddle River, N.J.: Prentice Hall, 41–95.

Balzer, N. (1992) "The Paradoxes", *Journal of Value Inquiry*, 26, 189–197.

Bambrough, Renford (1970) "Foundations", *Analysis*, 30, 190–197. Repr. in Roberts, George W. (ed.), *Bertrand Russell Memorial Volume*, London: Allen and Unwin, 1979, 414–421.

Barber, Benjamin R. (1979) "Solipsistic Politics: Russell's Empiricist Liberalism", in Roberts, George W. (ed.), *Bertrand Russell Memorial Volume*, London: Allen and Unwin, 455–478.

Bar-Elli, Gilead (1980) "Constituents and Denotation in Russell", *Theoria*, 46, 37–51.

Bar-Elli, Gilead (1989) "Acquaintance, Knowledge and Description in Russell", *Russell*, n.s. 9, 133–156.

Bar-Hillel, Yehoshua (1967) "Theory of Types", in Edwards, Paul (ed.), *The Encyclopedia of Philosophy*, Vol. 8, New York: Macmillan, 168–172.

Basson, A.H. (1960) "Propositional Functions", *Aristotelian Society*, Supplementary Vol. 34, 25–32.

Basu, Dilip K. (1983) "Russell on Denoting", *Analysis*, 43, 65–70.

Beanblossom, Ronald (1978) "Russell's Indebtedness to Reid", *Monist*, 61, 192–204.

Beck, Lewis W. (1950) "Constructions and Inferred Entities", *Philosophy of Science*, 17, 74–86.

Beerling, R.F. (1964) "Russell and Historical Truth", *Kant-Studien*, 55, 385–393.

Bell, D.R. (1972) "Philosophy", in Cox, Charles Brian, and Anthony Edward Dyson (eds), *The Twentieth-Century Mind*, Vol. 1, Oxford: Oxford University Press, 174–224.

Bell, John L., and William Demopoulos (1996) "Elementary Propositions and Independence", *Notre Dame Journal of Formal Logic*, 37, 112–124.

Bell, Robert H. (1983) "Bertrand Russell and the Eliots", *American Scholar*, 52, 309–325.

Benjamin, A.C. (1941) "Is Empiricism Self-Refuting?", *Journal of Philosophy*, 38, 568–573.

Bentley, A.F. (1946) "Logicians' Underlying Postulations: Russell's Approach", *Philosophy of Science*, 13, 3–19.

Bergmann, Gustav (1947) "Russell on Particulars", *Philosophical Review*, 56, 59–72. Repr. in Bergmann, Gustav, *The Metaphysics of Logical Positivism*, Madison: University of Wisconsin Press, 1954, 197–209, and in Klemke, E.D. (ed.), *Essays on Bertrand Russell*, Urbana: University of Illinois Press, 1970, 15–27.

Bergmann, Gustav (1948) "Descriptions in Nonextensional Contexts", *Philosophy of Science*, 15, 353–355.

Bergmann, Gustav (1956) "Russell's Examination of Leibniz Examined", *Philosophy of Science*, 23, 175–203. Repr. in Bergmann, Gustav, *Meaning and Existence*, Madison: University of Wisconsin Press, 1960, 155–188.

Bergmann, Gustav (1957, 1958) "The Revolt Against Logical Atomism", *Philosophical Quarterly*, 7, 323–339, and 8, 1–13. Repr. in Bergmann, Gustav, *Meaning and Existence*, Madison: University of Wisconsin Press, 1960, 39–72, and in Klemke, E.D. (ed.) *Essays on Bertrand Russell*, Urbana: University of Illinois Press, 1970, 28–64.

Berka, K. (1970) "Russell's Theory of Quantity and Magnitude", *Teorie a Metoda*, 2, 35–51.

Bernstein, B.A. (1931) "Whitehead and Russell's Theory of Deduction as a Mathematical Science", *Bulletin of the American Mathematical Society*, 37, 480–488.

Bernstein, B.A. (1932) "On Nicod's Reduction in the Number of Primitives of Logic", *Proceedings of the Cambridge Philosophical Society*, 28, 427–432.

Bernstein, B.A. (1932) "On Proposition *4.78 of *Principia Mathematica*", *Bulletin of the American Mathematical Society*, 38, 388–391.

Bernstein, B.A. (1932) "Relation of Whitehead and Russell's Theory of Deduction to the Boolean Logic of Propositions", *Bulletin of the American Mathematical Society*, 38, 589–593.

Bernstein, B.A. (1933) "On Section A of *Principia Mathematica*", *Bulletin of the American Mathematical Society*, 39, 788–792.

Bernstein, B.A. (1933) "Remarks on Propositions *1.1. and *3.35 of *Principia Mathematica*", *Bulletin of the American Mathematical Society*, 39, 111–114.

Bertolet, Rod (1982) "Russell and Strawson, Indexical and Improper Descriptions", *Theoria*, 48, 90–98.

Binet, F.E. (1954) "Notes on a Remark by Lord Russell", *British Journal for the Philosophy of Science*, 5, 67–69.

Black, Max (1933) "Logistic", in Black, Max, *The Nature of Mathematics*, London: Routledge and Kegan Paul, 13–144.

Black, Max (1944) "Russell's Philosophy of Language", in Schilpp, Paul Arthur (ed.), *The Philosophy of Bertrand Russell*, 3rd edn, New York: Tudor, 1951,

227–255. Repr. in Black, Max, *Language and Philosophy*, Ithaca: Cornell University Press, 1949, 109–138; and in Rorty, Richard (ed.), *The Linguistic Turn*, Chicago: University of Chicago Press, 136–146.

Blackburn, Simon (1972) "Searle on Descriptions", *Mind*, 81, 409–414.

Blackburn, Simon (1979) "Thought and Things", *Aristotelian Society*, Supplementary Vol. 53, 23–41.

Blackburn, Simon, and Alan Code (1978) "Reply to Geach's 'Russell on Denoting'", *Analysis*, 38, 206–207.

Blackburn, Simon, and Alan Code (1978) "The Power of Russell's Criticism of Frege: 'On Denoting' pp. 48–50", *Analysis*, 38, 65–77. Repr. as "The Power of Russell's Criticism of Frege", in Irvine, A.D., and G.A. Wedeking (eds), *Russell and Analytic Philosophy*, Toronto: University of Toronto Press, 1993, 22–36.

Blackman, Larry Lee (1983) "Russell on the Relations of Universals and Particulars", *Philosophy Research Archives*, 9, 265–278.

Blackwell, Kenneth (1969) "The Importance to Philosophers of the Bertrand Russell Archive", *Dialogue*, 7, 608–615.

Blackwell, Kenneth (1972) "An Essay on the Foundations of Geometry", *Russell*, o.s. 6, 3–4.

Blackwell, Kenneth (1972) "Russell's American Lecture Courses", *Russell*, o.s. 6, 8–9.

Blackwell, Kenneth (1972–73) "How Russell Wrote", *Russell*, o.s. 8, 13–15.

Blackwell, Kenneth (1973) "The Second Russell Archives", *Russell*, o.s. 10, 2–4.

Blackwell, Kenneth (1973–74) "Our Knowledge of 'Our Knowledge'", *Russell*, o.s. 12, 11–13.

Blackwell, Kenneth (1973–74) "Russell's Reply to Dewey", *Russell*, o.s. 12, 29–30.

Blackwell, Kenneth (1975–76) "A New Mythology? Russell as Archetypical Libertine", *Russell*, o.s. 20, 22–25.

Blackwell, Kenneth (1975–76) "A Non-Existent Revision of 'Introduction to Mathematical Philosophy'", *Russell*, o.s. 20, 16–17.

Blackwell, Kenneth (1981) "The Early Wittgenstein and the Middle Russell", in Block, Irving Leonard (ed.), *Perspectives on the Philosophy of Wittgenstein*, Oxford: Blackwell, 1–30.

Blackwell, Kenneth (1983) "'Perhaps You Will Think Me Fussy . . .': Three Myths in Editing Russell's *Collected Papers*", in Jackson, H.J. (ed.), *Editing Polymaths: Erasmus to Russell*, Toronto: Committee for the Conference on Editorial Problems.

Blackwell, Kenneth (1984–85) "Part I of *The Principles of Mathematics*", *Russell*, n.s. 4, 271–288.

Blackwell, Kenneth (1989) "Portrait of a Philosopher of Science", in Savage, C. Wade, and C. Anthony Anderson (eds), *Rereading Russell: Essays on Bertrand Russell's Metaphysics and Epistemology*, Minneapolis: University of Minnesota Press, 281–293.

Blackwell, Kenneth (1995) "Two Days in the Dictation of Bertrand Russell", *Russell*, n.s. 15, 37–52.

Blackwell, Kenneth, and Elizabeth R. Eames (1975) "Russell's Unpublished Book on Theory of Knowledge", *Russell*, o.s. 19, 3–14, 18.

Blanshard, Brand (1969) "Bertrand Russell in Retrospect", *Dialogue*, 7, 584–607.

Bloch, Werner (1967) "Russell's Concept of 'Philosophy'", in Schoenman, Ralph (ed.), *Bertrand Russell: Philosopher of the Century*, London: Allen and Unwin, 140–166.

Block, I. (1975) "'Showing' in the *Tractatus*: The Root of Wittgenstein and Russell's Basic Incompatibility", *Russell*, o.s. 17, 4–14, 19–22.

Bochenski, I.M. (1956) "Bertrand Russell", in Bochenski, I.M., *Contemporary European Philosophy*, Berkeley: University of California Press, 43–51.

Bode, Boyd H. (1918) "Mr Russell and Philosophical Method", *Journal of Philosophy, Psychology, and Scientific Methods*, 15, 701–710.

Bode, Boyd H. (1944) "Russell's Educational Philosophy", in Schilpp, Paul Arthur (ed.), *The Philosophy of Bertrand Russell*, 3rd edn, New York: Tudor, 1951, 619–642.

Boër, Steven E. (1973) "Russell on Classes as Logical Fictions", *Analysis*, 33, 206–208.

Boodin, John Elof (1944) "Russell's Metaphysics", in Schilpp, Paul Arthur (ed.), *The Philosophy of Bertrand Russell*, 3rd edn, New York: Tudor, 1951, 475–509.

Boolos, George (1993) "The Advantages of Honest Toil Over Theft", in George, Alexander (ed.), *Mathematics and Mind*, Oxford: Oxford University Press, 27–44.

Booth, Wayne C. (1974) "Bertrand Russell's Rhetoric and Dogmas of Doubt", *Modern Dogma and the Rhetoric of Assent*, Notre Dame: University of Notre Dame Press, 43–85.

Borg, Karl (1994) "Russell vs Dewey: Inquiry or Truth? Where is the Little Word?", in Camhy, Daniela G. (ed.), *Children: Thinking and Philosophy*, Graz: Academia Verlag, 72–84.

Borges, Jorge Luis (1964) "Two Books", in Borges, Jorge Luis, *Other Inquisitions, 1937–1952*, Austin: University of Texas Press, 129–133.

Borkowski, Ludwig (1958) "Reduction of Arithmetic to Logic Based on the Theory of Types", *Studia Logica*, 8, 283–295.

Bornet, Gerard (1982–83) "Has Kripke Refuted Russell?", *Russell*, n.s. 2, 31–40.

Bosanquet, Bernard (1914) "Science and Philosophy", *Proceedings of the Aristotelian Society*, 15, 1–21. Repr. in Bosanquet, Bernard, *Science and Philosophy*, London: George Allen and Unwin, 1927, 15–33.

Bourke, Judy (1994–95) "The Search for Plas Penrhyn", *Russell*, n.s. 14, 173–177.

Bouwsma, O.K. (1943) "Russell's Argument on Universals", *Philosophical Review*, 52, 193–199.

Bowden, Charles L. (1984) "Bertrand Russell: Liberalism, Science, and Religion", *Religious Humanism*, 18, 36–40.

Boyle, Edward (1970) "A Great British Philosopher", *Daily Telegraph*, 4 February, 16.

Bradie, Michael P. (1977) "The Development of Russell's Structural Postulates", *Philosophy of Science*, 44, 441–463.

Bradie, Michael P. (1988) "Russell's Scientific Realism", *Russell*, n.s. 8, 195–208. Repr. in Winchester, Ian, and Kenneth Blackwell (eds), *Antinomies and Paradoxes: Studies in Russell's Early Philosophy*, Hamilton: McMaster University Library Press, 195–208.

Bradley, Francis Herbert (1910) "On Appearance, Error and Contradiction", *Mind*, 19, 153–185.

Bradley, Francis Herbert (1911) "Reply to Mr Russell's Explanations", *Mind*, 20, 74–76.

Bradley, Francis Herbert (1914) "A Discussion of Some Problems in Connection with Mr Russell's Doctrine", in Bradley, Francis Herbert, *Essays on Truth and Reality*, Oxford: Clarendon, 293–309.

Bradley, Michael C. (1986) "Russell and the Identity of Indiscernibles", *History of Philosophy Quarterly*, 3, 325–333.

Braithwaite, R.B. (1938) "The Relevance of Psychology to Logic", *Aristotelian Society*, Supplementary Vol. 17, 19–41.

Braithwaite, R.B. (1970) "Bertrand Russell as Philosopher of Science", *British Journal for the Philosophy of Science*, 21, 129–32.

Brightman, Edgar Sheffield (1944) "Russell's Philosophy of Religion", in Schilpp,

Paul Arthur (ed.), *The Philosophy of Bertrand Russell*, 3rd edn, New York: Tudor, 1951, 537–556.

Brink, Andrew (1976) "Russell to Lady Ottoline Morrell", *Russell*, o.s. 3–15, 21–22.

Brink, Andrew (1979) "Love and Conflict in Bertrand Russell's Letters", *Queen's Quarterly*, 86, 1–15.

Brink, Andrew (1982) "Death, Depression and Creativity: A Psychobiological Approach to Bertrand Russell", *Mosaic*, 15, 89–103.

Brink, Andrew (1983) "Bertrand Russell's *The Pilgrimage of Life* and Mourning", *Journal of Psychohistory*, 10, 311–331.

Brink, Andrew (1984) "Bertrand Russell's Conversion of 1901, or the Benefits of a Creative Illness", *Russell*, n.s. 4, 83–99. Repr. in Moran, Margaret, and Carl Spadoni (eds), *Intellect and Social Conscience: Essays on Bertrand Russell's Early Work*, Hamilton: McMaster University Library Press, 1984, 83–99.

Brink, Andrew (1985) "Bertrand Russell: The Angry Pacifist", *Journal of Psychohistory*, 4, 497–514.

Brink, Andrew (1987) "Bertrand Russell and the Decline of Mysticism", *Russell*, n.s. 7, 42–52.

Brinton, Alan (1977) "Uses of Definite Descriptions and Russell's Theory", *Philosophical Studies*, 31, 261–267.

Britton, Karl (1948) "Truth and Knowledge: Some Comments on Russell", *Analysis*, 8, 39–43.

Broad, C.D. (1919) "Is There 'Knowledge by Acquaintance'?", *Aristotelian Society*, Supplementary Vol. 2, 206–220.

Broad, C.D. (1967) "Some Personal Impressions of Russell as a Philosopher", in Schoenman, Ralph (ed.), *Bertrand Russell: Philosopher of the Century*, London: Allen and Unwin, 100–108.

Broad, C.D. (1967) "Some Remarks on Sense-Perception", in Schoenman, Ralph (ed.), *Bertrand Russell: Philosopher of the Century*, London: Allen and Unwin, 108–121.

Broad, C.D. (1968) "Bertrand Russell's First Forty-Two Years: In Self-Portraiture", *Philosophical Review*, 77, 455–473.

Broad, C.D. (1973) "Bertrand Russell, as Philosopher", *Bulletin of the London Mathematical Society*, 5, 328–341.

Brogan, Denis (1970) "The Last of the Grand Whigs", *Spectator*, 14 February, 208–209.

Brown, Harold Chapman (1906) "On Some Difficulties in the Theory of Transfinite Numbers and Order Types", *Journal of Philosophy, Psychology, and Scientific Methods*, 3, 388–390.

Brown, Harold Chapman (1911) "The Logic of Mr Russell", *Journal of Philosophy, Psychology, and Scientific Methods*, 8, 85–91.

Brown, Harold Chapman (1944) "A Logician in the Field of Psychology", in Schilpp, Paul Arthur (ed.), *The Philosophy of Bertrand Russell*, 3rd edn, New York: Tudor, 1951, 445–473.

Brown, James M. (1976) "Bernays' Non-Circular Proof of the Non-Independence of the Fourth Axiom of *Principia Mathematica*", *Analysis*, 36, 207–208.

Buchler, Justus (1944) "Russell and the Principles of Ethics", in Schilpp, Paul Arthur (ed.), *The Philosophy of Bertrand Russell*, 3rd edn, New York: Tudor, 1951, 511–535.

Bunge, Mario (1973) "Bertrand Russell's *Regulae Philosophandi*", in Bunge, Mario (ed.) *The Methodological Unity of Science*, Dordrecht: Reidel, 3–12.

Burge, Tyler (1983) "Russell's Problem and Intentional Identity", in Tomberlin,

James E. (ed.), *Agent, Language, and the Structure of the World*, Indianapolis: Hackett, 79–110.

Burhop, Eric (1979) "The Einstein–Russell Statement", *Scientific World*, 23, 2, 11–13.

Butchvarov, Panayot (1959) "On an Alleged Mistake of Logical Atomism", *Analysis*, 19, 132–137.

Butchvarov, Panayot (1985/1986) "Our Robust Sense of Reality", *Grazer Philosophische Studien*, 25/26, 403–421.

Butchvarov, Panayot (1988) "Russell's Views on Reality", *Grazer Philosophische Studien*, 32, 165–167.

Butler, Ronald J. (1954) "The Scaffolding of Russell's Theory of Descriptions", *Philosophical Review*, 63, 350–364.

Byrd, Michael (1987) "Part II of *The Principles of Mathematics*", *Russell*, n.s. 7, 60–70.

Byrd, Michael (1989) "Russell, Logicism, and the Choice of Logical Constants", *Notre Dame Journal of Formal Logic*, 30, 343–361.

Byrd, Michael (1994) "Part V of *The Principles of Mathematics*", *Russell*, n.s. 14, 47–86.

Byrd, Michael (1996–97) "Parts III–IV of *The Principles of Mathematics*", *Russell*, n.s. 16, 145–168.

Calkins, Mary Whiton (1915) "Bertrand Russell on Neo-Realism", *Philosophical Review*, 24, 533–537.

Candlish, Stewart (1996) "The Unity of the Proposition and Russell's Theories of Judgement", in Monk, Ray, and Anthony Palmer (eds), *Bertrand Russell and The Origins of Analytical Philosophy*, Bristol: Thoemmes, 103–135.

Cappio, James (1981) "Russell's Philosophical Development", *Synthese*, 46, 185–205.

Carnap, Rudolf (1930) "The Old and the New Logic", in Ayer, A.J. (ed.), *Logical Positivism*, Glencoe, Ill.: The Free Press, 1959, 133–146.

Carnap, Rudolf (1931) "The Logicist Foundations of Mathematics", *Erkenntnis*, 2, 91–105. Repr. in Benacerraf, Paul, and Hilary Putnam (eds), *Philosophy of Mathematics*, 2nd edn, Cambridge: Cambridge University Press, 1983, 41–52; in Klemke, E.D. (ed.), *Essays on Bertrand Russell*, Urbana: University of Illinois Press, 1970, 341–354; and in Pears, David F. (ed.), *Bertrand Russell: A Collection of Critical Essays*, Garden City, N.Y.: Anchor Books, 1972, 175–191.

Carney, James D. (1980) "Russell's 'Proof', Again", *Canadian Journal of Philosophy*, 10, 587–592.

Carney, James D., and G.W. Fitch (1979) "Can Russell Avoid Frege's Sense?", *Mind*, 88, 384–393.

Carruthers, Peter (1987) "Russellian Thoughts", *Mind*, 96, 18–35.

Cartright, Richard (1966) "Substitutivity", *Journal of Philosophy*, 63, 684–685.

Cartwright, Richard (1987) "On the Origins of Russell's Theory of Descriptions", in Cartwright, Richard, *Philosophical Essays*, Cambridge, Mass.: MIT Press, 95–133.

Carus, Paul (1910) "The Nature of Logical and Mathematical Thought", *Monist*, 20, 33–75.

Cassin, Chrystine E. (1970) "Russell's Discussion of Meaning and Denotation: A Re-Examination", in Klemke, E.D. (ed.), *Essays on Bertrand Russell*, Urbana: University of Illinois Press, 256–272.

Cassin, Chrystine E. (1970) "Russell's Distinction between the Primary and Secondary Occurrence of Definite Descriptions", in Klemke, E.D. (ed.), *Essays on Bertrand Russell*, Urbana: University of Illinois Press, 273–284. Repr. in *Mind*, 80 (1971), 620–622.

Cassin, Chrystine E. (1971) "Existential Quantification in Russell's Analysis of Definite Descriptions", *Mind*, 10, 553–557.

Cassin, Chrystine E. (1976) "Variations on the Theme of Meaning", in Thomas, J.E., and Kenneth Blackwell (eds), *Russell in Review*, Toronto: Samuel Stevens, Hakkert and Co., 203–213.

Castañeda, Hector-Neri (1976) "Ontology and Grammar: I. Russell's Paradox and the General Theory of Properties in Natural Language", *Theoria*, 42, 44–92.

Castañeda, Hector-Neri (1988) "Negations, Imperatives, Colors, Indexical Properties, Non-existence, and Russell's Paradox", in Austin, David F. (ed.), *Philosophical Analysis*, Dordrecht: Kluwer, 169–205.

Casullo, Albert (1981) "Russell on the Reduction of Particulars", *Analysis*, 41, 199–205.

Casullo, Albert (1982) "Particulars, Substrata, and the Identity of Indescernibles", *Philosophy of Science*, 49, 591–603.

Casullo, Albert (1984) "The Contingent Identity of Particulars and Universals", *Mind*, 93, 527–541.

Caton, C.E. (1959) "Strawson on Referring", *Mind*, 68, 539–544.

Cayard, W. Wallace (1976) "Bertrand Russell and Existential Phenomenologists on Foundations of Knowledge", *Journal of the West Virginia Philosophical Society*, 17–22.

Cell, Edward (1971) "Logical Atomism and Russell: Analysis and Language Form", in Cell, Edward, *Language, Existence and God*, Nashville, Tenn.: Abingdon, 55–89.

Chalmers, Melanie, and Nicholas Griffin (1997) "Russell's Marginalia in his Copy of Bradley's *Principles of Logic*", *Russell*, n.s. 17, 43–70.

Chao, Yuen Ren (1972) "With Russell in China", *Russell*, o.s. 7, 14–17.

Chihara, Charles S. (1972) "Russell's Theory of Types", in Pears, David F. (ed.), *Bertrand Russell: A Collection of Critical Essays*, Garden City, N.Y.: Anchor Books, 245–289.

Chihara, Charles S. (1973) "Russell's Solution to the Paradoxes", in Chihara, Charles S., *Ontology and the Vicious-Circle Principle*, Ithaca, N.Y.: Cornell University Press, 1–59.

Chihara, Charles S. (1979) "A Diagnosis of the Liar and Other Semantical Vicious-Circle Paradoxes", in Roberts, George W. (ed.), *Bertrand Russell Memorial Volume*, London: Allen and Unwin, 52–80.

Chihara, Charles S. (1980) "Ramsey's Theory of Types: Suggestions for a Return to Fregean Sources", in Mellor, D.H. (ed.), *Prospects for Pragmatism*, Cambridge: Cambridge University Press, 21–47.

Childs, Donald J. (1986) "Mr. Apollinax, Professor Channing-Cheetah, and T. S. Eliot", *Journal of Modern Literature*, 13, 172–177.

Chisholm, Roderick M. (1944) "Russell on the Foundations of Empirical Knowledge", in Schilpp, Paul Arthur (ed.), *The Philosophy of Bertrand Russell*, 3rd edn, New York: Tudor, 1951, 419–444.

Chisholm, Roderick M. (1974) "On the Nature of Acquaintance: A Discussion of Russell's Theory of Knowledge", in Nakhnikian, George (ed.), *Bertrand Russell's Philosophy*, London: Duckworth, 47–56.

Church, Alonzo (1936) "A Note on the Entscheidungs-Problem", *Journal of Symbolic Logic*, 1, 40–41, 101–102.

Church, Alonzo (1940) "A Formulation of the Simple Theory of Types", *Journal of Symbolic Logic*, 5, 56–68.

Church, Alonzo (1960) "Mathematics and Logic", in Nagel, Ernest, Patrick Suppes, and Alfred Tarski (eds), *Logic, Methodology, and Philosophy of Science,*

Proceedings of the 1960 International Congress, Stanford: Stanford University Press, 181–186.

Church, Alonzo (1974) "Russellian Simple Type Theory", *Proceedings and Addresses of the American Philosophical Association*, 47, 21–33.

Church, Alonzo (1976) "A Comparison of Russell's Resolution of the Semantical Antinomies with that of Tarski", *Journal of Symbolic Logic*, 41, 747–760.

Church, Alonzo (1984) "Comparison of Russell's Resolution of the Semantical Antinomies With That of Tarski", in Martin, Robert L. (ed.), *Recent Essays on Truth and the Liar Paradox*, Oxford: Clarendon, 289–306.

Church, Alonzo (1984) "Russell's Theory of Identity of Propositions", *Philosophia Naturalis*, 21, 513–522.

Chwistek, Leon (1921) "Antynomje Logiki Formalng", *Przeglad Filozoficzny*, 24, 164–171. Repr. as "Antinomies of Formal Logic" in McCall, Storrs (ed.), *Polish Logic*, Oxford: Clarendon, 1967, 338–345.

Chwistek, Leon (1924, 1925) "The Theory of Constructive Types", *Annales de la Société Polonaise de Mathématique*, 2, 9–48; 3, 92–141.

Clark, Romane (1974) "Ontology and the Philosophy of Mind in Sellars' Critique of Russell", in Nakhnikian, George (ed.), *Bertrand Russell's Philosophy*, London: Duckworth, 101–116.

Clark, Romane (1981) "Acquaintance", *Synthese*, 46, 231–246.

Clarke, Peter (1984) "Bertrand Russell and the Dimensions of Edwardian Liberalism", *Russell*, n.s. 4, 207–221. Repr. in Moran, Margaret, and Carl Spadoni (eds), *Intellect and Social Conscience: Essays on Bertrand Russell's Early Work*, Hamilton: McMaster University Library Press, 1984, 207–221.

Clement, William C. (1953) "Russell's Structuralist Thesis", *Philosophical Review*, 62, 266–275.

Clements, Richard (1970) "Bertrand Russell; Man of the Century", *Central Literary Magazine*, 40 (Spring), 131–136.

Coates, Ken (1972) "The Internationalism of Bertrand Russell", in Coates, Ken (ed.), *Essays on Socialist Humanism*, Nottingham: Spokesman Books, 193–217.

Cocchiarella, Nino B. (1974) "Formal Ontology and the Foundations of Mathematics", in Nakhnikian, George (ed.), *Bertrand Russell's Philosophy*, London: Duckworth, 29–46.

Cocchiarella, Nino B. (1980) "The Development of the Theory of Logical Types and the Notion of a Logical Subject in Russell's Early Philosophy", *Synthese*, 45, 71–115.

Cocchiarella, Nino B. (1982) "Meinong Reconstructed Versus Early Russell Reconstructed", *Journal of Philosophical Logic*, 11, 183–214.

Cocchiarella, Nino B. (1989) "Russell's Theory of Logical Types and the Atomistic Hierarchy of Sentences", in Savage, C. Wade, and C. Anthony Anderson (eds), *Rereading Russell: Essays on Bertrand Russell's Metaphysics and Epistemology*, Minneapolis: University of Minnesota Press, 41–62.

Coffa, J. Alberto (1979) "The Humble Origins of Russell's Paradox", *Russell*, o.s. 33–34, 31–37.

Coffa, J. Alberto (1980) "Russell as a Platonic Dialogue: The Matter of Denoting", *Synthese*, 45, 43–70.

Coffa, J. Alberto (1981) "Russell and Kant", *Synthese*, 46, 247–263.

Cohen, Morris (1941) "A Scandalous Denial of Justice", in Dewey, John, and Horace M. Kallen (eds), *The Bertrand Russell Case*, New York: Viking, 131–147.

Cohen, Morris Raphael (1946) "New Philosopher's Stone", in Cohen, Morris Raphael, *Faith of a Liberal*, New York: Holt, 403–407.

Cohen, Morris Raphael (1946) "Scandalous Denial of Justice: The Bertrand Russell Case", in Cohen, Morris Raphael, *Faith of a Liberal*, New York: Holt, 198–210.

Collins, James (1947) "Bertrand Russell's *A History of Western Philosophy*: Book Two, Catholic Philosophy", *Franciscan Studies*, 7, 193–218.

Cooke, Alistair (1977) "Bertrand Russell: The Lord of Reason", in Cooke, Alistair, *Six Men*, New York: Knopf, 153–180.

Copi, Irving M. (1950) "The Inconsistency or Redundancy of *Principia Mathematica*", *Philosophy and Phenomenological Research*, 11, 190–199.

Copleston, Frederick (1966) "Bertrand Russell (1), (2) and (3)", in Copleston, Frederick, *A History of Philosophy*, vol. 8, pt 2, Garden City, N.Y.: Image Books, 185–254.

Cory, Daniel (1948) "Are Sense-Data 'In' the Brain?", *Journal of Philosophy*, 45, 533–548.

Cory, Daniel (1960) "A Philosophical Letter to Bertrand Russell", *Journal of Philosophy*, 57, 573–587.

Costello, Harry T. (1957) "Logic in 1914 and Now", *Journal of Philosophy*, 54, 245–264.

Costelloe, Karin (1914) "An Answer to Mr Bertrand Russell's Article on the Philosophy of Bergson", *Monist*, 24, 145–155.

Couture, Jocelyne (1988) "Are Substitutional Quantifiers a Solution to the Problem of the Elimination of Classes in *Principia Mathematica*?", *Russell*, n.s. 8, 116–132. Repr. in Winchester, Ian, and Kenneth Blackwell (eds), *Antinomies and Paradoxes: Studies in Russell's Early Philosophy*, Hamilton: McMaster University Library Press, 1988, 116–132.

Crawshay-Williams, Rupert (1983) "Profile – Bertrand Russell", *Russell*, n.s. 3, 25–28.

Crittenden, Charles (1970) "Ontology and the Theory of Descriptions", *Philosophy and Phenomenological Research*, 31, 85–96.

Croddy, W. Stephen (1976) "Russell on the Meaning of Descriptions", *Notre Dame Journal of Formal Logic*, 17, 424–428.

Croddy, W. Stephen (1979) "Do Descriptions Have Meaning?", *Logique et Analyse*, 22, 23–30.

Crosby, D.A., and R.G. Williams (1987) "Creative Problem-Solving in Physics, Philosophy, and Painting: Three Case Studies", in Amsler, Marc (ed.), *Creativity and the Imagination*, Newark: University of Delaware Press, 168–214.

Cross, Charles Byron (1979) "Time and the Russell Definition of Number", *Southwestern Journal of Philosophy*, 10, 177–180.

Cross, R. Nicol (1945) "Bertrand Russell's *History of Western Philosophy*", *Hibbert Journal*, 45, 193–201.

Crossley, J.N. (1973) "A Note on Cantor's Theorem and Russell's Paradox", *Australasian Journal of Philosophy*, 51, 70–71.

Cumming, L. (1989) "A Remarkable Philosophical Hybrid", *Quadrant*, 33 (January/February), 61–62.

Cunliffe, John William (1933) "Essays, Journalism and Travel", in Cunliffe, John William, *English Literature in the Twentieth Century*, New York: Macmillan, 259–280.

Cunningham, Suzanne (1994) "Herbert Spencer, Bertrand Russell, and the Shape of Early Analytic Philosophy", *Russell*, n.s. 14, 7–30.

Cunningham, Suzanne (1996) "Bertrand Russell and Evolutionism", in Cunningham, Suzanne, *Philosophy and the Darwinian Legacy*, Rochester: University of Rochester Press, 59–96.

Currie, Haver C. (1959) "Bertrand Russell on Values, with Allusions to Lord Byron", *The Personalist*, 40, 13–21.

Cusmariu, Arnold (1979) "Russell's Paradox Re-Examined", *Erkenntnis*, 14, 365–370.

Da Costa, Newton C.A., and Steven French (1991) "On Russell's Principle of Induction", *Synthese*, 86, 285–295.

Daniel, P.J. (1919) "Independence Proofs and the Theory of Implication", *Monist*, 29, 451–453.

DasGupta, R.K. (1973) "Russell as a Man of Letters", *Russell*, o.s. 9, 3–14.

Datta, Kritidipa (1987) "Russell's Notion of Existence", *Darshan-Manjari*, 5, 54–62.

Dau, Paolo (1985) "The Complex Matter of Denoting", *Analysis*, 45, 190–197.

Dau, Paolo (1986) "Russell's First Theory of Denoting and Quantification", *Notre Dame Journal of Formal Logic*, 27, 133–166.

Davant, James B. (1975) "Wittgenstein on Russell's Theory of Types", *Notre Dame Journal of Formal Logic*, 16, 102–108.

Davies, Mansel (1970) "Tribute to Bertrand Russell", *Humanist*, 85, 140–141.

Davies, Mansel (1991) "CND, Pugwash, and Eddington", *Russell*, n.s. 11, 193–199.

Dawes, Robyn M. (1988) "Plato Vs. Russell: Hess and the Relevance of Cognitive Psychology", *Religious Humanism*, 22, 20–26.

De Boer, J. (1953) "Critique of Continuity, Infinity, and Allied Concepts in the Natural Philosophy of Bergson and Russell", in Wild, John Daniel (ed.), *Return to Reason*, Chicago: Regnery, 92–124.

Degen, J. (1993) "Two Formal Vindications of Logicism", in Czermak, Johannes (ed.), *Philosophy of Mathematics*, Vienna: Verlag Hölder–Pichler–Tempsky, 243–250.

Dejnozka, Jan (1988) "A Reply to Butchvarov's 'Russell's Views on Reality'", *Grazer Philosophische Studien*, 32, 181–184.

Dejnozka, Jan (1988) "Russell's Robust Sense of Reality: A Reply to Butchvarov", *Grazer Philosophische Studien*, 32, 155–164.

Dejnozka, Jan (1990) "The Ontological Foundation of Russell's Theory of Modality", *Erkenntnis*, 32, 383–418.

Dejnozka, Jan (1991) "Russell's Seventeen Private Language Arguments", *Russell*, n.s. 11, 11–35.

Dejnozka, Jan (1995) "Quine: Whither Empirical Equivalence?", *South African Journal of Philosophy*, 14, 175–182.

De Laguna, Theodore (1915) "The Logical-Analytic Method in Philosophy", *Journal of Philosophy, Psychology, and Scientific Methods*, 12, 449–462.

Delany, Paul (1986) "Russell's Dismissal from Trinity: A Study in High Table Politics", *Russell*, n.s. 6, 39–61.

Demopoulos, William (1981) "New Work on Russell's Early Philosophy", *Russell*, n.s. 1, 163–170.

Demopoulos, William, and Michael Friedman (1985) "The Concept of Structure in *The Analysis of Matter*", *Philosophy of Science*, 52, 621–639. Repr. in Savage, C. Wade, and C. Anthony Anderson (eds), *Rereading Russell: Essays on Bertrand Russell's Metaphysics and Epistemology*, Minneapolis: University of Minnesota Press, 1989, 183–199.

Demos, Raphael (1917) "A Discussion of a Certain Type of Negative Proposition", *Mind*, 26, 188–196.

Demos, Raphael (1924) "Bertrand Russell – America's Distinguished Visitor", *Vanity Fair*, June, 54, 78.

Demos, Raphael (1945) "Mr Russell and Dogmatism", *Journal of Philosophy*, 42, 589–594.

Denonn, Lester E. (1975) "Russell as a Debater", *Russell*, o.s. 18, 10–14.

De Rouilhan, Philippe (1992) "Russell and the Vicious Circle Principle", *Philosophical Studies*, 65, 169–182.

Detlefsen, Michael (1993) "Poincaré vs Russell on the Role of Logic in Mathematics", *Philosophia Mathematica*, 1, 24–49. Repr. as "Logicism and the Nature of Mathematical Reasoning", in Irvine, A.D., and G.A. Wedeking (eds), *Russell and Analytic Philosophy*, Toronto: University of Toronto Press, 265–292.

Dewey, John (1915) "The Existence of the World as a Problem", *Philosophical Review*, 24, 357–370.

Dewey, John (1920) "Three Contemporary Philosophers", in Dewey, John, *The Middle Works*, Vol. 12, Carbondale: Southern Illinois University Press, 1982, 205–250. Repr. in part as "Russell's Philosophy and Politics", *Russell*, o.s. 11 (1973), 3–10, 15–20.

Dewey, John (1923) "China and the West", *Dial*, 74, 193–196.

Dewey, John (1926) "A Key to the New World", *New Republic*, 46, 410–411.

Dewey, John (1936) "Religion, Science, and Philosophy", *Southern Review*, 2, 53–62.

Dewey, John (1940) "The Bertrand Russell Case", *Nation*, 150 (June), 732–733.

Dewey, John (1941) "Propositions, Warranted Assertibility, and Truth", *Journal of Philosophy*, 38, 169–186.

Dewey, John (1941) "Social Realities Versus Police Court Fictions", in Dewey, John, and Horace M. Kallen (eds), *The Bertrand Russell Case*, New York: Viking, 55–74.

Dewey, John (1946) "Religion, Science and Philosophy", in Dewey, John, *Problems of Men*, New York: Philosophical Library, 169–179.

Dewey, John (1953) "Existence of the World as a Logical Problem", in Dewey, John, *Essays in Experimental Logic*, New York: Dover, 281–302.

Diamond, Cora (1988) "Throwing Away the Ladder", *Philosophy*, 63, 5–27.

Dingle, Herbert (1953) "Physics and Experience", in Dingle, Herbert, *Scientific Adventure*, New York: Philosophical Library, 263–268.

Domhoff, G. William (1963) "Sartre or Russell – Why Not Both?", *The Humanist*, 23, 116.

Donagan, A. (1971) "Universals and Metaphysical Realism", in Landesman, Charles (ed.), *The Problem of Universals*, New York: Basic Books, 98–118.

Donagan, Alan (1952) "Recent Criticisms of Russell's Analysis of Existence", *Analysis*, 12, 132–137.

Dong, Yu (1992) "Russell and Chinese Civilization", *Russell*, n.s. 12, 22–49.

Donnellan, Keith S. (1966) "Reference and Definite Descriptions", *Philosophical Review*, 75, 281–304.

Donnellan, Keith S. (1966) "Substitution and Reference", *Journal of Philosophy*, 63, 685–687.

Donnellan, Keith S. (1990) "Genuine Names and Knowledge by Acquaintance", *Dialectica*, 44, 99–112.

Dukelow, Owen W. (1976) "The Problem of Negative Facts in Russell's Logical Atomism", *Southwestern Journal of Philosophy*, 7, 7–13.

Dulckeit, Katharina (1989) "Hegel's Revenge on Russell: The 'Is' of Identity versus the 'Is' of Predication", in Desmond, William J. (ed.), *Hegel and His Critics*, Albany: SUNY Press, 111–131.

Duram, James C. (1977) "From Conflict to Cooperation: Russell, Norman Thomas and the Cold War", *Russell*, o.s. 25–28, 52–66.

Duran, Jane (1987) "Russell On Names", *Philosophy Research Archives*, 13, 463–470.

Duran, Jane (1994) "Russell On Pragmatism", *Russell*, n.s. 14, 31–38.

Durant, William James (1926) "Contemporary European Philosophers: Bergson, Croce and Bertrand Russell", in Durant, William James, *Story of Philosophy*, New York: Simon and Schuster, 487–529.

Durant, William James (1931) "Bertrand Russell on Marriage and Morals", in Durant, William James, *Adventures in Genius*, New York: Simon and Schuster, 212–224.

Eames, Elizabeth R. (1967) "The Consistency of Russell's Realism", *Philosophy and Phenomenological Research*, 27, 502–511.

Eames, Elizabeth R. (1968) "Bertrand Russell's Social Criticism", *Religious Humanism*, 2, 17–23.

Eames, Elizabeth R. (1968) "Contemporary British Criticism of Bertrand Russell", *Southern Journal of Philosophy*, 6, 45–51.

Eames, Elizabeth R. (1971–72) "Russell's Study of Meinong", *Russell*, o.s. 4, 4–7.

Eames, Elizabeth R. (1972) "Russell on 'What There Is'", *Revue Internationale de Philosophie*, 26, 483–498.

Eames, Elizabeth R. (1976) "Bertrand Russell's Philosophical Method", *Midwestern Journal of Philosophy*, 4, 3–13.

Eames, Elizabeth R. (1979–80) "Response to Mr Perkins", *Russell*, o.s. 35–36, 41–42.

Eames, Elizabeth R. (1986) "Russell and the Experience of Time", *Philosophy and Phenomenological Research*, 46, 681–682.

Eames, Elizabeth R. (1989) "Cause in the Later Russell", in Savage, C. Wade, and C. Anthony Anderson (eds), *Rereading Russell: Essays on Bertrand Russell's Metaphysics and Epistemology*, Minneapolis: University of Minnesota Press, 264–280.

Earman, John (1989) "Concepts of Projectability and the Problems of Induction", in Savage, C. Wade, and C. Anthony Anderson (eds), *Rereading Russell: Essays on Bertrand Russell's Metaphysics and Epistemology*, Minneapolis: University of Minnesota Press, 220–233.

Eastman, Max (1959) "Two Bertrand Russells", in Eastman, Max, *Great Companions*, New York: Farrar, Straus and Cudahy, 191–206.

Edgell, Beatrice (1919) "Is There 'Knowledge by Acquaintance'?", *Aristotelian Society*, Supplementary Vol. 2, 194–205.

Edman, Irwin (1917) "To Bertrand Russell after Reading *Why Men Fight*", *New York Tribune*, February 28, 11.

Edwards, Paul (1949) "Bertrand Russell's Doubts about Induction", *Mind*, 58, 141–163. Repr. in Flew, Antony G.N. (ed.), *Essays on Logic and Language*, New York: Philosophical Library, 55–79.

Edwards, Paul (1957) "How Bertrand Russell was Prevented from Teaching at the College of the City of New York", in Russell, Bertrand, *Why I Am Not a Christian*, London: Allen and Unwin, 207–259.

Edwards, Paul (1970) "Tribute to Bertrand Russell", *Humanist*, 85, 102–104.

Einstein, Albert (1944) "Remarks on Bertrand Russell's Theory of Knowledge", in Schilpp, Paul Arthur (ed.), *The Philosophy of Bertrand Russell*, 3rd edn, New York: Tudor, 1951, 277–291.

Eisler, R. (1949) "Scientific Inference According to Bertrand Russell, K.R. Popper and Feliz Hausdorff", *Hibbert Journal*, 47, 375–381.

Everdell, William (1997) "Bertrand Russell and Edmund Husserl: Phenomenology, Number, and the Fall of Logic", in Everdell, William, *The First Moderns*, Chicago: University of Chicago Press, 177–192.

Fahrnkopf, Robert (1976) "Stroll on Russell's 'Proof'", *Canadian Journal of Philosophy*, 6, 569–578.

Farley, Christopher (1972) "Reminiscences and Reflections on Russell", *Humanist in Canada*, 5, no. 4, 5–10.

Farley, Christopher (1976) "Bertrand Russell: Reminiscences and Reflections", in Thomas, J.E., and Kenneth Blackwell (eds), *Russell in Review*, Toronto: Samuel Stevens, Hakkert and Co., 5–20.

Feibleman, James Kern (1944) "A Reply to Bertrand Russell's Introduction to the Second Edition of *The Principles of Mathematics*", in Schilpp, Paul Arthur (ed.), *The Philosophy of Bertrand Russell*, 3rd edn, New York: Tudor, 1951, 155–174.

Feibleman, James Kern (1946) "Russell's Infidelity to Realism", in Feibleman, James Kern, *Revival of Realism*, Chapel Hill, N.C.: University of North Carolina Press, 269–287.

Feibleman, James Kern (1958) "Russell's Early Philosophy", in Feibleman, James Kern, *Inside the Great Mirror: A Critical Examination of the Philosophy of Russell, Wittgenstein, and Their Followers*, The Hague: Nijhoff, 1–47.

Feibleman, James Kern (1973) "Assumptions of Whitehead's and Russell's *Principia Mathematica*", *International Logic Review*, 4, 201–219.

Feigl, Herbert (1975) "Russell and Schlick: A Remarkable Agreement on a Monistic Solution of the Mind-Body Problem", *Erkenntnis*, 9, 11–34. Repr. in Roberts, George W. (ed.), *Bertrand Russell Memorial Volume*, London: Allen and Unwin, 1979, 321–338.

Feinberg, Barry, and Ronald Kasrils (1973) "Russell's Return to America", *Russell*, o.s. 10, 5–10.

Feuer, Lewis S. (1955) "Bertrand Russell: The Pilgrimage of Scientific Philosophy", *University of Toronto Quarterly*, 24, 217–233.

Findlay, J.N. (1949) "Is There Knowledge by Acquaintance?", *Aristotelian Society*, Supplementary Vol. 23, 111–128.

Fischer, Gilbert (1968) "Russell and the Philosopher's Fallacy", *The Personalist*, 49, 549–562.

Fisher, Herbert Albert Laurens (1939) "Philosopher's Paradise", in Fisher, Herbert Albert Laurens, *Pages From the Past*, Oxford: Oxford University Press, 182–190.

Fitch, Frederic (1938) "The Consistency of the Ramified *Principia*", *Journal of Symbolic Logic*, 3, 140–150.

Fitch, Frederic (1971) "Propositions as the Only Realities", *American Philosophical Quarterly*, 8, 99–103.

Fitch, Frederic (1974) "Towards Proving the Consistency of *Principia Mathematica*", in Nakhnikian, George (ed.), *Bertrand Russell's Philosophy*, London: Duckworth, 1–17.

Flathman, Richard E. (1996) "The Imagined and Wished for Imperium of Reason and Science: Russell's Empiricism and Its Relation to His and Our Ethics and Politics", *Philosophy of the Social Sciences*, 26, 162–180.

Fleischhacker, L.E. (1979) "Is Russell's Vicious Circle Principle False or Meaningless?", *Dialectica*, 33, 23–30.

Flew, Antony (1970) "The Passionate Sceptic", *Humanist*, 85 (April), 105–106.

Flew, Antony (1979) "Russell's Judgement on Bolshevism", in Roberts, George W. (ed.), *Bertrand Russell Memorial Volume*, London: Allen and Unwin, 428–454.

Fogelin, Robert J. (1974) "Negative Elementary Propositions", *Philosophical Studies*, 25, 189–197.

Folina, Janet (1990) "Russell Reread", *Philosophical Quarterly*, 40, 502–509.

Forte, Maria (1987) "Lucy Martin Donnelly: A Sojourn with the Russells", *Russell*, n.s. 7, 53–59.

Fortier, Evelyn (1996) "Was the Dispute Between Russell and Bradley About

Internal Relations?", in Mander, W.J. (ed.), *Perspectives on the Logic and Metaphysics of F.H. Bradley*, Bristol: Thoemmes, 25–37.

Foster, Thomas R. (1982) "Identity and Symmetry: Some Considerations of Russell's Definition", *Philosophy Research Archives*, 8, no. 1507.

Foster, Thomas R. (1983–84) "Russell on Particularized Relations", *Russell*, n.s. 3, 129–143.

Frege, Gottlob (1902) "Letter to Russell", in van Heijenoort, Jean, *From Frege to Gödel*, Cambridge, Mass.: Harvard University Press, 1967, 126–128.

Frege, Gottlob (1903) "The Russell Paradox", in Frege, Gottlob, *The Basic Laws of Arithmetic*, Berkeley: University of California Press, 1964, 127–143.

Friedman, Joel I. (1979) "On Some Relations Between Leibniz's Monadology and Transfinite Set Theory: A Complement to Russell's Thesis on Leibniz", in Roberts, George W. (ed.), *Bertrand Russell Memorial Volume*, London: Allen and Unwin, 182–221.

Fritz, Charles Andrew, Jr (1972) "Russell's Philosophy of Science", in Pears, David F. (ed.), *Bertrand Russell: A Collection of Critical Essays*, Garden City, N.Y.: Anchor Books, 147–167.

Fromm, Erich (1967) "Prophets and Priests", in Schoenman, Ralph (ed.), *Bertrand Russell: Philosopher of the Century*, London: Allen and Unwin, 67–79.

Fumerton, Richard (1989) "Russelling Causal Theories of Reference", in Savage, C. Wade, and C. Anthony Anderson (eds), *Rereading Russell: Essays on Bertrand Russell's Metaphysics and Epistemology*, Minneapolis: University of Minnesota Press, 108–118.

Gale, Richard M. (1959) "Russell's Drill Sergeant and Bricklayer and Dewey's Logic", *Journal of Philosophy*, 56, 401–406.

Gandy, R.O. (1956, 1959) "On the Axiom of Extensionality", *Journal of Symbolic Logic*, 21, 36–48; 24, 287–300.

Gandy, R.O. (1973) "Bertrand Russell, as Mathematician", *Bulletin of the London Mathematical Society*, 5, 342–348.

Ganeri, Jonardon (1995) "Contextually Incomplete Descriptions – A New Counterexample to Russell?", *Analysis*, 55, 287–290.

Garciadiego, Alejandro R. (1995) "*The Principles of Mathematics* of Bertrand Russell", in Ramirez, Santiago, and Robert S. Cohen (eds), *Mexican Studies in the History and Philosophy of Science*, Dordrecht: Kluwer, 213–234.

Garniner, Bennitt (1978) "1916", *Russell*, o.s. 29–32, 43–51.

Garvin, Ned S. (1991) "Russell's Naturalistic Turn", *Russell*, n.s. 11, 36–51.

Garvin, Ned S., *et al.* (1993) "*Human Knowledge* from Pen to Print", *Russell*, n.s. 13, 87–100.

Gass, William H. (1971) "Russell's Memoirs", in Gass, William H., *Fiction and the Figures of Life*, New York: Knopf, 242–246.

Gastwirth, Paul (1932) "φa, φx, and φx̂", *Monist*, 42, 313–315.

Gastwirth, Paul (1932) "The Hypothesis of Reducibility", *Monist*, 42, 384–387.

Gauvin, Marshall J. (1982) "The Bertrand Russell Case", *Russell*, n.s. 2, 47–58.

Gay, William (1990) "The Russell–Hook Debates of 1958: Arguments from the Extremes on Nuclear War and the Soviet Union", in Klein, Kenneth H. (ed.), *In the Interest of Peace: A Spectrum of Philosophical Views*, Wolfeboro: Longwood, 79–95.

Geach, P.T. (1950) "Russell's Theory of Descriptions", *Analysis*, 10, 84–88. Repr. in Macdonald, Margaret (ed.), *Philosophy and Analysis*, New York: Barnes and Noble, 1954, 32–36.

Geach, P.T. (1959) "Russell on Meaning and Denoting", *Analysis*, 19, 69–72. Repr.

in Klemke, E.D. (ed.), *Essays on Bertrand Russell*, Urbana: University of Illinois Press, 1970, 209–212.

Geach, P.T. (1970) "Two Paradoxes of Russell's", *Journal of Philosophy*, 67, 89–97.

Geach, P.T. (1978) "Russell on Denoting", *Analysis*, 38, 204–205.

Gellman, Jerome I. (1969) "Suter on Russell on Meinong", *Philosophy and Phenomenological Research*, 29, 441–445.

Gerrard, Steve (1997) "Desire and Desirability: Bradley, Russell and Moore versus Mill", in Tait, William W. (ed.), *Early Analytic Philosophy: Frege, Russell, Wittgenstein*, Chicago: Open Court, 37–74.

Ghose, A.G. (1977) "Whitehead's and Russell's *Principia Mathematica* and Formalization of Abstractions", *International Logic Review*, 8, 105–106.

Ghyka, Matila (1947) "Russell's Scientific Philosophy", *The Personalist*, 28, 129–139.

Goddard, L. (1964) "Sense and Nonsense", *Mind*, 63, 309–331.

Gödel, Kurt (1931) "Über formal unentscheidbare Sätze der *Principia mathematica* und verwandter Systeme I", *Monatshefte für Mathematik und Physik*, 38, 173–198. Trans. as "On Formally Undecidable Propositions of *Principia Mathematica* and Related Systems I", in Gödel, Kurt, *Collected Works*, Vol. 1, Oxford: Oxford University Press, 1986, 144–195, and in van Heijenoort, Jean, *From Frege to Gödel*, Cambridge, Mass.: Harvard University Press, 1967, 596–616.

Gödel, Kurt (1944) "Russell's Mathematical Logic", in Schilpp, Paul Arthur (ed.), *The Philosophy of Bertrand Russell*, 3rd edn, New York: Tudor, 1951, 123–153. Repr. in Benacerraf, Paul, and Hilary Putnam (eds), *Philosophy of Mathematics*, 2nd edn, Cambridge: Cambridge University Press, 1983, 447–469; and in Pears, David F. (ed.), *Bertrand Russell: A Collection of Critical Essays*, Garden City, N.Y.: Anchor Books, 1972, 192–226.

Goldfarb, Warren D. (1987) "Poincaré Against the Logicists", in Aspray, William, and Philip Kitcher (eds), *Essays in the History and Philosophy of Mathematics*, Minneapolis: University of Minnesota Press, 61–81.

Goldfarb, Warren D. (1989) "Russell's Reasons for Ramification", in Savage, C. Wade, and C. Anthony Anderson (eds), *Rereading Russell: Essays on Bertrand Russell's Metaphysics and Epistemology*, Minneapolis: University of Minnesota Press, 24–40.

Goodstein, R.L. (1979) "Post *Principia*", in Roberts, George W. (ed.), *Bertrand Russell Memorial Volume*, London: Allen and Unwin, 128–138.

Götlind, Erik J.A. (1953) "Note on a Formula in my *Bertrand Russell's Theories of Causation*", *Theoria*, 19, 177–178.

Graham, George (1986) "Russell's Deceptive Desires", *Philosophical Quarterly*, 36, 223–229.

Gram, M.S. (1970) "Ontology and the Theory of Descriptions", in Klemke, E.D. (ed.), *Essays on Bertrand Russell*, Urbana: University of Illinois Press, 118–143.

Grandy, Richard E. (1980) "Ramsey, Reliability and Knowledge", in Mellor, D.H. (ed.), *Prospects for Pragmatism*, Cambridge: Cambridge University Press, 197–210.

Grandy, Richard E. (1981) "Forms of Belief", *Synthese*, 46, 271–284.

Grant, George P. (1952) "Pursuit of an Illusion: A Commentary on Bertrand Russell", *Dalhousie Review*, 32, 97–109.

Grattan-Guinness, Ivor (1972) "Bertrand Russell on His Paradox and the Multiplicative Axiom", *Journal of Philosophical Logic*, 1, 103–110.

Grattan-Guinness, Ivor (1972–73) "Russell and Phillip Jourdain", *Russell*, o.s. 8, 7–12.

Grattan-Guinness, Ivor (1974) "Russell's Home at Bagley Wood", *Russell*, o.s. 13, 24–26.

Grattan-Guinness, Ivor (1974) "The Russell Archives: Some New Light on Russell's Logicism", *Annals of Science*, 31, 387–406.

Grattan-Guinness, Ivor (1975) "Russell's Election to the Royal Society", *Russell*, o.s. 17, 23–26.

Grattan-Guinness, Ivor (1975) "The Royal Society's Financial Support of the Publication of Whitehead and Russell's *Principia Mathematica*", *Notes and Records of the Royal Society of London*, 30, 89–104.

Grattan-Guinness, Ivor (1975) "Wiener on the Logics of Russell and Schröder", *Annals of Science*, 32, 103–132.

Grattan-Guinness, Ivor (1976) "On the Mathematical and Philosophical Background to Russell's *The Principles of Mathematics*", in Thomas, J.E., and Kenneth Blackwell (eds), *Russell in Review*, Toronto: Samuel Stevens, Hakkert and Co., 157–173.

Grattan-Guinness, Ivor (1978) "How Bertrand Russell Discovered His Paradox", *Historia Mathematica*, 5, 127–137.

Grattan-Guinness, Ivor (1980) "Georg Cantor's Influence on Bertrand Russell", *History and Philosophy of Logic*, 1, 61–93.

Grattan-Guinness, Ivor (1981) "On the Development of Logics Between the Two World Wars", *American Mathematical Monthly*, 88, 495–509.

Grattan-Guinness, Ivor (1984) "Notes on the Fate of Logicism from *Principia Mathematica* to Gödel's Incompletability Theorem", *History and Philosophy of Logic*, 5, 67–78.

Grattan-Guinness, Ivor (1985) "Bertrand Russell's Logical Manuscripts: An Apprehensive Brief", *History and Philosophy of Logic*, 6, 53–74.

Grattan-Guinness, Ivor (1985–86) "Russell's Logicism Versus Oxbridge Logics, 1890–1925: A Contribution to the Real History of Twentieth-Century English Philosophy", *Russell*, n.s. 5, 101–131.

Grattan-Guinness, Ivor (1990) "Bertrand Russell (1872–1970) After Twenty Years", *Notes and Records of the Royal Society London*, 44, 280–306.

Grattan-Guinness, Ivor (1991) "Russell and G.H. Hardy: A Study of Their Relationship", *Russell*, n.s. 11, 165–179.

Grattan-Guinness, Ivor (1991) "The Hon. Bertrand Russell and *The Educational Times*", *Russell*, n.s. 11, 86–91.

Grattan-Guinness, Ivor (1992) "Russell and Karl Popper: Their Personal Contacts", *Russell*, n.s. 12, 3–18.

Grattan-Guinness, Ivor (1996) "'I Never Felt Any Bitterness': Alys Russell's Interpretation of Her Separation from Bertie", *Russell*, n.s. 16, 37–44.

Grattan-Guinness, Ivor (1996–97) "How Did Russell Write *The Principles of Mathematics (1903)*?", *Russell*, n.s. 16, 101–127.

Graves, A. (1960) "Two Studies in Scientific Atheism", in Graves, Robert, *Food for Centaurs*, New York: Doubleday, 331–345.

Grayling, A.C. (1996) "Russell's Transcendental Argument in *An Essay on the Foundations of Geometry*", in Monk, Ray, and Anthony Palmer (eds), *Bertrand Russell and The Origins of Analytical Philsophy*, Bristol: Thoemmes, 245–267.

Green, Joe L. (1979) "Dewey, Russell, and the Integration of the Social", *Educational Theory*, 29, 285–296.

Greenfield, Howard (1987) *The Devil and Dr Barnes*, New York: Viking, 199–214, 215–230 (chapters 18 and 19).

Greenspan, Louis (1996) "Bertrand Russell and the End of Nationalism", *Philosophy of the Social Sciences*, 26, 348–368.

Greenspan, Louis (1996) "The History of Western Philosophy – Fifty Years Later", in Monk, Ray, and Anthony Palmer (eds), *Bertrand Russell and The Origins of Analytical Philsophy*, Bristol: Thoemmes, 363–383.

Grelling, Kurt (1929) "Realism and Logic: An Investigation of Russell's Metaphysics", *Monist*, 39, 501–520.

Griffin, Nicholas (1972) "Russell's Later Political Thought", *Russell*, o.s. 5, 3–6.

Griffin, Nicholas (1974–75) "Russell in Australia", *Russell*, o.s. 16, 3–12.

Griffin, Nicholas (1977) "Russell's 'Horrible Travesty' of Meinong", *Russell*, o.s. 25–28, 39–51.

Griffin, Nicholas (1979–80) "The Philosophical Importance of Russell's *Collected Papers*", *Russell*, o.s. 35–36, 17–23.

Griffin, Nicholas (1980) "Russell on the Nature of Logic (1903–1913)", *Synthese*, 45, 117–188.

Griffin, Nicholas (1981) "The Collected Papers of Bertrand Russell", *History and Philosophy of Logic*, 2, 121–131.

Griffin, Nicholas (1982) "New Work on Russell's Early Philosophy", *Russell*, n.s. 2, 69–83.

Griffin, Nicholas (1983) "Reply to Demopoulos", *Russell*, n.s. 3, 43–47.

Griffin, Nicholas (1984) "Bertrand Russell's Crisis of Faith", *Russell*, n.s. 4, 101–122. Repr. in Moran, Margaret, and Carl Spadoni (eds), *Intellect and Social Conscience: Essays on Bertrand Russell's Early Work*, Hamilton: McMaster University Library Press, 101–122.

Griffin, Nicholas (1985) "Russell's Critique of Meinong's Theory of Objects", *Grazer Philosophische Studien*, 25–26, 375–401.

Griffin, Nicholas (1985) "Russell's Multiple Relation Theory of Judgement", *Philosophical Studies*, 47, 213–248.

Griffin, Nicholas (1985) "Wittgenstein's Criticism of Russell's Theory of Judgement", *Russell*, n.s. 5, 132–145.

Griffin, Nicholas (1987–88) "Joachim's Early Advice to Russell on Studying Philosophy", *Russell*, n.s. 7, 119–123.

Griffin, Nicholas (1988) "The Tiergarten Programme", *Russell*, n.s. 8, 19–34. Repr. in Winchester, Ian, and Kenneth Blackwell (eds), *Antinomies and Paradoxes: Studies in Russell's Early Philosophy*, Hamilton: McMaster University Library Press, 19–34.

Griffin, Nicholas (1989) "Russell and Sidgwick", *Russell*, n.s. 9, 12–25.

Griffin, Nicholas (1992–93) "The Legacy of Russell's Idealism for His Later Philosophy: The Problem of Substance", *Russell*, n.s. 12, 186–196.

Griffin, Nicholas (1993) "Terms, Relations, Complexes", in Irvine, A.D., and G.A. Wedeking (eds), *Russell and Analytic Philosophy*, Toronto: University of Toronto Press, 159–192.

Griffin, Nicholas (1995) "Onto the Past! What the 1990s Mean to Bertrand Russell", *Free Inquiry*, 15, no. 4 (Fall), 45–46.

Griffin, Nicholas (1996) "Denoting Concepts in *The Principles of Mathematics*", in Monk, Ray, and Anthony Palmer (eds), *Bertrand Russell and The Origins of Analytical Philosophy*, Bristol: Thoemmes, 23–64.

Griffin, Nicholas, and Albert C. Lewis (1990) "Bertrand Russell's Mathematical Education", *Notes and Records of the Royal Society of London*, 44, 51–71.

Griffin, Nicholas, and Alison Miculan (1993) "The Decemviri", *Russell*, n.s. 13, 48–62.

Griffin, Nicholas, and Gad Zak (1982) "Russell on Specific and Universal Relations", *History and Philosophy of Logic*, 3, 55–67.

Griffiths, D.A. (1976) "Russell on Existence and Descriptions", *Philosophical Quarterly*, 26, 157–162.

Griffiths, D.A. (1981) "A Reconsideration of Russell's Early Ontological Development", *Philosophical Quarterly*, 31, 145–152.

Grossmann, Reinhardt (1972) "Russell's Paradox and Complex Properties", *Nous*, 6, 153–164.

Grossmann, Reinhardt (1975) "Definite Descriptions", *Philosophical Studies*, 27, 127–144.

Guthrie, Edwin (1915) "Russell's Theory of Types", *Journal of Philosophy, Psychology, and Scientific Methods*, 12, 381–385.

Gyekye, Kwame (1973) "An Examination of the Bundle-Theory of Substance", *Philosophy and Phenomenological Research*, 34, 51–61.

Hackett, Francis (1918) "Beyond Patriotism", in Hackett, Francis, *Horizons*, New York: Huebsch, 328–336.

Hager, Paul J. (1979) "Russell Resurrected", *Proceedings of the Russellian Society* (University of Sydney), 4, 1–13.

Hager, Paul J. (1987) "Russell and Zeno's Arrow Paradox", *Russell*, n.s. 7, 3–10.

Hager, Paul J. (1993–94) "Why Russell Didn't Think He Was a Philosopher of Education", *Russell*, n.s. 13, 150–167.

Hager, Paul J. (1995) "A Russellian Approach to Philosophy of Education", in Neiman, Alven (ed.), *Philosophy of Education*, Urbana: Philosophy of Education Society, 269–276.

Hager, Paul J. (1996) "Relational Realism and Professional Performance", *Educational Philosophy and Theory*, 28, 98–116.

Hailperin, Theodore, and Hughes Leblanc (1959) "Nondesignating Singular Terms", *Philosophical Review*, 68, 239–243.

Halbasch, Keith (1971) "A Critical Examination of Russell's View of Facts", *Nous*, 5, 395–409.

Haldane, John (1996) "Intentionality and One-Sided Relations", *Ratio*, 9, 95–114.

Haldane, John Burdon Sanderson (1933) "A Mathematician Looks at Science", in Haldane, John Burdon Sanderson, *Science and Human Life*, New York: Harper, 246–252.

Haldane, R.B. (1909) "The Logical Foundations of Mathematics", *Mind*, 18, 1–39.

Hall, Roland (1964) "The Term 'Sense-Datum'", *Mind*, 73, 130–131.

Halldén, Sören (1948) "Certain Problems Connected with the Definition of Identity and of Definite Descriptions Given in *Principia Mathematica*", *Analysis*, 9, 29–33.

Hambourger, Robert (1977) "A Difficulty with the Frege–Russell Definition of Number", *Journal of Philosophy*, 74, 409–414.

Hamilton, Walton H. (1941) "Trial by Ordeal, New Style", *Yale Law Journal*, 50, 778–786. Repr. in Dewey, John, and Horace M. Kallen (eds), *The Bertrand Russell Case*, New York: Viking, 1941, 75–90.

Hampshire, Stuart N. (1952) "Bertrand Russell: His Contribution to Philosophy", *Manchester Guardian*, 17 May, 4, 6.

Hampshire, Stuart N. (1967) "The Education of Bertrand Russell", *New York Review of Books*, 8/7 (20 April), 3–4.

Hampshire, Stuart N. (1970) "The Autobiography of Bertrand Russell – I and II", in Hampshire, Stuart N., *Modern Writers and Other Essays*, New York: Knopf, 111–119, 120–129.

Hampshire, Stuart N. (1972) "Russell, Radicalism, and Reason", in Held, Virginia, Kai Nielsen, and Charles Parson (eds), *Philosophy and Political Action*, New York: Oxford University Press, 258–274.

Hampshire, Stuart N. (1989) "Engaged Philosopher", *New York Review of Books*, 2 February, 7–10.

Hansson, Bengt (1967) "Some Incompatibilities in Russell's *Introduction to Mathematical Philosophy*", *Theoria*, 33, 133–138.

Hardin, Russell (1996) "Russell's Power", *Philosophy of the Social Sciences*, 26, 322–347.

Hardy, G.H. (1912) "The New Realism", *The Cambridge Magazine*, 1 (11 and 18 May), 314–315, 341–342.

Hardy, G.H. (1917) "Mr Russell as a Religious Teacher", *The Cambridge Magazine*, 6, 624–626, 650–653. Repr. in *Russell*, n.s. 1 (1981–82), 119–135.

Hare, William (1987) "Russell's Contribution to Philosophy of Education", *Russell*, n.s. 7, 25–41. Repr. in Hare, William, *Attitudes in Teaching and Education*, Calgary: Detselig, 1993, 27–43.

Hark, Michael Ter (1994) "Cognitive Science, Propositional Attitudes, and the Debate Between Russell and Wittgenstein", in Meggle, Georg, and Ulla Wessels (eds), *Analyomen 1: Proceedings of the First Conference: Perspectives in Analytical Philosophy*, Berlin: Walter de Gruyter, 612–617.

Harley, David (1979–80) "Beacon Hill School", *Russell*, o.s. 35–36, 5–16.

Harrell, Martha (1988) "Extension to Geometry of *Principia Mathematica* and Related Systems II", *Russell*, n.s. 8, 140–160. Repr. in Winchester, Ian, and Kenneth Blackwell (eds), *Antinomies and Paradoxes: Studies in Russell's Early Philosophy*, Hamilton: McMaster University Library Press, 1988, 140–160.

Harrison, Brian (1984) "Bertrand Russell: The False Consciousness of a Feminist", *Russell*, n.s. 4, 157–205. Repr. in Moran, Margaret, and Carl Spadoni (eds), *Intellect and Social Conscience: Essays on Bertrand Russell's Early Work*, Hamilton: McMaster University Library Press, 1984, 157–205.

Harrison, Royden (1985) "Bertrand Russell and the Webbs", *Russell*, n.s. 5, 44–49.

Harrison, Royden (1986) "Bertrand Russell: From Liberalism to Socialism?", *Russell*, n.s. 6, 5–38.

Harrison, Royden (1989) "'Science of Social Structure': Bertrand Russell as Communist and Marxist", *Russell*, n.s. 9, 5–11.

Hart, H.L.A. (1949) "Is There Knowledge by Acquaintance?", *Aristotelian Society*, Supplementary Vol. 23, 69–90.

Hart, W.D. (1983) "Russell and Ramsey", *Pacific Philosophical Quarterly*, 64, 193–210.

Hartshorne, Charles (1968) "Russell on Causality", in Hartshorne, Charles, *Beyond Humanism*, Lincoln: University of Nebraska Press, 211–224.

Hartshorne, Charles (1983) "Russell and Whitehead: A Comparison", in Hartshorne, Charles, *Insights and Oversights of Great Thinkers*, New York: State University of New York Press, 255–268.

Harwood, Larry D. (1997) "Russell's Reticence with Religion", *Russell*, n.s. 17, 27–41.

Hauerwas, Stanley (1978) "Sex and Politics: Bertrand Russell and *Human Sexuality*", *Christian Century*, 95, 417–422.

Hausman, David B. (1974) "Russell on Negative Facts", *Southwestern Journal of Philosophy*, 12, 49–53.

Hawkins, Benjamin (1997) "Peirce and Russell: The History of a Neglected 'Controversy'", in Houser, Nathan, Don D. Roberts, and James Van Evra (eds), *Studies in the Logic of Charles Sanders Peirce*, Bloomington, IND.: Indiana University Press, 111–146.

Hawkins, Denis John Bernard (1962) "Moore, Russell, and Sense-Data", in Hawkins, Denis John Bernard, *Crucial Problems of Modern Philosophy*, Notre Dame: University of Notre Dame Press, 55–65.

Hawthorne, James (1989) "Giving Up Judgement Empiricism: The Bayesian Epistemology of Bertrand Russell and Grover Maxwell", in Savage, C. Wade, and C. Anthony Anderson (eds), *Rereading Russell: Essays on Bertrand Russell's Metaphysics and Epistemology*, Minneapolis: University of Minnesota Press, 234–248.

Hay, William H. (1950) "Bertrand Russell on the Justification of Induction", *Philosophy of Science*, 17, 266–277.

Hayhurst, Stephen (1991) "Russell's Anti-Communist Rhetoric Before and After Stalin's Death", *Russell*, n.s. 11, 67–82.

Hayner, Paul (1969) "Knowledge by Acquaintance", *Philosophy and Phenomenological Research*, 29, 423–431.

Heath, A.E. (1919) "The Principle of Parsimony and Ethical Neutrality", *Monist*, 29, 448–450.

Heath, A.E. (1920) "Logical Atomism and the Law of Parsimony", *Monist*, 30, 309–310.

Hellman, Geoffrey (1981) "How to Gödel a Frege–Russell: Gödel's Incompleteness Theorems and Logicism", *Nous*, 15, 451–468.

Hempel, Carl G. (1966) "On Russell's Phenomenological Constructionism", *Journal of Philosophy*, 63, 668–669.

Hendley, Brian Patrick (1986) "Bertrand Russell and the Beacon Hill School", in Hendley, Brian Patrick, *Dewey, Russell, Whitehead: Philosophers as Educators*, Carbondale: Southern Illinois University Press, 43–74.

Henkin, Leon (1949) "Completeness in the Theory of Types", *Journal of Symbolic Logic*, 14, 159–166.

Henkin, Leon (1953) "Banishing the Rule of Substitution for Functional Variables", *Journal of Symbolic Logic*, 18, 201–208.

Henkin, Leon (1962) "Are Mathematics and Logic Identical?", *Science*, 138 (no. 3542, 16 November), 788–794.

Herrick, Jim (1985) "Bertrand Russell: A Passionate Rationalist", in Herrick, Jim, *Against the Faith*, Buffalo: Prometheus, 214–229.

Herzberger, Hans G. (1980) "New Paradoxes for Old", *Proceedings of the Aristotelian Society*, 81, 109–123.

Hicks, G. Dawes (1912) "The Nature of Sense-Data", *Mind*, 21, 399–409.

Hicks, G. Dawes (1919) "Is There 'Knowledge by Acquaintance'?", *Aristotelian Society*, Supplementary Vol. 2, 159–178.

Hill, Claire Ortiz (1991) "Presentations and Ideas", in Hill, Claire Ortiz, *Word and Object in Husserl, Frege, and Russell*, Athens: Ohio University Press, 125–135.

Hill, Thomas English (1961) "English Realism", in Hill, Thomas English, *Contemporary Theories of Knowledge*, New York: Ronald, 161–205.

Hinderliter, Hilton (1990) "More on Russell's Hypothesis", *Philosophy of Science*, 57, 703–711.

Hintikka, Jaakko (1959) "Existential Presuppositions and Existential Commitment", *Journal of Philosophy*, 63, 125–137.

Hintikka, Jaakko (1959) "Towards a Theory of Definite Descriptions", *Analysis*, 19, 79–85.

Hintikka, Jaakko (1970) "Objects of Knowledge and Belief: Acquaintances and Public Figures", *Journal of Philosophy*, 67, 869–883.

Hintikka, Jaakko (1972) "Knowledge by Acquaintance – Individuation by Acquaintance", in Pears, David F. (ed.), *Bertrand Russell: A Collection of Critical Essays*, Garden City, N.Y.: Anchor Books, 52–79.

Hintikka, Jaakko (1979) "Virginia Woolf and our Knowledge of the External World", *Journal of Aesthetics and Art Criticism*, 38, 5–14.

Hintikka, Jaakko (1981) "On Denoting What?", *Synthese*, 46, 167–183.

Hintikka, Jaakko (1981) "Russell, Kant, and Coffa", *Synthese*, 46, 265–270.

Hintikka, Jaakko, and Jack Kulas (1982) "Russell Vindicated: Towards a General Theory of Definite Descriptions", *Journal of Semantics*, 1, 387–397.

Hiz, H. (1977) "Descriptions in Russell's Theory and in Ontology", *Studia Logica*, 36, 271–283.

Hobhouse, L.T. (1907) "Sociology and Ethics", *The Independent Review*, 12, 322–331.

Hochberg, Herbert (1956) "Peano, Russell, and Logicism", *Analysis*, 16, 118–120. Repr. in Klemke, E.D. (ed.), *Essays on Bertrand Russell*, Urbana: University of Illinois Press, 1970, 369–371.

Hochberg, Herbert (1957) "Descriptions, Scope, and Identity", *Analysis*, 18, 20–22. Repr. in Klemke, E.D. (ed.), *Essays on Bertrand Russell*, Urbana: University of Illinois Press, 1970, 205–208.

Hochberg, Herbert (1959) "St Anselm's Ontological Argument and Russell's Theory of Descriptions", *The New Scholasticism*, 33, 319–330.

Hochberg, Herbert (1966) "Things and Descriptions", *American Philosophical Quarterly*, 3, 39–47. Repr. in Klemke, E.D. (ed.), *Essays on Bertrand Russell*, Urbana: University of Illinois Press, 1970, 65–80.

Hochberg, Herbert (1970) "Russell's Reduction of Arithmetic to Logic", in Klemke, E.D. (ed.), *Essays on Bertrand Russell*, Urbana: University of Illinois Press, 396–415.

Hochberg, Herbert (1970) "Strawson, Russell and the King of France", *Philosophy of Science*, 37, 363–384. Repr. in Klemke, E.D. (ed.), *Essays on Bertrand Russell*, Urbana: University of Illinois Press, 1970, 309–337.

Hochberg, Herbert (1976) "Russell's Attack on Frege's Theory of Meaning", *Philosophica*, 18, 9–34.

Hochberg, Herbert (1980) "Russell's Proof of Realism Reproved", *Philosophical Studies*, 37, 37–44.

Hochberg, Herbert (1987) "Russell, Ramsey, and Wittgenstein on Ramification and Quantification", *Erkenntnis*, 27, 257–281.

Hochberg, Herbert (1989) "Descriptions, Situations, and Russell's Extensional Analysis of Intentionality", *Philosophy and Phenomenological Research*, 49, 555–581.

Hochberg, Herbert (1989) "Russell's Paradox, Russellian Relations, and the Problems of Predication and Impredicativity", in Savage, C. Wade, and C. Anthony Anderson (eds), *Rereading Russell: Essays on Bertrand Russell's Metaphysics and Epistemology*, Minneapolis: University of Minnesota Press, 63–87.

Hochberg, Herbert (1994) "Causal Connections, Universals, and Russell's Hypothetico-Scientific Realism", *Monist*, 77, 71–92.

Hochberg, Herbert (1995) "Abstracts, Functions, Existence and Relations in the Russell–Meinong Dispute, the Bradley Paradox and the Realism–Nominalism Controversy", *Grazer Philosophische Studien*, 50, 273–291.

Hochberg, Herbert (1995) "Particulars as Universals: Russell's Ontological Assay of Particularity and Phenomenological Space–Time", *Journal of Philosophical Research*, 20, 83–111.

Hochberg, Herbert (1996) "Particulars, Universals and Russell's Late Ontology", *Journal of Philosophical Research*, 21, 129–137.

Hoensbroech, F. Graf (1939) "On Russell's Paradox", *Mind*, 48, 365–368.

Hoernlé, Reinhold F.A. (1916) "The Religious Aspect of Bertrand Russell's Philosophy", *Harvard Theological Review*, 9, 157–189.

Hoernlé, Reinhold Friedrich Alfred (1952) "On the Theory of Error in Mr Bertrand Russell's *Problems of Philosophy*", in Hoernlé, Reinhold Friedrich Alfred, *Studies in Philosophy*, Cambridge, Mass.: Harvard University Press, 98–124.

Holdcroft, D. (1980) "From the One to the Many: Philosophy, 1900–30", in Bell,

Michael (ed.), *In the Context of English Literature: 1900–1930*, New York: Holmes and Meier, 126–159.

Honderich, Ted (1969) "On the Theory of Descriptions", *Proceedings of the Aristotelian Society*, 69, 87–100.

Hook, Sidney (1941) "The General Pattern", in Dewey, John, and Horace M. Kallen (eds), *The Bertrand Russell Case*, New York: Viking, 185–210.

Hook, Sidney (1944) "Bertrand Russell's Philosophy of History", in Schilpp, Paul Arthur (ed.), *The Philosophy of Bertrand Russell*, 3rd edn, New York: Tudor, 1951, 643–678.

Hook, Sidney (1955) "A Question of Means and Ends in a World Threatened by Evil", *New York Times Book Review*, 30 January, sec. 7, 3.

Hook, Sidney (1966) "Lord Russell and the War Crimes Trial", *The New Leader*, 49 (24 October), 6–11. Repr. as "Bertrand Russell and Crimes Against Humanity", in Hook, Sidney, *Philosophy and Public Policy*, Carbondale: Southern Illinois University Press, 1980, 207–217.

Hook, Sidney (1984) "Bertrand Russell: A Portrait From Memory", *Encounter*, 62 (3 March), 9–20.

Hooker, C.A. (1972) "Definite Descriptions", *Philosophical Studies*, 23, 365–375.

Hookway, Christopher (1992) "Russell and the Possibility of Scepticism", *Journal of Speculative Philosophy*, 6, 95–110.

Hope, V. (1969) "The Picture Theory of Meaning in the *Tractatus* as a Development of Moore's and Russell's Theories of Judgement", *Philosophy*, 44, 140–148.

Hopkins, Kenneth (1985) "Bertrand Russell and Gamel Woolsey", *Russell*, n.s. 5, 50–65.

Horowitz, Irving Louis (1957) "Bertrand Russell on War and Peace", *Science and Society*, 21, 30–51. Repr. as "Bertrand Russell: Man Against Man", in Horowitz, Irving Louis, *The Idea of War and Peace in Contemporary Philosophy*, New York: Paine-Whitman, 1957, 107–123.

Hoskyn, F.P. (1930) "The Adjectival Theory of Matter", *Journal of Philosophy*, 27, 655–668.

Howard, Anthony (1980) "Bertrand Russell: The Patrician Rebel", *The Listener*, 103 (17 January), 70–72.

Hoy, Ronald C. (1973) "The Unverifiability of Unverifiability", *Philosophy and Phenomenological Research*, 33, 393–398.

Hughes, Emrys (1962) "Bertrand Russell – Ninety", *New Times*, 21, 18–20.

Hughes, G.F. (1935) "Good Adults – *Not* Good Children: Bertrand Russell on the Teacher's Job", *Senior Teacher's World*, 48, 297.

Hughes, George E. (1949) "Is There Knowledge by Acquaintance?", *Aristotelian Society*, Supplementary Vol. 23, 91–110.

Hughes, Percy (1916) "The Two Poles of the Philosophical Sphere", *Journal of Philosophy, Psychology, and Scientific Methods*, 13, 631–635.

Hulme, Thomas Ernest (1955) "North Staffs Continues Where He Left Off", in Hulme, Thomas Ernest, *Further Speculations*, Minneapolis: University of Minnesota Press, 199–205.

Hulme, Thomas Ernest (1955) "North Staffs Resents Mr Russell's Rejoinder", in Hulme, Thomas Ernest, *Further Speculations*, Minneapolis: University of Minnesota Press, 193–198.

Hunter, Graeme (1993) "Russell Making History: The Leibniz Book", in Irvine, A.D., and G.A. Wedeking (eds), *Russell and Analytic Philosophy*, Toronto: University of Toronto Press, 397–414.

Huntington, E.V. (1933) "New Sets of Independence Postulates for the Algebra of Logic, With Special Reference to Whitehead and Russell's *Principia Mathema-*

tica", *Transactions of the American Mathematical Society*, 35, 274–304, 557–558, 971.

Huntington, E.V. (1934) "Independent Postulates for an 'Informal' *Principia* System With Equality", *Bulletin of the American Mathematical Society*, 40, 137–143.

Huntington, E.V. (1934) "Independent Postulates for the 'Informal' Part of *Principia Mathematica*", *Bulletin of the American Mathematical Society*, 40, 127–136.

Huntington, E.V. (1935) "The Inter-Deducibility of the New Hilbert–Bernays Theory and *Principia Mathematica*", *Annals of Mathematics*, 36, 313–324.

Hurley, Patrick J. (1979) "Russell, Poincaré, and Whitehead's 'Relational Theory of Space'", *Process Studies*, 9, 14–21.

Hursthouse, Rosalind (1980) "Denoting in *The Principles of Mathematics*", *Synthese*, 45, 33–42.

Hussey, Charles (1962) "Earl, Philosopher, Logician, Rebel", *New York Times Magazine*, 13 May, sec. 6, 10, 102, 104.

Huxley, Aldous (1967) "The Relevance of Style", in Schoenman, Ralph (ed.), *Bertrand Russell: Philosopher of the Century*, London: Allen and Unwin, 91–94.

Hylton, Peter W. (1980) "Russell's Substitutional Theory", *Synthese*, 45, 1–31.

Hylton, Peter W. (1984) "The Nature of the Proposition and the Revolt Against Idealism", in Rorty, Richard, J.B. Schneewind, and Quentin Skinner (eds), *Philosophy in History*, Cambridge: Cambridge University Press, 375–397.

Hylton, Peter W. (1989) "The Significance of 'On Denoting'", in Savage, C. Wade, and C. Anthony Anderson (eds), *Rereading Russell: Essays on Bertrand Russell's Metaphysics and Epistemology*, Minneapolis: University of Minnesota Press, 88–107.

Hylton, Peter W. (1990) "Logic in Russell's Logicism", in Bell, David, and Neil Cooper (eds), *The Analytic Tradition: Philosophical Quarterly Monographs*, Vol. 1, Oxford: Blackwell, 137–172.

Hylton, Peter W. (1993) "Functions and Propositional Functions in *Principia Mathematica*", in Irvine, A.D., and G.A. Wedeking (eds), *Russell and Analytic Philosophy*, Toronto: University of Toronto Press, 342–360.

Hylton, Peter W. (1996) "Beginning with Analysis", in Monk, Ray, and Anthony Palmer (eds), *Bertrand Russell and The Origins of Analytical Philosophy*, Bristol: Thoemmes, 183–216.

Iglesias, M. Teresa (1977) "Russell's Introduction to Wittgenstein's 'Tractatus'", *Russell*, o.s. 25–28, 21–38.

Iglesias, M. Teresa (1981) "Russell and Wittgenstein: Two Views of Ordinary Language", *Philosophical Studies* (Ireland), 28, 149–163.

Iglesias, M. Teresa (1984) "Russell's *Theory of Knowledge* and Wittgenstein's Earliest Writings", *Synthese*, 60, 285–332.

Irvine, A.D. (1989) "Epistemic Logicism and Russell's Regressive Method", *Philosophical Studies*, 55, 303–327.

Irvine, A.D. (1996) "Bertrand Russell and Academic Freedom", *Russell*, n.s. 16, 5–36.

Irvine, William B. (1984) "Russell's Construction of Space from Perspectives", *Synthese*, 60, 333–348.

Iseminger, Gary (1986) "Russell's Much-Admired Argument Against Naive Realism", *Journal of Indian Council of Philosophical Research*, 4, 173–176.

Jacobson, Arthur (1970) "Russell and Strawson on Referring", in Klemke, E.D. (ed.), *Essays on Bertrand Russell*, Urbana: University of Illinois Press, 285–308.

Jadacki, Jacek Juliusz (1986) "Leon Chwistek–Bertrand Russell's Scientific Correspondence", *Dialectics and Humanism*, 13, 239–263.

Jager, Ronald (1960) "Russell's Denoting Complex", *Analysis*, 20, 53–62.

Jager, Ronald (1976) "Russell and Religion", in Thomas, J.E., and Kenneth Blackwell (eds), *Russell in Review*, Toronto: Samuel Stevens, Hakkert and Co., 91–113.

Jarrett, J.L. (1959) "D.H. Lawrence and Bertrand Russell", in Moore, Harry Thornton (ed.), *D.H. Lawrence Miscellany*, Carbondale: Southern Illinois University Press, 168–187.

Jeffreys, Harold (1938) "The Nature of Mathematics", *Philosophy of Science*, 5, 434–451.

Jeffreys, Harold (1950) "Bertrand Russell on Probability", *Mind*, 59, 313–319.

Joad, C.E.M. (1927) Bertrand Russell: The Man and the Things He Stands For", *The New Leader*, 14, no. 49, 8.

Joad, C.E.M. (1947) "Bertrand Russell's *History of Western Philosophy*", *Proceedings of the Aristotelian Society*, 47, 85–104.

Johnson, A.H. (1960) "Leibniz's Method and the Basis of his Metaphysics", *Philosophy*, 35, 51–61.

Johnson, P.O. (1992) "Wholes, Parts, and Infinite Collections", *Philosophy*, 67, 367–379.

Jones, E.E. Constance (1910) "Mr Russell's Objections to Frege's Analysis of Propositions", *Mind*, 19, 379–386.

Jones, Martin, and Clive Wood (1983) "A Conversation With Bertrand Russell", *Russell*, n.s. 3, 17–20.

Jourdain, Philip E.B. (1911, 1916) "The Philosophy of Mr B*rtr*nd R*ss*ll", *Monist*, 21, 481–508; 26, 24–62.

Jourdain, Philip E.B. (1912) "Mr Bertrand Russell's First Work on the Principles of Mathematics", *Monist*, 22, 149–158.

Jourdain, Philip E.B. (1919) "Cause and Effect", *Monist*, 29, 453–467.

Jourdain, Philip E.B. (1919) "The Logical Significance of 'Ockham's Razor'", *Monist*, 29, 450–451.

Judson, Lindsay (1987) "Russell on Memory", *Proceedings of the Aristotelian Society*, 88, 65–82.

Kaiser, Nolan (1972) "Russell's Paradox and the Residual Achilles", *Apeiron*, 6, 39–48.

Kalish, D., and R. Montague (1956) "Remarks on Descriptions and Natural Deduction (I and II)", *Archiv für Mathematische Logik und Grundlagenforschung*, 3, 50–64, 65–73.

Kallen, Horace M. (1940) "Behind the Bertrand Russell Case", *Twice a Year*, 5–6 (November), 441–466. Repr. in Dewey, John, and Horace M. Kallen (eds), *The Bertrand Russell Case*, New York: Viking, 1941, 13–53.

Kaplan, David (1970) "What is Russell's Theory of Descriptions?", in Yourgrau, Wolfgang, and Allen D. Breck (eds), *Physics, Logic, and History*, New York: Plenum, 277–288. Repr. in Pears, David F. (ed.), *Bertrand Russell: A Collection of Critical Essays*, Garden City, N.Y.: Anchor Books, 1972, 227–244.

Kaplan, David (1975) "How to Russell a Frege–Church", *Journal of Philosophy*, 72, 716–729.

Kaplan, David (1979) "The Logic of Demonstratives", in French, Peter A., Theodore E. Uehling, Jr, and Howard K. Wettstein (eds), *Contemporary Perspectives in the Philosophy of Language*, Minneapolis: University of Minnesota Press, 401–410.

Kattsoff, Louis Osgood (1948) "Frege's Definition of Number", in Kattsoff, Louis Osgood, *Philosophy of Mathematics*, Ames: Iowa State College Press, 24–47.

Kayden, Eugene M. (1930) "A Tract on Sex and Marriage", *Sewanee Review*, 38, 104–108.

Keane, E.F. (1961) "Bertrand Russell and the Emotive Theory", *Indian Journal of Philosophy*, 3, 26–36.

Keen, C.N. (1971) "The Interaction of Russell and Bradley", *Russell*, o.s. 3, 7–11.

Kennedy, H.C. (1973) "What Russell Learned from Peano", *Notre Dame Journal of Formal Logic*, 14, 367–371.

Kennedy, H.C. (1975) "Nine Letters from Guiseppe Peano to Bertrand Russell", *Journal of the History of Philosophy*, 13, 205–220.

Kennedy, Thomas C. (1972) "Philosopher as Father-Confessor", *Russell*, o.s. 5, 11–13.

Kennedy, Thomas C. (1974) "The Women's Man for Wimbledon", *Russell*, o.s. 14, 19–26.

Kennedy, Thomas C. (1984) "Nourishing Life: Russell and the Twentieth-Century British Peace Movement, 1900–1918", *Russell*, n.s. 4, 223–236. Repr. in Moran, Margaret, and Carl Spadoni (eds), *Intellect and Social Conscience: Essays on Bertrand Russell's Early Work*, Hamilton: McMaster University Library Press, 1984, 223–236.

Kenyon, Timothy A. (1991) "Russell on Pastness", *Dialogue (PST)*, 33, 57–59.

Kerss, Diane M. (1977) "Russell, Stopes and Birth Control", *Russell*, o.s. 25–28, 72–74.

Keyser, Cassius J. (1916) "Scientific Method in Philosophy", *Bulletin of the American Mathematical Society*, 23, 91–97.

Kilmister, C.M. (1996) "A Certain Knowledge? Russell's Mathematics and Logical Analysis", in Monk, Ray, and Anthony Palmer (eds), *Bertrand Russell and The Origins of Analytical Philosophy*, Bristol: Thoemmes, 269–286.

King-Farlow, John (1977) "Self-Enlargement and Union: Neglected Passages of Russell and Some Famous Ones of Proust", *Theoria to Theory*, 11, 105–115.

King-Hele, Desmond (1965) "Shelley and Nuclear Disarmament Demonstrations", *Keats–Shelley Memorial Bulletin*, 16, 39–41.

King-Hele, Desmond (1974–75) "A Discussion with Bertrand Russell at Plas Penrhyn, 4 August 1968", *Russell*, o.s. 16, 21–25.

Kleene, G.A. (1919) "Bertrand Russell on Socialism", *Quarterly Journal of Economics*, 34, 756–762.

Klemke, E.D. (1970) "Logic and Ontology in Russell's Philosophy", in Klemke, E.D. (ed.), *Essays on Bertrand Russell*, Urbana: University of Illinois Press, 416–444.

Kline, A. David (1985) "Humean Causation and the Necessity of Temporal Discontinuity", *Mind*, 94, 550–556.

Kneale, William C. (1934) "The Objects of Acquaintance", *Proceedings of the Aristotelian Society*, 34, 187–210.

Kneale, William C. (1936) "Is Existence a Predicate?", *Aristotelian Society*, Supplementary Vol. 15, 154–174.

Kneale, William C. (1968) "Methods of Designation", *Proceedings of the Aristotelian Society*, 68, 249–270.

Kneale, William C. (1971) "Russell's Paradox and Some Others", *British Journal for the Philosophy of Science*, 22, 321–338. Repr. in Roberts, George W. (ed.), *Bertrand Russell Memorial Volume*, London: Allen and Unwin, 1979, 34–51.

Kneale, William C., and Martha Kneale (1962) "The Philosophy of Mathematics After Frege", in Kneale, William C., and Martha Kneale, *The Development of Logic*, Oxford: Clarendon Press, 652–688.

Knight, Frank H. (1939) "Bertrand Russell on Power", *Ethics*, 49, 253–285.

Knowles, Owen (1988) "Conrad and Bertrand Russell: New Light on Their Relationship", *Conradiana: Journal of the Joseph Conrad Society*, 13, 192–202.

Koehler, Conrad J. (1972) "Studies in Bertrand Russell's Theory of Knowledge", *Revue Internationale de Philosophie*, 26, 499–512.

Kohl, Marvin (1969) "Bertrand Russell on Vagueness", *Australasian Journal of Philosophy*, 47, 31–41.

Kohl, Marvin (1984) "Russell and the Attainability of Happiness", *International Studies in Philosophy*, 16, 15–24.

Kohl, Marvin (1987) "Russell on the Utility of Religion: Copleston's Critique", *International Journal for Philosophy of Religion*, 22, 69–79.

Kohl, Marvin (1987) "Russell's Happiness Paradox", *Russell*, n.s. 7, 86–88.

Kohl, Marvin (1992–93) "Bertrand Russell's Characterization of Benevolent Love", *Russell*, n.s. 12, 117–134.

Kohl, Marvin (1995) "Russell and the Happy Life", *Free Inquiry*, 15, no. 4 (Fall), 43.

Korner, Stephan (1979) "On Russell's Critique of Leibniz's Philosophy", in Roberts, George W. (ed.), *Bertrand Russell Memorial Volume*, London: Allen and Unwin, 171–181.

Kreisel, Georg (1967) "Mathematical Logic: What Has it Done for the Philosophy of Mathematics?", in Schoenman, Ralph (ed.), *Bertrand Russell: Philosopher of the Century*, London: Allen and Unwin, 201–272, 315–316.

Kreisel, Georg (1972) "Bertrand Russell's Logic", in Pears, David F. (ed.), *Bertrand Russell: A Collection of Critical Essays*, Garden City, N.Y.: Anchor Books, 168–174.

Kreisel, Georg (1973) "Bertrand Arthur William Russell, Earl Russell: 1872–1970", *Biographical Memoirs of Fellows of the Royal Society*, 19, 583–620.

Kremer, Michael (1994) "The Argument of 'On Denoting'", *Philosophical Review*, 103, 249–297.

Krikorian, Yervant H., *et al.* (1941) "The College, The Community, and the Bertrand Russell Case", in Dewey, John, and Horace M. Kallen (eds), *The Bertrand Russell Case*, New York: Viking, 169–184.

Kripke, Saul A. (1972) "Naming and Necessity", in Davidson, Donald, and Gilbert Harman (eds), *Semantics of Natural Language*, Dordrecht: Reidel, 253–355, 763–769.

Kultgen, J.H. (1956) "Operations and Events in Russell's Empiricism", *Journal of Philosophy*, 53, 157–167.

Kuntz, Paul Grimley (1988) "Whitehead the Anglican and Russell the Puritan: The Traditional Origins of Muddleheadedness and Simplemindedness", *Process Studies*, 17, 40–44.

Kuroda, Sigekatu (1958) "An Investigation on the Logical Structure of Mathematics (V): Contradictions of Russell's Type", *Journal of Symbolic Logic*, 23, 393–407.

Lackey, Douglas P. (1972) "The Whitehead Correspondence", *Russell*, o.s. 5, 14–16.

Lackey, Douglas P. (1974–75) "Russell's Anticipation of Quine's Criterion", *Russell*, o.s. 16, 27–31.

Lackey, Douglas P. (1976) "Russell's Unknown Theory of Classes: The Substitutional System of 1906", *Journal of the History of Philosophy*, 14, 69–78.

Lackey, Douglas P. (1981) "Russell's 1913 Map of the Mind", *Midwest Studies in Philosophy*, 6, 125–142.

Lackey, Douglas P. (1984–85) "Russell's Contribution to the Study of Nuclear Weapons Policy", *Russell*, n.s. 4, 243–252.

Lackey, Douglas P. (1996) "Reply to Perkins on 'Conditional Preventive War'", *Russell*, n.s. 16, 85–88.

Laird, John (1919) "The Law of Parsimony", *Monist*, 29, 321–344.

Laird, John (1920) "Logical Atomism and the Law of Parsimony", *Monist*, 30, 307–309.

Laird, John (1944) "On Certain of Russell's Views Concerning the Human Mind", in Schilpp, Paul Arthur (ed.), *The Philosophy of Bertrand Russell*, 3rd edn, New York: Tudor, 1951, 293–316.

Lambert, Karel (1974) "Impossible Objects", *Inquiry*, 17, 303–314.

Lambert, Karel (1984) "What is Russell's Theory of Descriptions? An Addendum", *Pacific Philosophical Quarterly*, 65, 140–148.

Lambert, Karel (1990) "Russell's Theory of Definite Descriptions", *Dialectica*, 44, 137–152.

Lambert, Karel (1992) "Russell's Version of the Theory of Definite Descriptions", *Philosophical Studies*, 65, 153–167.

Lamond, Corliss (1973) "The Bertrand Russell Centenary Celebrations, *The Humanist*, 33, no. 1, 23.

Landini, Gregory (1987) "Russell's Substitutional Theory of Classes and Relations", *History and Philosophy of Logic*, 8, 171–200.

Landini, Gregory (1989) "New Evidence Concerning Russell's Substitutional Theory of Classes", *Russell*, n.s. 9, 26–42.

Landini, Gregory (1991) "A New Interpretation of Russell's Multiple-Relation Theory of Judgement", *History and Philosophy of Logic*, 12, 37–69.

Landini, Gregory (1992–93) "Russell to Frege, 24 May 1903: 'I Believe I Have Discovered That Classes are Entirely Superfluous'", *Russell*, n.s. 12, 160–185.

Landini, Gregory (1993) "Reconciling *PM*'s Ramified Type Theory with the Doctrine of the Unrestricted Variable of the *Principles*", in Irvine, A.D., and G.A. Wedeking (eds), *Russell and Analytic Philosophy*, Toronto: University of Toronto Press, 361–394.

Landini, Gregory (1996) "The 'Definability' of the Set of Natural Numbers in the 1925 *Principia Mathematica*", *Journal of Philosophical Logic*, 25, 597–615.

Landini, Gregory (1996) "Will the Real *Principia Mathematica* Please Stand Up? Reflections on the Formal Logic of the *Principia*", in Monk, Ray, and Anthony Palmer (eds), *Bertrand Russell and The Origins of Analytical Philosophy*, Bristol: Thoemmes, 287–330.

Langer, S.K. (1926) "Confusion of Symbols and Confusion of Logical Types", *Mind*, 35, 222–229.

Langford, C.H. (1929) "General Propositions", *Mind*, 38, 436–457.

Lazerowitz, Morris, (1979) "The Infinite", in Roberts, George W. (ed.), *Bertrand Russell Memorial Volume*, London: Allen and Unwin, 222–241.

Leavitt, Frank J. (1972) "On an Unpublished Remark of Russell's on 'If . . . Then'", *Russell*, o.s. 6, 10.

Lee, H.N. (1958) "Note on '⊃' and '⊢' in Whitehead and Russell's *Principia Mathematica*", *Mind*, 67, 250–253.

Lehman, Craig K. (1985) "Realism, Resemblances, and Russell's Regress", *Journal of Critical Analysis*, 8, 99–108.

Leithauser, Gladys Garner (1978) "'A Non-Supernatural Faust': Bertrand Russell and the Themes of Faust", *Russell*, o.s. 29–32, 33–41.

Leithauser, Gladys Garner (1984) "The Romantic Russell and the Legacy of Shelley", *Russell*, n.s. 4, 31–48. Repr. in Moran, Margaret, and Carl Spadoni (eds), *Intellect and Social Conscience: Essays on Bertrand Russell's Early Work*, Hamilton: McMaster University Library Press, 1984, 31–48.

Leithauser, Gladys Garner (1993) "Spirited Satire: The Fiction of Bertrand Russell", *Russell*, n.s. 13, 63–82.

Leithauser, Gladys Garner (1995) "Bertrand Russell's Intellectual Odyssey", *Free Inquiry*, 15, no. 4 (Fall), 39–41.

Leithauser, Gladys Garner, and Nadine Cowan Dyer (1982) "Bertrand Russell and T.S. Eliot: Their Dialogue", *Russell*, n.s. 2, 7–28.

Lejewski, Czeslaw (1960) "A Re-Examination of the Russellian Theory of Descriptions", *Philosophy*, 35, 14–29.

Lenz, John R. (1987–88) "Russell and the Greeks", *Russell*, n.s. 7, 104–118.

Lenzen, V.F. (1919) "Independence Proofs and the Theory of Implication", *Monist*, 29, 152–160.

Lenzen, V.F. (1971) "Bertrand Russell at Harvard, 1914", *Russell*, o.s. 3, 4–6.

Lenzen, V.F. (1974) "Peirce, Russell, and Achilles", *Transactions of the Charles S. Peirce Society*, 10, 3–7.

Leonard, Henry (1956) "The Logic of Existence", *Philosophical Studies*, 7, 49–64.

Levin, Bernard (1967) "Bertrand Russell – Prosecutor, Judge and Jury", *New York Times Magazine*, 19 February, 24, 55, 57, 60, 62, 67–68.

Lewis, Albert C. (1989) "The Influence of Roger Boscovich on Bertrand Russell's Early Philosophy of Physics", *Synthesis Philosophica*, 4, 649–658.

Lewis, Albert C., and Nicholas Griffin (1990) "Russell's Mathematical Education", *Notes and Records of the Royal Society*, 44, 51–71.

Lewis, C.I. (1913) "Interesting Theorems in Symbolic Logic", *Journal of Philosophy, Psychology, and Scientific Methods*, 10, 239–242.

Lewis, C.I. (1917) "The Issues Concerning Material Implication", *Journal of Philosophy, Psychology, and Scientific Methods*, 14, 350–356.

Lewis, C.I. (1918) "The Logic of *Principia Mathematica*", in Lewis, C.I., *A Survey of Symbolic Logic*, New York: Dover, 1960, 279–290.

Lichtheim, George, (1973) "The Birth of a Philosopher", in Lichtheim, George, *Collected Essays*, New York: Viking, 104–110.

Lindberg, Jordan J. (1990) "From Russell to Quine: Basic Statements, Foundationalism, Truth, and Other Myths", *Dialogue (PST)*, 33, 27–31.

Lindeman, E.C. (1944) "Russell's Concise Social Philosophy", in Schilpp, Paul Arthur (ed.), *The Philosophy of Bertrand Russell*, 3rd edn, New York: Tudor, 1951, 557–577.

Lindsay, James (1920) "The Logic of the New Realism", *Philosophical Review*, 29, 476–480.

Linsky, Bernard (1988) "Propositional Functions and Universals in *Principia Mathematica*", *Australasian Journal of Philosophy*, 66, 447–460.

Linsky, Bernard (1990) "Was the Axiom of Reducibility a Principle of Logic?", *Russell*, n.s. 10, 125–140. Reprinted in Tait, William W. (ed.), *Early Analytic Philosophy: Frege, Russell, Wittgenstein*, Chicago: Open Court, 1997, 107–122.

Linsky, Bernard (1993) "Why Russell Abandoned Russellian Propositions", in Irvine, A.D., and G.A. Wedeking (eds), *Russell and Analytic Philosophy*, Toronto: University of Toronto Press, 193–209.

Linsky, Bernard (1995) "Russell's Logical Constructions", *Studies in Dialectics of Nature* (Beijing), Supplementary Vol. 11, 129–148.

Linsky, Leonard (1962) "Reference and Referents", in Caton, C.E. (ed.), *Philosophy and Ordinary Language*, Urbana: University of Illinois Press, 74–89. Repr. in Klemke, E.D. (ed.), *Essays on Bertrand Russell*, Urbana: University of Illinois Press, 1970, 220–235.

Linsky, Leonard (1966) "Substitutivity and Descriptions", *Journal of Philosophy*, 63, 673–683.

Linsky, Leonard (1967) "Russell's Theory of Descriptions", in Linsky, Leonard, *Referring*, London: Routledge and Kegan Paul, 49–66.

Linsky, Leonard (1983) "Russell's Solution to Frege's Paradox", in Linsky, Leonard, *Oblique Contexts*, Chicago: University of Chicago Press, 13–43.

Linsky, Leonard (1983) "Russell's Theory of Oblique Contexts", in Linsky, Leonard, *Oblique Contexts*, Chicago: University of Chicago Press, 69–81.

Linsky, Leonard (1987) "Russell's 'No-Classes' Theory of Classes", in Thomson, Judith Jarvis (ed.), *On Being and Saying*, Cambridge: MIT Press, 21–39.

Linsky, Leonard (1988) "Terms and Propositions in Russell's *Principles of Mathematics*", *Journal of the History of Philosophy*, 26, 621–642.

Linsky, Leonard (1992) "The Unity of the Proposition", *Journal of the History of Philosophy*, 30, 243–273.

Lipkind, Donald (1979) "Russell on the Notion of Cause", *Canadian Journal of Philosophy*, 9, 701–720.

Lippincott, Mark S. (1990) "Russell's Leviathan", *Russell*, n.s. 10, 6–29.

Lockwood, Michael (1981) "What *Was* Russell's Neutral Monism?", *Midwest Studies in Philosophy*, 6, 143–158.

Lovejoy, Arthur O. (1929) "Mr Bertrand Russell and the Unification of Mind and Matter", in Lovejoy, Arthur O., *The Revolt Against Dualism*, Chicago: Open Court, 190–256.

Lowe, Victor (1974) "Whitehead's 1911 Criticism of *The Problems of Philosophy*", *Russell*, o.s. 13, 3–10.

Lucas, B.J. (1971) "Moore's Influence on Russell", *Russell*, o.s. 1, 9–10.

Lucas, B.J. (1975) "Russell on the Socratic Question", *Russell*, o.s. 18, 3–9.

Lucas, George R. (1988) "'Muddleheadedness' Versus 'Simplemindedness' – Comparisons of Whitehead and Russell", *Process Studies*, 17, 26–39.

Lucas, George R. (1989) "Whitehead and Russell", in Lucas, George R., *The Rehabilitation of Whitehead*, New York: State University of New York Press, 109–125.

Ludlow, Peter (1991) "Indefinite Descriptions: In Defense of Russell", *Linguistics and Philosophy*, 14, 171–202.

Lycan, William G. (1970) "Transformational Grammar and the Russell–Strawson Dispute", *Metaphilosophy*, 1, 335–337.

Lycan, William G. (1981) "Logical Atomism and Ontological Atoms", *Synthese*, 46, 207–229.

Lycan, William G. (1993) "Russell's Strange Claim That '*a* exists' Is Meaningless Even When *a* Does Exist", in Irvine, A.D., and G.A. Wedeking (eds), *Russell and Analytic Philosophy*, Toronto: University of Toronto Press, 140–156.

McCawley, J.D. (1988) "Actions and Events Despite Bertrand Russell", in LePore, Ernest, and Brian P. McLaughlin (eds), *Actions and Events*, Oxford: Blackwell, 177–192.

MacColl, Hugh (1905) "The Existential Import of Propositions", Mind, 14, 401–402. Repr. in Russell, Bertrand, *Essays in Analysis*, London: George Allen and Unwin, 1973, 317–319.

MacColl, Hugh (1905) "The Existential Import of Propositions", *Mind*, 14, 578–579. Repr. in Russell, Bertrand, *Essays in Analysis*, London: George Allen and Unwin, 1973, 319–322.

McCollum, Dannel Angus (1977) "Tea With Bertrand Russell in 1961", *Russell*, o.s. 25–28, 67–71.

McDermott, Michael (1988) "A Russellian Account of Belief Sentences", *Philosophical Quarterly*, 38, 141–157.

Macdonald, Margaret (1936) "Russell and McTaggart", *Philosophy*, 11, 322–335.

McDonough, Richard (1994) "A Note on Frege's and Russell's Influence on Wittgenstein's *Tractatus*", *Russell*, n.s. 14, 39–46.

McGeehan, J. (1940) "Decision of Justice McGeehan", in Dewey, John, and Horace M. Kallen (eds), *The Bertrand Russell Case*, New York: Viking, 1941, 213–225.

McGill, V.J. (1944) "Russell's Political and Economic Philosophy", in Schilpp, Paul Arthur (ed.), *The Philosophy of Bertrand Russell*, 3rd edn, New York: Tudor, 1951, 579–617.

McGilvary, Evander Bradley (1939) "Relations in General and Universals in Particular", *Journal of Philosophy*, 36, 5–15, 29–40.

McGuinness, Brian (1972) "Bertrand Russell's and Ludwig Wittgenstein's 'Notes on Logic'", *Revue Internationale de Philosophie*, 26, 444–460.

McGuinness, Brian, and G.H. Von Wright (1990–91) "Unpublished Correspondence Between Russell and Wittgenstein", *Russell*, n.s. 10, 101–124.

McKenney, John L. (1958) "Concerning Russell's Analysis of Value Judgements", *Journal of Philosophy*, 55, 382–389.

McKenney, John L. (1959) "Dewey and Russell: Fraternal Twins in Philosophy", *Educational Theory*, 9, 24–30.

McKeon, Richard (1941) "The Problems of Education in a Democracy", in Dewey, John, and Horace M. Kallen (eds), *The Bertrand Russell Case*, New York: Viking, 91–130.

McKinney, J.P. (1957) "Philosophical Implication of Logical Analysis", *Hibbert Journal*, 55, 249–259.

McKinsey, J.C.C. (1935) "On a Redundancy in *Principia Mathematica*", *Mind*, 44, 270–271.

McKinsey, Michael (1979) "The Ambiguity of Definite Descriptions", *Theoria*, 45, 78–89.

McLaughlin, Brendan (1970) "Russell, Philosopher King", *Month*, 1 (April), 235–237.

McLendon, Hiram J. (1952) "Has Russell Answered Hume?", *Journal of Philosophy*, 49, 145–159.

McLendon, Hiram J. (1956) "Has Russell Proved Naive Realism Self-Contradictory?", *Journal of Philosophy*, 53, 289–302.

McLendon, Hiram J. (1957) "Russell's Portraits and Self-Portraits from Memory", *Journal of Philosophy*, 54, 264–279.

MacLennan, Hugh (1991) "The Clearest Intellect of Our Age", *Russell*, n.s. 11, 83–85.

McMahon, M. Brian (1976) "Russell's Denoting Relation", *The Personalist*, 57, 345–350.

Magee, Brian, and Anthony Quinton (1970) "Conversations with Philosophers: Russell, Moore, Wittgenstein and Austin", *Listener*, 84 (10 December), 805–809.

Magee, Brian, and Anthony Quinton (1970) "Conversations with Philosophers: Stuart Hampshire Talks to Bryan Magee About Bertrand Russell's Contribution to Philosophy", *Listener*, 84 (17 December), 839–842.

Magee, Brian, Peter Strawson, and Geoffrey Warnock (1970) "Bertrand Russell's Theory of Descriptions", *Listener*, 83 (21 May), 685–686.

Magee, Bryan, *et al.* (1971) "The Philosophy of Russell: I and II", in Magee, Bryan, *Modern British Philosophy*, London: Secker and Warburg, 17–30, 131–149.

Magnell, Thomas (1991) "The Extent of Russell's Modal Views", *Erkenntnis*, 34, 171–185.

Makin, Gideon (1995) "Making Sense of 'On Denoting'", *Synthese*, 102, 383–412.

Makin, Gideon (1996) "Why the Theory of Descriptions?", *Philosophical Quarterly*, 46, 158–167.

Malleson, Constance (1967) "Fifty Years: 1916–1966", in Schoenman, Ralph (ed.), *Bertrand Russell: Philosopher of the Century*, London: Allen and Unwin, 17–25.

Maracchia, S. (1971) "Plato and Russell on the Definition of Mathematics", *Scientia*, 106, 216–223.

Marcus, Ruth Barcan (1993) "On Some Post-1920s Views of Russell on Particularity, Identity, and Individuation", in Marcus, Ruth Barcan, *Modalities*, Oxford: Oxford University Press, 177–188.

Marquis, Jean-Pierre (1993) "Russell's Logicism and Categorical Logicisms", in Irvine, A.D., and G.A. Wedeking (eds), *Russell and Analytic Philosophy*, Toronto: University of Toronto Press, 293–324.

Marseille, Walter W. (1958) "Not War, Not Peace", *Bulletin of the Atomic Scientists*, 14, 140–143, 159.

Marsh, Robert C. (1972) "Russell's Educational Views in the World of 1972", in Thomas, J.E., and Kenneth Blackwell (eds), *Russell in Review*, Toronto: Samuel Stevens, Hakkert and Co., 1976, 115–133.

Marsh, Robert C. (1995) "Talking with Russell: 1951–55", *Russell*, n.s. 15, 21–35.

Martin, Richard M. (1952) "On the Berkeley–Russell Theory of Proper Names", *Philosophy and Phenomenological Research*, 13, 221–231.

Martin, Richard M. (1964) "The Philosophic Import of Virtual Classes", *Journal of Philosophy*, 61, 377–386.

Martin, Richard M. (1979) "Truth, Belief and Modes of Description", in Roberts, George W. (ed.), *Bertrand Russell Memorial Volume*, London: Allen and Unwin, 253–263.

Martinich, Aloysius P. (1975) "Russell, Frege and the Puzzle of Denoting", *International Studies in Philosophy*, 7, 145–154.

Martinich, Aloysius P. (1976) "Russell's Theory of Meaning and Descriptions", *Journal of the History of Philosophy*, 14, 183–201.

Martinich, Aloysius P. (1983) "Sense, Reference, and Russell's Theory of Descriptions", *Journal of the History of Philosophy*, 21, 85–92.

Mason, Daniel Gregory (1921) "Bertrand Russell on Music and Mathematics", in Mason, Daniel Gregory, *Music as a Humanity*, New York: H.W. Gray, 91–94.

Mason, Marilyn (1983–84) "'The Sins of Civilization': Bertrand Russell in Toronto", *Russell*, n.s. 3, 145–156.

Mason, Richard (1996) "Russell, Bertrand Arthur William", in Brown, Stuart, Dianē Collinson, and Robert Wilkinson (eds), *Biographical Dictionary of Twentieth-Century Philosophers*, London: Routledge, 683–687.

Mates, Benson (1973) "Descriptions and Reference", *Foundations of Language*, 10, 409–418.

Matson, W.I. (1979) "Russell's Ethics", in Roberts, George W. (ed.), *Bertrand Russell Memorial Volume*, London: Allen and Unwin, 422–427.

Mattai, Bansraj (1990–91) "Education and the Emotions: The Relevance of the Russellian Perspective", *Russell*, n.s. 10, 141–157.

Maurer, A.A. (1966) "Return to Realism", in Gilson, Etienne Henry (ed.), *Recent Philosophy, Hegel to the Present*, New York: Random House, 485–519.

Maxwell, Grover (1972) "Russell on Perception: A Study in Philosophical Method", in Pears, David F. (ed.), *Bertrand Russell: A Collection of Critical Essays*, Garden City, N.Y.: Anchor Books, 110–146.

Maxwell, Grover (1974) "The Later Bertrand Russell: Philosophical Revolutionary", in Nakhnikian, George (ed.), *Bertrand Russell's Philosophy*, London: Duckworth, 169–182.

Maxwell, Grover (1975) "Russell on Perception and Mind–Body: A Study in Philosophical Method", in Cheng, Chung-ying (ed.), *Philosophical Aspects of the Mind-Body Problem*, Honolulu: University of Hawaii Press, 131–153.

Maziarz, Edward A. (1949) "Russell and Human Knowledge", *The New Scholasticism*, 23, 318–328.

Mehta, Ved Parkash (1963) "Argument Without End", in Mehta, Ved Parkash, *Fly and the Fly-Bottle: Encounters with British Intellectuals*, London: Weidenfeld and Nicolson, 106–192.

Menzel, Christopher (1993) "Singular Propositions and Modal Logic", *Philosophical Topics*, 21, 113–148.

Mercier, Louis J.A. (1947) "A Symposium on Bertrand Russell's *History of Western Philosophy* – Introduction", *Franciscan Studies*, 7, 72–77.

Meyer, Adolph Erich (1934) "Russell and Beacon Hill", in Meyer, Adolph Erich, *Modern European Educators and Their Work*, Englewood Cliffs, N.J.: Prentice-Hall, 183–196.

Meyers, Robert G. (1970) "Knowledge by Acquaintance: A Reply to Hayner", *Philosophy and Phenomenological Research*, 31, 293–296.

Miah, Sajahan (1987) "The Emergence of Russell's Logical Construction of Physical Objects", *Russell*, n.s. 7, 11–24.

Michell, Joel (1993) "The Origins of the Representational Theory of Measurement: Helmholtz, Hölder, and Russell", *Studies in History and Philosophy of Science*, 24, 185–206.

Mijuskovic, Ben (1976) "The Simplicity Argument in Wittgenstein and Russell", *Critica*, 8, 85–103.

Monk, Ray (1994–95) "The Madness of Truth: Russell's Admiration for Joseph Conrad", *Russell*, n.s. 14, 119–134.

Monk, Ray (1996) "The Tiger and the Machine: D.H. Lawrence and Bertrand Russell", *Philosophy of the Social Sciences*, 26, 205–246.

Monk, Ray (1996) "What is Analytical Philosophy?", in Monk, Ray, and Anthony Palmer (eds), *Bertrand Russell and The Origins of Analytical Philosophy*, Bristol: Thoemmes, 1–22.

Monro, D.H. (1960) "Russell's Moral Theories", *Philosophy*, 35, 30–50. Repr. in Pears, David F. (ed.), *Bertrand Russell: A Collection of Critical Essays*, Garden City, N.Y.: Anchor Books, 1972, 325–355.

Montague, William P. (1906) "The Meaning of Identity, Similarity, and Non-Entity: A Criticism of Mr Russell's Logical Puzzles", *Journal of Philosophy, Psychology, and Scientific Methods*, 3, 127–131.

Moorcroft, Francis (1993) "Why Russell's Paradox Won't Go Away", *Philosophy*, 68, 99–104.

Moore, A.W. (1914) "Isolated Knowledge", *Journal of Philosophy, Psychology, and Scientific Methods*, 11, 393–408.

Moore, G.E. (1918) "Some Judgments of Perception", *Proceedings of the Aristotelian Society*, 19, 1–29. Repr. in Moore, G.E., *Philosophical Studies*, London: Routledge and Kegan Paul, 1951, 220–252.

Moore, G.E. (1919) "Is There 'Knowledge by Acquaintance'?", *Aristotelian Society*, Supplementary Vol. 2, 179–193.

Moore, G.E. (1936) "Is Existence a Predicate?", *Aristotelian Society*, Supplementary Vol. 15, 175–188.

Moore, G.E. (1944) "Russell's 'Theory of Descriptions'", in Schilpp, Paul Arthur (ed.), *The Philosophy of Bertrand Russell*, 3rd edn, New York: Tudor, 1951, 175–225. Repr. in Moore, G.E., *Philosophical Papers*, London: George Allen and Unwin, 1959, 151–195.

Moore, G.E. (1959) "Russell's Theory of Descriptions", in Moore, G.E., *Philosophical Papers*, New York: Macmillan, 151–195.

Moore, Gregory H. (1988) "The Roots of Russell's Paradox", *Russell*, n.s. 8, 46–56. Repr. in Winchester, Ian, and Kenneth Blackwell (eds), *Antinomies and Paradoxes: Studies in Russell's Early Philosophy*, Hamilton: McMaster University Library Press, 1988, 46–56.

Moran, Margaret (1982) "Men of Letters: Bertrand Russell and Joseph Conrad", *Russell*, n.s. 2, 29–46.

Moran, Margaret (1983) "Bertrand Russell's First Short Story", *Dalhousie Review*, 63, 575–589.

Moran, Margaret (1984) "Bertrand Russell as Scogan in Aldous Huxley's *Crome Yellow*", *Mosaic*, 17, 117–131.

Moran, Margaret (1984) "Bertrand Russell's Early Approaches to Literature", *University of Toronto Quarterly*, 54, 56–78.

Moran, Margaret (1985) "'The World as It Can Be Made': Bertrand Russell's Protest Against the First World War", *Prose Studies*, 8, 51–68.

Moran, Margaret (1991) "Bertrand Russell Meets His Muse: The Impact of Lady Ottoline Morrell (1911–12)", *Russell*, n.s. 11, 180–192.

Morris, Charles W. (1929) "Has Russell Passed the Tortoise?", *Journal of Philosophy*, 26, 449–459.

Morris, Charles W. (1932) "Mind as Relation", in Morris, Charles W., *Six Theories of Mind*, Chicago: University of Chicago Press, 102–148.

Morris, William Edward (1979) "Moore and Russell on Philosophy and Science", *Metaphilosophy*, 10, 111–138.

Morscher, E. (1977) "Russell's Theory of Description as a Vehicle for a Translation from 'Ought' to 'Is' and *Vice Versa*", *Logique et Analyse*, 20, 129–133.

Moss, J.M.B. (1972) "Some B. Russell's Sprouts (1903–1908)", in Hodges, Wilfrid (ed.), *Conference in Mathematical Logic – London '70* (Lecture Notes in Mathematics, 255), Berlin: Springer Verlag, 211–250.

Moulder, James (1974) "Is Russell's Paradox Genuine?", *Philosophy*, 49, 295–302.

Mudrick, Marvin (1979) "Aged Eagles and Dirty Old Men", in Mudrick, Marvin, *Books Are Not Life, but Then What Is?*, Oxford: Oxford University Press, 132–142.

Muehlmann, Robert (1969) "Russell and Wittgenstein on Identity", *Philosophical Quarterly*, 19, 221–230.

Murray, Joseph (1991) "Acquaintance with Logical Objects in *Theory of Knowledge*", *Russell*, n.s. 11, 147–164.

Mursell, James L. (1919) "The Critical Philosophy and the Theory of Types", *Journal of Philosophy, Psychology, and Scientific Methods*, 16, 347–352.

Musgrave, Alan (1977) "Logicism Revisited", *British Journal for the Philosophy of Science*, 28, 99–127.

Myhill, John (1951) "Report of Some Investigations Concerning the Consistency of the Axiom on Reducibility", *Journal of Symbolic Logic*, 16, 35–42.

Myhill, John (1974) "The Undefinability of the Set of Natural Numbers in the Ramified *Principia*", in Nakhnikian, George (ed.), *Bertrand Russell's Philosophy*, London: Duckworth, 19–27.

Myhill, John (1979) "A Refutation of an Unjustified Attack on the Axiom of Reducibility", in Roberts, George W. (ed.), *Bertrand Russell Memorial Volume*, London: Allen and Unwin, 81–90.

Nagel, Ernest (1941) "Mr Russell on Meaning and Truth", *Journal of Philosophy*, 38, 253–270.

Nagel, Ernest (1944) "Russell's Philosophy of Science", in Schilpp, Paul Arthur (ed.), *The Philosophy of Bertrand Russell*, 3rd edn, New York: Tudor, 1951, 317–349.

Nagel, Ernest (1954) "Basis of Human Knowledge", in Nagel, Ernest, *Sovereign Reason*, New York: Free Press, 211–215.

Nagel, Ernest (1954) "Mr Russell on Meaning and Truth", in Nagel, Ernest, *Sovereign Reason*, New York: Free Press, 190–210.

Nagel, Ernest (1954) "Philosophy of Bertrand Russell", in Nagel, Ernest, *Sovereign Reason*, New York: Free Press, 161–189.

Najjar, Ibrahim (1987) "Russell's Criticisms of 'The Common-Sense View of Desire'", *Russell*, n.s. 7, 124–136.

Najjar, Ibrahim, and Heather Kirkconnell (1975) "Russell's Foreword to the First German Translation of *The Problems of Philosophy*", *Russell*, o.s. 17, 27–29.

Nakhnikian, George (1974) "Some Questions about Bertrand Russell's Liberalism", in Nakhnikian, George (ed.), *Bertrand Russell's Philosophy*, London: Duckworth, 221–226.

Narskii, I.S., and Pomogaeva, E.F. (1973) "Bertrand Russell – Philosopher and Humanist", *Soviet Studies in Philosophy*, 12, 33–50.

Nathanson, Stephen (1985) "Russell's Scientific Mysticism", *Russell*, n.s. 5, 14–25.

Neale, Stephen (1993) "Grammatical Form, Logical Form, and Incomplete Symbols", in Irvine, A.D., and G.A. Wedeking (eds), *Russell and Analytic Philosophy*, Toronto: University of Toronto Press, 97–139.

Nelson, E.J. (1934) "Whitehead and Russell's Theory of Deduction as a Non-Mathematical Science", *Bulletin of the American Mathematical Society*, 40, 478–486.

Nelson, John O. (1964) "On Sommers' Reinstatement of Russell's Ontological Program", *Philosophical Review*, 73, 517–521.

Nemesszeghy, E.Z., and E.A. Nemesszeghy (1971) "Is $(p \supset q) = (\sim p \vee q)$ Df. A Proper Definition in the System of *Principia Mathematica*?", *Mind*, 80, 282–283.

Neumann, Henry (1930) "How to be Happy with Russell", *Survey*, 65, 284.

Newberry, Jo (1971) "1916", *Russell*, o.s. 2, 9–10.

Newberry, Jo (1972) "How World War I Changed Bertrand Russell", *Humanist in Canada*, 5, no. 4, 17–19.

Newberry, Jo (1974) "Russell as Ghost-Writer", *Russell*, o.s. 15, 19–23.

Newberry, Jo (1976) "Russell and the Pacifists in World War I", in Thomas, J.E., and Kenneth Blackwell (eds), *Russell in Review*, Toronto: Samuel Stevens, Hakkert and Co., 33–55.

Newman, M.H.A. (1928) "Mr Russell's 'Causal Theory of Perception'", *Mind*, 37, 137–148.

Nicholson, Katherine (1993) "The Psychiatrist's Nightmare", *Russell*, n.s. 13, 83–86.

Nicod, Jean G.P. (1916) "A Reduction in the Number of Primitive Propositions of Logic", *Proceedings of the Cambridge Philosophical Society*, 19, 32–41.

Nielsen, Kai (1958) "Bertrand Russell's New Ethic", *Methodos*, 10, 151–182.

Noonan, Harold (1996) "The 'Gray's Elegy' Argument – and Others", in Monk, Ray, and Anthony Palmer (eds), *Bertrand Russell and The Origins of Analytical Philosophy*, Bristol: Thoemmes, 65–102.

Norman, Jack (1969) "Russell and *Tractatus* 3: 1432", *Analysis*, 29, 190–192.

Novak, John (1995) "Why I Am Not a Russellian", *Free Inquiry*, 15, no. 4 (Fall), 38–39.

Nubiola, Jaime (1994–95) "Russell, Crexells, and d'Ors: Barcelona, 1920", *Russell*, n.s. 14, 155–161.

Nusenoff, Ronald E. (1978) "Russell's External World: 1912–1921", *Russell*, o.s. 29–32, 65–82.

O'Briant, Walter H. (1979) "Russell on Leibniz", *Studia Leibnitiana*, 11, 159–222.

O'Connor, D.J. (1964) "Bertrand Russell", in O'Connor, D.J. (ed.), *A Critical History of Western Philosophy*, New York: The Free Press, 473–491.

O'Connor, D.J. (1979) "Russell's Theory of Perception", in Roberts, George W. (ed.), *Bertrand Russell Memorial Volume*, London: Allen and Unwin, 304–320.

O'Grady, Paul (1995) "The Russellian Roots of Naturalized Epistemology", *Russell*, n.s. 15, 53–63.

O'Leary, Daniel J. (1988) "The Propositional Logic of *Principia Mathematica* and

Some of its Forerunners", *Russell*, n.s. 8, 92–115. Repr. in Winchester, Ian, and Kenneth Blackwell (eds), *Antinomies and Paradoxes: Studies in Russell's Early Philosophy*, Hamilton: McMaster University Library Press, 1988, 92–115.

O'Leary, Daniel J. (1991) "*Principia Mathematica* and the Development of Automated Theorem Proving", in Drucker, Thomas (ed.) *Perspectives on the History of Mathematical Logic*, Basle: Birkhäuser, 47–53.

Oaklander, L. Nathan (1982) "Does the Russellian Theory of Time Entail Fatalism?", *The Modern Schoolman*, 59, 206–212.

Oaklander, L. Nathan (1983) "The Russellian Theory of Time", *Philosophia*, 12, 363–392.

Oaklander, L. Nathan, and Silvano Miracchi (1980) "Russell, Negative Facts, and Ontology", *Philosophy of Science*, 47, 434–455.

Ogden, Suzanne P. (1982) "The Sage and the Inkpot: Bertrand Russell and China's Social Reconstruction in the 1920s", *Modern Asian Studies*, 16, 529–600.

Organ, Troy (1986) "The Humor of Bertrand Russell", *The Humanist*, 46 (6), 24–27.

Orilia, Francesco (1991) "Type-Free Property Theory, Exemplification and Russell's Paradox", *Notre Dame Journal of Formal Logic*, 32, 432–447.

Over, D.E. (1987) "Russell's Hierarchy of Acquaintance", *Philosophical Papers*, 16, 107–124.

Padia, Chandrakala (1986–87) "Is Russell a Political Philosopher: A Critique of His Critiques", *Russell*, n.s. 6, 134–143.

Pakaluk, Michael (1992) "The Doctrine of Relations in Bertrand Russell's *Principles of Mathematics*", *Topicos*, 2, 153–182.

Pakaluk, Michael (1993) "The Interpretation of Russell's 'Gray's Elegy' Argument", in Irvine, A.D., and G.A. Wedeking (eds), *Russell and Analytic Philosophy*, Toronto: University of Toronto Press, 37–65.

Pal, Jagat (1993) "Balzer's Solution to Russell's Paradox", *Journal of Value Inquiry*, 27, 539–540.

Palmer, Anthony (1996) "The Complex Problem and the Theory of Symbolism", in Monk, Ray, and Anthony Palmer (eds), *Bertrand Russell and The Origins of Analytical Philosophy*, Bristol: Thoemmes, 155–182.

Pap, Arthur (1953) "Logic, Existence and the Theory of Descriptions", *Analysis*, 13, 97–111.

Pape, Helmut (1982) "Peirce and Russell on Proper Names", *Transactions of the Charles S. Peirce Society*, 18, 339–348.

Parker, DeWitt H. (1945) "Knowledge By Acquaintance", *Philosophical Review*, 54, 1–18.

Parker, DeWitt H. (1945) "Knowledge by Description", *Philosophical Review*, 54, 458–488.

Parkinson, G.H.R. (1970) "Bertrand Russell, 1872–1970", *Studia Leibnitiana*, 2, 161–170.

Parris, Henry (1965) "The Political Thought of Bertrand Russell", *Durham University Journal*, 58, 86–94.

Parsons, Terence D. (1988) "Russell's Early Views on Denoting", in Austin, David F. (ed.), *Philosophical Analysis*, Dordrecht: Kluwer, 17–44.

Passmore, John Arthur (1957) "Moore and Russell", in Passmore, John Arthur, *A Hundred Years of Philosophy*, New York: Macmillan, 203–41.

Passmore, John Arthur (1969) "Russell and Bradley", in Brown, Robert, and C.D. Rollins, *Contemporary Philosophy in Australia*, London: Allen and Unwin, 21–30.

Passmore, John Arthur (1994–95) "Editing Russell's Papers: A Fragment of Institutional History", *Grazer Philosophische Studien*, 49, 189–205.

Patterson, Wayne A. (1996) "The Logical Structure of Russell's Negative Facts", *Russell*, n.s. 16, 45–66.

Patton H.J. (1941) "The Purpose of Words", *The Spectator*, 166, 150, 152.

Pauling, Linus (1967) "Would Civilization Survive a Nuclear War?", in Schoenman, Ralph (ed.), *Bertrand Russell: Philosopher of the Century*, London: Allen and Unwin, 80–88.

Pears, David F. (1956) "Logical Atomism: Russell and Wittgenstein", in Ayer, A.J., *et al.*, *The Revolution in Philosophy*, London: Macmillan, 41–55.

Pears, David F. (1972) "Russell's Logical Atomism", in Pears, David F. (ed.), *Bertrand Russell: A Collection of Critical Essays*, Garden City, N.Y.: Anchor Books, 23–51.

Pears, David F. (1974) "Russell's Theories of Memory 1912–1921", in Nakhnikian, George (ed.), *Bertrand Russell's Philosophy*, London: Duckworth, 117–138.

Pears, David F. (1975) "Russell's Theory of Desire", in Pears, David F., *Questions in the Philosophy of Mind*, London: Duckworth, 251–272. Repr. in Thomas, J.E., and Kenneth Blackwell (eds), *Russell in Review*, Toronto: Samuel Stevens, Hakkert and Co., 1976, 215–235.

Pears, David F. (1977) "The Relation Between Wittgenstein's Picture Theory and Russell's Theories of Judgement", *Philosophical Review*, 86, 177–196.

Pears, David F. (1979) "A Comparison Between Ayer's Views about the Privileges of Sense-Datum Statements and the Views of Russell and Austin", in Macdonald, G.F. (ed.), *Perception and Identity*, New York: Cornell University Press, 61–83.

Pears, David F. (1981) "The Function of Acquaintance in Russell's Philosophy", *Synthese*, 46, 149–166.

Pears, David F. (1989) "Russell's 1913 *Theory of Knowledge* Manuscript", in Savage, C. Wade, and C. Anthony Anderson (eds), *Rereading Russell: Essays on Bertrand Russell's Metaphysics and Epistemology*, Minneapolis: University of Minnesota Press, 169–182.

Pelham, Judy (1993) "Russell's Philosophy of Logic", in Irvine, A.D., and G.A. Wedeking (eds), *Russell and Analytic Philosophy*, Toronto: University of Toronto Press, 325–341.

Pelletier, Francis Jeffrey, and John King-Farlow (1975) "Relations: Turning Russell's Other Flank", *Southern Journal of Philosophy*, 13, 359–367.

Perkins, Ray, Jr (1971) "On Russell's Alleged Confusion of Sense and Reference", *Analysis*, 32, 45–51.

Perkins, Ray, Jr (1972) "Urmson on Russell's Incomplete Symbols", *Analysis*, 32, 200–203.

Perkins, Ray, Jr (1973) "Russell on Memory", *Mind*, 82, 600–601.

Perkins, Ray, Jr (1976) "Russell's Realist Theory of Remote Memory", *Journal of the History of Philosophy*, 14, 358–360.

Perkins, Ray, Jr (1979–80) "Russell's Unpublished Book on Theory of Knowledge", *Russell*, o.s. 35–36, 37–40.

Perkins, Ray, Jr (1982) "Russell, Frege, and the Meaning of the Theory of Descriptions (or): Did Russell Know his Frege?", *Journal of the History of Philosophy*, 20, 407–424.

Perkins, Ray, Jr (1994–95) "Bertrand Russell and Preventive War", *Russell*, n.s. 14, 135–153.

Perkins, Ray, Jr (1996–97) "Response to Lackey on 'Conditional Preventive War'", *Russell*, n.s. 16, 169–170.

Perrott, Roy (1970) "In Search of Bertrand Russell", *Observer*, 8 February, 21.

Perry, Ralph Barton (1916) "A Realistic Theory of Knowledge", in Perry, Ralph Barton, *Present Philosophical Tendencies*, New York: Longmans Green, 306–328.

Perry, Ralph Barton (1927) "Realism in England and America", in Perry, Ralph Barton, *Philosophy of the Recent Past*, London: Charles Scribner's Sons, 211–220.

Perszyk, Kenneth J. (1984) "The Nyaya and Russell on Empty Terms", *Philosophy East and West*, 34, 131–146.

Peters, Franz (1963) "Russell on Class Theory", *Synthese*, 15, 327–335.

Phillips, Cliff (1983) "The Pipe of Peace", *Russell*, n.s. 3, 21–23.

Philpot, Terry (1969) "The Russells and Beacon Hill", *Humanist*, 84, 173–175.

Pigden, Charles R. (1996) "Bertrand Russell: A Neglected Ethicist", in Monk, Ray, and Anthony Palmer (eds), *Bertrand Russell and The Origins of Analytical Philosophy*, Bristol: Thoemmes, 331–361.

Pigden, Charles R. (1996) "Bertrand Russell: Meta-Ethical Pioneer", *Philosophy of the Social Sciences*, 26, 181–204.

Pineau, Lois (1990) "Russell on Ordinary Names and Synonymy", *History of Philosophy Quarterly*, 7, 93–108.

Pitt, Jack (1971) "With Russell at the Archives", *Russell*, o.s. 2, 3–7.

Pitt, Jack (1974) "Russell and Recent Psychology", *Russell*, o.s. 14, 26–31.

Pitt, Jack (1975) "Russell on Religion", *International Journal for Philosophy of Religion*, 6, 40–53.

Pitt, Jack (1980–81) "Russell and Marx: Similarities and Differences", *Russell*, o.s. 37–40, 9–16.

Pitt, Jack (1981–82) "Russell and the Cambridge Moral Sciences Club", *Russell*, n.s. 1, 103–118.

Poincaré, Henri (1909) "La Logique de l'Infini", *Revue de Métaphysique et de Morale*, 17, 451–482. Trans. as "The Logic of Infinity", in Poincaré, Henri, *Mathematics and Science: Last Essays*, New York: Dover, 1963, 45–64.

Poincaré, Henri (1912) "The Latest Effort of the Logisticians", *Monist*, 22, 524–539.

Poincaré, Henri (1912) "The New Logics", *Monist*, 22, 243–256.

Poincaré, Henri (1913) "Mathematics and Logic", in Poincaré, Henri, *Mathematics and Science: Last Essays*, New York: Dover, 1963, 65–74.

Pollanen, Michael S. (1993) "On Balzer's Small Set Solution to Russell's Paradox", *Journal of Value Inquiry*, 27, 541.

Pollock, John L. (1970) "On Logicism", in Klemke, E.D. (ed.), *Essays on Bertrand Russell*, Urbana: University of Illinois Press, 388–395.

Polonoff, I.I. (1973) "Bertrand Russell", in Kidd, Walter E. (ed.), *British Winners of the Nobel Literary Prize*, Norman: University of Oklahoma Press, 168–201.

Popper, Karl R. (1956) "The History of Our Time: An Optimist's View", in Popper, Karl R., *Conjectures and Refutations*, London: Routledge and Kegan Paul, 4th edn, 1972, 364–376.

Popper, Karl R., and F. Hansdorff (1949) "Scientific Inference According to Bertrand Russell", *Hibbert Journal*, 47, 375–381.

Popper, Karl R., Geoffrey Warnock, and Bryan Magee (1970) "The Philosophy of Bertrand Russell", *Listener*, 83 (14 May), 633–634.

Prichard, H.A. (1915) "Mr Bertrand Russell on Our Knowledge of the External World", *Mind*, 24, 145–185.

Prichard, H.A. (1928) "Mr Bertrand Russell's *Outline of Philosophy*", *Mind*, 37, 265–282.

Priest, Graham (1994) "The Structure of the Paradoxes of Self-Reference", *Mind*, 103, 25–34.

Priest, Stephen (1990) "Russell", in Priest, Stephen, *The British Empiricists: Hobbes to Ayer*, London: Penguin, 200–228.

Pringle-Pattison, A.S. (1913) "'The Free Man's Worship': A Consideration of Mr Bertrand Russell's Views on Religion", *Hibbert Journal*, 12, 47–63.

Prior, A.N. (1956) "Definitions, Rules, and Axioms", *Proceedings of the Aristotelian Society*, 56, 199–216.

Prior, A.N. (1965) "Existence in Lesniewski and in Russell", in Crossley, John N., and Michael A.E. Dummett (eds), *Formal Systems and Recursive Functions*, Amsterdam: North-Holland, 149–155.

Prior, A.N. (1966) "Some Problems of Self-Reference in John Buridan", in Findlay, John Niemayer (ed.), *Studies in Philosophy*, Oxford: Oxford University Press, 241–259.

Prior, A.N. (1967) "Russell's Correspondence Theory", in Edwards, Paul (ed.), *The Encyclopedia of Philosophy*, Vol. 2, New York: Macmillan, 226–228.

Purcell, Victor (Myra Buttle, pseud.) (1967) "Fifty Years' Influence", in Schoenman, Ralph (ed.), *Bertrand Russell: Philosopher of the Century*, London: Allen and Unwin, 33–55.

Putnam, Hilary (1967) "The Thesis that Mathematics is Logic", in Schoenman, Ralph (ed.), *Bertrand Russell: Philosopher of the Century*, London: Allen and Unwin, 273–303. Repr. in Putnam, Hilary, *Mathematics, Matter and Method*, Cambridge: Cambridge University Press, 1975, 12–42.

Quine, Willard Van Orman (1932) "A Note on Nicod's Postulate", *Mind*, 41, 345–350.

Quine, Willard Van Orman (1936) "On the Axiom of Reducibility", *Mind*, 45, 498–500.

Quine, Willard Van Orman (1937) "New Foundations for Mathematical Logic", *American Mathematical Monthly*, 44, 70–80.

Quine, Willard Van Orman (1938) "On the Theory of Types", *Journal of Symbolic Logic*, 3, 125–139.

Quine, Willard Van Orman (1939) "Designation and Existence", *Journal of Philosophy*, 36, 701–709.

Quine, Willard Van Orman (1941) "Whitehead and the Rise of Modern Logic", in Schilpp, Paul Arthur (ed.) *The Philosophy of Alfred North Whitehead*, La Salle: Open Court, 125–164.

Quine, Willard Van Orman (1941–42) "Russell's Paradox and Others", *Technology Review*, 44, 16–17.

Quine, Willard Van Orman (1948) "On What There Is", *Review of Metaphysics*, 2, 21–38.

Quine, Willard Van Orman (1963) "Russell's Theory of Types", in Quine, Willard Van Orman, *Set Theory and Its Logic*, Cambridge, Mass.: Harvard University Press, 241–265. Repr. in Klemke, E.D. (ed.), *Essays on Bertrand Russell*, Urbana: University of Illinois Press, 1970, 372–387.

Quine, Willard Van Orman (1966) "Russell's Ontological Development", *Journal of Philosophy*, 63, 657–667. Repr. in Schoenman, Ralph (ed.), *Bertrand Russell: Philosopher of the Century*, London: Allen and Unwin, 1967, 304–314; in Klemke, E.D. (ed.), *Essays on Bertrand Russell*, Urbana: University of Illinois Press, 1970, 3–14; in Pears, David F. (ed.), *Bertrand Russell: A Collection of Critical Essays*, Garden City, N.Y.: Anchor Books, 1972, 290–304; and in Quine, Willard Van Orman, *Theories and Things*, Cambridge: Belknap Press, 1981, 73–85.

Quine, Willard Van Orman (1972) "Remarks for a Memorial Symposium", in Pears, David F. (ed.), *Bertrand Russell: A Collection of Critical Essays*, Garden City, N.Y.: Anchor Books, 1–5.

Quine, Willard Van Orman (1988) "Logical Correspondence with Russell", *Russell*, n.s. 8, 225–231. Repr. in Winchester, Ian, and Kenneth Blackwell (eds), *Antinomies and Paradoxes: Studies in Russell's Early Philosophy*, Hamilton: McMaster University Library Press, 1988, 225–231.

Quinton, Anthony (1960) "Russell's Philosophical Development", *Philosophy*, 35, 1–13. Repr. in Quinton, Anthony, *Thoughts and Thinkers*, New York: Holmes and Meier, 1982, 277–287.

Quinton, Anthony (1972) "Russell's Philosophy of Mind", in Pears, David F. (ed.), *Bertrand Russell: A Collection of Critical Essays*, Garden City, N.Y.: Anchor Books, 80–109.

Radek, Karl (1935) "Mr Bertrand Russell's Sentimental Journey to Russia", in Radek, Karl, *Portraits and Pamphlets*, London: Wishart, 210–216.

Radford, Colin (1995) "MacColl, Russell, the Existential Import of Propositions, and the Null-Class", *Philosophical Quarterly*, 45, 316–331.

Radner, Michael (1975) "Philosophical Foundations of Russell's Logicism", *Dialogue*, 14, 241–253.

Ramachandran, Murali (1993) "A Strawsonian Objection to Russell's Theory of Descriptions", *Analysis*, 53, 209–212.

Ramachandran, Murali (1995) "Bach on Behalf of Russell", *Analysis*, 55, 283–287.

Ramsey, Frank Plumpton (1925) "The Foundations of Mathematics", *Proceedings of the London Mathematical Society*, series 2, 25, 338–384. Repr. in Ramsey, Frank Plumpton, *The Foundations of Mathematics*, London: Kegan Paul, Trench, Trubner, 1931, 1–61; in Ramsey, Frank Plumpton, *Foundations*, London: Routledge and Kegan Paul, 1978, 152–212; and in Ramsey, Frank Plumpton, *Philosophical Papers*, Cambridge: Cambridge University Press, 1990, 164–224. Repr. in part as "Predicative Functions and the Axiom of Reducibility", in Klemke, E.D. (ed.), *Essays on Bertrand Russell*, Urbana: University of Illinois Press, 1970, 355–368.

Ramsey, Frank Plumpton (1925) "Universals", *Mind*, 34, 401–417. Repr. in Ramsey, Frank Plumpton, *The Foundations of Mathematics*, London: Kegan Paul, Trench, Trubner, 1931, 112–134; in Ramsey, Frank Plumpton, *Foundations*, London: Routledge and Kegan Paul, 1978, 17–39; and in Ramsey, Frank Plumpton, *Philosophical Papers*, Cambridge: Cambridge University Press, 1990, 8–30.

Ramsey, Frank Plumpton (1926) "Mathematical Logic", *Mathematical Gazette*, 13, 185–194. Repr. in Ramsey, Frank Plumpton, *The Foundations of Mathematics*, London: Kegan Paul, Trench, Trubner, 1931, 62–81; in Ramsey, Frank Plumpton, *Foundations*, London: Routledge and Kegan Paul, 1978, 213–232; and in Ramsey, Frank Plumpton, *Philosophical Papers*, Cambridge: Cambridge University Press, 1990, 225–244.

Ramsey, Frank Plumpton (1927) "Facts and Propositions", *Aristotelian Society*, Supplementary Vol. 7, 153–170. Repr. in Ramsey, Frank Plumpton, *The Foundations of Mathematics*, London: Kegan Paul, Trench, Trubner, 1931, 138–155; in Ramsey, Frank Plumpton, *Foundations*, London: Routledge and Kegan Paul, 1978, 40–57; and in Ramsey, Frank Plumpton, *Philosophical Papers*, Cambridge: Cambridge University Press, 1990, 34–51.

Read, Herbert (1967) "A Philosophical Debt", in Schoenman, Ralph (ed.), *Bertrand Russell: Philosopher of the Century*, London: Allen and Unwin, 95–99.

Reeves, Alan (1973) "In Defence of a Simple Solution", *Australasian Journal of Philosophy*, 51, 17–38.

Reeves, J.W. (1934) "The Origin and Consequences of the Theory of Descriptions", *Proceedings of the Aristotelian Society*, 34, 211–230.

Reichenbach, Hans (1944) "Bertrand Russell's Logic", in Schilpp, Paul Arthur (ed.), *The Philosophy of Bertrand Russell*, 3rd edn, New York: Tudor, 1951, 21–54.

Reichenbach, Hans (1949) "A Conversation Between Bertrand Russell and David Hume", *Journal of Philosophy*, 46, 545–549.

Reichenbach, Hans (1967) "An Early Appreciation", in Schoenman, Ralph (ed.), *Bertrand Russell: Philosopher of the Century*, London: Allen and Unwin, 129–133.

Reichenbach, Maria (1967) "Rudolf Carnap: The Cross Currents", in Schoenman, Ralph (ed.), *Bertrand Russell: Philosopher of the Century*, London: Allen and Unwin, 134–139.

Reimer, Marga (1992) "Incomplete Descriptions", *Erkenntnis*, 37, 347–363.

Rempel, R.A. (1979) "From Imperialism to Free Trade: Couturat, Halévy and the Development of Russell's First Crusade", *Journal of the History of Ideas*, 40, 423–443.

Rempel, R.A. (1996) "Pacifism and Revolution: Bertrand Russell and Russia, 1914–1920", in Dyck, Harvey L., *The Pacifist Impulse in Historical Perspective*, Toronto: University of Toronto Press, 341–361.

Rescher, Nicholas (1959) "On the Logic of Existence and Denotation", *Philosophical Review*, 68, 157–180.

Rescher, Nicholas (1979) "Russell and Modal Logic", in Roberts, George W. (ed.), *Bertrand Russell Memorial Volume*, London: Allen and Unwin, 139–149.

Rescher, Nicholas (1979) "Russell's Criticism of Leibniz on Relations", in Rescher, Nicholas, *Leibniz: An Introduction to his Philosophy*, Totowa, N.J.: Rowman and Littlefield, 59–61.

Resnik, Michael D. (1969) "A Set Theoretic Approach to the Simple Theory of Types", *Theoria*, 35, 239–258.

Richards, Joan L. (1988) "Bertrand Russell's *Essay on the Foundations of Geometry* and the Cambridge Mathematical Tradition", *Russell*, n.s. 8, 59–80. Repr. in Winchester, Ian, and Kenneth Blackwell (eds), *Antinomies and Paradoxes: Studies in Russell's Early Philosophy*, Hamilton: McMaster University Library Press, 1988, 59–80.

Richards, John (1976) "Pre-'On Denoting' Manuscripts in the Russell Archives", *Russell*, o.s. 21–22, 28–34.

Richards, John (1980) "Propositional Functions and Russell's Philosophy of Language, 1903–1914", *Philosophical Forum*, 11, 315–339.

Richardson, Alan (1990) "How Not to Russell Carnap's *Aufbau*", *Proceedings of the Biennial Meetings of the Philosophy of Science Association*, 1, 3–14.

Richardson, Robert P., and Edward H. Landis (1915) "Numbers, Variables, and Mr Russell's Philosophy", *Monist*, 25, 321–364.

Ripley, Charles (1980–81) "Moore and Russell on Existence as a Predicate", *Russell*, o.s. 37–40, 17–30.

Riska, Augustin (1980) "Knowledge by Acquaintance Reconsidered", *Grazer Philosophische Studien*, 11, 129–140.

Riverso, Emanuele (1992) "Ayer's Treatment of Russell", in Hahn, Lewis Edwin (ed.), *The Philosophy of A.J. Ayer*, La Salle, Ill.: Open Court, 517–541.

Roberts, George W. (1979) "Some Aspects of Knowledge (I)", in Roberts, George W. (ed.), *Bertrand Russell Memorial Volume*, London: Allen and Unwin, 348–383.

Roberts, Joy H. (1976) "An Error in Searle's Criticism of Russell's Theory of Descriptions", *Southwestern Journal of Philosophy*, 7, 15–19.

Roberts, Lawrence (1984) "Russell on the Semantics and Pragmatics of Indexicals", *Philosophia*, 14, 111–128.

Robinson, Abraham (1979) "On Constrained Denotation", in Roberts, George W. (ed.), *Bertrand Russell Memorial Volume*, London: Allen and Unwin, 91–104.

Robinson, H. (1975) "The Class as One and as Many", *International Logic Review*, 6, 172–182.

Robson, Ann (1972) "Bertrand Russell and his Godless Parents", *Russell*, o.s. 7, 3–9.

Rockler, Michael J. (1992) "The Curricular Role of Russell's Scepticism", *Russell*, n.s. 12, 50–60.

Rockler, Michael J. (1995) "Russell vs Dewey on Religion", *Free Inquiry*, 15, no. 4 (Fall), 36–38.

Rodríguez-Consuegra, Francisco A. (1987) "Russell's Logistic Definitions of Numbers, 1898–1913: Chronology and Significance", *History and Philosophy of Logic*, 8, 141–169.

Rodríguez-Consuegra, Francisco A. (1989) "Russell's Theory of Types, 1901–1910: Its Complex Origins in the Unpublished Manuscripts", *History and Philosophy of Logic*, 10, 131–164.

Rodríguez-Consuegra, Francisco A. (1989) "The Origins of Russell's Theory of Descriptions According to the Unpublished Manuscripts", *Russell*, n.s. 9, 99–132. Repr. as "The Origins of Russell's Theory of Descriptions", in Irvine, A.D., and G.A. Wedeking (eds), *Russell and Analytic Philosophy*, Toronto: University of Toronto Press, 1993, 66–96.

Rodríguez-Consuegra, Francisco A. (1990) "The First Technical Philosophy of Bertrand Russell", *History and Philosophy of Logic*, 11, 225–230.

Rodríguez-Consuegra, Francisco A. (1991) "A Global Viewpoint on Russell's Philosophy", *Diálogos*, 57, 173–186.

Rodríguez-Consuegra, Francisco A. (1992) "Russell's Philosophical Exchanges", *Russell*, n.s. 12, 93–104.

Rodríguez-Consuegra, Francisco A. (1992–93) "A New Angle on Russell's 'Inextricable Tangle' Over Meaning and Denotation", *Russell*, n.s. 12, 197–207.

Rodríguez-Consuegra, Francisco A. (1993) "Russell, Gödel and Logicism", in Czermak, Johannes (ed.), *Philosophy of Mathematics*, Vienna: Hölder–Pichler–Tempsky, 233–242.

Rodríguez-Consuegra, Francisco A. (1994) "Mathematical Logic and Logicism from Peano to Quine", in Grattan-Guinness, Ivor (ed.), *Companion Encyclopaedia of the History and Philosophy of the Mathematical Sciences*, London: Routledge, Vol. 1, 617–628.

Rodríguez-Consuegra, Francisco A. (1995) "Bertrand Russell and Bradley's Ghost (I)", in Hintikka, J., and K. Puhl (eds), *The British Tradition in Twentieth Century Philosophy*, Vienna: Hölder–Pichler–Tempsky, 353–366.

Rodríguez-Consuegra, Francisco A. (1996) "Russell's Perilous Journey From Atomism to Holism 1919–1951", in Monk, Ray, and Anthony Palmer (eds), *Bertrand Russell and The Origins of Analytical Philosophy*, Bristol: Thoemmes, 217–243.

Rolf, Bertil (1982) "Russell's Theses on Vagueness", *History and Philosophy of Logic*, 3, 69–83.

Rolston, John (1973) "Bradley on Russell and Relations", *Philosophical Forum*, 4, 513–530.

Rorty, Richard (1982) "Is There a Problem about Fictional Discourse?", in Rorty, Richard, *Consequences of Pragmatism*, Minneapolis: University of Minnesota Press, 110–138.

Rosenbaum, S.P. (1976) "Bertrand Russell: The Logic of a Literary Symbol", in

Thomas, J.E., and Kenneth Blackwell (eds), *Russell in Review*, Toronto: Samuel Stevens, Hakkert and Co., 57–87.

Rosenbaum, S.P. (1976) "Gilbert Cannan and Bertrand Russell", *Russell*, o.s. 21–22, 16–25.

Rosenbaum, S.P. (1984) "Bertrand Russell in Bloomsbury", *Russell*, n.s. 4, 11–29. Repr. in Moran, Margaret, and Carl Spadoni (eds), *Intellect and Social Conscience: Essays on Bertrand Russell's Early Work*, Hamilton: McMaster University Library Press, 1984, 11–29.

Rosenberg, Alexander (1989) "Russell Versus Steiner on Physics and Causality", *Philosophy of Science*, 56, 341–347.

Rosenberg, Jay F. (1972) "Russell on Negative Facts", *Nous*, 6, 27–40.

Rosenberg, Jay F. (1979) "Russell and the Form of Outer Sense", in Roberts, George W. (ed.), *Bertrand Russell Memorial Volume*, London: Allen and Unwin, 285–303.

Roshwald, Mordecai (1986–87) "Encounters with Bertrand Russell", *Russell*, n.s. 6, 150–153.

Ross, William T. (1994) "Bertrand Russell and the Colonialist Assumption", *Centennial Review*, 38, 387–399.

Rotblat, Joseph (1967) "The Russell–Einstein Manifesto", in Rotblat, Joseph, *Pugwash – The First Ten Years: History of the Conferences of Science and World Affairs*, New York: Humanities, 12.

Rowse, Alfred Leslie (1947) "Debacle of European Liberalism", in Rowse, Alfred Leslie, *End of an Epoch*, New York: Macmillan, 170–180.

Rowse, Alfred Leslie (1947) "Questions in Political Theory", in Rowse, Alfred Leslie, *End of an Epoch*, New York: Macmillan, 291–309.

Ruffino, Marco Antonio (1994) "The Context Principle and Wittgenstein's Criticism of Russell's Theory of Types", *Synthese*, 93, 401–414.

Ruja, Harry (1968) "Principles of Polemic in Russell", *Inquiry*, 11, 282–294.

Ruja, Harry (1972, 1973) "Russell's American Lecture Tours", *Russell*, o.s. 6, 6–8; o.s. 10, 22–23.

Ruja, Harry (1984) "Russell on the Meaning of 'Good'", *Russell*, n.s. 4, 137–156. Repr. in Moran, Margaret, and Carl Spadoni (eds), *Intellect and Social Conscience: Essays on Bertrand Russell's Early Work*, Hamilton: McMaster University Library Press, 1984, 137–156.

Ruja, Harry (1995–96) "Bertrand Russell's Life in Pictures", *Russell*, n.s. 15, 101–152.

Russell, Conrad (1972) "Memories of My Father", *Sunday Times Magazine*, 14 May, 32–33, 35, 37.

Russell, Dora Winifred Black (1934) "Beacon Hill", in Blewit, Trevor (ed.), *The Modern Schools Handbook*, London: Victor Gollancz, 29–42.

Russell, Dora Winifred Black (1967) "What Beacon Hill Stood For", *Anarchy*, 7, 11–16.

Russell, L.J. (1908) "Space and Mathematical Reasoning", *Mind*, 17, 321–349.

Russell, L.J. (1945) "The Philosophy of Bertrand Russell", *Philosophy*, 20, 172–182.

Ryan, Alan (1995) "Russell at Century's End", *Free Inquiry*, 15, no. 4 (Fall), 44–45.

Ryan, Alan (1996) "Russell: the Last Great Radical?", *Philosophy of the Social Sciences*, 26, 247–266.

Ryan, William F. (1978) "Bertrand Russell and Haldeman-Julius: Making Readers Rational", *Russell*, o.s. 29–32, 53–64.

Ryle, Gilbert (1931) "Systematically Misleading Expressions", *Proceedings of the Aristotelian Society*, 32, 139–170.

Ryle, Gilbert (1970) "Bertrand Russell, 1872–1970", *Proceedings of the Aristotelian Society*, 71, 77–84. Repr. in *Revue Internationale de Philosophie*, 26 (1972),

436–443, and in Roberts, George W. (ed.), *Bertrand Russell Memorial Volume*, London: Allen and Unwin, 1979, 15–21.

Saarinen, Esa (1982) "How to Frege a Russell–Kaplan", *Nous*, 16, 257–276.

Sainsbury, Richard Mark (1980) "Russell on Constructions and Fictions", *Theoria*, 46, 19–36.

Sainsbury, Richard Mark (1986) "Russell on Acquaintance", in Vesey, Godfrey (ed.), *Philosophers Ancient and Modern*, Cambridge: Cambridge University Press, 219–244.

Sainsbury, Richard Mark (1989) "On Induction and Russell's Postulates", in Savage, C. Wade, and C. Anthony Anderson (eds), *Rereading Russell: Essays on Bertrand Russell's Metaphysics and Epistemology*, Minneapolis: University of Minnesota Press, 200–219.

Sainsbury, Richard Mark (1993) "Russell on Names and Communication", in Irvine, A.D., and G.A. Wedeking (eds), *Russell and Analytic Philosophy*, Toronto: University of Toronto Press, 3–21.

Sainsbury, Richard Mark (1996) "How Can We Say Something?", in Monk, Ray, and Anthony Palmer (eds), *Bertrand Russell and The Origins of Analytical Philosophy*, Bristol: Thoemmes, 137–153.

Salmon, Merrilee H. (1974–75) "On Russell's 'Brief but Notorious Flirtation with Phenomenalism'", *Russell*, o.s 16, 13–20.

Salmon, Wesley C. (1974) "Memory and Perception in *Human Knowledge*", in Nakhnikian, George (ed.), *Bertrand Russell's Philosophy*, London: Duckworth, 139–167.

Salmon, Wesley C. (1974) "Russell on Scientific Inference or Will the Real Deductivist Please Stand Up?", in Nakhnikian, George (ed.), *Bertrand Russell's Philosophy*, London: Duckworth, 183–208.

Salmon, Wesley C. (1975) "Note on Russell's Anticipations", *Russell*, o.s. 17, 29.

Santayana, George (1911) "Russell's Philosophical Essays", *Journal of Philosophy, Psychology, and Scientific Methods*, 8, 57–63, 113–124, 421–432.

Santayana, George (1913) "The Philosophy of Mr Bertrand Russell", in Santayana, George, *Winds of Doctrine*, London: J.M. Dent and Sons, 110–154.

Santayana, George (1968) "Bertrand Russell's Search-light", in Santayana, George, *The Birth of Reason and Other Essays*, New York: Columbia University Press, 125–129.

Santayana, George (1969) "Essences not Abstractions", in Santayana, George, *Physical Order and Moral Liberty*, Nashville, Tenn.: Vanderbilt University Press, 96–101.

Santayana, George (1969) "What are Data?", in Santayana, George, *Physical Order and Moral Liberty*, Nashville, Tenn.: Vanderbilt University Press, 87–96.

Sard, Arthur (1973) "Russell, Searle, and Hamlet", *Journal of the History of Philosophy*, 11, 392.

Saunders, L.P. (1917) "Mr Russell's Lowell Lectures", *Mind*, 26, 29–52.

Savage, C. Wade (1989) "Sense-Data in Russell's Theories of Knowledge", in Savage, C. Wade, and C. Anthony Anderson (eds), *Rereading Russell: Essays on Bertrand Russell's Metaphysics and Epistemology*, Minneapolis: University of Minnesota Press, 138–168.

Sayward, Charles (1993) "Definite Descriptions, Negation, and Necessitation", *Russell*, n.s. 13, 36–47.

Scales, Ronald (1977) "A Russellian Approach to Truth", *Nous*, 11, 169–174.

Scheer, Robert (1967) "Lord Russell", *Ramparts*, 5/11, 16–23.

Schiller, Ferdinand Canning Scott (1922) "Mr Russell's Psychology", *Journal of Philosophy*, 19, 281–292.

Schiller, Ferdinand Canning Scott (1934) "Tribulations of Truth", in Schiller, Ferdinand Canning Scott, *Must Philosophers Disagree?*, New York: Macmillan, 182–193.

Schiller, Ferdinand Canning Scott (1939) "Must Empiricism be Limited?", in Schiller, Ferdinand Canning Scott, *Our Human Truths*, New York: Columbia University Press, 32–47.

Schilpp, Paul Arthur (1971) "Some Recollections of Bertrand Russell, 1872–1970", *Journal of Thought*, 6, 68–79.

Schilpp, Paul Arthur (1996) "Bertrand Russell", in Schilpp, Paul Arthur, *Reminiscing*, Carbondale: Southern Illinois University Press, 116–121.

Schnitzer, Marc L. (1971) "Presupposition, Entailment, and Russell's Theory of Descriptions", *Foundations of Language*, 7, 297–299.

Schock, Rolf (1962) "Some Remarks on Russell's Treatment of Definite Descriptions", *Logique et Analyse*, 5, 77–80.

Schoenman, Ralph (1974) "Bertrand Russell and the Peace Movement", in Nakhnikian, George (ed.), *Bertrand Russell's Philosophy*, London: Duckworth, 227–252.

Schultz, Bart (1992) "Bertrand Russell in Ethics and Politics", *Ethics*, 102, 594–634.

Schultz, Bart (1996) "Bertrand Russell in Ethics and Politics, Philosophy and Power", *Philosophy of the Social Sciences*, 26, 317–321.

Schultz, Bart (1996) "Bertrand Russell in Ethics and Politics, the Vicissitudes of Growth and Power", *Philosophy of the Social Sciences*, 26, 157–161.

Schutte, Karl (1960) "Syntactical and Semantical Properties of Simple Type Theory", *Journal of Symbolic Logic*, 25, 305–326.

Schwarcz, Vera (1991) "Between Russell and Confucius: China's Russell Expert, Zhang Shenfu (Chang Sung-nian)", *Russell*, n.s. 11, 117–146.

Schweitzer, A.R. (1914) "Some Critical Remarks on Analytical Realism", *Journal of Philosophy, Psychology, and Scientific Methods*, 11, 169–183.

Scott, Dana (1967) "Existence and Description in Formal Logic", in Schoenman, Ralph (ed.), *Bertrand Russell: Philosopher of the Century*, London: Allen and Unwin, 181–200.

Scott, Michael (1967) "Civil Disobedience and Morals", in Schoenman, Ralph (ed.), *Bertrand Russell: Philosopher of the Century*, London: Allen and Unwin, 63–66.

Searle, John R. (1958) "Russell's Objections to Frege's Theory of Sense and Reference", *Analysis*, 18, 137–143. Repr. in Klemke, E.D. (ed.), *Essays on Frege*, Urbana: University of Illinois Press, 1968, 337–345.

Seckel, Al (1984–85) "Russell and the Cuban Missile Crisis", *Russell*, n.s. 4, 253–261.

Sellars, Wilfrid (1949) "Acquaintance and Description Again", *Journal of Philosophy*, 46, 496–504.

Sellars, Wilfrid (1954) "Presupposing", *Philosophical Review*, 63, 197–215. Repr. in Klemke, E.D. (ed.), *Essays on Bertrand Russell*, Urbana: University of Illinois Press, 1970, 173–189.

Sellars, Wilfrid (1963) "Classes as Abstract Entities and the Russell Paradox", *Review of Metaphysics*, 17, 67–90.

Sellars, Wilfrid (1974) "Ontology and the Philosophy of Mind in Russell", in Nakhnikian, George (ed.), *Bertrand Russell's Philosophy*, London: Duckworth, 57–100.

Seymour, Michel (1988) "The Referential Use of Definite Descriptions", *Russell*, n.s. 8, 133–139. Repr. in Winchester, Ian, and Kenneth Blackwell (eds), *Antinomies and Paradoxes: Studies in Russell's Early Philosophy*, Hamilton: McMaster University Library Press, 1988, 133–139.

Shanker, Stuart (1993) "Wittgenstein versus James and Russell on the Nature of Willing", in Canfield, John V., and Stuart Shanker (eds), *Wittgenstein's Intentions*, New York: Garland, 195–243.

Shanker, Stuart (1993) "Wittgenstein versus Russell on the Analysis of Mind", in Irvine, A.D., and G.A. Wedeking (eds), *Russell and Analytic Philosophy*, Toronto: University of Toronto Press, 210–242.

Sharvy, Richard (1980) "A More General Theory of Definite Descriptions", *Philosophical Review*, 89, 607–624.

Shaw, James Byrnie (1912) "What is Mathematics?", *Bulletin of the American Mathematical Society*, 18, 386–411.

Shearn, Martin (1950) "Whitehead and Russell's Theory of Types – A Reply to J.J.C. Smart's 'Whitehead and Russell's Theory of Types'", *Analysis*, 11, 45–48.

Shearn, Martin (1951) "Russell's Analysis of Existence", *Analysis*, 11, 124–131.

Sheffer, Henry Maurice (1913) "A Set of Five Independent Postulates for Boolean Algebras, with Applications to Logical Constants", *Transactions of the American Mathematical Society*, 14, 481–488.

Sherman, Edward F. (1974) "Bertrand Russell and the Peace Movement: Liberal Consistency or Radical Change?", in Nakhnikian, George (ed.), *Bertrand Russell's Philosophy*, London: Duckworth, 253–263.

Shipler, Guy Emery (1941) "The Attitude of the Episcopal Church", in Dewey, John, and Horace M. Kallen (eds), *The Bertrand Russell Case*, New York: Viking, 149–155.

Shoemaker, Sydney (1960) "Logical Atomism and Language", *Analysis*, 20, 49–52.

Shosky, John (1995) "Russell and the Contemplation of Philosophy", *Free Inquiry*, 15, no. 4 (Fall), 41–42.

Shosky, John (1997) "Russell's Use of Truth-Tables", *Russell*, n.s. 17, 11–26.

Shulka, J.J. (1979) "Failure of Russell's Theory of External Relations", *Indian Philosophical Quarterly*, 6, 697–704.

Shusterman, Richard (1983) "Russell's Fiction and the Vanity of Human Knowledge", *Modern Fiction Studies*, 29, 680–688.

Siitonen, Arto (1993) "Logical Atomism Reconsidered", in Puhl, Klaus (ed.) *Wittgenstein's Philosophy of Mathematics*, Vienna: Verlag Hölder–Pichler–Tempsky, 201–206.

Simon, Bennett, and Nancy Simon (1974) "The Pacifist Turn: An Episode of Mystic Illumination in Russell's Life", *Russell*, o.s. 13, 11–12, 17–24.

Simon, Herbert A. (1991) "The Logic Theorist is Conceived", *Models of My Life*, New York: Basic Books, 205–212.

Simons, Peter, (1992) "On What There Isn't: The Meinong–Russell Dispute", in Simons, Peter, *Philosophy and Logic in Central Europe From Bolzano to Tarski*, Dordrecht: Kluwer, 159–191.

Sinha, L.P.N. (1972) "Bertrand Russell and the Problem of Perception", *Indian Philosophy and Culture*, 17, 5–13.

Sinisi, Vito F. (1976) "Lesniewski's Analysis of Russell's Antimony", *Notre Dame Journal of Formal Logic*, 17, 19–34.

Skosnik, Jeffrey (1972) "Russell's Unpublished Writings on Truth and Denoting", *Russell*, o.s. 7, 12–13.

Skyrms, Brian (1993) "Logical Atoms and Combinatorial Possibility", *Journal of Philosophy*, 90, 219–232.

Slater, B.H. (1979) "Internal and External Negations", *Mind*, 88, 588–591.

Slater, John G. (1971) "Bertrand Russell and 'The Tribunal'", *Russell*, o.s. 1, 6–7.

Slater, John G. (1971–72) "What Happened at Leeds?", *Russell*, o.s. 4, 9–10.

Slater, John G. (1976) "One Hundred Years of Bertrand Russell", *Russell*, o.s. 23–24, 4–25.

Slater, John G. (1976) "The Political Philosophy of Bertrand Russell", in Thomas, J.E., and Kenneth Blackwell (eds), *Russell in Review*, Toronto: Samuel Stevens, Hakkert and Co., 135–154.

Slater, John G. (1982–83) "Bertrand Russell and the Volkhovsky Letters, 1920–26", *Russell*, n.s. 2, 7–19.

Slater, John G. (1988) "Russell's Conception of Philosophy", *Russell*, n.s. 8, 163–178. Repr. in Winchester, Ian, and Kenneth Blackwell (eds), *Antinomies and Paradoxes: Studies in Russell's Early Philosophy*, Hamilton: McMaster University Library Press, 1988, 163–178.

Slezak, Gary, and Donald W. Jackanicz (1977) "The Town is Beastly and the Weather was Vile: Bertrand Russell in Chicago, 1938–1939", *Russell*, o.s. 25–28, 5–20.

Smart, Harold R. (1929) "Is Mathematics a 'Deductive' Science?", *Philosophical Review*, 38, 232–245.

Smart, Harold R. (1943) "Cassirer Versus Russell", *Philosophy of Science*, 10, 167–175.

Smart, J.J.C. (1950) "Whitehead and Russell's Theory of Types", *Analysis*, 10, 93–96.

Smart, J.J.C. (1951) "The Theory of Types Again", *Analysis*, 11, 131–133.

Smiley, T.J. (1960) "Propositional Functions", *Aristotelian Society*, Supplementary Vol. 34, 33–46.

Smith, Helen M. (1932) "Bertrand Russell on Perception", *Proceedings of the Aristotelian Society*, 32, 207–226.

Smith, Janet Farrell (1985) "The Russell–Meinong Debate", *Philosophy and Phenomenological Research*, 45, 305–350.

Smith, Janet Farrell (1988) "Russell's Re-Evaluation of Meinong, 1913–14: An Analysis of Acquaintance", *Russell*, n.s. 8, 179–194. Repr. in Winchester, Ian, and Kenneth Blackwell (eds), *Antinomies and Paradoxes: Studies in Russell's Early Philosophy*, Hamilton: McMaster University Library Press, 1988, 179–194.

Smith, Janet Farrell (1989) "Russell on Indexicals and Scientific Knowledge", in Savage, C. Wade, and C. Anthony Anderson (eds), *Rereading Russell: Essays on Bertrand Russell's Metaphysics and Epistemology*, Minneapolis: University of Minnesota Press, 119–137.

Smith, Joseph Wayne, and Sharyn Ward (1984) "Are We Only Five Minutes Old? A Cock on the Age of the Universe", *Philosophy of Science*, 51, 511–513.

Smith, Vincent Edward (1950) "Russell's Ascent to Logic", in Smith, Vincent Edward, *Idea-Men of Today*, Milwaukee: Bruce, 105–132.

Smullyan, Arthur F. (1948) "Modality and Description", *Journal of Symbolic Logic*, 13, 31–37.

Smullyan, Arthur F. (1958) "Incomplete Symbols", *Philosophical Review*, 67, 237–242.

Soles, Deborah Hansen (1981) "Russell's Causal Theory of Meaning", *Russell*, n.s. 1, 27–37.

Solomon, Graham (1989) "An Addendum to Demopoulos and Friedman (1985)", *Philosophy of Science*, 56, 497–501.

Solomon, Graham (1989) "What Became of Russell's 'Relation-Arithmetic'?", *Russell*, n.s. 9, 168–173.

Somerville, James (1992) "Futures Past and Futures Future", *Journal of the History of Philosophy*, 30, 103–121.

Somerville, John (1946) "An Open Letter to Bertrand Russell", *Philosophy of Science*, 13, 67–71.

Sommers, Fred (1963) "Types and Ontology", *Philosophical Review*, 72, 327–363. Repr. in Strawson, Peter F. (ed.), *Philosophical Logic*, Oxford: Oxford University Press, 1967, 138–169.

Sorensen, Roy A. (1988) "Precisification by Means of Vague Predicates", *Notre Dame Journal of Formal Logic*, 29, 267–274.

Spadoni, Carl (1972–73) "Reply to Mr Leavitt", *Russell*, o.s. 8, 16–18.

Spadoni, Carl (1976) "Great God in Boots! – The Ontological Argument is Sound!", *Russell*, o.s. 23–24, 37–41.

Spadoni, Carl (1978) "Philosophy in Russell's Letters to Alys", *Russell*, o.s. 29–32, 17–31.

Spadoni, Carl (1984) "Bertrand Russell on Aesthetics", *Russell*, n.s. 4, 49–82. Repr. in Moran, Margaret, and Carl Spadoni (eds), *Intellect and Social Conscience: Essays on Bertrand Russell's Early Work*, Hamilton: McMaster University Library Press, 1984, 49–82.

Spadoni, Carl (1986) "Who Wrote Bertrand Russell's *Wisdom of the West?*", *The Papers of the Bibliographical Society of America*, 80, 349–367.

Spadoni, Carl, and David Harley (1985) "Bertrand Russell's Library", *Journal of Library History*, 20, 25–45.

Spaulding, Edward Gleason (1912) "A Defense of Analysis", in Holt, Edwin, *et al.*, *The New Realism*, New York: Macmillan, 155–247.

Spiegelberg, Herbert (1980) "The Correspondence Between Bertrand Russell and Albert Schweitzer", *International Studies in Philosophy*, 1, 1–45.

Sprigge, Timothy (1979) "Russell and Bradley on Relations", in Roberts, George W. (ed.), *Bertrand Russell Memorial Volume*, London: Allen and Unwin, 150–170.

Stabler, E.R. (1935) "An Interpretation and Comparison of Three Schools of Thought in the Foundations of Mathematics", *Mathematics Teacher*, 28, 5–35.

Stace, W.T. (1944) "Russell's Neutral Monism", in Schilpp, Paul Arthur (ed.), *The Philosophy of Bertrand Russel*, 3rd edn, New York: Tudor, 1951, 351–384.

Standen, Anthony (1972) "Russell's Paradox Resolved", *New Scientist*, 55 (24 August), 383–385.

Stander, Philip (1974) "Bertrand Russell on the Aims of Education", *Educational Forum*, 38, 447–456.

Stapledon, Olaf (1927) "Mr Bertrand Russell's Ethical Beliefs", *International Journal of Ethics*, 37, 390–402.

Stawell, F. Melian (1914) "Some Problems of Philosophy", *Mind*, 23, 194–206.

Stebbing, L. Susan (1930) "Logical Constructions", in Stebbing, L. Susan, *A Modern Introduction to Logic*, 6th edn, London: Methuen, 1948, 502–505.

Steel, T. (1971) "In Reply to a Paradox", *Mind*, 80, 616.

Steiner, George (1970) "Russell: The Voice of Passionate Reason", *Sunday Times*, 8 February, 12.

Stephen, Karin C. (1914) "Comparison of the Data and Philosophical Methods of Mr Russell and Mr Bergson", *Proceedings of the Aristotelian Society*, 15, 271–303.

Stock, G. (1972) "Russell's Theory of Judgment in Logical Atomism", *Revista Portuguesa de Filosophia*, 28, 458–489.

Stock, G. (1974) "Wittgenstein on Russell's Theory of Judgment", in Royal Institute of Philosophy, *Understanding Wittgenstein*, New York: St Martin's Press, 62–75.

Stone, I.F. (1967) "To Oppose the Stream", in Schoenman, Ralph (ed.), *Bertrand Russell: Philosopher of the Century*, London: Allen and Unwin, 56–60.

Stone, I.F. (1981) "Bertrand Russell as a Moral Force in World Politics", *Russell*, n.s. 1, 7–25.

Stout, George F. (1915) "Mr Russell's Theory of Judgment", *Proceedings of the Aristotelian Society*, 15, 332–352.

Stove, David C. (1960) "Bertrand Russell, Andersonian", *Nation*, 35 (16 January), 22–23.

Strachey, Oliver (1915) "Mr Russell and Some Recent Criticisms of His Views", *Mind*, 24, 16–28.

Strawson, Peter F. (1950) "On Referring", *Mind*, 59, 320–344. Repr. in Flew, Anthony (ed.), *Essays in Conceptual Analysis*, London: Macmillan, 1960, 21–52, and in Klemke, E.D. (ed.), *Essays on Bertrand Russell*, Urbana: University of Illinois Press, 1970, 147–172.

Strawson, Peter F. (1954) "A Reply to Mr Sellars", *Philosophical Review*, 63, 216–231. Repr. in Klemke, E.D. (ed.), *Essays on Bertrand Russell*, Urbana: University of Illinois Press, 1970, 190–204.

Strawson, Peter F. (1964) "Identifying Reference and Truth-Values", *Theoria*, 30, 96–118. Repr. in Klemke, E.D. (ed.), *Essays on Bertrand Russell*, Urbana: University of Illinois Press, 1970, 236–255.

Stroll, Avrum (1973) "Descriptions Again", *Analysis*, 34, 27–28.

Stroll, Avrum (1975) "Russell's 'Proof'", *Canadian Journal of Philosophy*, 4, 653–662.

Stroll, Avrum (1978) "Four Comments on Russell's Theory of Descriptions", *Canadian Journal of Philosophy*, 8, 147–155.

Strong, Charles A. (1922) "Mr Russell's Theory of the External World", *Mind*, 31, 307–320.

Suter, Ronald (1967) "Russell's 'Refutation' of Meinong in 'On Denoting'", *Philosophy and Phenomenological Research*, 27, 512–516.

Swinnerton, Frank Arthur (1934) "Bloomsbury", in Swinnerton, Frank Arthur, *Georgian Scene*, New York: Farrar and Rinehart, 337–377.

Tait, Katharine (1978) "Russell and Feminism", *Russell*, o.s. 29–32, 5–16.

Tait, Katharine (1982–83) "Portrait of the Philosopher as Father", *Russell*, n.s. 2, 21–30.

Tait, Katharine (1987–88) "The Beacon Hill School Materials", *Russell*, n.s. 7, 137–140.

Tallon, Hugh, J. (1939) "Russell's Doctrine of the Logical Proposition", *New Scholasticism*, 13, 31–48.

Taqi, Syed Mohammad (1955) "Bertrand Russell and Formal Logic", *Pakistan Philosophical Congress*, 2, 119–128.

Taschek, William W. (1992) "Frege's Puzzle, Sense, and Information Content", *Mind*, 101, 767–791.

Tawney, G.A. (1914) "Transcendentalism and the Externality of Relations", *Journal of Philosophy, Psychology, and Scientific Methods*, 11, 431–436.

Taylor, Gerald (1993–94) "Acquaintance, Physical Objects, and Knowledge of the Self", *Russell*, n.s. 13, 168–184.

Taylor, Gladys G. (1981) "The Analytic and Synthetic in Russell's Philosophy of Mathematics", *Philosophical Studies*, 39, 51–59.

Taylor, Gladys G. (1984) "The *Double Entente* of Russell's Thesis that Mathematics is Logic", *International Logic Review*, 15, 105–117.

Thayer, H.S. (1947) "Two Theories of Truth: The Relation Between the Theories of John Dewey and Bertrand Russell", *Journal of Philosophy*, 44, 516–527.

Tibbetts, Paul (1972) "Phenomenological and Empirical Inadequacies of Russell's Theory of Perception", *Philosophical Studies (Ireland)*, 20, 98–108.

Trevelyan, Julian (1967) "An Old Friendship", in Schoenman, Ralph (ed.), *Bertrand Russell: Philosopher of the Century*, London: Allen and Unwin, 26–31.

Tully, Robert E. (1988) "Russell's Neutral Monism", *Russell*, n.s. 8, 209–224. Repr. in Winchester, Ian, and Kenneth Blackwell (eds), *Antinomies and Paradoxes: Studies in Russell's Early Philosophy*, Hamilton: McMaster University Library Press, 1988, 209–224.

Tully, Robert E. (1988) "Wittgenstein, Russell, and the Self", *University of Toronto Quarterly*, 57, 516–528.

Tully, Robert E. (1993) "Regarding Privacy", in Irvine, A.D., and G.A. Wedeking (eds), *Russell and Analytic Philosophy*, Toronto: University of Toronto Press, 243–262.

Tully, Robert E. (1993–94) "Three Studies of Russell's Neutral Monism", *Russell*, n.s. 13, 5–35, 185–202.

Turcon, Sheila (1983–84) "A Quaker Wedding: The Marriage of Bertrand Russell and Alys Pearsall Smith", *Russell*, n.s. 3, 103–128.

Turcon, Sheila (1986) "Russell Sold Up", *Russell*, n.s. 6, 71–78.

Turing, A.M. (1948) "Practical Forms of Type Theory", *Journal of Symbolic Logic*, 13, 80–94.

Turnau, Pawel (1991) "Russell's Argument Against Frege's Sense-Reference Distinction", *Russell*, n.s. 11, 52–66.

Turner, J.E. (1914) "Mr Russell on Sense-Data and Knowledge", *Mind*, 23, 251–255.

Turner, J.E. (1915) "Mr Strachey's Defence of Mr Russell's Theory", *Mind*, 24, 532–535.

Umphrey, Stewart (1988) "The Meinongian–Antimeinongian Dispute Reviewed: A Reply to Dejnozka and Butchvarov", *Grazer Philosophische Studien*, 32, 169–179.

Unna, Sarah (1919) "Bertrand Russell – Then and Now", *Journal of Philosophy, Psychology, and Scientific Methods*, 16, 393–403.

Untermeyer, Louis (1955) "Bertrand Russell", in Untermeyer, Louis, *Makers of the Modern World*, New York: Simon and Schuster, 450–457.

Unwin, Philip (1970) "Bertrand Russell as His Publishers Knew Him", *Bookseller*, 7 February, 388.

Urmson, J.O. (1956) "Philosophical Analysis and Logical Atomism", in Urmson, J.O., *Philosophical Analysis: Its Development Between the Two World Wars*, Oxford: Oxford University Press, 1–98.

Urmson, J.O. (1969) "Russell on Acquaintance with the Past", *Philosophical Review*, 78, 510–515.

Urmson, J.O. (1973) "Russell's Incomplete Symbols", *Analysis*, 33, 111–112.

Urmson, J.O. (1986) "Russell on Universals", in Vesey, Godfrey (ed.), *Philosophers Ancient and Modern*, Cambridge: Cambridge University Press, 245–258.

Urquhart, Alasdair (1988) "Russell's Zigzag Path to the Ramified Theory of Types", *Russell*, n.s. 8, 82–91. Repr. in Winchester, Ian, and Kenneth Blackwell (eds), *Antinomies and Paradoxes: Studies in Russell's Early Philosophy*, Hamilton: McMaster University Library Press, 1988, 82–91.

Urquhart, Alasdair (1994–95) "G.F. Stout and the Theory of Descriptions", *Russell*, n.s. 14, 163–171.

Ushenko, Andrew Paul (1933) "The Problem of General Propositions", *Monist*, 43, 285–289.

Ushenko, Andrew Paul (1934) "A Modification of the Theory of Types", *Monist*, 44, 147–149.

Ushenko, Andrew Paul (1941) "Comments on Russell's *An Inquiry into Meaning and Truth*", *Philosophy and Phenomenological Research*, 2, 98–100.

Ushenko, Andrew Paul (1944) "Russell's Critique of Empiricism", in Schilpp, Paul

Arthur (ed.), *The Philosophy of Bertrand Russell*, 3rd edn, New York: Tudor, 1951, 385–417.

Ushenko, Andrew Paul (1956) "A Note on Russell and Naive Realism", *Journal of Philosophy*, 53, 819–820.

van Fraassen, Bas C. (1967) "A Note on Bacon's Alternative to Russell", *Philosophical Studies*, 18, 47–48.

van Fraassen, Bas C. (1979) "Russell's Philosophical Account of Probability", in Roberts, George W. (ed.), *Bertrand Russell Memorial Volume*, London: Allen and Unwin, 384–413.

van Horn, C.E. (1916) "An Axiom in Symbolic Logic", *Proceedings of the Cambridge Philosophical Society*, 19, 22–31.

van Patten, James (1965) "Some Reflections on Bertrand Russell's Philosophy", *Educational Theory*, 15, 58–65.

Vardy, P. (1979) "Some Remarks on the Relationship Between Russell's Vicious-Circle Principle and Russell's Paradox", *Dialectica*, 33, 3–19.

Veatch, Henry B. (1970) "The Philosophy of Logical Atomism: A Realism *Manqué*", in Klemke, E.D. (ed.), *Essays on Bertrand Russell*, Urbana: University of Illinois Press, 102–117.

Vesey, G.N.A. (1979) "Self-Acquaintance and the Meaning of 'I'", in Roberts, George W. (ed.), *Bertrand Russell Memorial Volume*, London: Allen and Unwin, 339–347.

Vuillemin, Jules (1972) "Logical Flaws on Philosophical Problems: On Russell's *Principia Mathematica*", *Revue Internationale de Philosophie*, 26, 534–556.

Vuillemin, Jules (1972) "Platonism in Russell's Early Philosophy and the Principle of Abstraction", in Pears, David F. (ed.), *Bertrand Russell: A Collection of Critical Essays*, Garden City, N.Y.: Anchor Books, 305–324.

Wagner, Hilmar (1967) "A Comparison of Bertrand Russell and Alfred North Whitehead on Education", *Journal of Thought*, 2, 65–74.

Wahl, Russell (1984–85) "Knowledge by Description", *Russell*, n.s. 4, 262–270.

Wahl, Russell (1986) "Bertrand Russell's Theory of Judgement", *Synthese*, 68, 383–407.

Wahl, Russell (1993) "Russell's Theory of Meaning and Denotation and 'On Denoting'", *Journal of the History of Philosophy*, 31, 71–94.

Wang, Hao (1965) "Russell and His Logic", *Ratio*, 7, 1–34.

Wang, Hao (1966) "Russell and Philosophy", *Journal of Philosophy*, 63, 670–672.

Wang, Hao (1974) "Bertrand Russell as an Example", in Wang, Hao, *From Mathematics to Philosophy*, London: Routledge and Kegan Paul, 346–353.

Wang, Hao (1984) "Wittgenstein's and Other Mathematical Philosophies", *Monist*, 67, 18–28.

Wang, Hao (1986) "Russell and Philosophy in This Century", in Wang, Hao, *Beyond Analytic Philosophy*, Cambridge, Mass.: MIT Press, 45–73.

Warnock, G.J. (1958) "Bertrand Russell", in Warnock, G.J., *English Philosophy Since 1900*, 2nd edn, Oxford: Oxford University Press, 1969, 25–33.

Washburne, Carleton (1941) "The Case as a School Administrator Sees It", in Dewey, John, and Horace M. Kallen (eds), *The Bertrand Russell Case*, New York: Viking, 157–167.

Waterlow, S. (1910) "Some Philosophical Implications of Mr Bertrand Russell's Logical Theory of Mathematics", *Proceedings of the Aristotelian Society*, 10, 132–188.

Watkin, Edward Ingram (1937) "Lord Russell: Religion Without Reason", in Watkin, Edward Ingram, *Men and Tendencies*, London: Sheed and Ward, 49–92.

Watson, George (1947) "Russell's Basic Propositions", *The Personalist*, 28, 140–146.

Wedberg, A. (1937) "Bertrand Russell's Empiricism", in Hedenius, Ingemar, *et al.* (eds), *Philosophical Essays*, Uppsala: Almqvist and Wiksell, 345–387.

Weiss, Bernard (1994) "On Russell's Argument for Restricting Modes of Specification and Domains of Quantification", *History and Philosophy of Logic*, 15, 173–188.

Weiss, Paul (1928) "The Theory of Types", *Mind*, 37, 338–348.

Weiss, Paul (1932) "The Metaphysics and Logic of Classes", *Monist*, 42, 112–154.

Weiss, Paul (1938) "Thoughts Out of Season", *The New Republic*, 95, 193–194.

Weitz, Morris (1944) "Analysis and the Unity of Russell's Philosophy", in Schilpp, Paul Arthur (ed.), *The Philosophy of Bertrand Russell*, 3rd edn, New York: Tudor, 1951, 55–121.

Welding, S.O. (1971) "Frege's Conception of Sense and Reference Related to Russell's Theory of Definite Descriptions", *Revue Internationale de Philosophie*, 25, 389–402.

Welding, S.O. (1972) "Russell's Theory of Definite Description as Opposed to Quine's Singular Terms", *Revue Internationale de Philosophie*, 26, 513–533.

Wells, Donald A. (1954) "Basic Propositions in Ayer and Russell", *Journal of Philosophy*, 51, 124–127.

Wenderoth, Christine (1986) "Bertrand Russell's Thought", *Religious Humanism*, 20, 18–27.

Wertz, S.K. (1991) "On Russell's Argument Concerning Philosophic Contemplation", *South West Philosophical Studies*, 13, 117–128.

Wettstein, Howard K. (1981) "Demonstrative Reference and Definite Descriptions", *Philosophical Studies*, 40, 241–258.

Wettstein, Howard K. (1990) "Frege–Russell Semantics?", *Dialectica*, 44, 113–135. Repr. in Wettstein, Howard K., *Has Semantics Rested on a Mistake?*, Stanford: Stanford University Press, 1991, 86–108.

White, Alan R. (1959) "The 'Meaning' of Russell's Theory of Descriptions", *Analysis*, 20, 8–9.

White, Alan R. (1979) "Belief as a Propositional Attitude", in Roberts, George W. (ed.), *Bertrand Russell Memorial Volume*, London: Allen and Unwin, 242–252.

White, Alan R. (1979) "Propositions and Sentences", in Roberts, George W. (ed.), *Bertrand Russell Memorial Volume*, London: Allen and Unwin, 22–33.

White, Alan R. (1981) "Knowledge, Acquaintance, and Awareness", *Midwest Studies in Philosophy*, 6, 159–172.

White, Morton Gabriel (1955) "Mathematics, Logic, and Analysis: Bertrand Russell", in White, Morton Gabriel, *Age of Analysis*, Boston: Houghton and Mifflin, 189–203.

Whitehead, Alfred North (1986) "To the Masters and Fellows of Trinity College, Cambridge", *Russell*, n.s. 6, 62–70.

Whitman, Alden (1970) "Governed By Three Passions", *New York Times*, 3 February, 1, 30.

Wickham, Harvey (1930) "Visual Black Dot Occurs: Bertrand Russell", in Wickham, Harvey, *The Unrealists*, New York: Dial Press, 165–195.

Wiener, Norbert (1914) "A Simplification of the Logic of Relations", *Proceedings of the Cambridge Philosophical Society*, 17, 387–390. Repr. in van Heijenoort, Jean, *From Frege to Gödel*, Cambridge, Mass.: Harvard University Press, 1967, 224–227.

Wiener, Norbert (1914) "Studies in Synthetic Logic", *Proceedings of the Cambridge Philosophical Society*, 18, 14–28.

Wiener, Norbert (1916) "Mr Lewis and Implication", *Journal of Philosophy, Psychology, and Scientific Methods*, 13, 656–662.

Wiener, Phillip P. (1944) "Method in Russell's Work on Leibniz", in Schilpp, Paul Arthur (ed.), *The Philosophy of Bertrand Russell*, 3rd edn, New York: Tudor, 1951, 257–276.

Wilder, Raymond L. (1952) "The Frege–Russell Thesis: Mathematics as an Extension of Logic", in Wilder, Raymond L., *The Foundations of Mathematics*, New York: John Wiley and Sons, 209–229.

Wilder, Raymond L. (1952) "The Russell Contradiction", in Wilder, Raymond L., *The Foundations of Mathematics*, New York: John Wiley and Sons, 55–57.

Will, Frederick L. (1979) "The Concern About Truth", in Roberts, George W. (ed.), *Bertrand Russell Memorial Volume*, London: Allen and Unwin, 264–284.

Williams, C.J.F. (1985) "Aristotle's Theory of Descriptions", *Philosophical Review*, 94, 63–80.

Williams, C.J.F. (1993) "Russelm", *Philosophical Quarterly*, 43, 496–499.

Williams, D.C. (1932) "On Having Ideas in the Head", *Journal of Philosophy*, 29, 617–631.

Williams, H.H. (1919) "Professor Russell's Infinite", *Monist*, 29, 616–619.

Willis, Kirk (1976) "The Critical Reception of 'German Social Democracy'", *Russell*, o.s. 21–22, 35–45.

Willis, Kirk (1984) "The Adolescent Russell and the Victorian Crisis of Faith", *Russell*, n.s. 4, 123–135. Repr. in Moran, Margaret, and Carl Spadoni (eds), *Intellect and Social Conscience: Essays on Bertrand Russell's Early Work*, Hamilton: McMaster University Library Press, 1984, 123–135.

Willis, Kirk (1989) "'This Place is Hell': Bertrand Russell at Harvard, 1914", *New England Quarterly*, 62, 3–26.

Willis, Kirk (1996–97) "Russell and His Biographers", *Russell*, n.s. 16, 129–143.

Wilson, Edmund (1995) "A.N. Whitehead and Bertrand Russell", in Wilson, Edmund, *From the Uncollected Edmund Wilson*, Columbus: Ohio University Press, 45–49.

Wilson, Edwin Bidwell (1904) "The Foundations of Mathematics", *Bulletin of the American Mathematical Society*, 11, 74–93.

Wilson, Fred (1995) "Burgersdijck, Bradley, Russell, Bergmann: Four Philosophers on the Ontology of Relations", *Modern Schoolman*, 72, 283–310.

Wilson, N.L. (1953) "Description and Designation", *Journal of Philosophy*, 50, 369–383.

Wilson, N.L. (1953) "In Defense of Proper Names Against Descriptions", *Philosophical Studies*, 4, 72–78.

Wilson, N.L. (1976) "The Semantics of the Philosophy of Logical Atomism", in Thomas, J.E., and Kenneth Blackwell (eds), *Russell in Review*, Toronto: Samuel Stevens, Hakkert and Co., 237–250.

Wilson, Thomas A. (1985) "Russell's Later Theory of Perception", *Russell*, n.s. 5, 26–43.

Wilson, W. Kent (1980) "Incomplete Symbols and Russell's Proof", *Canadian Journal of Philosophy*, 10, 233–250.

Winchester, Ian (1988) "The Antinomy of Dynamical Causation in *Leibniz* and the *Principles* and Russell's Early Picture of Physics", *Russell*, n.s. 8, 35–45. Repr. in Winchester, Ian, and Kenneth Blackwell (eds), *Antinomies and Paradoxes: Studies in Russell's Early Philosophy*, Hamilton: McMaster University Library Press, 1988, 35–45.

Winslade, William J. (1970) "Russell's Theory of Relations", in Klemke, E.D. (ed.), *Essays on Bertrand Russell*, Urbana: University of Illinois Press, 81–101.

Wisdom, John (1953) "Bertrand Russell and Modern Philosophy", in Wisdom, John, *Philosophy and Psychoanalysis*, Oxford: Blackwell, 195–209.

Wittgenstein, Ludwig (1957) "Notes on Logic, September, 1913", *Journal of Philosophy*, 54, 231–245.

Wittgenstein, Ludwig (1974) "Letters to Bertrand Russell 1912–1935", in Wittgenstein, Ludwig, *Letters to Russell, Keynes, and Moore*, Oxford: Basil Blackwell, 7–104.

Wolff, Karen Ann (1970) "Russell on Sense and Reference", *Dianoia*, 13–18.

Wollheim, Richard (1974) "Bertrand Russell and the Liberal Tradition", in Nakhnikian, George (ed.), *Bertrand Russell's Philosophy*, London: Duckworth, 209–220.

Wood, Alan (1959) "Russell's Philosophy: A Study of its Development", in Russell, Bertrand, *My Philosophical Development*, London: George Allen and Unwin, 255–277.

Wood, Herbert George (1924) "Logic and Pessimism", in Wood, Herbert George, *Living Issues in Religious Thought*, London: Allen and Unwin, 26–50.

Wood, Herbert George (1924) "Moral Scepticism of Today", in Wood, Herbert George, *Living Issues in Religious Thought*, London: Allen and Unwin, 51–64.

Wood, Joanne A. (1994) "Lighthouse Bodies: The Neutral Monism of Virginia Woolf and Bertrand Russell", *Journal of the History of Ideas*, 55, 483–502.

Woodger, J.H. (1930) "Russell's Theory of Perception", *Monist*, 40, 621–636.

Woodhouse, Howard (1974) "On a Suggested Contradiction in Russell's Educational Philosophy", *Russell*, o.s. 15, 3–14.

Woodhouse, Howard (1983) "The Concept of Growth in Bertrand Russell's Educational Thought", *Journal of Educational Thought*, 17 (April), 12–21.

Woodhouse, Howard (1985–86) "Science as Method: The Conceptual Link Between Russell's Philosophy and His Educational Thought", *Russell*, n.s. 5, 150–161.

Woodhouse, Howard (1987) "More Than Mere Musings: Russell's Reflections on Education as Philosophy", *Russell*, n.s. 7, 176–178.

Woodhouse, Howard (1992–93) "Russell and Whitehead on the Process of Growth in Education", *Russell*, n.s. 12, 135–159.

Woodhouse, Howard (1994–95) "Russell as Philosopher of Education: Reply to Hager", *Russell*, n.s. 14, 193–205.

Wrinch, Dorothy Maud (1917) "Mr Russell's Lowell Lectures", *Mind*, 26, 448–452.

Wrinch, Dorothy Maud (1918) "Recent Work in Mathematical Logic", *Monist*, 28, 620–623.

Yourgrau, Palle (1985) "Russell and Kaplan on Denoting", *Philosophy and Phenomenological Research*, 46, 315–321.

Zytaruk, George J. (1983) "Lectures on Immortality and Ethics: The Failed D.H. Lawrence–Bertrand Russell Collaboration", *Russell*, n.s. 3, 7–15.

3. Additional Reviews

Armstrong, David M. (1959) Review of *My Philosophical Development* and *The Wisdom of the West*, *The Observer* (Sydney), 2, 24 (28 November), 31.

Ayer, Alfred Jules (1984) Review of *Theory of Knowledge*, *The Times Literary Supplement*, no. 4262, December 7, 1404.

Bedau, Hugo (1958) Review of *Logic and Knowledge, Philosophy of Science*, 25, 136–139.

Bergmann, Gustav (1949) Review of *Human Knowledge*, *Physics Today*, 2(4), 27–28.

Berlin, Isaiah (1947) Review of *A History of Western Philosophy*, *Mind*, 56, 151–166.

Bernstein, B.A. (1926) Review of *Principia Mathematica*, Vol. 1 (2nd edn), *Bulletin of the American Mathematical Society*, 32, 711–713.

Bosanquet, Bernard (1912) Review of *Problems of Philosophy*, *Mind*, 21, 556–564.

Bosanquet, Bernard (1915) Review of *Our Knowledge of the External World*, *Philosophical Review*, 24, 431–439.

Bosanquet, Bernard (1917) Review of *Principles of Social Reconstruction*, *Mind*, 26, 233–234.

Britton, Karl (1960) Review of *John Stuart Mill*, *Philosophy*, 35, 62–65.

Broad, C.D. (1918) Review of *Mysticism and Logic*, *Mind*, 27, 484–492.

Broad, C.D. (1928) Review of *Analysis of Matter*, *Mind*, 37, 88–95.

Burns, C. Delisle (1930) Review of *Marriage and Morals*, *International Journal of Ethics*, 40, 435–436.

Carnap, Rudolf (1931) Review of *Principia Mathematica, Vols 1, 2 and 3* (2nd edn), *Erkenntnis*, 2, 73–75.

Catlin, George E. (1936) Review of *Freedom Versus Organization*, *Philosophical Review*, 45, 81–82.

Church, Alonzo (1928) Review of *Principia Mathematica, Vols 2 and 3* (2nd edn), *Bulletin of the American Mathematical Society*, 34, 237–240.

Cohen, Morris R. (1912) Review of *Principia Mathematica, Vol. 1*, *Philosophical Review*, 21, 87–91.

Couturat, Louis (1898) Review of *Essay on the Foundations of Geometry*, *Revue de Métaphysique et de Morale*, 6, 354–380.

Couturat, Louis (1904) Review of *Principles of Mathematics*, *Bulletin des Sciences Mathematiques*, 28, 129–147.

Denonn, Lester E. (1941) Review of *An Inquiry Into Meaning and Truth*, *Philosophic Abstracts*, 4, 12–13.

Dewey, John (1926) Review of *Education and the Good Life*, *New Republic*, 46, 410–411.

Duncan, George Martin (1901) Review of *A Critical Exposition of the Philosophy of Leibniz*, *Philosophical Review*, 10, 288–297.

Eddington, Arthur S. (1928) Review of *Analysis of Matter*, *Journal of Philosophical Studies*, 3, 93–95.

Edgley, R. (1956) Review of *Human Society in Ethics and Politics*, *Mind*, 65, 551–557.

Eliot, T.S. (1927) Review of *Why I Am Not a Christian*, *Criterion*, 6, 177–179.

Ewing, A.C. (1932) Review of *The Scientific Outlook*, *Philosophy*, 7, 233–235.

Ewing, A.C. (1955) Review of *Human Society in Ethics and Politics*, *Philosophy*, 30, 283–285.

Fite, Warner (1922) Review of *The Analysis of Mind*, *Philosophical Review*, 31, 298–303.

Forder H.G. (1938) Review of *The Principles of Mathematics* (2nd edn), *Mathematical Gazette*, 22, 300–301.

Halsted, George Bruce (1897) Review of *The Foundations of Geometry*, *Science*, 5, 487–491.

Handcock, W.D. (1948) Review of *Philosophy and Politics*, *Philosophy*, 23, 270–272.

Hook, Sidney (1969) Review of *The Autobiography of Bertrand Russell*, *New York Times*, 26 October, sec. 7, 7, 24.

Kaufmann, Felix (1947) Review of *A History of Western Philosophy*, *Philosophy and Phenomenological Research*, 7, 461–466.

Kennard, E.H. (1928) Review of *The Analysis of Matter*, *Philosophical Review*, 37, 382–385.

Kneale, William C. (1949) Review of *Human Knowledge*, *Mind*, 58, 369–378.

Knight, Frank H. (1939) Review of *Power*, *Ethics*, 49, 253–285.

Krikorian, Y.H. (1949) Review of *Human Knowledge*, *Scientific American*, 180(2), 56–59.

Lamprecht, S.P. (1939) Review of *Power*, *Journal of Philosophy*, 36, 387–389.

Langer, Susanne K. (1938) Review of *The Principles of Mathematics* (2nd edn), *Journal of Symbolic Logic*, 3, 156–157.

Langford, C.H. (1928) Review of *Principia Mathematica, Vols 2 and 3* (2nd edn), *Isis*, 10, 513–519.

Larrabee, H.A. (1936) Review of *Religion and Science*, *Journal of Philosophy*, 33, 55–56.

Latta, Robert (1901) Review of *A Critical Exposition of the Philosophy of Leibniz*, *Mind*, 10, 525–533.

Lenzen, V.F. (1929) Review of *The Analysis of Matter* and *Philosophy*, *Journal of Philosophy*, 26, 637–639.

Lewis, C.I. (1914) Review of *Principia Mathematica, Vol. 2*, *Journal of Philosophy, Psychology, and Scientific Methods*, 11, 497–502.

Lewis, C.I. (1928) Review of *Principia Mathematica, Vols 1, 2 and 3* (2nd edn), *American Mathematical Monthly*, 35, 200–205.

Lewis, John (1949) Review of *Authority and the Individual*, *Modern Quarterly* (London), 4, 341–365.

Macbeath, A. (1955) Review of *Human Society in Ethics and Politics*, *Philosophical Quarterly*, 5, 379–380.

McGill, V.J. (1952) Review of *The Impact of Science on Society*, *Journal of Philosophy*, 49, 79–81.

McGill, V.J. (1952) Review of *Unpopular Essays*, *Journal of Philosophy*, 49, 79–81.

McGilvary, Evander Bradley (1911) Review of *Philosophical Essays*, *Philosophical Review*, 20, 422–426.

MacIver, R.M. (1930) Review of *Marriage and Morals*, *New Republic*, 61, 256–257.

Malcolm, Norman (1950) Review of *Human Knowledge*, *Philosophical Review*, 59, 94–106.

Meder, Albert E. (1940) Review of *The Principles of Mathematics* (2nd edn), *Scripta Mathematica*, 7, 138–141.

Milne, E.A. (1948–49) Review of *Human Knowledge*, *Hibbert Journal*, 47, 297–299.

Moore, G.E. (1899) Review of *An Essay on the Foundations of Geometry*, *Mind*, 8, 397–405.

Murray, D.A. (1899) Review of *An Essay on the Foundations of Geometry*, *Philosophical Review*, 8, 49–57.

Mursell, James L. (1922) Review of *The Analysis of Mind*, *Journal of Philosophy*, 19, 163–166.

Nagel, Ernest (1932) Review of *The Scientific Outlook*, *Journal of Philosophy*, 29, 386–388.

Nagel, Ernest (1938) Review of *Principles of Mathematics* (2nd edn), *Journal of Philosophy*, 35, 191–192.

Nagel, Ernest (1941) Review of *An Inquiry into Meaning and Truth*, *Journal of Philosophy*, 38, 253–70.

Niebuhr, Reinhold (1957) Review of *Why I Am Not a Christian*, *New York Times*, September 22, sec. 7, 6, 30.

Nott, Kathleen (1959) Review of *Wisdom of the West*, *The Bookman*, October, 49.

Paton, H.J. (1942) Review of *An Inquiry into Meaning and Truth*, *Philosophy*, 17, 82–85.

Peirce, C.S. (1903) Review of *The Principles of Mathematics*, *The Nation*, 77 (October), 308.

Popper, Karl R. (1992) Broadcast review of *The History of Western Philosophy*, *Russell*, n.s. 12, 19–21.

Ramsey, Frank Plumpton (1925) Review of *Principia Mathematica* (2nd edn), *Mind*, 34, 506–507.

Ramsey, Frank Plumpton (1925) Review of *Principia Mathematica* (2nd edn), *Nature*, 116 (July), 127–128.

Randall, John Herman, Jr (1960) Review of *Wisdom of the West*, *Journal of Philosophy*, 57, 365–368.

Ratner, Joseph (1946) Review of *Physics and Experience*, *Journal of Philosophy*, 43, 276–278.

Ratner, Joseph (1947) Review of *A History of Western Philosophy*, *Journal of Philosophy*, 44, 39–49.

Riedl, John (1941) Review of *An Inquiry Into Meaning and Truth*, *Thought*, 16, 740–742.

Ritchie, A.D. (1946) Review of *History of Western Philosophy*, *Mind*, 55, 256–262.

Ritchie, A.D. (1946) Review of *History of Western Philosophy*, *The Observer*, 24 November, 4.

Ritchie, A.D. (1949) Review of *Human Knowledge*, *Nature*, 163, 267–268.

Russell, L.J. (1928) Review of *An Outline of Philosophy*, *Journal of Philosophical Studies*, 3, 231–235.

Russell, L.J. (1938) Review of *A Critical Exposition of the Philosophy of Leibniz*, *Philosophy*, 13, 217–220.

Russell, L.J. (1944) Review of *An Inquiry into Meaning and Truth*, *Mind*, 53, 332–340.

Russell, L.J. (1946) Review of *Physics and Experience*, *Philosophy*, 21, 276–279.

Russell, L.J. (1949) Review of *Human Knowledge*, *Philosophy*, 24, 253–260.

Russell, L.J. (1953) Review of *New Hopes for a Changing World*, *Philosophy*, 28, 79–81.

Russell, L.J. (1957) Review of *The Analysis of Matter*, *Philosophy*, 32, 364–365.

Schiller, F.C.S. (1931) Review of *The Conquest of Happiness*, *Mind*, 40, 238–241.

Shaw, James Byrnie (1912) Review of *Principia Mathematica*, *Bulletin of the American Mathematical Society*, 18, 386–411.

Shearman, A.T. (1907) Review of *Principles of Mathematics*, *Mind*, 16, 254–265.

Sheffer, Henry M. (1926) Review of *Principia Mathematica, Vol. 1* (2nd edn), *Isis*, 8, 226–231.

Smith, Huston (1960) Review of *The Wisdom of the West*, *Saturday Review*, 42 (7 May), 34.

Sparshott, F.E. (1958) Review of *Why I Am Not a Christian*, *Tamarack Review*, 6, 90–94.

Stebbing, L. Susan (1929) Review of *Sceptical Essays*, *Journal of Philosophical Studies*, 4, 263–264.

Stebbing, L. Susan (1938) Review of *The Principles of Mathematics* (2nd edn), *Philosophy*, 13, 481–483.

Tait, Katharine (1992–93) Review of *The Selected Letters of Bertrand Russell*, *Russell*, n.s. 12, 211–221.

Turner, John Pickett (1913) Review of *The Problems of Philosophy*, *Journal of Philosophy, Psychology, and Scientific Methods*, 10, 161–164.

Ushenko, Andrew Paul (1941) Review of *An Inquiry Into Meaning and Truth*, *Philosophy of Science*, 8, 391–392.

Waters, Bruce (1940–41) Review of *An Inquiry Into Meaning and Truth*, *Philosophy and Phenomenological Research*, 1, 499–504.

Wellmuth, John J. (1942) Review of *An Inquiry Into Meaning and Truth*, *New Scholasticism*, 16, 180–182.

Will, Frederick L. (1942) Review of *An Inquiry into Meaning and Truth*, *Philosophical Review*, 51, 327–331.

Wilson, Edwin B. (1904) Review of *Principles of Mathematics*, *Bulletin of the American Mathematical Society*, 11, 74–93.

Wollheim, Richard (1959) Review of *The Wisdom of the West*, *The Spectator*, 9 October, 482.

Woolf, Leonard (1938) Review of *Power*, *London Mercury*, 39, 74–76.

4. Encyclopedia and Dictionary Entries

Anon. (1977) "Russell, Bertrand Arthur William", in Bullock, Alan, and Oliver Stallybrass (eds), *The Harper Dictionary of Modern Thought*, New York: Harper and Row, 551.

Anon. (1981) "Russell, Bertrand", in Maurer, James F. (ed.), *Concise Dictionary of Scientific Biography*, New York: Charles Scribner's Sons, 597–598.

Anon. (1994) "Russell, Bertrand (Arthur William)", in Crystal, David (ed.), *The Cambridge Biographical Encyclopedia*, Cambridge: Cambridge University Press, 821.

Anon. (1994) "Russell, Bertrand (Arthur William)", in Trosky, Susan M. (ed.), *Contemporary Authors*, New Revision Series Vol. 44, Detroit: Gale, 371–376.

Ayer, Alfred Jules (1960) "Russell, Bertrand Arthur William", in Urmson, J.O. (ed.), *Western Philosophy and Philosophers*, New York: Hawthorn, 331–335.

Ayer, Alfred Jules (1989) "Russell", in Urmson, J.O., and Jonathan Rée (eds), *The Concise Encyclopedia of Western Philosophy and Philosophers*, London: Unwin Hyman, 281–285.

Biddiss, Michael (1990) "Russell, Bertrand (Arthur William)", in Robbins, Keith (ed.), *The Blackwell Biographical Dictionary of British Political Life in the Twentieth Century*, London: Blackwell, 363–365.

Black, Max (1942) "Russell, Bertrand A.W.", in Runes, Dagobert D. (ed.), *Dictionary of Philosophy*, New York: Philosophical Library, 274.

Blackburn, Simon (1994) "Russell, Bertrand Arthur William", in Blackburn, Simon, *The Oxford Dictionary of Philosophy*, Oxford: Oxford University Press, 335–336.

Borowski, E.J., and J.M. Borwein (1989) "Russell, Lord Bertrand Arthur William", in Borowski, E.J., and J.M. Borwein, *Dictionary of Mathematics*, London: Collins, 517–518.

Collinson, Diané (1987) "Bertrand Russell", in Collinson, Diané, *Fifty Major Philosophers*, London: Routledge, 134–138.

Crawshay-Williams, Rupert (1974) "Russell, Bertrand", in Benton, Helen Hemingway (pub.), *The New Encyclopaedia Britannica*, Micropaedia Vol. 10, 15th edn, Chicago: Encyclopedia Britannica, Inc., 249–250.

Daintith, John, and R.D. Nelson (1989) "Russell, Bertrand Arthur William", in Daintith, John, and R.D. Nelson, *The Penguin Dictionary of Mathematics*, London: Penguin Books, 287.

Edwards, Paul, William P. Alston, and A.N. Prior (1967) "Russell, Bertrand Arthur William", in Edwards, Paul (ed.), *The Encyclopedia of Philosophy*, Vol. 7, New York: Macmillan, 235–258.

Flew, Antony (1979) "Russell, Bertrand Arthur William", in Flew, Antony, *A Dictionary of Philosophy*, London: Pan Books, 308–309.

Frolov, I. (1967) "Russell, Bertrand", in Frolov, I., *Dictionary of Philosophy*, Moscow: Progress Publishers, 365–366.

Griffin, Nicholas, and David B. Martens (1995) "Russell, Bertrand (Arthur William)", in Audi, Robert (ed.), *The Cambridge Dictionary of Philosophy*, Cambridge: Cambridge University Press, 699–702.

Lacey, A.R. (1976) "Russell, Bertrand Arthur William", in Lacey, A.R., *A Dictionary of Philosophy*, London: Routledge and Kegan Paul, 187.

Leiser, M. (1992) "Russell, Bertrand", in McGreal, Ian P. (ed.), *Great Thinkers of the Western World*, New York: HarperCollins, 465–468.

Martin, Robert M. (1991) "Russell, Bertrand (Arthur William)", in Martin, Robert M., *The Philosopher's Dictionary*, Peterborough, Ont.: Broadview Press, 205.

Quinton, Anthony (1981) "Russell, Bertrand Arthur William", in Williams, E.T., and C.S. Nicholls (eds), *The Dictionary of National Biography, 1961–1970*, Oxford: Oxford University Press, 901–908.

Quinton, Anthony (1983) "Russell, Bertrand Arthur William", in Bullock, Alan, and R.B. Woodings (eds), *The Fontana Dictionary of Modern Thinkers*, London: Fontana, 661–662.

Reese, William L. (1980) "Russell, Bertrand", in Reese, William L., *Dictionary of Philosophy and Religion*, Atlantic Highlands, N.J.: Humanities, 500–503.

Rockler, Michael (1996) "Russell, Bertrand", in Chambliss, J.J. (ed.), *Philosophy of Education: An Encyclopedia*, New York: Garland, 573–575.

Rodríguez-Consuegra, F.A. (1994) "Mathematical Logic and Logicism From Peano to Quine, 1890–1940", in Grattan-Guinness, I. (ed.), *Companion Encyclopedia of the History and Philosophy of the Mathematical Sciences*, Vol. 1, London: Routledge, 617–628.

Sainsbury, R.M. (1992) "Russell, Bertrand Arthur William", in Dancy, Jonathan, and Ernest Sosa (eds), *A Companion to Epistemology*, Oxford: Blackwell, 450–452.

Sainsbury, R.M. (1995) "Russell, Bertrand", in Honderich, Ted (ed.), *The Oxford Companion to Philosophy*, Oxford: Oxford University Press, 781–785.

Sainsbury, R.M. (1995) "Russell, Bertrand Arthur William", in Kim, Jaegwon, and Ernest Sosa (eds), *A Companion to Metaphysics*, Oxford: Blackwell, 446–450.

Sainsbury, R.M. (1996) "Frege and Russell", in Bunnin, Nicholas F. and E.P. Tsui-James (eds), *The Blackwell Companion to Philosophy*, Cambridge: Blackwell, 662–677.

Stewart, Ralph (1990) "Bertrand Russell", in Beum, Robert (ed.), *Modern British Essayists, Second Series*, (*Dictionary of Literary Biography*, vol. 100), Detroit: Gale Research, 268–284.

Thomas, Henry (1965), "Russell, Bertrand", in Thomas, Henry, *Biographical Encyclopedia of Philosophy*, Garden City, N.Y.: Doubleday, 216–217.

Tice, Terrence N., and Thomas P. Slavens (1983) "Bertrand Russell", in Tice, Terrence N., and Thomas P. Slavens (eds), *Research Guide to Philosophy*, Chicago: American Library Association, 172–181.

Vellacott, Jo (1985) "Russell, Bertrand Arthur William", in Josephson, Harold (ed.), *Biographical Dictionary of Modern Peace Leaders*, Westport, Conn.: Greenwood, 825–827.

White, Alan (1996) "Russell, Bertrand Arthur William, Third Earl Russell", in Mautner, Thomas (ed.), *A Dictionary of Philosophy*, Oxford: Blackwell, 374–375.

Willis, Kirk (1995) "Russell, Bertrand", in Leventhal, F.M. (ed.), *Twentieth-Century Britain: An Encyclopedia*, New York: Garland, 691–693.

5. Bibliographies

Andersson, Stefan (1987–88) "A Secondary Religious Bibliography", *Russell*, n.s. 7, 147–161.

Blackwell, Kenneth (1967) "Manuscripts of Books, Articles and Speeches", in Feinberg, Barry (ed.), *A Detailed Catalogue of the Archives of Bertrand Russell*, London: Continuum 1, 61–96.

Blackwell, Kenneth (1973) "Russell's Writings on Logic", in Russell, Bertrand, *Essays in Analysis*, London: Allen and Unwin, 329–336.

Blackwell, Kenneth (1979) "A Secondary Political Bibliography of Russell", *Russell*, o.s. 33–34, 39–44.

Blackwell, Kenneth (1981–82) "A Secondary Bibliography of Russell's 'The Essence of Religion'", *Russell*, n.s. 1, 143–146.

Blackwell, Kenneth (1990) "A.J. Ayer on Russell: A Secondary Bibliography", *Russell*, n.s. 10, 80–81.

Blackwell, Kenneth, and Carl Spadoni (1992) *A Detailed Catalogue of the Second Archives of Bertrand Russell*, Bristol: Thoemmes Press.

Blackwell, Kenneth, and Harry Ruja (1994) *A Bibliography of Bertrand Russell*, 3 vols, London: Routledge.

Denonn, Lester E. (1963) "Bibliography of the Writings of Bertrand Russell to 1962", in Schilpp, Paul Arthur (ed.), *The Philosophy of Bertrand Russell*, 3rd edn, New York: Harper and Row, 743–828.

Feinberg, Barry (ed.) (1967) *A Detailed Catalogue of the Archives of Bertrand Russell*, London: Continuum 1, 61–96.

Harley, David (1982) "A Secondary Educational Bibliography of Bertrand Russell", *Russell*, n.s. 2, 59–68.

Jacob, Gertrude (1929–30) "Bertrand Russell: An Essay Toward a Bibliography", *Bulletin of Bibliography and Dramatic Index*, 13, 198–199; 14, 28–30.

Martin, Werner (1981) *Bertrand Russell: A Bibliography of His Writings, Eine Bibliographie seiner Schriften, 1895–1976*, Munich: K.G. Saur.

Ruja, Harry (1968–69) "Bertrand Russell: A Classified Bibliography 1929–1967", *Bulletin of Bibliography and Magazine Notes*, 25, 182–190, 192; 26, 29–32.

Ruja, Harry (1972) "A Selective, Classified Bertrand Russell Bibliography", in Pears, David F. (ed.), *Bertrand Russell: A Collection of Critical Essays*, New York: Doubleday, 357–387.

Ruja, Harry (1975) "Bibliography of Russell's 'Hearst' Articles", *Russell*, o.s. 18, 18–19; o.s. 19, 19–28.

6. Internet Resources

Bertrand Russell Archives,
   http://www.mcmaster.ca/ russdocs/russell1.htm#beginning
Bertrand Russell Editorial Project,
   http://www.humanities.mcmaster.ca/~russell/brhome.htm
Bertrand Russell Society,
   http://daniel.drew.edu/~jlenz/brs.html
Russell: The Journal of the Bertrand Russell Archives,
   http://websites.mcmaster.ca/mupress/journals/russell/journal.html
Stanford Encyclopedia of Philosophy – Principia Mathematica,
   http://plato.stanford.edu/entries/principia-mathematica/

Stanford Encyclopedia of Philosophy – Russell, Bertrand,
   http://plato.stanford.edu/entries/russell/
Stanford Encyclopedia of Philosophy – Russell's paradox,
   http://plato.stanford.edu/entries/russell-paradox/
*University of St Andrew's MacTutor History of Mathematics Archive – Russell,
   Bertrand,*
   http://www-groups.dcs.st-and.ac.uk/~history/Mathematicians/Russell.html